RR Whit.

D1201502

REDWOOD

LIBRARY
NEWPORT
R.I.

GIFT OF
RUTH WHITMAN

WITHDRAWN

The Poetic Vision of
MURIEL RUKEYSER

LOUISE KERTESZ

Foreword by Kenneth Rexroth

LOUISIANA STATE UNIVERSITY PRESS

Baton Rouge and London

COPYRIGHT © 1980 BY LOUISIANA STATE UNIVERSITY PRESS
ALL RIGHTS RESERVED
MANUFACTURED IN THE UNITED STATES OF AMERICA

DESIGN: DWIGHT AGNER
TYPEFACE: VIP SABON
COMPOSITION: LSU PRESS

LIBRARY OF CONGRESS CATALOGING IN PUBLICATION DATA

Kertesz, Louise, 1939–
The poetic vision of Muriel Rukeyser

Bibliography: p.
Includes index.
1. Rukeyser, Muriel, 1913–   —Criticism and
interpretation.   I. Title.
PS3535.U4Z74   811'.5'2   79–1131
ISBN 0–8071–0552–X

PS
3535
.U4
Z74
1980

OCT 0 2 2000

177146

WITH LOVE AND THANKS TO MY MOTHER,
ANNETTA MERLI CRISTINA

Contents

List of Illustrations

Following page 172

Myra Rukeyser and Muriel at age one
At Yaddo, Saratoga Springs, 1934
At Yaddo, 1938
A photograph by Imogen Cunningham
Bollingen Poetry Prize Committee, 1954
In front of Monet's *Waterlilies*, Museum of Modern Art, 1963
With son Bill in San Francisco, 1947
With grandson Jacob, Berkeley, 1976
At Papitos, Cyprus, 1974
A tree planting for peace, Central Park, 1975
In support of poet Kim Chi-Ha, Korea, 1975
At Sarah Lawrence College for "A Day in Honor of
    Muriel Rukeyser"
At Sarah Lawrence College, 1978

Foreword

Muriel Rukeyser is the best poet of her exact generation. Kenneth Patchen, the only other claimant, spoke of himself as "born in one world and doomed to die in another." It was not a good time for poetry, because poetry was dominated by ideologies—and Left and Right—the so-called Proletarians and the self-styled Reactionary Generation. Today, if you return to these people you will be surprised at the flimsiness of their accomplishments. The Marxists do not sound like Mayakovsky or Neruda, and the Reactionary Generation most certainly do not sound like John Donne. Most of the Left broke with their political mentors and became so embittered that they stopped writing—like Herman Spector—or died young—like Sol Funaroff, or both—like Kenneth Fearing. Walter Lowenfels wasted years as a "functionary," but came back to vigorous poetic life in old age. Only Patchen, singularly intractable, and never a joiner, survived, and somewhat later the much unappreciated Thomas McGrath, who is still writing one of the best of the long poems of the period, *Letter to an Unknown Friend*. For all their emphasis on "form," poets of the Reactionary Generation simply didn't write well.

Vasari said of Tintoretto, "His was the most profound mind ever to lend itself to the art of painting." It is curious to read in this book the attacks on Muriel Rukeyser by what were, in fact, political opponents, for her lack of "depth." Purely as a thinker, she is certainly more profound than anyone else in her generation. It's just that her thoughts were not their thoughts. She is one of the most

important writers of the Left of her time, and now with the death of
Neruda and the ever-increasing sterility of Louis Aragon, she ranks
very high indeed. Unlike the other writers of the Left, she never paid
much, if any, attention to the corkscrew twists of the party line. So
the critics of the Left alternately embraced and damned her. It is
impossible to believe that she ever was a member of the Communist
party; if she ever joined, she must have been quickly expelled. She
does not have an ideology grafted into her head like these devices
they attach to the brains of monkeys. She has a philosophy of life
which comes out of her own flesh and bones. It is not a foreign
body. So, likewise, this philosophy was totally unlike the superficial
fadism of the *jeunesse dorée* of English Stately Home Weekend
Soviets. She never gave it all up to enter the Anglican Church or edit
a magazine for the CIA. Muriel Rukeyser is a traditionalist. But
when everybody was running about talking about one tradition or
another but doing nothing about it, her tradition was not recognized or was despised. Muriel Rukeyser is not a poet of Marxism,
but a poet who has written directly about the tragedies of the
working class. She is a poet of liberty, civil liberty, woman's liberty,
and all the other liberties that so many people think they themselves
just invented in the last ten years.

Today the only poet of the early twentieth century who wrote in
the tradition of the fulfilled "American Dream" is Carl Sandburg.
The intervening writers, especially the women, have been forgotten.
Sandburg long ago succumbed to his Chicago police reporter senti-
mentality and the shallow patriotism, verging on jingoism. After all,
poetry in the tradition of the "American Dream" must necessarily be
tragic, because the community of love of Whitman and of all the
communalist communities that flourished in his youth have not
been realized. Muriel Rukeyser believes in the community of love,
not because she is convinced that it is going to win, but because it is
true, it is the right way for human beings to live. She has been
accused of "optimism," and this in a country where the Left thinks
the revolution is just around the corner and the rest of the population continuously invents new euphemisms for graveyards. (I think

gravediggers [undertakers] now call themselves bereavement coun-
selors.) In America you're either an optimist or a pessimist. Hardly
anyone knows that "The world is a tragedy for those who feel, and
a comedy for those who think." Muriel Rukeyser thinks and feels;
and not only that, she seems to enjoy placing herself as an obstacle
in the way of evil. Book after book has involved action—from
personal investigation of the fate of miners doomed to die of
silicosis in *U.S.1*, to her fairly recent personal confrontation of a
South Korean dictatorship in the case of a Catholic radical poet,
Kim Chi-Ha, who had been condemned to death. Everywhere she
went in Korea, she had only one message: "Free Kim Chi-Ha." They
haven't freed him yet, but at least they commuted his sentence, and
he undoubtedly owes his life to the worldwide agitation of the
"nonpolitical" international writers organization PEN, which Muriel
Rukeyser was representing. It takes guts, in middle age when most
radicals have calmed down and embraced Zen or scientology or the
Reader's Digest, to put yourself physically in the way of the Dictator
Park, the KCIA, and the CIA, for a colleague on the other side of the
world of whom few people had heard.

"Revenons à nos moutons." What about Muriel's poetry? Her
enemies have called it rhetorical, as though the "Ode to the Con-
federate Dead" was anything but rhetoric uncontaminated by intellect. She has a sonority as deep as her deep laughter, and it is this
sense of the power over language that distinguishes her from the
women who preceded her in her tradition, Lola Ridge, Evelyn
Scott, Beatrice Ravenel, or men like James Oppenheim, or Wallace
Gould. Except for Gould, they weren't anywhere near as good
writers, and Lola Ridge can sometimes be embarrassing in her na-
ïve exhortations.

Muriel Rukeyser does not embrace Zen, but she has more and
more internalized her philosophy of life—but this in a special
sense. It's one thing to be a suffragette, it's another thing to insist
on being a woman, completely, in every sense of the word. All the
years that Louise Bogan was poetry reviewer for the *New Yorker*,
she carried on what can only be called a malevolent vendetta with

Muriel Rukeyser, which can only be accounted for by some unknown personal motivation. She was herself a militant feminist
and "free woman," and much of her poetry is either a celebration
of her womanhood or intensely, but cryptically erotic. In fact, she
could be called a lesser and greatly more cooked Muriel Rukeyser.
She never reviewed Muriel's books, but as each came out she took
the opportunity to insert a few catty remarks in her column. Most
extraordinary is the accusation that Muriel's poetry was devoid of
human affection and sexual passion. One of her most anthologized poems derived from a famous love poem in the Chinese
Book of Songs, "Effort at Speech Between Two People," beginning:

> Speak to me. Take my hand. What are you now?
> I will tell you all. I will conceal nothing.
> When I was three, a little child read a story about a rabbit
> who died, in the story, and I crawled under a chair:
> a pink rabbit: it was my birthday, and a candle
> burnt a sore spot on my finger, and I was told to be happy.

"Ajanta" is purportively a poem about the great painted caves
in India, one of the high points of the world's art. When she wrote
it, Muriel had never been to India, although, of course, she had
seen the great portfolio of accurate reproductions. I have seen
Ajanta, and I must say that the poem conveys, amongst other
things, the feeling, the emotion, the very sensibility, of those long-
gone Buddhist monks, that overwhelms you in the same way the
poem does. "Ajanta" is an exploration with continuous discoveries
of new meanings, of her own interior—in every sense. It is the interior of her mind as a human being, as a poet, and as a woman. It
is the interior of her self as her own flesh. It is her womb. I am sure
that she did not know, in those days, of the womb mandala of Ti-
betan and Japanese Shingon Buddhism, but in a sense that is what
the poem is. We did not need Carl Jung to tell us that the mandalas
of Buddhism and Hinduism are paradigms of the interior life, and
that that life with its symbolic patterns is shared by all human
beings to the extent that we all have the same physiology. After
"Ajanta," in fact, she wrote a poem of introspection into her own
womb where, to use Buddhist symbolism, Maitreya was seated in

Peace. It is in nine parts, one for each month of pregnancy, and it is unique in the literature of feminine poetry.

Like Walt Whitman, as the horizons darkened and the community of love seemed to grow more distant, Muriel has sought ever deeper into her self for its meaning. She is far from being a member of that most profitable fraternity—a disillusioned radical. The message now is not, if it ever was, "All power to the people!" Kenneth Burke once turned to me as we were marching up Fifth Avenue chanting that slogan and said in his wispy way, "What do we mean by *all*? What do we mean by *power*? What do we mean by people? We don't even know what we mean by *to* or *the*." Power has fascinated Muriel since her first book, *Theory of Flight*. As is self-evident from her biography of Willard Gibbs, power has always meant to her not the power of Stalin or Mao that "comes out of the mouth of a gun." Power for her is the great dynamo within what used to be called the soul. Her later poems and her life have been devoted to research into the dynamics of that power, and as always, this has led her to actual physical confrontation with the mechanical power of despotism and exploitation. "Free Kim Chi-Ha!" she said to the Dictator Park, and nothing more.

I think it is wonderful that a big comprehensive book should at last be devoted to Muriel Rukeyser. The establishments of varied colors and stripe that dominate, they think, with their mechanical powers have given her few honors in comparison with far lesser poets. And considering the committees who have awarded Bollingen Prizes, and poetry consultants to the Library of Congress, it is almost ludicrous to think of her in such a position. It would be amusing if the Nobel committee sneaked up behind them and gave her a Nobel Prize, because she is certainly a better poet than Gabriela Mistral or, in fact, any other woman who has ever received the prize.

I hope this book, which will accompany the publication, by another publisher, of her complete collected poems, will help bring her to the attention of the youngest generation of liberated women and men who, alas, know so little of their antecedents.

As Whitman said:

Courage yet, my brother or my sister!
Keep on—Liberty is to be subserv'd whatever occurs;
That is nothing that is quell'd by one or two failures, or
    any number of failures,
Or by the indifference or ingratitude of the people, or by
    any unfaithfulness,
Or the show of the tushes of power, soldiers, cannon,
    penal statutes.

What we believe in waits latent forever through all the
    continents,
Invites no one, promises nothing, sits in calmness and
    light, is positive and composed, knows no
    discouragement.
Waiting patiently, waiting its time.

KENNETH REXROTH

Preface

THIS BOOK traces the progress of images and themes Muriel Rukeyser found compelling as she wrote about the "rhymed scenes"
that made up her life and those of "axiom-breaking" men and
women. Since she is a responsive and committed human being, uncompromising in her art, despite negative criticism and change in
poetic fashion, her work reflects the deepest concerns of many
who experienced American life from the thirties to the present.
Lewis Mumford wrote her, "I know no one else in your generation
who has stood up better to the bitter challenges of our day, without either whine or snarl." Her finest art reaches beyond our
American span into the currents of hope and love that have always
nourished the spirit.[1]

In the course of my discussion, I explore her traditions and her
contemporaries as these serve to highlight her distinctive voice and
vision. This book is also a record of the reception Muriel Rukeyser's work has enjoyed—and endured—through the years. It is a
record of both generous and remarkably mean response, revealing
the gratifications and the perils of the vocation of poetry in mid–
twentieth-century America.

Most of the research for this book was done at the libraries of
Smith College and the Forbes Library at Northampton, Massachu-
setts. I am grateful for their services and especially for those of
Mrs. George Snook, interlibrary loan librarian at the Forbes. I
gratefully acknowledge permission from the Trustees of Amherst
College to quote from letters in the Rolfe Humphries Papers, and

1. Lewis Mumford to Muriel Rukeyser, September 28, 1958, in the Berg Collection of
the New York Public Library.

for permission to quote from the papers of Muriel Rukeyser now in the Henry W. and Albert A. Berg Collection I am grateful to the New York Public Library, Astor, Lenox and Tilden Foundations. Thanks to Monica McCall. Thanks to Muriel Rukeyser—for herself, her work, and her trust.

Abbreviations

The Poetic Vision of
MURIEL RUKEYSER

The Bridge, *"Theory of Flight," and the Spirit of Whitman: An Introduction to Rukeyser's Work and to Her Critics*

ROBERT SPILLER in *The Cycle of American Literature* singles out Hart Crane's *The Bridge* as a poem of the thirties which "sought an American tradition of unity and faith." Crane, invoking the spiritual patronage of Whitman, had attempted to create a myth of modern America that would embody a vision of its achievements and possibilities. But Spiller and other critics concur that "the poem remained an expression of a brilliant and confused personality rather than of a united people." Spiller concludes, "If Walt Whitman had been called back to answer the nihilism of Eliot's *The Waste Land*, but had been given an insufficiently rugged sensibility, he might have produced something like . . . *The Bridge*."[1] Published in 1930, it is irrevocably associated with a despairing poet who committed suicide two years later at the age of thirty-three. It is not technological America's mythic poem, expressing the human values and meanings of the world in which modern Americans live and strive. However, Crane's brilliant and extremely difficult poem has received a good deal of critical attention in books and articles since its publication.

Muriel Rukeyser published *Theory of Flight*, which won the Yale Younger Poets Prize, in 1935 when she was twenty-one. In her long poem "Theory of Flight" she uses, like Crane, a technological achievement, the airplane, to symbolize the successes and possibilities of American civilization. As an embodiment of Whitman's spirit, "Theory of Flight" succeeds where *The Bridge* fails.

1. Robert Spiller, *The Cycle of American Literature* (New York, 1957), 217.

But the work of Muriel Rukeyser has received little attention from scholars. In the major works of literary criticism that deal with American poetry from the thirties to the present, Rukeyser has never been given the good part of a chapter. If mentioned at all, at best she has received a few paragraphs in which no attempt has been made to trace the development or outline the sweep of her work. The one exception is Kenneth Rexroth's brief discussion of Rukeyser in *American Poetry in the Twentieth Century* (1971) in which he comments on the development of her work and on its eminent virtue of responsibility. Though her poems have been widely anthologized and are featured in recent anthologies of feminist verse, Rukeyser has been omitted from standard anthologies such as *Chief Modern Poets of Britain and America* (ed. Gerald Sanders *et al.*) and *The Norton Anthology of Modern Poetry.*

The only substantial articles on Rukeyser in scholarly publications have been M. L. Rosenthal's. One chapter of his dissertation (unpublished, 1949) is devoted to Rukeyser's work in the thirties, and he published an article on her longer poems in 1953 in *New Directions in Prose and Poetry.* In the 1949 dissertation Rosenthal offered a largely nonjudgmental close reading of Rukeyser's poems. In the otherwise elucidative article of 1953, however, Rosenthal is the New Critic who finds not enough irony, too much raw personal material, and "unaccountable optimism" in Rukeyser's work. The first paragraphs and other passages read like an apology for the subject under discussion.

To readers nourished on Eliot and Yeats and disciplined by analytical criticism, the faults in Muriel Rukeyser's work may seem more obvious than its merits. Though they do not define her work and are very often absent from it, these faults are real. . . . But if the faults . . . are undoubtedly present, it is also true that they are by-products—though at times more important than the chief fruits of her labor. . . . It is not a matter so much of the reservations one must bear in mind (just look, after all, at some of Pound's minor pieces and major aberrations . . .).[2]

---

2. M. L. Rosenthal, "Muriel Rukeyser: The Longer Poems," in James Laughlin (ed.), *New Directions in Prose and Poetry*, XIV (New York, 1953), 202.

An article in *American Poetry Review* by Virginia R. Terris (1974) is the first discussion of Rukeyser to appear since Rosenthal's in 1953 and the first substantial response to Rukeyser's work published by a woman. Terris suggests that Rukeyser has been ignored by scholars because she had been "written off" as a poet of social protest in an age—the forties and fifties—when poetry was supposed to be primarily concerned with form.[3] But Terris' explanation is only part of the story.

Because scholars have not discussed Rukeyser's work in books and articles, I turned to the reviews which appeared regularly in publications such as the *New Republic* and from time to time in academic journals such as *Yale Review*. In these often brief reviews I found a genuine response to her work, as opposed to categorizing mention in a scholarly book. Reviewers have been passionate in their response; some have loved or hated her, depending on their politics and their preconceptions of what poetry should be and what poetry by a woman should be. Louise Bogan, reviewing in the *New Yorker*, could not mention Rukeyser without bristling sarcasm. But Rukeyser has been fortunate in that many reviewers have been generous in their responses. Eunice Clark, reviewing *Theory of Flight* in *Common Sense* in 1936, wrote: "Her art is the kind that makes people act a little more valiantly when they have understood it." James Caldwell, reviewing several of her works in the *Saturday Review* in 1950, wrote that "she discovers . . . especially for youth, invigoration and a brilliant hope."[4] Such reviewers have compensated in part for the lack of scholarly attention given Rukeyser's work.

The long poem "Theory of Flight," which is comparable to *The Bridge*, is printed as the middle section of Rukeyser's first book, *Theory of Flight*. The first section of the book contains lyrics dealing with the poet's childhood and adolescence, and the first of these poems, "Poem out of Childhood," provides, as Rosenthal says, the

3. Virginia R. Terris, "Muriel Rukeyser: A Retrospective," *American Poetry Review*, III (May/June, 1974), 10.
4. Eunice Clark, review of *Theory of Flight* in *Common Sense*, V (January, 1936), 28; James R. Caldwell, "Invigoration and a Brilliant Hope," *Saturday Review*, March 11, 1950, p. 26.

key to the rest of her work. "Breathe-in experience, breathe-out poetry," she begins, avowing her program as a poet, an honest "making," based on experience. The first section of the poem presents an
experience universal to Americans who have intensely experienced
their education.

> Not Angles, angels   :   and the magnificent past
> shot deep illuminations into high-school.
> I opened the door into the concert-hall
> and a rush of triumphant violins answered me
> while the syphilitic woman turned her mouldered face
> intruding upon Brahms.[5]

The young (romantic) woman here becomes aware of her context in
history, of the achievements of the human imagination; like all of us
in modern America, however, she also becomes aware in adolescence, if not sooner, of the misery in society and the violence in
America.

> We sat on the steps of the unrented house
> raining blood down on Loeb and Leopold,
> creating again how they removed his glasses
> and philosophically slit his throat.

The referents are headliners of the thirties; but the poem is timeless
in its embodiment of the idealism and outrage of adolescence.

> They who manipulated and misused our youth,
> smearing those centuries upon our hands,
> trapping us in a welter of dead names,
> snuffing and shaking heads at patent truth. . . .

Rukeyser's adolescence corresponds to that of some generations
more closely than to others, for hers was a rebellious generation
whose thoughts and concerns could not remain on the literary or
abstract level. The events of the times were too obtrusive.

> We were ready to go the long descent with Virgil
> the bough's gold shade advancing forever with us,
> entering the populated cold of drawing-rooms;

5. Muriel Rukeyser, *Theory of Flight* (New Haven, 1935).

Sappho, with her drowned hair trailing along Greek waters
. . . .
Not Sappho, Sacco.

Daniel Aaron in *Writers on the Left* has said that the one event that turned thoughtful people, intellectuals, and artists to political involvement in the late twenties was the execution of Sacco and Vanzetti. It became apparent to many during the trial that there was a dual system of justice in America: one for the rich, another for the poor and politically unorthodox.[6] But the poet's moral engagement, like that of most adolescents, is as yet undirected, and there are many paths she might follow, to many unknown destinations.

Rosenthal noted in 1949 that Rukeyser's special method in this opening section is "a new kind of directness, a refusal to admit that what is true of life is not also true for art."[7] The directness of the style, the "ordinariness" of the details, and their juxtaposition with public events—high school, sitting on the steps discussing the headlines, the adolescent's impulsive responses—surprise us in this poem published in 1935. It has been said that the unornamented presentation of private, often painful details mingled with references to public events originated with W. D. Snodgrass, Robert Lowell, and the "confessional school" of the 1950s.

In the third section we are given the poet's decision in adolescence about what to do with her memories of a childhood in a suffering world and her own experience of suffering and conflict.

> Organize the full results of that rich past
> open the windows : potent catalyst,
> harsh theory of knowledge, running down the aisles
> crying out in the classrooms, March ravening on the plain,
> inexorable sun and wind and natural thought.

This theory of knowledge and natural thought is a way of understanding and organizing experience. She will no longer simply

6. Daniel Aaron, *Writers on the Left: Episodes in American Literary Communism* (New York, 1961), 168.
7. M. L. Rosenthal, "Chief Poets of the American Depression: Contributions of Kenneth Fearing, Horace Gregory, and Muriel Rukeyser to Contemporary American Poetry" (Ph.D. dissertation, New York University, 1949), 389.

"breathe-in experience, breathe-out poetry," but she will breathe out the poetry based on her experience with the help of an organizing vision. The vision is intensely personal, "harsh" perhaps in that it is hard won, and also because it is associated with the Hegelian theory which maintains that natural development occurs through inexorable tension, that in order to grow beings must change into their opposites in which they are fulfilled.

> Dialectically our youth unfolds   :
> the pale child walking to the river, passional
> in ignorance   in loneliness   demanding
> its habitation for the leaping dream, kissing
> quick air, the vibrations of transient light,
> not knowing substance or reserve

Youth begins as a simple, passionate response to life, without much intellection. But for youth to be fulfilled in adulthood the dialectic, the change, must occur.

> Listening at dead doors,
> our youth assumes a thousand differing flesh
> summoning fact from abandoned machines of trade,
> knocking on the wall of the nailed-up power plant,
> telephoning hello, the deserted factory, ready
> for the affirmative clap of truth
> ricochetting from thought to thought among
> the childhood, the gestures, the rigid travellers.

The youth no longer simply throws stones at the deserted plant, as in the second section of the poem; now she knocks at the wall, she questions its meaning, its social implications. In all her questioning and organizing of experience she is ready to affirm, for she is not by nature predisposed to gloom and pessimism. She gives play to her thought, ready to affirm, but she implies that no guides ("travellers") will receive her allegiance if they are "rigid."

In 1949 Rosenthal wrote that the conclusion of the poem is a vision of life as a whole in language both Marxist and mystic. Perhaps the use of "dialectically" in a poem written in 1935 inevitably calls up the figure of Marx to some readers. Today, however, one can appreciate the poem's meanings in fundamental rather than purely ideological terms, the way Rukeyser herself intended. James Caldwell, writing in the *Saturday Review* in 1950, noted that a major key to her work is the dialectical process "seen not as a tight and easy rationale of class struggle but in a poetic vision of the eternal counterpoise and reconcilement of forces."[8] The fact is, youth does unfold dialectically, for most of us, and our "leaping dream" finds substance and "habitation," finally, in the realities of everyday life. The whole movement of growth the poet has shown us in this poem has been dialectical, proceeding through the poet's experiencing of opposites. In high school the triumphant violins in the concert hall and the ravaged face of the syphilitic woman developed her social consciousness and led her to respond later on: "Not Sappho, Sacco." And in a rush of insight (which has the force of all important recognitions occuring in banal circumstances) she admits to her father who is "scraping his jaw" in the bathroom that when she grows up she will be " 'Maybe : something : like : Joan : of : Arc. . . .' "

"Poem out of Childhood" is a rich evocation of the psychological progress of childhood and adolescence in the modern world. The poem shows us a poetic nature at the beginning of her career: fully responsive, honest, growing. Rosenthal found, however, that "the facile puns of Auden, the overtones of Eliot's obsession with Jacobean melodramatic horror and gnarled rhythms, the selfpitying childhood characteristic of Crane, and the sour language of Marxist criticism make for something of an aesthetic hash." This criticism is a good example of an academic tendency to take no writer's expression as her own, the need always to listen for and find "patent echoes" of other (usually "greater") writers. But the young poet is obviously not mainly concerned with sounding like no one else; she is not straining for originality. As Philip Blair Rice wrote in *The Nation*, "Her originality consists in making something new and making it well with the tools at hand, rather than in devising new instruments for others to use." Willard Maas in the New York *Her-*

8. *Ibid.*, 390; Caldwell, "Invigoration and a Brilliant Hope," 26.

ald Tribune recognized that she made no self-conscious effort to be modern or revolutionary but that her poems show a healthy intelligence making use of the materials she knows.[9] When she does echo a voice—Eliot's, for instance, or Crane's, or Whitman's—the attentive reader can sense why. Rukeyser made use of modern poetic instruments, moreover, with "a new kind of directness," as Rosenthal noted in 1949. It is, in part, this directness that makes "Theory of Flight" more nearly the "myth" of America's technological age than Crane's.

In the same way Crane set out to make *The Bridge* an answer to Eliot's *The Waste Land*, to "overcome its debilitating influence," Rukeyser also wanted "to stand against the idea of the fallen world, a powerful and destructive idea overshadowing Western poetry. In that sense there is no lost Eden, and God is the future. The child walled-up in our life can be given his growth. In this growth is our security." [10] The fundamental difference between Crane's and Rukeyser's positions in refuting Eliot is that Crane considered himself a visionary poet, one who expressed in words an approximation of ecstatic, mystical experiences transcending the waste land of materialist America. Waldo Frank said in his introduction to Crane's *Collected Poems* that *The Bridge* is a "challenging synthesis of life, wherein all the modern multiverse is accepted and transfigured without loss into One." Rukeyser, on the other hand, though reviewers have labeled her a "pythoness" and a "sybil" because she emphasizes the deep insights poetry affords us into reality, does not write as a visionary of Crane's type. In *The Life of Poetry* she describes her plans at the beginning of her career. "We did not want a sense of Oneness with the One so much as a sense of Many-ness with the Many. Multiplicity no longer stood against unity. Einstein, Picasso, Joyce, gave us our keys." Rukeyser seeks no transcendent mystical vision. She wants a more complete apprehension of ordinary reality,

9. Rosenthal, "Chief Poets of the American Depression," 390; Philip Blair Rice, "New Poet," *Nation*, January 29, 1936, p. 134; Willard Maas, review of TF, in *New York Herald Tribune Books*, January 19, 1936, p. 7.

10. Brom Weber (ed.), *The Letters of Hart Crane: 1916–1932* (New York, 1952), 351; Muriel Rukeyser, *The Life of Poetry* (New York, 1949), 221.

as in Whitman's assuming all phases of life in "Song of Myself." In *The Life of Poetry* she writes of "experience taken into the body, breathed-in, so that reality is the completion of experience, and poetry is what is produced. And life is what is produced." Kenneth Burke said of *Theory of Flight*, "This work is an experience involving the entire personality," and William Rose Benét said of her first volume, "When you hold this book in your hand you hold a living thing." [11] Moreover, Rukeyser stands as a complement to Hart Crane in that from her poems emerges the image of the affirmative, productive female poet, and her long career is a testament of courage and endurance.

Horace Gregory in his brief review of *Theory of Flight* in the *New Republic* in 1936 entitled "A Hope for Poetry" offered a link between the two poets: " 'Theory of Flight' is for the most part an articulate translation of machine images into poetry, and may be regarded as a logical development of a technique that was brilliantly exhibited in the poetry of Hart Crane." Gregory didn't explain what he meant by "logical development," and it is perhaps more accurate to say that the use of machine imagery in Rukeyser's poem is more the result of her personality and philosophy than of any "logical development" in poetic theory from 1930 to 1935, though the development was in the air. In the early thirties poets of the "Dynamo" school such as Kenneth Fearing and Sol Funaroff were concerned with making poetry out of the most characteristic feature of their world: the machine. They sought to depict the machine not as an evil (as did Eliot and the imagists who were nostalgic for a preindustrial era) but as a good and a hope for the human race, an exciting embodiment of its energy and vitality. Crane chose the Brooklyn Bridge as a technological marvel which would symbolize America's (and the race's) striving, achievement, and potential; but he could not keep the bridge from also symbolizing his personal quest for an

11. Waldo Frank (ed.), *The Collected Poems of Hart Crane* (New York, 1933), xix; Rukeyser, *The Life of Poetry*, 223, 221; Kenneth Burke, "Return after Flight," *New Masses*, XVIII (February 4, 1936), 26; William Rose Benét, review of TF, in *Saturday Review*, December 7, 1935, p. 47.

ideal or absolute which transcends a degenerate present. The bridge is wrapped in shrouds of ineffability, invoked as the deity—anything but an ordinary engineering marvel. For Rukeyser (and the poets of the "Dynamo" school) each machine, such as the airplane, is above all ordinary. The miracle for her is in what has become usual, and she is concerned in her poetry to give the flavor of the precise, often flat prose of engineering and science that, in its ordinariness, conveys miracles of understanding and achievement. In this sense "Theory of Flight" anticipates her study of the scientist Willard Gibbs.[12]

The Bridge and "Theory of Flight" develop their themes in comparable structures. Crane's poem of 1,200 lines is divided into eight sections, with a "Proem," and Rukeyser's, of 950 lines, has six sections, with a "Preamble." (An outline of both poems follows this chapter.) Crane's "Proem: To Brooklyn Bridge," addresses the bridge in prayer, as an image of the divinity, as "Thou." He stands in the shadow of the bridge and contemplates its beauty which "condense[s] eternity."[13] He petitions the bridge to infuse his life and that of other ordinary mortals he describes—the clerks, the moviegoers—with its spiritually uplifting meanings: "Unto us lowliest sometime sweep, descend / And of the curveship lend a myth to God." Crane's language is courtly, as befits one who petitions a higher power; the "Proem" is in regular four-line stanzas with occasional rhyme, and the effect of this form is to set the speaking voice in a traditional context of formal supplicators. The images are in the tradition of beautiful poetry, such as the opening one of the seagull's flight.

> How many dawns, chill from his rippling rest
> The seagull's wings shall dip and pivot him,
> Shedding white rings of tumult, building high
> Over the chained bay waters Liberty—
>
> Then, with inviolate curve, forsake our eyes

12. Horace Gregory, "A Hope for Poetry," *New Republic*, February 5, 1936, p. 374; Estelle G. Novak, "The Dynamo School of Poets," *Contemporary Literature*, XI (1970), 526–39.
13. Frank (ed.), *The Collected Poems of Hart Crane*, 4.

As apparitional as sails that cross
Some page of figures to be filed away;
—Till elevators drop us from our day . . .

Even the image of the suicide plunging from the bridge has a fairy-tale loveliness.

A bedlamite speeds to thy parapets,
Tilting there momently, shrill shirt balooning,
A jest falls from the speechless caravan.

Rukeyser's opening "prayer" is to elemental nature, to all the productive natural powers which negate death and weakness. Despite failures and distractions, the human mind has always sought to harness these powers for its own uses and to discover in itself the powers which are the counterparts of those it observes in the universe.

Earth, bind us close, and time   ; nor, sky, deride[14]
how violate we experiment again.
In many Januaries, many lips
have fastened on us while we deified
the waning flesh : now, fountain, spout for us,
mother, bear children : lover, yet once more :
in final effort toward your mastery.
Many Decembers suffered their eclipse
death, and forgetfulness, and the year bore round ;
now years, be summed in one access of power.
Fortresses, strengths, beauties, realities,
gather together, discover to us our wings
new special product of mortality.

The "Preamble" is in jagged stanzas of irregular length which, with the colons and semicolons, visually emphasize the urging to effort, to experiment. The use of the jarring word "violate" in the second line seems a deliberate contrast to Crane's poetic "inviolate" in his fifth line. The harshness of Rukeyser's language is part of her emphasis on "strengths." Because she, too, seeks to dispel the gloom of *The Waste Land*, she states at the beginning of her poem that Eliot's expression of the utter debility of modern persons actually "liber-

14. This line is reminiscent of Crane's "Voyages II": "Bind us in time, O Seasons clear, and awe."

ated" the modern psyche. In Eliot the poetic expression of indecision and prostration reached its limit.

> Fortuitously have we gained loneliness,
> fallen in waste places liberated,
> relieved ourselves from weakness' loveliness :
> remain unpitied now, never descend
> to that soft howling of the prostrate mind.

There will be no cult of the loveliness of weakness and indecision in her poem, and loveliness of expression will deliberately be minimal. Her aspirations will not be dreamy, for "wish gnawed clean by plans precurses flight." Her images will be hard, to match her determination: "Distinguish the metaphor most chromium clear." The poet abjures the "frail mouthings" and "dusty whispers" of dead traditions. If we are resolved to be strong, "nor may we replica / ourselves in hieroglyphs and broken things." (Hear Eliot's "These fragments I have shored against my ruins.") What chromium-clear metaphor shall we choose to represent our new mood, our resolve? We will replica ourselves in the metaphor of flight.

> Look! Be : leap ;
> paint trees in flame
> bushes burning
> roar in the broad sky
> know your color : be :
> produce that the widenesses
> be full and burst their wombs
> riot in redness, delirious with light,
> swim bluely through the mind
> shout green as the day breaks
> put up your face to the wind
> FLY

Rosenthal writes of this striking passage, "It demonstrates . . . the immaturity of the style—how the poet tries at times to solve technical problems through the simple device of shouting or groaning, or ecstacizing." This is decidedly not shouting and groaning, and if it is ecstacizing it is not of the passive, so-called "feminine" variety. It is intense Emersonian exhortation, based on the insight that what can be for the material world can also be for the spirit and the personality. We can fly if we learn from the "fortresses, strengths, beauties, realities" of the universe: they will "discover to us our wings." We *do* have wings, in the poet's view. Rosenthal says "the plane's phallic power must bear her away, reveal new vistas, teach her and the reader to 'fly' on their own."[15] Yet no phallic power is invoked in these lines, only the power common to all active beings. The poet is not asking to be borne away: she is urging herself and all humans to fly on their own.

History has come to fruition in this moment of time, says the poet. This is cause for a sense of power. The strength of the past is contained in the present, which is giving birth to the future.

> Leonardo's tomb
> not in Italian earth
> but in a fuselage
> designed
> in the historic mind
> time's instrument
> blue-print of birth.

Crane chose the bridge to symbolize the "unfractioned idiom" of eternity, ever present in any moment we choose to contemplate. Rukeyser's symbol for eternity, that sweep which contains all history, is the plane in flight. Translated into human terms, it is the human spirit in the exercise of its power that finds "unity in knowing / all space in one unpunctuated flowing." We fly when we know this and live by the strength of this knowledge.

> We bear the seeds of our return forever,
> the flowers of our leaving, fruit of flight,
> perfect for present, fertile for its roots
> in past   in future   in motility.

Rosenthal notes perceptively that Rukeyser's plane differs from Crane's bridge "in that it is something to be used by the intelligence, not something in which the intelligence seeks to lose itself." This in-

15. Rosenthal, "The Longer Poems," 209.

sight penetrates to the essential difference between Crane's poem and Rukeyser's and explains why "Theory of Flight" is the more active counter-thrust to Eliot's waste land. Whereas Crane's poem contains symbols for pure contemplation, Rukeyser's contains symbols which urge the intelligence to make personal and social applications. Harold Rosenberg in his review of *Theory of Flight* in *Poetry* (1936) found the book "remarkable for its self-confidence and lack of hesitation." He said her poetry "contains a moral will, a will to make itself useful as statement and a will to warm itself against the major human situations of our day." [16]

Crane's poem goes on from the "Proem" to explore incidents of the American past in order to find examples of man's successful bridging of the gap between time and eternity, the imperfect and the absolute. For his spiritual purposes Crane seeks a "usable past," as did Van Wyck Brooks, Lewis Mumford, Waldo Frank, and other intellectuals of the twenties who sought examples in American history of their countrymen's higher striving, as opposed to the depressingly universal materialistic competing. Crane finds in Columbus' voyage into the unknown what Vincent Quinn calls "an analogue of the ascension of the spirit from time to eternity." [17] Columbus is the symbol of intense desire, like the poet's own, for unity with the absolute. For Crane, the absolute is always, despite the seekers and the yearners, "still one shore beyond desire!" But the poet is always on its track: "Elohim, still I hear thy sounding heel!" The language of this section, entitled "Ave Maria," is like that of the "Proem": courtly, preindustrial. Such language is appropriate to a monologue spoken by Columbus as he is returning to Spain from America, and there are several invocations to Mary the Mother of God for safe voyage. The poetry is splendid, the images lush in a Miltonic rendering of the sailor's perception of the watery globe.

> Series on series, infinite,—till eyes
> Starved wide on blackened tides, accrete—enclose

16. Rosenthal, "Chief Poets of the American Depression," 412; Harold Rosenberg, "Youth in Protest," *Poetry*, XLVIII (May, 1936), 107–10.
17. Vincent Quinn, *Hart Crane* (New York, 1963), 77, 83.

This turning rondure whole, this crescent ring
Sun-cusped and zoned with modulated fire
Like pearls that whisper through the Doge's hands

The concluding stanzas are an invocation to God who, as prime mover, draws all to himself, who is the originator of all intense desire.

O Thou who sleepest on Thyself, apart

. . . .

Into thy steep savannahs, burning blue,
Utter to loneliness the sail is true.

The section following the "Preamble" in Rukeyser's poem is entitled "The Gyroscope." Like Crane's "Ave Maria" it is about desire as the energy of the universe, opening with "But this is our desire, and of its worth. . . ." The gyroscope represents both the constant movement and the stillness and stability of the universe and is like Crane's God who sleeps on himself.

Centrifugal power, expanding universe
within expanding universe, what stillnesses
lie at your center resting among motion?

. . . .

Here is the gyroscope whirling out pulsing in tides illimitably
          widening, live force contained
in a sphere of rigid boundary   ;   concentrate
at the locus of all forces, spinning with black speed
revolving outward perpetually, turning with its torque
all the developments of the secret will.

Because Rukeyser finds in the gyroscope a replica of the self-renewing life of the universe, she can extrapolate its principles to all levels of human and cosmic desiring.

Rukeyser's father was a construction engineer, and she tells us in *The Life of Poetry* that she was fascinated as a child by technology and the physical principles behind it. She also tells us, on the same page, that her mother read Emerson, and Emerson's method of extrapolating spiritual principles from physical is seen in Rukeyser's comment about what she learned as a child. "Concrete must contain expansion joints, the strips of material that allow the forcing heat of these summers, the forcing cold of these violent white winters, to do their work. The principle of the expansion joint, you learn, runs through all" (LP, 212). Similarly, in "The Gyroscope," Rukeyser finds a physical principle of constant renewal which applies to the attraction of one human being for another.

> Power electric-clean, gravitating outward at all points,
> moving in savage fire, fusing all durable stuff
> but never itself being fused with any force
> homing in no hand nor breast nor sex
> for buried in these lips we rise again,
> bent over these plans, our faces raise to see.

The principle also applies to the human being's relationship with God. Rukeyser's idea of God as the current of the universe is opposed to Crane's concept of Elohim perpetually evading the yearning human spirit.

> The dynamics of desire are explained
> in terms of action outward and reaction to a core
> obscured and undefined, except, perhaps, as "God in
> Heaven," "God in Man,"
> Elohim intermittent with the soul, recurrent
> as Father and Holy Ghost, Word and responsive Word,
> merging with contact in continual sunbursts,
> the promise, the response, the hands laid on,
> the hammer swung to the anvil, mouth fallen on mouth,
> the plane nose up into an open sky.

The use of the term *Elohim* here seems a pointed response to Crane ("Elohim, still I hear thy sounding heel!"). To Rukeyser the desire in the universe and in human beings implies its fulfillment, and she experiences and renders this insight by focusing on human technological achievement.

> Roads are cut, purchase is gained on our wish,
> the turbines gather momentum, tools are given   :
> whirl in desire, hurry to ambition, return,
> maintaining the soul's polarity ; be : fly.

After Crane's description of the voyage of Columbus, which symbolizes the passage of the spirit from the imperfect to the absolute, he turns to the actual progress of American history in which the land is raped and its questing heroes, the Indians, the seafarers, are forgotten or destroyed. Similarly, after the description of desire as the energy of the universe, as "Elohim intermittent with the soul," Rukeyser shows the perversion or frustration of desire in the murders of those men and women who have desired most intensely the spiritual advancement of humanity. The second sections of both poems therefore have as their theme the frustration of that very desire which is celebrated in the first. Reality obtrudes upon the ideal; the actual does not support theory.

Rukeyser's "The Lynchings of Jesus," which is subdivided into three sections, corresponds to Crane's "Powhatan's Daughter," "Cutty Sark," and "Cape Hatteras" in that it too shows how the energy of desire has operated in actual human history. The first section, "Passage to Godhead," echoes Whitman's "Passage to India" in which he sang the past and present achievements of Adam and Eve's "myriad progeny . . . / Wandering, yearning, curious, with restless explorations" and insisted that the human soul will someday achieve "Passage to more than India!" By this Whitman meant that someday human beings would achieve a sense of unity with the mythic vision of the race ("primal thought") and "the great achievements of the present," exemplified in "the strong light works of engineers," and the universe we now live in, "The whole earth, this cold, impassive, voiceless earth, shall be completely justified." When we achieve this sense of unity, this "passage," it will be a passage to ultimate reality, to God.

Rukeyser's idea of "Passage to Godhead" is similar to Whitman's. That which is divine in human beings, she says, is the striving to pierce the limitations imposed on us by materialism and custom. Each person who tries to break through these barriers is a revolutionary. The first stanza refers to the attempt of Jesus.

> Passage to godhead, fitfully glared upon
> by bloody shinings over Calvary
> this latest effort to revolution stabbed
> against a bitter crucificial tree

The second stanza affirms her belief that desire will triumph, ultimately, despite its recurrent setbacks throughout history. She offers as proof the fact that in the airplane "Icarus' phoenix-flight fulfils itself." Taking the physical accomplishment as a harbinger of future achievements for the human race, the poet continues:

> desire's symbol swings full circle here,
> eternal defeat by power, eternal death
> of the soul and body in murder or despair
> to be followed by eternal return, until
> the thoughtful rebel may triumph everywhere.

Seeking a "usable past" she calls upon those who have achieved passage beyond barriers in the past: "Bruno, Copernicus, Shelley, Karl Marx : you / makers of victory for us : how long?" How long will we be unable to break through the barriers of our present age to achieve that passage to the human development now required of us and our society? We need rebellion but "benevolent bugles smother rebellion's song, / blowing protection for the acquiescent, / and we need many strengths to continue strong." We must find strength in our world, with the inspiration of our past achievements and of what we have discovered about reality. Once human beings believed that sheer physical power, the military panoplies of nationalism, meant strength. America still believes this, "and freedom's eagles scream above our faces, / misleading, sly, perverse, and unprofound." But we must take a lesson from the very methods of technology that have served us well in the past. These are based on steady observation and demand minds free from all chauvinism.

> Passage to godhead, shine illuminated
> by other colors than blood and fire and pride.
> Given wings, we looked downward on earth, seen
> uniform from distance; and descended, tied
> to the much-loved near places, moved to find
> what numbers of lynched Jesuses have not been deified

Observation will yield us heroes in our ordinary world; their example will give us strength to pass the barriers into the new society.

In the second section, "The Committee Room," the poet looks closely at our society as it is now constituted. Rukeyser sees what Crane saw from the Twentieth Century Limited: an America trivialized and vulgarized. But her emphasis is on the country's being run by abstracted men in a committee room who have no real contact with the people outside. Crane writes about the individual's loss of contact with the land; Rukeyser goes a step further and writes of the abstractedness of those in power. She writes political poetry. The romantic Eliotesque fogginess of Crane's "The Harbor Dawn" ("long, tired sounds, fog-insulated noises: / Gongs in white surplices . . . / Far strum of fog horns . . . / signals dispersed in veils") becomes in Rukeyser's poem the foggy bottom of modern bureaucracy.

> Let us be introduced to our superiors, the voting men.
> They are tired ; they are hungry ; from deciding all day around the committee-table.
>> Is it foggy outside? It must be very foggy
>> The room is white with it

Rukeyser, like Crane, points up the contrast between the heroes in our tradition and degraded commercial contemporaries, "the flab faces." As Crane summoned a vision of the Indian, she summons a vision of her Jewishness.

> Those people engendered my blood swarming
> over the altar to clasp the scrolls and Menorah
> the black lips, bruised cheeks, eye-reproaches :
> as the floor burns, singing Shema

Contrasted to the profound truths of "the scrolls" and of "Shema" (the central creed of Judaism) we have today the mountains of newsprint.

> Our little writers go about, hurrying the towns along,
> running from mine to luncheon, they can't afford
> to let one note escape their holy jottings:
> today the mother died, festering : he shot himself : the
>> bullet entered
> the roof of the mouth, piercing the brain-pan

In school children learn history as a colorful blur of conquest and power. But they don't learn much about America because its teachers and leaders have recently been closemouthed and evasive.

>   What did you do in school today, my darling?
>   Tamburlaine rode over Genghis had a sword
>   holding riot over Henry V Emperor of and
>   the city of Elizabeth the tall sails
>   crowding England into the world and Charles
>   his head falling many times onto a dais
>   how they have been monarchs and
>   Calvin Coolidge who wouldn't say
>   however, America

What is there to learn about America? The poem pans to the committee room where the bureaucratic machine grinds out meaningless decisions and abdicates responsibility.

>   All day we have been seated around a table
>   all these many days
>   One day we voted on whether he was Hamlet
>   or whether he was himself and yesterday
>   I cast the deciding vote to renounce our mouths.

There is a sinister note of warning: the committee decides many meaningless questions, but it will one day decide to remake the impassive governed into its image.

>   Tomorrow
>   the vote's to be cast on the eyes, and sex, and brain.
>   Perhaps we will vote to disavow all three.

In the end the committee is transformed into all governments and bureaucracies which, while the people "look the other way, and cough," have persecuted the rebellious and the powerless.

>   We are powerful now   :   we vote
>   death to Sacco a man's name
>   and Vanzetti, a blood-brother;
>   death
>   to Tom Mooney, or a wall, no
>   matter;
>   poverty to Piers Plowman,

                    shrieking anger
               to Shelley, a cough and Fanny to
                    Keats;
               thus to Blake in a garden; thus to
                    Whitman;
               thus to D. H. Lawrence.
                              And to all you women,
               dead and unspoken-for, what
                    sentences,
               to you dead children, little in the
                    ground
          :   all you sweet generous rebels,
               what sentences

Such passages as these are surely the basis of T. C. Wilson's observation in *Poetry* in 1940. Comparing Rukeyser's work with *The
Bridge* he says, "As an interpretation of American life hers is the
more mature and closely observed. Where Crane was rhetorical
and mystic, she is hard and clear and concrete." [18]

The concluding stanza describes a demonstration in which the
poet sees hope, despite history's record of massacring rebels and
misfits. The figure of the crowd ascending repeats the poem's redeeming motif of flight:

          all night they carried leaves
          bore songs and garlands up the gradual hill
          the noise of singing kept the child awake
               but they were dead
               all Shakespeare's heroes   the saints   the Jews   the rebels
               but the noise stirred their graves' grass
               and the feet all falling in those places
               going up the hill with sheaves and tools
               and all the weapons of ascent together.

The third section, "The Trial," focuses on the potentially
lynched Jesuses of the thirties: the nine black boys who were sen-
tenced to be electrocuted in Alabama for allegedly raping two
white girls on a freight gondola in Scottsboro in the spring of

18. T. C. Wilson, review of *A Turning Wind,* in *Poetry*, LV (January, 1940), 216.

1931. (Rukeyser herself had driven south to cover the trial for the leftist *Student Review* but she was arrested by the police when they found her and two friends talking to black reporters and discovered in her valise thirty posters advertising a black student conference at Columbia.) The "Scottsboro Boys" were, like Sacco and Vanzetti, symbols of the victimization of the weak by what Rukeyser and others saw as the dual system of justice in the United States.

As in Crane's "The River," Rukeyser describes the vast land.

> The South is green with coming spring   ;   revival
> flourishes in the fields of Alabama.   Spongy with rain,
> plantations breathe April   :   carwheels suck mud in the roads,
> the town expands warm in the afternoons.   At night the
>   black boy
> teeters no-handed on a bicycle, whistling The St. Louis Blues,
> blood beating, and hot South.

But her picture of trains and hoboes bears the stamp of social concern.

> Grass is green now in Alabama; Birmingham dusks are quiet
> relaxed and soft in the park, stern at the yards:
> a hundred boxcars shunted off to sidings, and the hoboes
> gathering grains of sleep in forbidden corners.
> In all the yards   :   Atlanta, Chattanooga,
> Memphis, and New Orleans, the cars, and no jobs.

The poem goes on to place the scene of the Scottsboro trial in its historical context. If Rukeyser seeks and finds "ancestors," as Crane sought Van Winkle, the Indian, the pioneer, and the seafarer, hers are the ancestors with a specific dream of social justice, of betterment of the human condition.

> . . . the air is populous beyond our vision:
> all the people's anger finds its vortex here
> as the mythic lips of justice open, and speak.
>
> .   .   .   .
>
> John Brown, Nat Turner, Toussaint stand in this courtroom,
> Dred Scott wrestles for freedom there in the dark corner,
> all our celebrated shambles are repeated here   :   now again

> Sacco and Vanzetti walk to a chair, to the straps and rivets
> and the switch spitting death and Massachusetts' will.

By comparing the "mythic" heroes chosen by Crane and Rukeyser one understands Rukeyser's statement in *The Life of Poetry* that an earlier generation had tried to make a mysticism out of materialism. "Looking back from what I knew in Spain, I must remember . . . a world of constriction and fear, a materialist world that exposed the American danger, in materialism, to be mystical about material values" (LP, 222). To Rukeyser it is not enough to glory in human power and achievement if those are used to exploit the less fortunate.

> Wreaths are brought out of history
> here are the well-nourished flowers of France, grown strong on
>   blood,
> Caesar twisting his thin throat toward conquest . . .
> the Istrian galleys slide again to sea.

One remembers that in Crane's seafaring fantasy at the conclusion of "Cutty-Sark" he dreams of the glory of trading vessels, Yankee and British, calling them

>   skil-
> ful savage sea-girls
> that bloomed in the spring—Heave, weave
> those bright designs the trade winds drive . . .

His refrain is "Sweet opium and tea, Yo-ho!" as he pictures "clipper dreams indelible and ranging, / baronial white on lucky blue!" Crane indiscriminately sings the hobo and the entrepreneur, empire and Indian. His mythicizing is without social consciousness. (Peter Viereck in "The Crack-Up of American Optimism" has written an incisive article on Crane's and Vachel Lindsay's perpetrating the heedless optimism, the exalted materialism, of their time.)[19] But Rukeyser's heroes are always those on the side of the people. As she wrote in the first section of "The Lynchings of Jesus," "Passage to godhead, shine illuminated / by other colors than blood and fire and

19. Peter Viereck, "The Crack-Up of American Optimism: Vachel Lindsay, the Dante of the Fundamentalists," *Modern Age*, IV (Summer, 1960), 269–84.

pride." She continues this theme in "The Trial."

> The fastidious Louis', cousins to the sun, stamping
> those ribboned heels on Calas, on the people;
> the lynched five thousand of America.
> Tom Mooney from San Quentin, Herndon : here
> is an army for audience

The last stanzas of "The Trial" are a surreal dialectical vision of opposites merging.

> Earth, include sky   ;   air, be stable to our
> feet, which have need of stone and iron stance

Finally the elemental opposites in nature are associated with the opposites which are Jesus and the enemies of Jesus; and these too merge. Rukeyser's belief in the dialectical growth of all parts of the universe makes possible the hopeful final vision of the resurrection of the lynched Jesus.

> Shall we then straddle Jesus in a plane
> the rigid crucified revived at last
> the pale lips flattened in a wind a rain
> of merging conquered blast and counterblast.
> Shout to us : See !
> the wind   !
> Shout to us :
> FLY

In the "Cape Hatteras" section of *The Bridge* Crane also takes the airplane as the symbol of human desire and achievement and the hope of overcoming difficulties in other realms of experience. In this section Crane celebrates Walt Whitman as the first to see the divinity in the "Years of the Modern!"

> Our Meistersinger, thou set breath in steel;
> And it was thou who on the boldest heel
> Stood up and flung the span on even wing
> Of that great Bridge, our Myth, whereof I sing!

"Cape Hatteras" is one of the more difficult sections of *The Bridge*. It is filled with images of technology, for here the poet is at the core of his theme: the birth of the glorious future of America out of "this new realm of fact." At this exciting moment in history, "man hears himself an engine in a cloud!" The difficulty arises from the style in which Crane treats this theme. First of all, one senses the incongruousness of Miltonic rhetoric and diction in dealing with technology.

> But that star-glistered salver of infinity,
> The circle, blind crucible of endless space,
> Is sluiced by motion,—subjugated never.
> Adam and Adam's answer in the forest
> Left Hesperus mirrored in the lucid pool.

Then, Crane's description of the machine builds up into a frenzy of adoration, as if the machine itself, and not the laboring brain of the inventor, were divine.

With his hand in Walt Whitman's, Crane invokes the older poet as the spirit permeating the modern age, even calling him *Panis Angelicus*. Whitman's spiritual guidance and that of the poet who follows in Whitman's footsteps are supposed to direct the use of machinery to humane ends. This is a big order for Whitman and for the modern poet. There must be a bridge between the intense wish on the part of the poet that human beings view the machine as an emblem of their higher powers, Whitman as a bringer of "a pact, new bound, / Of living brotherhood," and the exercise of those higher powers and ideals of brotherhood in modern life. That bridge may be found in the social statement explicit in "Theory of Flight," a poem also infused with the spirit of Whitman, who sang "the strong light works of engineers" but who also wrote *Democratic Vistas*, a severe indictment of materialism in American life and corruption in government. "Theory of Flight" is closer to the spirit of Whitman than is *The Bridge* in that Rukeyser and Whitman manifest a social consciousness and an attentiveness to the concrete details of modern life that Crane often leaves far behind in his mystic climb to the absolute.

Rukeyser's "The Tunnel" (in three sections) corresponds to "Three Songs," in which Crane turns to the theme of unsatisfied sexual desire: "I wanted you, nameless Woman of the South." The first section of "The Tunnel" describes unemployed miners who never owned their lives and despite sex and procreation never knew the luxury of love relationships. There is no time or energy for love— "year in and out, seeing no color but coal"—and even to have sex with one's wife is a dangerous luxury.

> These are the valley's losses
>
> which even the company fails to itemize
> in stubborn black and red in the company stores :
> the empty breasts like rinds, the father's hands,
> the sign, the infected whores,
>
> a puppy roasted for pregnant Mary's dinner . . .

Contrast this to the Mary in Crane's third song, "Virginia," where the working-class girl is romanticized:

> O blue-eyed Mary with the claret scarf,
> Saturday Mary, mine!
>
> . . . .
>
> O Mary, leaning from the high wheat tower,
>   Let down your golden hair!

The second section of Rukeyser's "The Tunnel" is spoken by a woman whose love has been rejected. Like the speaker in Crane's "Three Songs" the speaker in Rukeyser's poem is at first all physical desire for the beloved and finally desire to pass beyond the particular beloved. For Crane the "beyond" is "through a fleshless door" to a mystic union with an ideal love. "Magdalene" becomes "blue-eyed Mary" and finally "Cathedral Mary." But the speaker in Rukeyser's poem wants to pass beyond the throes of desire for the particular beloved to her self. Desire for the beloved, that particular idol, has meant death to her self.

> You have been stone set upon fine-grained woods, buildings
> of granite standing in a street of stone, roads
> full of fallen flowers wet under the foot, ships
> pointing an index to voyage among islands,
>
> blue archipelagoes :   your body being an island
> set about with magnetic flowers and flesh and fruit :
> the sons I might bear you, the sons, the fragrant daughters.

The speaker desires the return of her self, which she sees as more real than her former passion.

> Intrudes on this the bleak authentic voice   :
> wherefore does the mouth stiffen, the cheeks freeze austere
> as stone, affording special grief among the days
> and cold days catalogued of comfort murdered,
> the iron passage, estranged eyes, and the death
> of all my logic   :   pale with the weakness of one
> dead and not yet arisen, a hollow bath of flame
> with my fire low along the oils of grace
> how many deaths, body so torn from spirit.
> Body, return   :   I love you   :   soul, come home!

In the return of her self she will have the restoring world. In the abandoning of particular, idolizing desire, she will know the power of her desire in its authentic wholeness and its counterpart in the power of the modern world.

> Open me a refuge where I may be renewed. Speak to me
> world hissing over cables, shining among steel strands,
> plucking speech out on a wire, linking voices,
> reach me now in my fierceness, or I am drowned

The imagery here reflects the change from the inauthentic desire to abandon herself to an idol (traditionally feminine) to the desire of one seeking a creative communion with her self and the world.

In the third section of "The Tunnel" we are given a dawn conversation between a pilot who must arise and fly that day and his wife who is in her sixth month of pregnancy. Desire is embodied in the child growing in her and in her will that it grow and fulfill his desire. (This is not the same as a "desire to please" him.)

> She faces him, hands brought to her belly's level, offering,
> wordless, looking upon him. She carries his desire well.

The pilot is a good-humored, decent, efficient modern man who disclaims the notion (suggested by his wife) that he is a hero. "No personal hero's left / to make a legend. Those centuries have gone." The reader sees, however, that in the pilot's steady, matter-of-fact approach to his dangerous job he is the modern hero. His will to live is great. He goes to his death that day as a result of a failure of "desire" in the machine. The poet here again unites the energy of desire in human beings with the desire in the so-called "inanimate" universe of things. As in "The Gyroscope" we see that a current runs through the whole cosmos.

> She does not imagine how the propeller turns
> in a blinding speed, swinging the plane through space;
> she never sees the cowling rattle and slip
> forward and forward against the grim blades' grinding
> Cruising speed 1700 R.P.M.
> Slipping, a failing desire   ;   slipping like death
> insidious against the propeller, until the blades shake,
> bitten by steel, jagged against steel, broken,
> and his face angry and raked by death, staring.

The coda to the three sections of "The Tunnel" which describe three kinds of unsatisfied desire, or failure (in the miners, the rejected lover, and the dead pilot) is an exhortation to *use* the human experience of loss, defeat, and death to gain strength to meet the future. We must not fear, says the poet, "the natural calm inclusiveness of time."

> We have prayed torrents of humility, open
> in anguish to be hurt, in terror to be fooled.
> We are beyond demand, waiting a minute
> unconscious in attendance   :   here is strength to be used
> delicately, most subtly on the controls and levers.
> They begged that time be condensed. Extend space for us,
> let us include this memory in ourselves,
> time and our dividend of history.

Rukeyser's stance in the coda corresponds with Crane's at the conclusion of "Quaker Hill," which follows "Three Songs." Both Crane and Rukeyser attempt to make use of the human experience of unsatisfied longing, of defeat. But Crane's answer to that experience is "patience." Rukeyser also counsels "waiting," but she foresees a more active role for those who have been, for a moment, "unconscious in attendance." There are "controls and levers" to be manipulated. There is an extended space in which to act. "The tunnel," for Rukeyser, is a state through which we travel in our progress toward the light. It is the descent into hell which precedes vision and understanding.

The seventh section of Crane's poem is also called "The Tunnel," and it is about a ride in a subway tunnel during which the poet feels despair at modern life as the train plunges into the ground and then regains hope as the train rises again into the light. The poem is Crane's descent into hell which precedes the vision of his final section, "Atlantis." "The Tunnel" obviously continues to develop Crane's theme of questing for the ideal, despairing, and regaining hope to seek it again. Rukeyser has developed her related theme (of striving to ascend into a fuller personal and social humanity) by focusing on the phenomenon of flight and on scenes of social injustice; but critics have had a difficult time showing that the sections of Crane's poem are effectively related to a developing theme. M. L. Rosenthal concluded that "Theory of Flight" has an "organic unity perhaps superior to that of *The Bridge*." [20]

"Atlantis," the conclusion of *The Bridge*, is the poet's final vision of the ideal, which has been the object of the poem's entire quest. This section contains the most exalted, ecstatic, and difficult passages in *The Bridge*. The subject of "Atlantis"—the ideal—makes paraphrase impossible, and explication, which is ultimately inadequate for any poem, is here almost pointless. The bridge is apotheosized to an "Ever-presence, beyond time," a symbol which is to resolve all actual human difficulties.

> Thy pardon for this history, whitest Flower,
> O Answerer of all,—Anemone—

From "the tunnel" of actual modern urban despair, Crane rises to this vision of the absolute. But the irony has been pointed out by Monroe K. Spears: "The poet prays, 'Atlantis,—hold thy floating singer late!' The image is a pathetic one, since the singer is floating because Atlantis is not there, and the poem ends on an unanswered question." [21]

20. Rosenthal, "Chief Poets of the American Depression," 442.
21. Monroe K. Spears, *Hart Crane*, University of Minnesota Pamphlets on American Writers, XLVII (Minneapolis, 1965), 38.

When the poet emerges from despair in "Theory of Flight" she focuses not on an Atlantis, an ineffable vision, but on the practicalities of modern (miraculous) theories and inventions. These are the "controls and levers" (referred to in "The Tunnel") that we can manipulate in order to sense our strengths. The section following "The Tunnel" is entitled "The Structure of the Plane." In the first part we are given a quotation from the Wright brothers.

> "To work intelligently" (Orville and Wilbur Wright)
> "one needs to know the effects of variations
>   incorporated in the surfaces. . . . The pressures on squares
>   are different from those on rectangles, circles, triangles, or
>   ellipses . . .
> The shape of the edge also makes a difference."

Rosenthal writes of this passage that it is "one of the things she does best . . . a general statement of technical theory, exact and economical in diction, foreshadowing her fascination with the language of Willard Gibbs."[22] From this statement of theory we pass immediately to a human being's putting it to test.

> The plane is wheeled out of the hangar. The sleeves shake
> fixing the wind, the four o'clock blue sky
> blinks in the goggles swinging over his wrist.
> The plane rests, the mechanic in cream-colored overalls
> encourages the engine into idling speed.
> The instructor looks at his class
> and begins the demonstration.

We flash back to the Wright brothers again, and to their great will to fly.

> "We finally became discouraged, and returned to kite-flying.
> But as we grew older we had to give up this sport,
> it was unbecoming to boys of our ages."

Then the voice of the instructor resumes its description of the Wrights' dream achieved; the voice eventually sounds like Whitman's.

> On the first stroke of the piston the intake valve opens,
> the piston moves slowly from the head of the cylinder,

22. Rosenthal, "Chief Poets of the American Depression," 435.

drawing in its mixture of gas and air. On the second stroke
the piston returns, the valve closes. The mixture is
     compressed.
A spark occurs, igniting America, opening India,
finding the Northwest Passage, Cipango spice

The effect of this piling-up of technical details and their expansive
implications, physical and spiritual, for human beings is Whitmanesque. Yet the language always returns to the ordinary, for the
point of the poem is that the miraculous has been achieved by the
mind laboring with the ordinary.

Blue smoke from the exhaust signifies too much oil.
Save yourselves from excesses, dirt, and tailspins.
These are the axioms   :   stability, control,
and equilibrium   :   in a yaw, in a roll, or pitch.
Here, gentlemen, are the wings, of fabric doped and painted
here is the rudder
here the propeller spins
  :   BE   hammers in the brain
FLY and the footbeat of that drum
may not be contradicted

How better portray the immense will of the human being to live,
to develop, to evolve than to yoke it with that of the inventor, the
one who dares attempt mastery of conditions not yet human?

   The conclusion of this part describes a student pilot who becomes afraid and parachutes out of a plane in flight. At the beginning of the flight he is seen as a being about to ascend in
evolutionary movement.

Centuries fall behind his brain, the motor
pushes in a four-beat rhythm, his blood moves,
he dares look at the levels mounting in clouds
the dropping fields of the sky the diminishment of earth

But he is held back in fear by his immaturity, by an insufficient development outward from his own ego:

now he thinks I am the child crying Mother
this rim is the threshold into the hall's night
or the windowsill livened with narcissus.

The student's panic and unwillingness to fly cause him to regress to childhood's emotional associations. These are in fact suicidal, for there can be no real return to the haven of childhood, and the best approximation is death.

> The white edge of the bath a moment before
> slipping into watery ease, the windowsill
> eager for the jump into the street
> the hard stone under my back. . . .
>
> . . . .
>
> take me back the bath had fronds of steam
> escaping the hands held my head
> my eyes slipped in oil looking along your beauty
> earth is painful the distance hurts
> mother the night, the distance, dear

With "a long scream" he leaps from the plane, cursing his instructor; but his leap to "safety" has the emotional context of a suicidal leap. The flight, symbol of the mature will to ascend, goes on:

> his parachute opens a bright plume surrendering downward,
> the plane heads up again, no good in following,
> continues unfascinated by night or land or death.

In the second part, "The Strike," the poem shifts focus again from an aspect of flight to a scene of conflict in contemporary society. Here a strikebreaker, "George," repeats the pattern of the student pilot and surrenders to the seduction of defeat. Whereas death was implied in the student's surrender, the strikebreaker's surrender causes his actual death. At first, like the student, he had shown resolve to transcend his situation.

> "Well," he said, "George, I never thought you were with us.
> You walked out of the shaft as if you'd spent years of your life
> planning some day to walk out once without blinking
> and not stop for a smoke but walk over to our side."

But when George saw "how the child chewed its shoe to strips" in hunger and when he had endured all the hardships he could bear, death seduced him to break the strike line.

> "George!" he heard.   That had once been his name.
> Very carefully he had stepped from his place,

> walked over his ground, over the last line.
> It seemed impossible he should not die.
>> When a gun faces you, look down the bore,
>> that is the well of death   :   when it confronts you
>> it is not satisfied, it draws you steadily
>> more loving than love, eagerer than hunger,
>> resolving all unbalance.   He went to it.

Ironically, this miner's death, this surrender, causes the company to concede. The strikers' victory is ambiguous, as is any victory which does not radically alter the pattern of an exploiting society and whose cost is the death of even one human being.

> Perhaps the strike might equal victory,
> a company funeral, and the trucks of coal
>> ladled up from the earth,
>> heaped on this grave.

But the position of this ironic death in the center of "The Structure of the Plane" gives it a positive significance.

The third and last part, "The Lover," is an exhortation to answer the ambiguities, the questions posed by the weaknesses and the destructive forces in society.

> Answer with me these certainties
>
> . . . .
> Answer the men walking toward death
> leaping to death meeting death in a kiss
> able to find of equilibrium none
> except that last of hard stone kissing stone

The poet seeks an equilibrium which is not death, but a balance, a Zen-like poise that unlocks the power of each being:

> all surfaces of flight are pared to planes
>
> equal, equilibrated, solid in fulfilment. No way
> is wanted to escape, no explosions craved,
> only this desire must be met, this motion
> be balanced with passion

The desire or motion of the cosmos and of society (first presented in "The Gyroscope") is here interpreted as need, as love, to be answered by responsive love. Love will create the equilibrium of the living:

> in the wreaths of time given to us what love
> may reach us in the streets   the books   the years
> what wreaths of love may touch our dreams,
> what skeins of fine response may clothe our flesh,
> robe us in valor brave as our dear wish

The failures and the sufferings of society are here projected upon a female lover; in the overcoming of love's inadequacies is found the secret of all overcoming:

> lover haunting the ghosts of rivers, letting time
> slide a fluid runner into darkness
> give over the sad eyes the marble face of pain
> do not mourn . . .
>
> . . . .
>
> take to yourself the branches of green trees
> watch the clean sky signed by the flight of planes
> know rivers of love   be flooded thoroughly
> by love and the years and the past and know
> the green tree perishes and green trees grow.

This lover, once forsaken, is seen awaiting her next encounter; she is described in metaphors from modern technology which, we see, are consistent with what we know of the personality in its smoothest functioning.

> Taut with a steel strut's singing tautness she
> clinches her softness anguished at postponement
>
> . . . .
>   The opened door
> adjusts such things   ;   responsive, she relaxes
> ringing in answer to a word before
>
> all tensity is changed to eagerness.
> Translated and resolved, the anguish through,
> sensitive altogether to the present   :
> "Now?"   "Yes," she says, "yes," she says, "do."

(This is, of course, a more modern Molly Bloom.) To fly is to meet life with life, to decide to be adequate to whatever situation life presents, not to give in to the disequilibrium of despair or the final equilibrium of death.

> Answer motion with motion, be birds flying
> be the enormous movements of the snows,
> be rain, be love, remain equilibrated
> unseeking death,
>   if you must have pilgrimages
> go traveling to balance need with answer
> suiting the explosion to the ensuing shock
> the foil to the airstream running over it
> food to the mouth, tools to the body, mind
> to the bright mind that leaps in necessity
> go answering   answering   FLY

But the next section, "Night Flight: New York," catapults us again to a vision of hell. We are given a rich, beautiful description of planes bombing New York City in a mock air raid. The irony of aerial bombardment is that it is

> Failure encompassed in success, the warplanes
> dropping flares, as a historic sum of knowledge,
>
> . . . .
>
> Icarus' passion, Da Vinci's skill, corrupt,
> all rotted into war

Rosenthal refers to the conclusion of this section as a " 'triumphant' tendentious" conclusion which can't offset "the sense of intransigent evil [which] had 'taken over' the poem by the end." Elsewhere he objects to Rukeyser's early poems' "jamming an unaccountable optimism down our throats." "The unearned triumphant conclusion" is one of the chief faults of her work, according to Rosenthal.[23] This is the conclusion of "Night Flight: New York":

> Between murmur and murmur, birth and death,
> is the earth's turning which follows the earth's turning,
> a swift whisper of life, an ambiguous word spoken   ;
> morning travelling quiet on mutinous fields,
> muscles swollen tight in giant effort   ;   rain   ;   some
>   stars   ;

23. Rosenthal, "The Longer Poems," 213, 219, 202.

a propeller's glimpsing silver whirl, intensely upward,
intensely forward, bearing the plane   :   flying.
. . . .
Believe that we bloom upon this stalk of time   ;
and in this expansion, time too grows for us
richer and richer towards infinity.
They promised us the gold and harps and seraphs.
Our rising and going to sleep is better than future pinions.
We surrender that hope, drawing our own days in,
covering space and time draped in tornadoes,
lightning invention, speed crushing the stars upon us,
stretching the accordion of our lives, sounding the same chord
longer and savoring it until the echo fails.
Believe that your presences are stong,
O be convinced without formula or rhyme
or any dogma   ;   use yourselves   :   be   :   fly.
Believe that we bloom upon this stalk of time

The first two lines are a clear evocation of Eliot's "The Hollow
Men."

> Between the idea
> And the reality
> Between the motion
> And the act
> Falls the Shadow

For Thine is the Kingdom

Rukeyser's stanzas are a direct rebuttal of Eliot's pessimistic mood
and withdrawal into High Church religion. ("The accordion of
our lives" is an aptly "common" metaphor.) Eliot's debility was
the result of his belief that the individual consciousness could no
longer remain integrated because it lacked the fixed relations to
the world afforded by traditional religion and philosophy. But if
an individual consciousness does not demand fixed relations to the
world but rather sees security in change which is growth, then pessimism will not necessarily follow a vision of traumatic change,
such as the vision in "Night Flight: New York." The incessant
swift whispers of life, the trillions of words spoken (though ambiguous), the muscles swollen in giant efforts, the planes flying,

these are proof for the consciousness which is like Rukeyser's that all is well. We bloom upon a stalk of time; and there will be other stalks, other blooms. No shadow of inadequacy falls on our daily round of effort and result.

Rosenthal has called attention to the similarity of thought between Rukeyser and the Marxist critic Kenneth Burke, especially in his *Attitudes Toward History* (1937). Both Burke and Rukeyser expressed attitudes that were "in the air" in the thirties: for example, the politically and philosophically hopeful perspective that in any circumstance there is the seed (dialectically) of the development of its opposite. Rukeyser explained to Rosenthal that in her poems she uses experience "to show the seed, or the arrangement" of a desired change. Burke and Rukeyser are in the tradition of American meliorism of Emerson, Whitman, and William James. Meliorism holds that there are no absolutes, that a person need be neither an optimist nor a pessimist; the reasonable way to relate to the universe is to accept it and work to make it better. Burke calls his meliorism a "comic frame of motives" for dealing with and thinking about society.[24] He would use "secular prayer," which is a self-coaching of reasonable attitudes toward any circumstance, no matter how adverse. Secular prayer involves the use of terms that transcend conflicts by adopting a point of view in which opposites cease to be opposites. Burke notes in *Attitudes Toward History* that primitives use secular prayer, the giving of a symbol of transcendence or reconciliation, in initiation rites during which a member of the tribe assumes a new stance toward life, a new identity. He or she is urged to grow into a new stance. In *The Life of Poetry* Rukeyser writes approvingly of primitive societies where members are molded "toward emotion, toward the experience of crises of realization and of conscience" (LP, 43). She says poetry should do this for modern people.

When Crane sings the bridge as "harp and altar," evoking the "white choiring wings" of angels, ultimately the bridge is "Ev-

24. *Ibid.*, Note, 203, 205, 208; Kenneth Burke, *Attitudes Toward History* (2 vols.; New York, 1937), I, 1–4, 214; II, 220 ff.

erpresence, beyond time." Rukeyser does not seek to go beyond time, believing the promised "harps and seraphs" are a false hope. She seeks the exaltation of human life intensely lived. Crane answered Eliot with Eliot's own traditional Anglo-Catholic terminology, accepting the value Eliot placed on transcending time and the ordinary world. Rukeyser would savor the marvels of the ordinary turning world which harbors all its seeds. Because of her focus on "our rising and going to sleep," on "our own days" rather than on "future pinions" or on a vanished, supposedly glorious past, she does earn her "triumphant" conclusions to her visions of hell. In her system, hell is simply the temporary inability to focus on the strong presences of good, growth, and renewal in the midst of universal perishing.

The final section, "Theory of Flight," restates the theme of the poem. "Flight is intolerable contradiction," but it can be accomplished because human beings have chosen to "ride" with contradictions, to use them. "Use yourselves," the poet has urged in the previous section. To fly is to "open your flesh . . . to opposites," to live with contradictions, to respond to the prophets and rebels of the past who have urged growth and change. We can choose what part of the past will pass to the future:

> the guns are dying the past is born again
> into these future minds the incarnate past
> gleaming upon the present.

Because we can choose, the poet affirms that "we go to victory / in a commune of regenerated lives." The technological achievement of flight is here urged as a symbol of what can be accomplished in human relationships, private and public. Society is ripe for regeneration, for abandoning futile wars of "brain versus brain for absolutes." Society is ready to emphasize human responsiveness to human needs.

> Now we can look at our subtle jointures, study our hands,
> the tools are assembled, the maps unrolled, propellers spun,
> do we say **all is in readiness** :
> **the times approach, here is the signal shock** : ?

Master in the plane shouts "Contact" :
master on the ground : "Contact!"
    he looks up : "Now?" whispering : "Now."
    "Yes," she says.   "Do."
    Say yes, people.
    Say yes.
    YES

Kenneth Burke, in his review of *Theory of Flight* for the *New Masses* in 1936 found these final lines "magnificent in their context." [25]

Joseph Warren Beach in *Obsessive Images* did not appreciate Rukeyser's method and attitude in "Theory of Flight," noting that " 'The Structure of the Plane' . . . ends with an effusive peroration in favor of an affirmative attitude toward life." He complained that "she could not resist the temptation to patch up her symbolism with the mortar of prosy abstractions: and here she constantly ran into the baldness of cliché. What is needed to give proper effect to such outlandish combinations of tone and reference as are found throughout *Theory of Flight* is a solvent capable of assimilating them all to itself—such as irony, for example, in the later Auden. Without that one is frequently repelled by the raw gobbets, the unstyled crudities of rhetoric and self-revelation." [26]

Literary criticism is perhaps the most relative of all attempts to evaluate the productions of human beings. What is a bald cliché, a prosy abstraction, an outlandish combination, a raw gobbet to one decade of critics and readers may be a stunning method to another. Since the "confessional school" of poets, we have come to accept, even to prize, as Stephen Stepanchev said, "experience in all its rawness and directness." [27] Literary critics, however, still have difficulty with the nonironic. The situation is not so rigid as in the heyday of irony—the fifties—when Rosenthal wrote in his article

25. Burke, " Return After Flight," 26.
26. Joseph Warren Beach, *Obsessive Images: Symbolism in Poetry of the 1930's and 1940's,* ed. W. V. O'Connor (Minneapolis, 1960), 256–57.
27. Stephen Stepanchev, review of *Waterlily Fire,* in *Shenandoah,* XIV (Spring, 1963), 58.

on Rukeyser, "Now current criticism responds well to the poetry of pure and ironic sensibility; less surely, though constrained to recognize its power, to the poetry of incantation. It does by far the least justice, however, to the rhetoric of romantic expression, in which the speaker dares to give the game away because he counts on a relationship of some personal sympathy with the reader."[28] Since Allen Ginsberg, the new Black writing, and the new feminist writing, critics have been forced to accommodate the speaking voice seeking the reader's sympathy, even in affirmation. It isn't necessary to be ironic anymore to be taken seriously as a poet.

Joseph Warren Beach found Rukeyser's affirmative attitude unacceptable because there was no leaven of irony in her poetry. Yet he could write, at the conclusion of *Obsessive Images*, that "our poets" have failed their audience—the great mass of readers of poetry—because poets have not been able to write out of the humanist perspective in which the good in the world is stressed, without supernatural guarantee. Most people, said Beach, can't identify with "the moral terrors, the mental anguish or 'anxiety' . . . the macabre moral scenery and atmosphere to which our poets have invited them." He continued:

Our poets are not in a position to complain of the philistine insensitiveness of the public so long as they represent so meagerly the concerns, the attitudes, the joys and exultances, the agonies and aspirations, the disenchantments and the braveries of the great mass of the population—including most of those who read books, trust to scientific method for the solution of scientific problems, enjoy driving cars and planes and monkeying with machines, prefer comfort to discomfort, see many evidences of progress in the material world and in the world of human relations, accept their responsibilities in family life and take some pleasure in them, try to keep their vicious propensities under control, but think more of the good life they aim at than of the devil they dodge, and maintain some measure of what used to be called 'faith in humanity.'[29]

Other critics have praised Rukeyser's "faith in humanity." Eunice Clark in her review of *Theory of Flight* in *Common Sense* found "deep positive humanity" in Rukeyser's work. The poet has

28. Rosenthal, "The Longer Poems," 203.
29. Beach, *Obsessive Images*, 374–75.

"an intellect alive to history, respectful of science and eager for revolution. . . .She is an artist who is not afraid to have a message, a loving and fighting message to her own generation." *Time* magazine praised *Theory of Flight*, saying, "The mood of spiritual desolation expressed in T. S. Eliot's *The Waste Land* and echoed by a thousand imitators has no place in *[her work]*. On the contrary, the poet gives an impression of eagerness and determination in facing the experiences of contemporary life, even the most brutal, and making a passionate effort to understand them and incorporate them into her verse." Richard Eberhart wrote in 1948 that in each of her books we find a rich nature expressing itself positively, addressing itself to the large, elemental concepts of love, freedom, and peace. M. L. Rosenthal, in a completely positive review in the *New York Herald Tribune* (1948), said she has "eschewed the reach for an artificial myth, or tradition . . . or . . . approved . . . formulas including the Pure and Absolute Horror of it All" and "has the effrontery to take science seriously." [30]

According to these reviewers, Rukeyser is a humanist poet who has represented the concerns and "the braveries of the great mass of the population," in Beach's words. Yet Beach, who called for such a poet in *Obsessive Images*, objected in that book to "the confident self-assurance of the young woman taking on the Whitman mantle of prophecy":

Somehow, in Whitman, one feels that the 'I' of the poet is actually *possessed* by his prophetic vision and raised out of himself; he is merely the challenger of old shells of thought, and the vehicle or medium through which the revelation declares itself. Besides, he has no confidently worked out ideological system like Miss Rukeyser's revolutionary doctrine. He does not have anything like so pretentious a program, and is not so prone to take his own personal vitality as the proof of this and that social dogma. It is the uncritical cheekiness of this young woman that does much to prevent her from writing really fine poetry. [31]

The last sentence of Beach's evaluation reveals the preconception

30. Eunice Clark, review of TF; unsigned review of TF, in *Time*, December 16, 1935, p. 81; Richard Eberhart, "Art and *Zeitgeist*," *Poetry*, LXXIII (December, 1948), 173; M. L. Rosenthal, review of *The Green Wave*, in *New York Herald Tribune Books*, June 27, 1948, p. 4.
31. Beach, *Obsessive Images*, 257.

that underlies the whole: a woman should not sound like Walt Whitman. But Rukeyser's personal vitality, so like Whitman's, is not a program proving "this and that social dogma." Her faith in life is not "cheekiness" but a rare and inspiring positiveness.

Rukeyser's work has suffered at the hands of critics who felt she did not, as a woman, write the right kind of poetry. She was too bold for some critics, too sweeping and assertive. Surprisingly enough, the poet Louise Bogan was one of Rukeyser's harshest reviewers. (Bogan's published and unpublished correspondence and the unpublished letters of Rolfe Humphries and Morton Dauwen Zabel to Bogan reveal their shared acid personal dislike of Rukeyser and her close friends during the thirties, the poets Horace Gregory and [his wife]Marya Zaturenska.)[32] Critics have pointed out that as an artist and critic, Bogan had difficulty because of her view of her own sex—as expressed in her poem "Women":

> Women have no wilderness in them,
> They are provident instead,
> Content in the tight hot cell of their hearts
> To eat dusty bread.
>
> . . . .
>
> They wait, when they should turn to journeys,
> They stiffen, when they should bend.
> They use against themselves that benevolence
> To which no man is friend.

Bogan was impatient with women poets. Consider the deprecatory tone and the generalizations in her review of Rukeyser's *Beast in View* (1944): "The sentiment of a given period is nowhere so well distilled as in the contemporary verse . . . by women either as a serious literary exercise or merely to get something off their minds. The fashionable attitude, the decorative emotion, the sweeping empty enthusiasm, the sigh that is not yet a tear come through in the works of female versifiers so vividly that we are at once carried off into a 'period' mood of one kind or another." Bogan insists that women poets must rise above their time "if their work is not to re-

32. Ruth Limmer (ed.), *Selected Letters of Louise Bogan, 1920–1970* (New York, 1973). Letters from Rolfe Humphries and Morton Dauwen Zabel in the Bogan Papers, Amherst College.

semble, after twenty years . . . the dated illustrations in a household magazine." But she adds, "Muriel Rukeyser has always stood four-square in her time."

Several years later, in 1951, praising Adrienne Rich's first volume for its modesty of form and scope, Bogan called Rukeyser's work unconvincing because it did not measure up to the best female lyricism. "The chief virtue of women's poetry is its power to pin down, with uncanny accuracy, moments of actual experience. From the beginning of the record, female lyricism has concerned itself with minute particulars, and at its best seems less a work of art than a miracle of nature—a flawless distillation, a pure crystallization of thought, circumstance, and emotion." Rukeyser's work, on the other hand, is "a deflated Whitmanian rhetoric. . . . Muriel Rukeyser is the one woman poet of her generation to put on sibyl's robes, nowadays truly threadbare." (It is an irony of literary history that Adrienne Rich, whose first book Bogan reviewed with one of Rukeyser's, developed into a feminist political poet in Rukeyser's tradition. The Adrienne Rich of the seventies sounds more like Muriel Rukeyser than like the "modest" poet whom Bogan faintly praised in 1951. Rich has undergone an amazing evolution since she wrote in her first volume, "a too compassionate art is half an art.")[33]

A woman Whitman, a woman whose work recalls the boldness and scope of Whitman's, was offensive to critics of the forties and fifties. When one asks why Rukeyser has been given little attention in published scholarly discussions, the answer seems to be: she didn't fit. She didn't fit into critics' notions of what poetry should be, what poetry by a woman should be. In addition, her politics often offended, both as politics and as ideas which seemed incongruous in their development from her stance of the thirties. One of

33. Gloria Bowles, "Louise Bogan: To Be (Or Not To Be?) Woman Poet," *Women's Studies*, V, 2 (1977), 131–35; Louise Bogan, "Women," *The Blue Estuaries: Poems 1923–1968* (New York, 1977), 19; Louise Bogan, review of *Beast in View*, in *New Yorker*, October 21, 1944, p. 91; Louise Bogan, review of *Selected Poems*, in *New Yorker*, November 3, 1951, p. 150; Adrienne Rich, "At a Bach Concert," *Poems Selected and New, 1950–1974* (New York, 1975), 7.

the objects of this study is to trace the organic growth of Rukeyser's political ideas in their relationship to her larger philosophy of life.

Comparative Outline of *The Bridge* and "Theory of Flight"

The Bridge	"Theory of Flight"
Proem: To Brooklyn Bridge	Preamble
I. Ave Maria	The Gyroscope
II. Powhatan's Daughter	
The Harbor Dawn	
Van Winkle	The Lynchings of Jesus
The River	I. Passage to Godhead
The Dance	II. The Committee-Room
Indiana	III. The Trial
III. Cutty Sark	
IV. Cape Hatteras	
V. Three Songs	The Tunnel
Southern Cross	I.
National Winter Garden	II.
Virginia	III.
VI. Quaker Hill	
VII. The Tunnel	
	The Structure of the Plane
	I. The Structure of the Plane
	II. The Strike
VIII. Atlantis	III. The Lover
	Night Flight: New York
	Theory of Flight

TWO

Traditions and Contemporaries

AT THE BEGINNING of her career, Muriel Rukeyser was identified
with what Elizabeth Drew and others called "the Auden-Spender
group," who "dictated the fashion *[when]* it came to be considered
intellectually a trifle dowdy if verse did not wear red."[1] Rukeyser
herself says that as a young poet she admired Auden's first poems
very much. But she is markedly unlike Auden in her early volumes
(her later poems are quite simply a different species from the later
Auden); one is struck by the facileness with which critics repeatedly placed them in the same "school." However, today we have
the advantage of hindsight, a view of the developing body of both
poets' work, and we can recognize the seeds better for our view of
the harvest.

Nor can one mistake her for earlier American poets of social
concern such as Carl Sandburg, Stephen Vincent Benét, Genevieve Taggard, and Lola Ridge (though of all these Ridge is her
closest kin). Some of these older poets came late to social awareness and did not have to juxtapose in their poems both youthful
personal struggles and the agonized awareness of a world out of
joint. Others did not share Rukeyser's belief in poetry as a process
of sharing discovery, which means an open poetry whose images
invite and demand the reader's intense participation. Rukeyser is
obviously in the line of those who sang the land, more often the

1. Elizabeth Drew, *Directions in Modern Poetry* (New York, 1940), 97.

city, and its people, from Whitman to Sandburg, but from the very beginning another tradition found a new voice in her poems, and that is the impulse in this century of Van Wyck Brooks, Paul Rosenfeld, and Hart Crane to make an art to irrigate men's spirits in an acquisitive society. Such an art had to explore as well as celebrate and had to go beyond Whitman who, Brooks claimed, could only say he was glad to be alive but was "unable to imagine what can be made of life." Brooks said artists must teach us how to imagine. Sandburg sang the people and the land but never attempted or invited creative exploration with poetry (as Whitman did when he said the reader "must himself or herself construct . . . the poem"), nor did he ever "take the risk of even a tentative solution or suggestion for the world's ills." As Horace Gregory noted in 1941, "Miss Rukeyser's 'Say yes, people, Say yes. Yes' made its spectacular reappearance in the title of Carl Sandburg's book *The People, Yes.*" His is the famous and less complex exhortation.[2]

Rukeyser is essentially a modern poet of possibility (a word which recurs in her writing and conversation) in the tradition of the transcendental writers of America's Golden Day: Emerson, Whitman, Thoreau. In his introduction to *The Collected Poems of Hart Crane*, Waldo Frank explains that Crane grounded the older vision of possibility, the belief that human beings can transcend material concerns and achieve an organic relationship with the cosmos, in twentieth-century technology. In *The Bridge* Crane rose from the machines he loved to an embrace of the unity of all energy, the One. Rukeyser's vision of possibility is also based in part on the marvels of technology, but her times—times of war, waiting for war, and living with the vast human devastation of the mid- and later twentieth century—and her personal exploration of the struggle of the individual in a corrupt society (Alabama, West Virginia, Catalonia, Vietnam, East Harlem, South Korea) cause

2. Van Wyck Brooks, *Letters and Leadership* (New York, 1918), 109; Richard Crowder, *Carl Sandburg* (New York, 1964), 119; Horace Gregory, "American Poetry 1930–40," *Decision*, I (January, 1941), 28. Sandburg's *The People, Yes* was published in 1936, a year after *Theory of Flight*.

her vision of possibility to rise from a more inclusive complexity than Crane's. Yet the basic source of her vision is her self (in the Emersonian sense), which she sounds in poetic exploration and extends in human involvement thereby discovering the possibility to which all may aspire, despite repression, war, genocide, and the chorus of poets who sing, in Rosenthal's words, that "the humanistic way . . . has already been defeated." [3] She believes that all her involvements, political, scholarly, artistic, are "ways of reaching the world and the Self," those two ever fertile sources of possibility. Her early prose comments on poetry all point to her acceptance of Emerson's urging in "The Poet" to write out of a thoroughly individual and fresh relationship with the continually fresh world, denying none of its complexities and rendering them in whatever "axiom-breaking" form they demand (LP, 63).

In *The Life of Poetry*, in two pages of dense, concrete detail, Rukeyser describes the "richness even to the most contradictory" of America. "I think of the concrete landscapes of airfields, where every line prolongs itself straight to the horizon, and the small cabin in the Appalachians under the steep trail streaming its water down; of the dam at Shasta. . . . And I think of the wretched houses of Gamoca where the Negroes lived and were brave, who are dead now of silicon in the lungs. And of the pride of the Embarcadero" (LP, 65–66). These elements in conflict are to her, as to Emerson, "process or moment, gods or half-gods . . . immortal necessities, which are not checks and balances, but phases, if you will, of essence—all to be fought for, realized, and sung" (LP, 68). She says we have had poems which offer these phases, these truths of outrage and of possibility. Whitman, trusting in possibility, strove to be inclusive "in an identification with America as a people, multitudinous and full of contradictions," accepting his entire nature, trusting finally to his body rhythms (LP, 75). "Whitman's fight for reconciliation was of profound value as a symbol. The fight was the essential process of democracy: to remake and

3. M. L. Rosenthal, *The New Poets: American and British Poetry Since World War II* (New York, 1967), 5.

acknowledge the relationships, to find the truth and power in diversity, among antagonists; and a poet of that democracy would have to acknowledge and make that truth emerge from the widest humanity in himself, among the horizons of his contradicted days and nights" (LP, 80–81). Melville, on the other hand, spoke for outrage in his day: "he touched perpetual evil." In our time, says Rukeyser with her characteristic sympathy when discussing the work of a contemporary, Robinson Jeffers touches that evil constantly. He represents outrage in poetry of "beautiful strength." In our day Rukeyser embodies possibility for she, like all poets who "lived toward their forms," has given voice, in a more complex world, to Whitman's and Emerson's inclusive, hopeful theme (LP, 86, 87).

It is the merging and extending of these philosophical and aesthetic traditions (as well as her use of the modern poetic techniques of Eliot and Crane) in the early poems which makes Rukeyser so unlike the proletarian poets with whom she was invariably grouped in the thirties and along with whom she was berated in the disillusioned forties by critics such as Randall Jarrell who could see only the "Perfect State" in her visions of a more humanly satisfying world. After the war, when poetry of social concern was strictly outmoded to academic poets and critics (and there were few who were not associated with the academy), Jarrell could say of Rukeyser, "One feels about most of her poems almost as one feels about the girl on last year's calendar." But critics failed to see in their categorizing that Rukeyser never wrote poetry that was a simple commentary on the political or social scene. (Many proletarian poets often did that; Sandburg also did that. There is little of Sandburg himself in his poems. As Daniel Hoffman said, we find in them, "collective emotions divorced from the individual consciousness.") Louise Bogan said in 1939 that Rukeyser is "interested in the state of society to the almost complete exclusion of any conscious 'personal expression.'" But quite the opposite is true. It is precisely the intense exploration of what it means and feels like to be the kind of person she is in a certain span of the twentieth century that has been Rukeyser's work in poetry and prose from *Theory of Flight* to *The Gates*. This personal exploration, against the background of a world of increasing terror and inhumanity, draws the contemporary reader into the poems of the thirties and gives the latest volumes a rich personal-historical dimension which is absent in the work of younger poets simply because they haven't lived through and imagined through as much of this stunning century.[4] Through the unsettling decades since the thirties and the shifts in critical fashion, Rukeyser has been steadily productive. Through all her work run the impulses and ideals of *Theory of Flight*; as Kenneth Rexroth noted, "while still in college she had already discovered her own special vocation, the poetic material, and the philosophical attitudes, which would endure throughout her work."[5] Rukeyser's harvest of forty years is a genuine inspiration to those who believe that the practice of poetry can expand the personality and the imagination, that poetry (and prose that shares poetry's urge to the fullest realization of meaning) can explore reality and discover its often otherwise unutterable truths.

The School of Auden

Every student of American literature learns that Auden was the most important English-language poet of the thirties and that his poetic style and leftist politics influenced a whole generation on both sides of the Atlantic. Rukeyser is assumed to have been influenced by Auden, to have taken her philosophical, political, and artistic cues from him and his group. But how useful to the understanding of her poetry and its development is this assumption? Auden was six years Rukeyser's senior, and by the time her first volume of poetry appeared in 1935 he had published three volumes of

4. Randall Jarrell, *Poetry and the Age* (New York, 1953), 163; Daniel Hoffman, quoted in Crowder, *Carl Sandburg*, 166; Louise Bogan, review of TW, in *New Yorker*, December 16, 1939, p. 120.

5. Kenneth Rexroth, *American Poetry in the Twentieth Century* (New York, 1971), 123.

poetry (1928, 1930, 1933). These early poems are not at all like the poems in *Theory of Flight*. Nor is the verse in his plays, burlesques, and travel book (*Letters from Iceland*, 1937) like Rukeyser's poetry in her second volume, *U.S.1* (1938). Essentially, the difference in Auden's and Rukeyser's early poetry is based on the fact that the original rebelliousness of the Auden group was distinctly nonpolitical. Auden claimed that in the 1920s when he was at Oxford people were unaffected by world events: the Russian Revolution, inflation in Germany and Austria, fascism in Italy. But Rukeyser in "Poem out of Childhood" (above, p. 3) says her school and college days were disturbed by the First World War, the Sacco and Vanzetti trial, the Depression, and a general keen awareness of "horrors." There is an awareness of horrors in Auden's early poetry, to be sure. Untermeyer said Auden's early work was written mainly out of revulsion, in a desperate and morose tone which emphasized, in Auden's words, "immeasurable neurotic dread." There are "barricades," "armies," and forebodings of catastrophe in Auden's early poems—but there are few proper names. Auden's first work was not a grappling with the emerging self in the context of a society in turmoil about which he cared intensely and specifically. Auden said, "Before 1930, I never opened a newspaper." That would have made him twenty-four by the time he (presumably) opened a newspaper on a fairly regular basis. But by the time she was twenty-four Rukeyser had already tried to cover the Scottsboro trials for a student newspaper and contracted typhoid in an Alabama jail, given streetcorner speeches in New York, made her investigative journey to Gauley, West Virginia, and studied congressional reports of the miners' deaths there for her long poem in *U.S.1,* and witnessed the first fighting of the Spanish Civil War.[6]

Let us examine some of Auden's poetry before *Theory of Flight* to see why critics have placed Rukeyser in the "school of Auden."

6. George Wright, *W. H. Auden* (New York, 1969), 33; Louis Untermeyer (ed.), *Modern American Poetry and Modern British Poetry* (Mid-century edition; New York, 1950), 429; W. H. Auden, *Poems*(New York, 1934), 54; W. H. Auden, "As It Seemed to Us," *New Yorker*, April 3, 1965, p. 180.

The sense of a doomed world in turmoil which makes individual lives and strivings comparatively meaningless is present in both Auden's and Rukeyser's poetry. But where the speaker in Auden is engulfed in this sense of doom, even to the point of denying the validity of personal love, Rukeyser invariably redeems the meaninglessness by an act of hope, a compelling, often complex vision of a better world, or an aggressive will to change which is quite unlike the resignation that marks even the young Auden.

There is nothing in *Theory of Flight* that parallels the mood of the following lines from Auden's *Poems* (1934):

> It wasn't always like this?
> Perhaps it wasn't, but it is.
> Put the car away; when life fails,
> What's the good of going to Wales?
> Here am I, here are you:
> But what does it mean? What are we going to do? (no. IX)

> A bird used to visit this shore:
> It isn't going to come any more.
> I've come a very long way to prove
> No land, no water, and no love.
> Here am I, here are you:
> But what does it mean? What are we going to do? (no. IX)

The ironic lilt of these lines gives a poignancy to the sense of futility and loss. One poem in *Theory of Flight* that resembles Auden's is entitled "Eccentric Motion." Here Rukeyser, with similar questions and short lines, treats the theme of frantic activity against the backdrop of an ailing society.

> Dashing in glass we race,
> New York to Washington :
> . . . .
> Have we reached the last limits?
> What have we not done?
> Shut into velvet we
> survey the scene,
> the locked-up building,
> the frozen pier   :
> . . . .

> This is not the way
> to save the day.
> Get up and dress and go
> nobly to and fro :
> Dashing in glass we race,
> New York to Mexico. . . .

But here the frenzy and boredom are parodied, whereas in Auden's early poems the answer to the anxiety felt by the speaker is resignation. The background of the early Auden poems is some unexplained great defeat for the human spirit, even after "we made all possible preparations." The only course now is a stoical acceptance.

> As for ourselves there is left remaining
> Our honour at least,
> And a reasonable chance of retaining
> Our faculties to the last. (no. XII)

This note of weariness and the sense of irreparable damage is absent from Rukeyser's poems.

Both Auden and Rukeyser write of the inadequacy of parents and elders who have little wisdom to offer the young in a world which demands a new vision, new modes of behavior. No poem of Auden's, however, is as personal ("confessional") about the wrenching apart of generations as Rukeyser's "Four in a Family," which begins:

> The father and mother sat, and the sister beside her.
> I faced the two women across the table's width,
> speaking, and all the time he looked at me,
> sorrowing, saying nothing, with his hard tired breath.

Both Auden and Rukeyser seek ancestors in world civilization to inspire and direct youthful idealisms. But Auden's search for ancestors is a futile one. He finds certain culture heroes irrelevant to our times: "Those who have betrayed us nicely while we took them to our rooms / Newman, Ciddy, Plato, Fronny, Pascal, Bowdler, Baudelaire." And the most enlightened of our ancestors are effective no longer:

> Lawrence, Blake and Homer Lane, once healers in our English land;

> These are dead as iron for ever; these can never hold our hand.
> Lawrence was brought down by smut-hounds, Blake went
>   dotty as he sang,
> Homer Lane was killed in action by the Twickenham Baptist
>   gang. (no. XXII)

Rukeyser's search for ancestors is more fruitful, though she must turn from those whose toil and energy she admires but whose vision was limited. Unlike Auden (whose expressions of loss are never without a touch of irony) she expresses a sad love for American forebears whom she must betray. Philip Blair Rice, reviewing *Theory of Flight* in *The Nation*, said that the most moving poems in the book are those in which she develops the thesis that she can "establish 'continuance' with the American dream, but only by turning against its traditional forms." These poems, Rice sensed, were "evidently conceived in some anguish of spirit."[7] Consider these lines from "The Blood Is Justified."

> How did they wish, grandparents of these wars,
> what cataracts of ambition fell across their brains?   :
>
> The heavy boots kicked stones down Wisconsin roads,
> Augusta Coller danced her début at Oshkosh   :
> they spoke these names   :   Milwaukee, Waukesha,
>
> . . . .
> What treason to their race has fathered us?
>
> . . . .
> I do not say   :   Forgive, to my kindred dead,
> only   :   Understand my treason, See I betray you kissing,
> I overthrow your milestones weeping among your tombs.

Unlike Auden, Rukeyser does not think that Blake, Lawrence, and other visionaries and healers of the human spirit are "dead as iron for ever." In "Theory of Flight" all the heroes and rebels are alive in those whose feet follow, "going up the hill with sheaves and tools / and all the weapons of ascent together." She says of those who have sought beauty and truth through the ages, "These braveries are permanent. These gifts / flare on our lives, clarifying, revealed" ("Ci-

7. Philip Blair Rice, "New Poet," *Nation*, January 29, 1936, p. 134.

tation for Horace Gregory"). Her series of "Lives," begun in 1939, is proof that she continues to find ancestors.

To come to the fundamental difference between Auden and Rukeyser, one can cite Auden's famous prayer (XXX) in the *Poems* of 1934.

> Sir, no man's enemy, forgiving all
>
> . . . .
>
> Send to us power and light, a sovereign touch,
> Curing the intolerable neural itch,
>
> . . . .
>
> The exhaustion of weaning
>
> . . . .
>
> look shining at
> New styles of architecture, a change of heart.

Rukeyser's prayer, "Earth, bind us close, and time," at the beginning of "Theory of Flight" is unlike Auden's in every respect save one. In Rukeyser there is no supplication to an Anglican "Sir," no assertion that maturing is inevitably exhausting and riddled with neuroses— there are mistakes, loneliness, losses, fears, but not unbearable neuroses. In 1934, however, Auden as well as Rukeyser could pray for "new styles of architecture, a change of heart." One assumes he meant to affirm, like Rukeyser, the physical face of the modern world as well as new modes of personal behavior which bespeak possibility in human development.

But in the foreword to his *Collected Shorter Poems* (1967) Auden repudiated his prayer of 1934. "Some poems . . . I have thrown out because they were dishonest. . . . A dishonest poem is one which expresses, no matter how well, feelings or beliefs which its author never felt or entertained. For example, I once expressed a desire for 'New styles of architecture'; but I have never liked modern architecture. I prefer *old* styles." As both poets develop through several decades, their philosophies, aesthetics, and poetic styles become increasingly different. Auden's bear out his assertion, "I have always been a formalist." His poems become discursive, and the world view they embody grows increasingly "civilized" in the eighteenth-century sense: "closed, finished." Titles are indicative: in 1972

Auden published a book of poems entitled *Epistle to a Godson*; Rukeyser in 1973 published *Breaking Open*. In Auden's book, "Moon Landing" complains of "our lack of decorum":

> give me a watered
> lively garden, remote from blatherers
> about the New, the von Brauns and their ilk, where
> . . . .
> no engine can shift my perspective.

In the title poem he says, "Let us leave rebellions to the choleric who need them." But these are the later poems. The point here is that Auden's supposed influence on Rukeyser's early poems is not significant; from the beginning, she spoke in her own voice, out of native traditions, and her response to the world of the thirties was quite unlike Auden's. His early poems were essentially noncommittal. His later poems (and editing) renounce his young "enthusiasms." But Rukeyser's early poems reveal, as Philip Blair Rice noted in 1936, a genuine "revolutionary attitude," one that is "carefully reasoned and deeply felt." M. L. Rosenthal noted that her work of the thirties is radically different from Auden's despite superficial resemblances because "her work does not aim to set the reader exploring ambiguities, possibilities, freedoms, without indicating goals." Rosenthal summed up this difference as a "sense of responsibility."[8]

Stephen Spender is the English leftist poet who most resembles Rukeyser in her first volume. Unlike Auden, Spender was a romantic poet of "revolutionary fervor." In his *Poems*, 1933, there is exhortation in the metaphors of the machine age, like that of "Theory of Flight," to live fully in this world and to try to improve it. From XXXIII, "Not palaces, an era's crown":

> It is too late for rare accumulation
> For family pride, for beauty's filtered dusts;
> I say, stamping the words with emphasis,
> Drink from here energy and only energy,

8. W. H. Auden, *Collected Shorter Poems* (New York, 1967), 15; "Craft Interview with W. H. Auden," in William Packard (ed.), *The Craft of Poetry* (Garden City, N.Y., 1974), 1; W. H. Auden, *Epistle to a Godson* (New York, 1972), 22; Rice, "New Poet"; Wright, *W. H. Auden*, 53; Rosenthal, "Chief Poets of the American Depression," 494.

> As from the electric charge of a battery,
> To will this Time's change.
>
> . . . .
>
> Touch, love, all senses;
> Leave your gardens, your singing feasts,
> Your dreams of suns circling before our sun,
> Of heaven after our world.
> Instead, watch images of flashing brass
> . . . the polished will
> Flag of our purpose which the wind engraves.

Yet in this second volume, published when Spender was twenty-four years old, there is, as in Auden, the recurrent note that the world is diminished somehow, that we have suffered an irreparable loss. From "What I expected," XIII:

> What I had not foreseen
> Was the gradual day
> Weakening the will
> Leaking the brightness away,
> The lack of good to touch

There are poems which praise the achievements of modern technology in a spirit shared by Rukeyser but in language which, despite some modern phrasing, is still more like Yeats than like the Wright Brothers. "The Express," XXVI:

> . . . gliding like a queen, she leaves the station.
>
> . . . .
>
> And always light, aerial, underneath
> Goes the elate meter of her wheels.
>
> . . . .
>
> Ah, like a comet through flames she moves entranced
> Wrapt in her music no bird song, no, nor bough
> Breaking with honey buds, shall ever equal.

Similarly, in "The Landscape Near an Aerodrome," Spender's description of the airplane is, unlike Rukeyser's, reminiscent of an older world.

> More beautiful and soft than any moth
> With burring furred antennae feeling its huge path

Through dusk, the air liner with shut-off engines
Glides. . . .[9]

Thus we see that Rukeyser's early poetry reflects an involvement
with the contemporary world, its living heritage, and its possibility
which is not characteristic of "the Auden-Spender group."

The Proletarians

Proletarian literature is the term used to describe the writing of social consciousness and revolution of the thirties. Allen Guttmann
says "proletarian poetry as an American literary movement of permanent importance began in 1929, with the publication of Kenneth
Fearing's first book [Angel Arms], and ended—to assign an arbi-
trary date—in 1939, with the start of World War II." [10] At first, self-
proclaimed proletarian writers were a small group of militants who
denounced Archibald MacLeish as a Nazi for writing Frescoes for
Mr. Rockefeller's City. But after the Seventh Congress of the Communist International called, in the summer of 1935, for a popular
front against fascism, leftist writers of all persuasions were hailed as
proletarian. The Communist-sponsored American Writers Con-
gresses of 1935 and 1937 were attended by a wide spectrum of
writers concerned with demonstrating and discussing their commitment as artists to social justice and social change. (Rukeyser made a
brief appearance at the first congress.)

Two anthologies of proletarian literature appeared in the thirties: We Gather Strength (1933), which included the poetry of Herman Spector, Joseph Kalar, Edwin Rolfe, and Sol Funaroff, and
Proletarian Literature in the United States (1935), edited by Granville Hicks. Marcus Klein calls Hicks's anthology the most nearly
"official" compendium.[11] It included, along with a poem of Rukey-

9. Untermeyer (ed.), Modern American Poetry, 450; Stephen Spender, Poems (London, 1933).
10. Allen Guttmann, "The Brief Embattled Course of Proletarian Poetry," in David
Madden (ed.), Proletarian Writers of the Thirties (Carbondale, Illinois, 1968), 252.
11. Marcus Klein, "The Roots of Radicals: Experience in the Thirties," in David Madden (ed.), Proletarian Writers of the Thirties (Carbondale, Illinois, 1968), 138.

ser's, the work of twenty-eight other poets, among whom were
Stanley Burnshaw, Kenneth Fearing, Michael Gold, Horace Gregory, Langston Hughes, Alfred Kreymborg, Kenneth Patchen, Genevieve Taggard, Isidor Schneider, and Richard Wright. These poets
display, in a wide variety of styles and a great range of competence,
a concern with the lives of ordinary Americans often as they fall mi-
serably short of the ideals of social justice and freedom.

The manifestos and arguments about proletarian literature in
periodicals and in the prefaces to these anthologies and to individual volumes of poetry boggle the mind of the contemporary
reader and apparently didn't do much to enlighten writers of the
thirties. In his foreword to *Theory of Flight*, Stephen Vincent Benét
said, "I do not intend to add, in this preface, to the dreary and unreal discussion about unconscious fascists, conscious proletarians,
and other figures of straw which has afflicted recent criticism with
head noises and small specks in front of the eyes." In these discussions writers were accused of not being proletarian enough or for
being too proletarian and therefore propagandistic and sloganeer-
ing. Some were attacked for wavering—for not coming out squarely
in favor of the Communist party (Horace Gregory, Edmund Wilson). It was asserted that there could really be no such thing as proletarian literature because writers inevitably came from the
bourgeoisie and were constantly falling into preoccupation with the
self and with "irrelevant" modernist fashions such as the subconscious and symbolism. Rukeyser was accused of such "romantic,
bourgeois" concerns. But at the same time she was hailed as an asset
to the Communists.[12]

The editorial commentary in *Proletarian Literature in the United
States* is helpful in considering Rukeyser's "proletarianism," but not
because the commentary strictly applies to her poetry as it developed through 1939. Certainly the main argument applies; Marcus
Klein says that in Hicks's anthology "it is a matter of constant insistence that literature must live, and the life of literature is its involve-

12. Burke, "Return After Flight."

ment with ordinary, insistent, real experience. . . . In the absence of any binding definitions, one may say that the proletarian movement as a whole is primarily characterized by this sense, that literature is of the present, that it is to be rescued into contemporaneity." Joseph Freeman's introduction asserted that social themes are simply more interesting today than those involving "nightingales, the stream of the middle-class unconscious, or love in Greenwich Village." One can recognize Rukeyser's poetry in these statements, if one doesn't pursue their restrictive innuendos.

But Freeman makes other assertions that cannot be applied to Rukeyser's poetry because they are too limiting. He says the revolutionary writer sees the world "through the illuminating concepts of revolutionary science [Marxism]. The feelings of the proletarian writer are molded by his experience and by the science which explains that experience, just as the bourgeois writer's feelings are molded by his experience and by the science which explains that experience." The science of the bourgeois was, among others, Freudianism, the exploration of the subconscious and its symbols. Rukeyser's work has from the beginning made use of this modern knowledge; Freud is mentioned as a hero in "Theory of Flight." Her poems are involved with the buried contents of the mind, with dream and with the dreamlike movement and transformation of images. (She has associated this movement of images with cinematic montage.) Moreover, Rukeyser's interest in the achievements of science, particularly as they reveal the relating power of the imagination, would have seemed a luxurious dalliance to a more thoroughgoing proletarian (to use an imprecise terminology), for she by no means considered science only in its social implications. In sum, Rukeyser's poetry was not simply "literature which describes the lives and concerns of the working class." [13]

The preface to the poetry section of Hicks's anthology states that many poems had to be omitted because, though very good, they

13. Marcus Klein, "The Roots of Radicals: Experience in the Thirties," 138, 141; Joseph Freeman, Introduction, in Granville Hicks *et al.* (eds.), *Proletarian Literature in the United States* (New York, 1935), 16, 19, 13.

were indecisive. Their "colors were too iridescent, the red tints too faint and too vanishing." Though the charge of vagueness and indecision is made against Rukeyser's first two volumes by John Wheelwright in *Partisan Review* (1938), the editors of *Proletarian Literature* apparently felt her "City of Monuments" was decisive and "red" enough. But in fact the poem stands out in its company by its complexity and insistence on "nothing certain but the risk." Hope prevails in all the poems in this anthology (except in Fearing's bitter "Dirge"). But in most of them the enemy is simplistically caricatured: "the ruling swine," "the miserly dog who fired you." The styles of most poets are less metaphorical, more narrative than Rukeyser's, telling stories of hunger, unemployment, the slum-poor, the farm-poor, the steelworker buried alive by molten steel, capitalists like beasts in a jungle whom greed, graft, and indulgence have scarred. Again and again is voiced the hope in communism, in Russia, in Communists fighting Nazis in Germany. Rukeyser's is the only poem which meditates on American history, further back than Sacco and Vanzetti and Joe Hill, and on the possibility of the historical American Dream blossoming in the revolt of the present.[14]

"City of Monuments" is dated "Washington 1934," and one begins to read with the idea that Washington is the city of monuments. But the first stanza alludes to a cemetery:

> Be proud   you people   of these graves
> these chiseled words   this precedent
> From these blind ruins shines our monument.

Are the monuments of Washington the graves of the American Dream? Yes; but since the poem refers later to the "slain" of the Civil War and to Gettysburg and the "tended graves," the title also designates the cemetery at Gettysburg. The voice in the poem may be speaking from the cemetery. When one has read through the poem and returns to the first stanza, the ambiguity intensifies. The city of Washington and the cemetery at Gettysburg are now in a double exposure. And though we are told to be proud of our prece-

---

14. Granville Hicks *et al.* (eds.), *Proletarian Literature in the United States*, 145.

dent and our monument which shine "from these ruins" (*i.e.*, we fought a war to free the slaves, and we may lay claim to other buried ideals), we are told, in the third stanza:

> Entrust no hope to stone although the stone
> shelter the root :   see too-great burdens placed
> with nothing certain but the risk
> set on the infirm column of
> the high memorial obelisk

We have no monument, then, nothing solidly achieved; for nothing is certain but risk, and there are "still unemancipated slaves."

"Anacostia" and "the anguish of the poor" allude to the plight of the "Bonus Army," thousands of unemployed, impoverished veterans who converged on the capital in the summer of 1932, many with wives and children, camping in the Anacostia Flats. They were petitioning the government for money they felt was due them for their military service. The U.S. Army dispersed the veterans and their families with guns and tear gas.

The last section of the poem speaks from a definite locale: the streets of Washington. But the voice is not certain if the vision it describes is the result of heightened perception (achieved in the light of the resurrected slaves) or of the simple confusion of the senses which may occur in traffic:

> Blinded by chromium or transfiguration
> we watch, as through a microscope, decay :
>   down the broad streets the limousines
> advance in passions of display.

The final "triumphant" sight is not uncomplicated since it comes as part of that uncertain vision.

> Split by a tendril of revolt
> Stone cedes to blossom everywhere.

"City of Monuments" shows how hope for social change and revived ideals can exist simultaneously with anxiety that the ideals can be rescued from the ruins, the graveyard of American society. Allen Guttmann said that Rukeyser's poem "is probably the best of the many poems that surveyed symbolic cities and warned of the old order's doom." [15]

The book reviews Rukeyser wrote in the thirties are relevant in considering her goals as a writer and in comparing her theory and achievement with those of her contemporaries. Rukeyser believed at the outset of her career, as did other proletarian "theorists" such as Granville Hicks, that any depiction in literature of the victims of social injustice should give them enough consciousness to see the meanings of their lives, to interpret the horrors. For this reason she criticized William Faulkner's *Dr. Martino and Other Stories*, saying his characters remain half-people, "touching no others, being touched by nothing," showing violent reactions "from the stomach alone." Summarizing her judgment that the stories are not a full enough picture of human beings in our world, she says, "These pieces are terse and ingenious; they might be vehicles for something of more account than unconcern. . . . Because of his gift for manipulation and disinterest, Faulkner falls into the list of precious writers. Less erudite than the academic authors concentrating on a society they would never remake, he nevertheless is in a position parallel to those writers of vignettes of the macabre who portray a civilization without explaining it." It is apparent from this review that Rukeyser's demand of literature is that it portray people in society fully, that no crucial meanings be evaded. Yet she never believed that these meanings could be simplified. In a review of the poet John Wheelwright's *Rock and Shell* for *New Masses*, she insists that "fine poetry which is not obviously propagandistic has confused the critics again and again." She calls Wheelwright's a fine book and reviews it generously. "His work cannot be dismissed as confused or confusing. Too many poets whose work might be exhibited as vital influences have been too faintly praised. Their poems may not be accessible to a large number of readers who must be reached, but they are writing the fine Left poetry of our time. Such writers are laying a base of literary activity and revolutionary creation which must be realized as

15. "City of Monuments" appeared in *Theory of Flight*; Guttmann, "The Brief Embattled Course of Proletarian Poetry," 259.

one of the important fronts in the growing cultural movement."
Clearly she is not insisting, as did the editor of *Proletarian Literature
in the United States*, that revolutionary tints be uniformly bold.
Like Horace Gregory, who was then poetry editor of *New Masses*,
she admits a revolutionary poetry which is highly individualistic. In
her broad sympathy she contrasts sharply with Granville Hicks in
his judgment of Wheelwright. In *The Great Tradition* Hicks dismissed the poet as a follower of Eliot, a regressive "defender of the
faith," and one who snobbishly turned to Catholicism because of
"its complacent assertion of a realm of values outside the compre-
hension of the average American business man." [16] Ironically Wheelwright went on to write a simplistic, intolerant review of *Theory of
Flight* and *U.S.1* for *Partisan Review* (see p. 112 herein), citing their
inexperienced socialism.

Rukeyser's reviews have always been generously sympathetic,
since, except for two of her earliest pieces, she sought to review
books whose merits she could defend and praise. This attitude in a
reviewer is rare in any age. The modest, temperate voice of her reviews was especially rare in *New Masses* where reviewers roasted
books and authors who erred politically. (It was in *New Masses*
that Granville Hicks, using a pseudonym, called MacLeish a "dirty
Nazi" and Horace Gregory's *Chorus for Survival* was branded luxurious liberal obscurantism and "cryptic soul-scratchings.")[17]

In a 1939 review of *The Collected Poems of Robert Frost*, Rukeyser reveals her own goals for poetry. She begins by admiring
Frost's beautiful rendering of New England people, places, and
things. But, she emphasizes, "Frost has his theme. He was recognizable from the beginning, and he never chose again." Nevertheless,
she continues, to appreciate Frost "one need not require a line of de-

16. Muriel Rukeyser, review of Faulkner's *Dr. Martino and Other Stories*, in *New
Masses*, XI (May 22, 1934), 25; Muriel Rukeyser, review of John Wheelwright's *Rock and
Shell*, "With Leftward Glances," *New Masses*, XII (July 10, 1934), 28; Granville Hicks,
The Great Tradition (revised ed.; New York, 1968), 270–71.
    17. Granville Hicks ["M. Mather"], "Der Schöne Archibald," *New Masses*, X (Janu-
ary 16, 1934), 26; Moishe Nadir, "Poetry Out of Season," review of Gregory's *Chorus
for Survival*, in *New Masses*, XV (June 18, 1935), 25–26.

velopment from [him], any more than from Fearing—these are people working and always working with one implement." The value of Frost's poetry, however, is limited. "He drew a circle around himself early in life and said 'I will deal with this.' The attitude does not come through as self-control, but as a rigid preconception of life." Frost is guarded; "he is a village-spirit, deep in village life," and he cannot show the speed of the modern imagination, seizing hold and letting go fast. "This is not poetry that strikes immediately at invention and the spirit." She concludes, "He cultivates his own garden, grouping with art so that everything there may be discussed in the same tone of voice. Meet him on these his own terms, and there is fine work, rewarding place-love, folk-love, solemn or gay recognitions. They are the recognitions of a man desperately determined that this is really all there is, and that this will be enough. It is not all, and it is not enough." [18]

To Rukeyser poetry which does not "allow people to feel the meeting of their consciousness and the world, to feel the full value of the meanings of emotions and ideas in their relations with each other" is not enough. A recent columnist in *American Poetry Review*, writing on the narrowing of contemporary poetry and its subsequent lack of intensity, says that the ideal poetry has the intensity which comes from "seeing with all of the eyes of the mind at once." Rukeyser wanted that of poetry from the beginning of her career. That is why "proletarian" and other narrower modes were not enough for her. [19]

Youthful enthusiasm, eroticism, revolutionary idealism, the exaltation of the machine are all exuberantly mingled in the proletarian anthology *We Gather Strength* (Spector, Kalar, Rolfe, and Funaroff, 1933) as they are in Rukeyser's volumes of the thirties. But there is no attempt at the fullness or the personal revelation evident in her very first volume with its experiments with the filmlike

18. Muriel Rukeyser, review of *The Collected Poems of Robert Frost*, in *Poetry*, LIV (July, 1939), 218–24.
19. Rukeyser, *The Life of Poetry*, unpaged section before the Introduction; Charles M. Fair, "The Poet as Specialist," *American Poetry Review*, IV (November–December, 1975), 20.

juxtaposition of images. There are echoes of Eliot and of Joyce in *We Gather Strength*, but these are heavy-handed parodies, never as effective as Rukeyser's echoing well-known lines and rhythms of those great moderns in "Theory of Flight." [20]

Many poems in Kenneth Patchen's two volumes of the thirties are blunt leftist oratory with an abundance of lines like "Boo! you well-fed bastards" and "Hey! Fatty, don't look now but that's a Revolution breathing down your neck." Patchen rejects the literary establishment across the board in "The Old Lean Over the Tomb-stones" in which, unlike Rukeyser in "Citation for Horace Gregory," he sees no value in the work of Eliot, Pound, Jeffers ("Literature, Inc."), Auden, Spender, Lewis ("Mr. Triumvirate"), and a character he calls "Gregory MacLeish Millay." In Patchen's proletarian stage much of his revolutionary poetry, often surreal, doesn't attempt to come to terms with the complexities of that turbulent period. [21]

Kenneth Fearing's early poems, especially those of his second book (*Poems*, 1935), try to show the complexity of hope and the meanings working against hope in the contemporary world. Fear-ing's cutting, ironic tone and stark city imagery and vocabulary set him apart stylistically from every other proletarian poet. The mono-tone of despair builds in intensity through his first volumes, how-ever, and he never succeeds in creating images of the dream achieved (as in Rukeyser's "Lives" and her poems with the motif of the jour-ney.) In "Denouement" (from *Poems*, 1935), which Edward Dahl-berg called in the introduction "a foreshadowing of the doom of the whole capitalistic society," there is exhortation which reminds one of the opening rhythms and mood of "Theory of Flight."

> Sky be blue, and more than blue; wind, be flesh
> and blood; flesh and blood be deathless;
> walls, streets, be home;
> desire of millions, become more real than warmth and
> breath and strength and bread. . . .

20. Herman Spector and Joseph Kalar, *We Gather Strength* (New York, 1933).
21. Kenneth Patchen, *Before the Brave* (New York, 1936); Kenneth Patchen, *First Will and Testament* (Norfolk, Connecticut, 1939), 61–69.

But the poem goes on to compare society's dream to the perfect denouement of a Hollywood movie! The very image implies that the "desire of millions" is wishful thinking. The poem concludes with descriptions of a rotten harbor city where revolutionaries are beaten, gassed, imprisoned. That Fearing's vision is what Dahlberg called "the poet looking beyond the horizon toward a socialist civilization, a Vita Nuova of the workers" is not at all clear.

Fearing's poetry in *Dead Reckoning* (1938) makes no attempt to portray a tension of forces; there is a simple and bleak admission that the revolutionary dream is impossible. *Poems* was issued by Dynamo, a publishing company dedicated to revolutionary poetry, for Fearing was, for a time, considered a proletarian poet with "Marxian insights," despite the heavy gloom of all his volumes. But when the *Collected Poems* appeared in 1940, Alexander Bergman wrote in *New Masses* that the book in its fatalism and despair is "a cancellation of his identification with the progressive forces among the people." [22]

Isidor Schneider, poetry critic and editor of *New Masses*, was the one poet associated with the proletarian school who by his own admission made a conscious effort to change his poetry to fit the tenets of the movement as he interpreted them. The essay "Toward Revolutionary Poetry" is his abjuration of his early personal and romantic preoccupation with his individual life, marriage, and children. "The poet who is making his beginnings now is to be envied. He does not have to remake himself as does the older poet. The process, as I know from my own experience, is a painful one." Unlike Rukeyser, who continues to find, through personal love, a means of reaching and touching the greater world, here is Schneider:

> So, vain and doomed is personal love.
> If it has destiny, it is like a potted tree,

22. Kenneth Fearing, *Angel Arms* (New York, 1929); Kenneth Fearing, *Poems* (New York, 1935); Kenneth Fearing, *Dead Reckoning* (New York, 1938); Kenneth Fearing, *Collected Poems of Kenneth Fearing* (New York, 1940); Alexander Bergman, review of Fearing's *Collected Poems*, in *New Masses*, XXXVII (November 19, 1940), 26.

that as it grows must break the pot,
and if it reach not more abundant earth, must die.
My love has cracked its pot; but has struck
the more abundant earth; the earth of comradeship,
and I can, all my length grow out,
in revolutionary act.

The poetry Schneider wrote after "remaking" himself, however, is in the flat oratorical style of the dullest proletarian verse.

Schneider published no more volumes of poetry after *Comrade Mister* (1934). He continued for many years as an editor of *New Masses* and reviewed books of poetry always with the intention of showing how they fit into one of the two traditions he discerned in American poetry: the "recherché," isolate, expatriate, and irresponsible (poetry for the cultural elite) or the social and populist (poetry for the people.) He felt the latter to be the genuinely American tradition. Schneider's simplistic division of traditions caused him to disparage poetry that did not squarely belong in the popular tradition. In 1944 he attacked former social poets who "in despair or opportunism have turned renegade and are producing a sort of parody of the twenties. . . . A new era of little magazines, patronage, and cult snobbery has come in." (Rukeyser was affiliated with the little magazine *Decision*, which was issued in 1941–1942, and she published prose and poetry in *Twice-a-Year*. See p. 171 herein.) Schneider noted that "in the new esthete circles" poets were substituting "a mysticism sunk to incantation" for social consciousness. He claimed that social poets who continued in the genuine American tradition were left with *New Masses* as virtually their sole medium. Rukeyser's last contribution to *New Masses* is dated 1939. Her work after *U.S.1* (1938) was not reviewed there. Obviously Schneider felt that her work was no longer in the genuine tradition. In 1940 he wrote that proletarian poetry is "unkillable. The realities out of which proletarian literature draws its subjects are largely and heavily with us; and the understanding from which it takes its light and faith has become an ineradicable knowledge." But Schneider did not see how poetry of social consciousness became transformed, in a poet such as Rukeyser, into a richer testament of the responsible artist.[23]

Rukeyser owes to Horace Gregory her early development as a poet of social consciousness using the methods developed by the great moderns (Eliot, Crane) and the newer suggestions of the cinema. Fifteen years her senior, Gregory was on the faculty at Sarah Lawrence College when she sought his help before publishing *Theory of Flight*. Essentially he pointed out to her where her poems began. She says that when she showed them to him "they were lifted from the river dripping wet." He helped her with notions of the dramatic moment, the beginning. Gregory's poetry itself also influenced Rukeyser, for it combined those elements of form toward which she was herself drawn. In addition, Gregory's political and philosophical beliefs were similar to hers. The description of Gregory's poems in Untermeyer's anthology could serve for Rukeyser's as well: "They indulge in a freedom of form and effect; they employ the montage of cinema, the interrupting voice of the radio, the summons of the quick–changing telephone dial. Like Eliot, Gregory is fond of the dissonant chord and the unresolved suspense; like Hart Crane, he crowds image upon image to increase sensation and suggest new perspectives. But he does not share Eliot's disillusions or Crane's disorganization. There is constant control as well as positive belief in Gregory's poetry; his faith is a social faith." (The element of "*constant* control" is not what strikes one in Rukeyser, but the rest of the description is apt.) Gregory, like Rukeyser, was criticized for not being a thoroughgoing Marxist, for not becoming a Communist, for continuing to write complex poems which do not simply affirm the revolution. His poetry and his political and aesthetic statements were attacked in *New Masses*.

But Gregory's work is not Rukeyser's. Of another generation, he could have no poems about being young with the youth of the revo-

23. Isidor Schneider, *The Temptation of Anthony* (New York, 1928); Isidor Schneider, *Comrade Mister* (New York, 1934); Isidor Schneider, "Poetry: Red-baiting Victim," *New Masses*, L (January 18, 1944), 24–25.

lution. (Untermeyer says Gregory destroyed a first book of traditional lyrics when he came to New York from his native Wisconsin.)
His first lyrical collection, *No Retreat* (1933), is spoken in a grave
voice whose characteristic tone is heard in the supplication, "give me
the power / to stay in no retreat and not to die." There are already
elegiac poems such as "Poems for my Daughter" in which he imagines his life in his young daughter's after he is dead. In Gregory's
urging the need to change America, in *Chorus for Survival*, there is
none of Rukeyser's aggressiveness; the emphasis is on how to survive and face each day in a confusing time. If his tone is positive it is
muted. Rukeyser's "Say yes!" sounds brash by comparison. In "For
You, my Son" there is pity, similar to that in Rukeyser's "The Blood
Is Justified," for strong ancestors whose dreams could not be realized in America. But there is pity as well for his own misguided
generation:

> Turn here, my son
> (No longer turn to what we were)
> Build in the sunlight with strong men,
> Beyond our barricade:
> For even I remember the old war
> And death in peace:
> The neon sign 'Success' across our foreheads.

Gregory's hope, unlike Rukeyser's, is not for his generation.[24]

Rosenthal aptly concluded his discussion of Rukeyser in his dissertation by saying that though Fearing and Gregory also dealt in
their poetry of the thirties with the theme of individual sensibility in
the midst of betrayal and destruction, "she has made by far the
greatest effort of the three to give [that sensibility] an identity that
will link it with the most vital meaning and potentialities of human
life."[25]

Since the thirties Rukeyser has admired and been a personal
friend of the Scots poet Hugh MacDiarmid, literary innovator and

---

24. Untermeyer (ed.), *Modern American Poetry*, 547; Horace Gregory, *No Retreat*
(New York, 1933), 10; Horace Gregory, *Chorus for Survival* (New York, 1935), 510.
25. Rosenthal, "Chief Poets of the American Depression," 613.

theorist and ardent Scottish nationalist and Communist. He dedicated his "Third Hymn to Lenin" to Rukeyser. When asked today
which contemporary poet had the most influence on her vision of
possibility, she answers "MacDiarmid." In an essay entitled "The
Politics and Poetry of Hugh MacDiarmid" which he himself wrote
in 1952 under the pseudonym "Arthur Leslie," we recognize Rukeyser's themes:

As Miss Nan Shepherd has said of him in a critical essay in the *Aber-
deen University Review*, the vision behind MacDiarmid's creed—that focuses everything he has written in a point of light—"Never changes.
Always he sees man 'filled with lightness and exaltation,' living to the full
reach of his potentialities. In that clear world 'all that has been born de-
served birth.' Man 'will flash with the immortal fire,' will

> rise
> To the full height of the imaginative act
> That wins to the reality in the fact.

until all life flames in the vision of

> the light that breaks
> From the whole earth seen as a star again
> In the general life of man.

The actuality is different. Men are obtuse, dull, complacent,
vulgar. They love the third-rate, live on the cheapest terms with
themselves, 'the engagement between man and being forsaken,'
their 'incredible variation nipped in the bud.' Their reading is
'novels and newspapers,' their preoccupations 'fitba' and
'weemen,' their thinking 'treadmills of rationalizing.' They have
hardly issued yet,

> Up frae the slime, that a' but a handfu' o men
> Are grey wi' still.

They refuse to explore the largeness of life. This refusal he sees
as a cowardice." Like Geddes he holds that "our greatest need
today is to grasp life as a whole, to see its many sides in their
proper relations." [26]

---

26. Duncan Glen (ed.), *Selected Essays of Hugh MacDiarmid* (Berkeley, 1970), 35–
36.

A New "Female Lyricism"

In Rukeyser's early work one encounters an open, growing spirit, an intense young woman who from adolescence was seriously interested in and troubled by social issues while at the same time seeking and sharing deep personal involvements. (Her young associates in New York City were enthusiastic radicals, organizers, and aspiring artists.) *Theory of Flight* contains the poems of a rebelling daughter of affluence: her father, Lawrence Rukeyser, cofounded Colonial Sand and Stone. Her mother, Myra, who had once struggled as a bookkeeper, was unable to enjoy her comfortable life because— among other fears—she was terrified that her daughter would one day be found "dead in a ditch." Not surprisingly, these first poems are concerned with the possibilities and the responsibilities of love in a troubled society. They manifest an unusual lyricism.

"In a Dark House" explores the inadequacy of possessive sexual love, which is engulfing and which shuts out the world and prevents growth. In the scheme of the poem growth involves a real awareness of others in the world. A woman moved toward this awareness, but then she fell back on a secure way of life, sharing a house with a man, shutting the world out.

> She had believed in the quick response to pain,
> in union of crowds living in one belief,
> a social order kept by a cooperative strain
> steadily toward one thing, but aware of all   :
> she had reached out her hand with the gesture of one who
>   dares,
> and found   :   these stairs.

The real world outside the sheltering but dark house might be revealed if the walls "should slide into the night." (This image will recur in other poems.) It is a world of the "bitter, impotent, angered," of "toolless arms," of "silent mouths / opened to cry for law." Though the man and woman go on climbing their "fateful road" (as people continue to pair off and wall the world out), the dreams of the speaker continue, dreams of a world in which the words chiseled on public buildings correspond to reality: "Beauty Old Yet Ever

New: Eternal Voice / And Inward Word." Now the reality is that "the pock-bitten pass to spit / gelatinously and obscenely on the bird-marked stones."

The last stanza establishes the speaker's will to break the hold which the ideal of romantic love has on her generation.

> . . . Cool Brow.   Athenian lips.
> The creaking stairs.   Stupid stupid stupidly stupidly
> we go a long voyage on the stairs of a house
>
> . . . .
>
> up   mounting   up   O lovely stairs, hideous and cruel
> we propitiate you with incensuous
> words   stairs   lovely   loved
> rise, idol of our waking days and nights

The speaker sees "the crackled lips of the mass / that must be there waiting for law at the wall's decay." The last three lines envision a new ascent for lovers, one whereby they are equals and open to the world.

> Large female   :   male   :   come tiredness and sleep
> come peace   come generous power over no other, come Order
>   here.

The poem is a good example of Rukeyser's merging in her early poems of themes of youthful sensibility and social awareness. One can see the poem as a young woman's struggling with the attractive but inadequate values of her society. It is a young person's poem—the loneliness and fears are expressed as though they fill the whole world, as they are felt at twenty-one: "We cry, fling our arms abroad, and there is no one." There is a stiffness in the description of people spitting on monuments, making the "shallow-carven letters fade," but the speaking voice is convincing in her feeling both for herself and her world.

"Effort at Speech Between Two People," a classic dialogue, is, according to Untermeyer in 1940, "one of the period's most moving love poems." But the theme here is not isolating romantic love. Though the poem was written when Rukeyser was a young woman in college, it is a mature expression of the human need to communicate with another, to share experience, to touch; in Untermeyer's words, the poem "reveals the tension and terror of the contemporary world." [27] The key words in the poem will be found throughout Rukeyser's work: *effort, speech, touch, open*. There is no explicit asking for love in the poem. Rather the emphasis in the refrain (occurring rhythmically but not in the predictable pattern of traditional prosody) is "Grow to know me." The speakers in the poem are trying desperately to reveal themselves to one another in a world where people move in crowds and do not speak a word. The crowds are ominous—"everyone silent, moving," and a voice is saying, "If we could touch one another. . . ." ("Breathing Landscape" and "Sonnet" are also on the theme of the great need for openness and contact.)

How much more powerful now are these lines published in 1935 on the eve of the most terrible span of distrust and terror in history. The scientist Jacob Bronowski stood in the pond at Auschwitz for television viewers in the 1970s and picked up a fistful of sludge, explaining that into that pond were flushed the ashes of four million people. He urged his audience to adopt the humble attitude of the atomic scientists who were discovering, ironically, just as Nazism was flourishing, that no certainty is possible, that no dogmatism is justified. What is important, said Bronowski, holding his fistful of sludge, is that "we touch human beings." Rukeyser's theory of poetry is essentially that it is a touching: a complete responsiveness to experience on the part of the poet and a complete responsiveness to the poem on the part of the reader. Poetry is, to Rukeyser, "the confession to oneself made available to all. This is confession as a means to understanding, as testimony to the truths of experience as they become form and ourselves." "The poet, intellectually giving form to emotional and imaginative experience, with the music and history of a lifetime behind the work, offers a total response. And the witness receives the work, and offers a total response, in a most human communication." (LP, 228) This concept may seem in

27. Louis Untermeyer, "The Language of Muriel Rukeyser," *Saturday Review*, August 10, 1940, p. 11; Untermeyer (ed.), *Modern American Poetry*, 655.

no need of apologetics. We know we must communicate, to feel with one another, as fully as possible. But we must be reminded of this need, for in our ordinary lives we learn to conceal, prudently, to allow only certain emotions at certain levels to show. The writing and receiving of poetry, says Rukeyser, is an activity where we can be "full-valued," where we can offer a full response to another. This activity is an essential exercise for human beings, lest our capacities for response atrophy. We must constantly exercise the skill of "reaching that makes a meeting-place." Poets teach us how. In our world of "embarrassment before disclosure, or intensity" poetry keeps alive those vital impulses to reach out, to touch, for a poem invites us to take its meaning "in a blaze of discovery and love." Muriel Rukeyser says, "We will not be saved by poetry. But poetry is the type of the creation in which we may live and which will save us" (LP, 46, 200, 228).

These ideas were set down in the early forties when millions of human beings had sufficiently inured themselves to emotion to permit the murder of other millions of human beings. The prose which conveys these ideas is passionate in its conviction that feeling must not be forgotten, that imagination capable of receiving another's feeling must be exercised. (This is not the prose of analytical criticism.) The course of events since World War II has not demonstrated that people have become less tolerant of killing on a vast scale. Rukeyser's poems have continued to stress touch and communication; and her credo *The Life of Poetry* was reissued in 1974, without revision. Besides being what David Daiches called "a refreshing change from the cold ingenuity of so much contemporary criticism of poetry," *The Life of Poetry* still stands very much behind all her volumes of poetry and prose.[28]

28. David Daiches, review of LP, in *New York Herald Tribune Book Review*, June 25, 1950, p. 8. Rukeyser says of *The Life of Poetry* that she "got it down" so that she could give a series of lectures and teach at the California Labor School. She later published the essays (1949) and issued them again in 1974. John Malcolm Brinnin slighted the book in a review of five books about poetry in the *New York Times Book Review* (March 2, 1975), saying in one brief (last) paragraph that the book "has been reissued without having been revised." He did not attempt to dispel the implication that the unrevised book is therefore outdated. But as far as their helping to illuminate Rukeyser's poems, the ideas about poetry in *The Life of Poetry* need no revision.

The human need for touch and speech in a world where people learn the destructive habit of silence is a major theme of Rukeyser's latest volumes, *The Speed of Darkness, Breaking Open,* and *The Gates.* In the early poems of the thirties we find all the directness on this theme that bursts through in the volumes of the sixties and seventies. She will write in more complex and symbolic ways, but she always returns to this early directness. Louise Bogan said that Rukeyser's gift was "in no way lyrical." We have seen that Bogan had limited ideas of what "female lyricism" was permitted. "Effort at Speech" is not the lyricism of Edna St. Vincent Millay, whose love poems idealized the romantic passion Rukeyser found inadequate in "In a Dark House." But it is not that familiar tradition that was to Bogan the epitome of the feminine poetic gift. She cited, rather, Christina Rossetti, Emily Dickinson, and Emily Brontë as women lyricists whose poetry belongs to the region of the sublime. Their poetry, concerned with "minute particulars . . . at its best seems less a work of art than a marvel of nature—a flawless distillation, a pure crystallization of thought, circumstance, and emotion." The work of these supreme women lyricists has a "transcendent quality" which they brought "in a clearly traceable line from antiquity into the modern bourgeois world." [29]

Words that come to mind after a reading of Rukeyser's lyrics are "strength" and "movement." Hers is not a tender but a strong lyricism that does not aim to distill or crystallize an emotion or an experience. Rukeyser's aim is to follow the powerful rhythms of experience in herself (and often in her imagining of another) in a world which in its fears about economics and war has conspired to be silent about the deepest human values and to repress impulses which interfere with "getting ahead." Rukeyser would not deny these rhythms, these impulses. She has said that talk about poetry which is "in terms of the start, the image, the crystallization" is inadequate. "The passion, the intensity in form, of a great poem, are not here. They do not stand: they fly through, and over. The luck of the book is that we then may go back to the top of the page, and be-

29. Louise Bogan, review of *The Green Wave,* in *New Yorker,* May 8, 1948, p. 115; Bogan, review of *Selected Poems.*

gin to arrive again" (LP, 182). Richard Eberhart, in looking back at the time when Rukeyser began to write, has said that the disturbing scene of the mid-thirties "had to be coped with directly, with passionate insight." Rukeyser's lyrics are probing explorations of a complex of emotions in the face of a world which denies their relevance. The pressure of this world on a lyric impulse in Rukeyser's case made for a positive, often aggressive response rendered in "a long, fierce, loose, informative" verse line. Rukeyser today uses the image of "the river" to refer to that movement of rhythm, emotion, and image into which she plunges for her poetry. The poems contain the strong current of that river. They are no crystallizations. They are, in Eberhart's phrase, "primordial and torrential." [30]

The probing quality of Rukeyser's lyrics caused Philip Blair Rice in his review of *Theory of Flight* to conclude that she was not primarily a lyricist because her poems "not only present and celebrate experience but evaluate it. Here is a well-stored, vigorous mind attempting to bring its world into some kind of imaginative and human order." [31] In Emily Dickinson one finds the rigorous concentration and impulse to a definition of a state of soul, in a poetic line that is appropriately spare. In Rukeyser there is the no less rigorous, wide-ranging exploration of emotion and experience and the attempt to project them onto an imagined other, often a whole society; Rukeyser's world is always *there,* in her poetry. Dickinson is severely alone; there is little expression of an effort to reach another, through touch and speech, as in Rukeyser. Nor is there the expansive impulse (given form in Rukeyser's long lines) to reach the world, to include and transform an unfeeling other. There is no such impulse at exploration and inclusion in Rossetti and Brontë whose poetry is meditative—a distillation, again, a crystallization of very private emotions and experiences.

These general remarks about Dickinson, Brontë, and Rossetti need a chapter in themselves. I have merely tried to indicate what is

30. Richard Eberhart, review of *Selected Poems*, in *New York Times Book Review*, September 23, 1951, p. 30.
31. Rice, "New Poet."

to my mind the chief difference between Rukeyser's lyricism and that of the women poets who (along with those of the school of Millay) had given "female lyricism" its reputation. In sum, one could say that Rukeyser's lyricism shows a freer, more active and exploring impulse than that of the other three women poets.

"Letter, Unposted," on the traditional theme of waiting for a lover, is distinguished from poems of pining by the speaker's very inability to pine and to see nature as pining with her. The letter is unposted; she *cannot* write "earth sickens, as I sicken, with waiting," because, in fact, to this complete personality, "summer lives / and minds grow, and nerves are sensitized to power" even in the lover's absence. This is a very unusual love poem, especially for a young poet. It casts a strong light on the strong mind and heart behind "Theory of Flight":

> the door stands open for you, and other figures pass,
> and I receive them joyfully and live   :   but wait for you.

The sensibility manifest in the two-part "Wedding Presents" is of the same strong character. The first part of the poem is compact and difficult, describing a "fantastic juxtapose": the "anthropoid hunger" for love and all the forces which are set against love in the personality. The last two lines foresee a more developed human being to whom love will come more naturally, more beautifully and imaginatively, "until evolved man hears with each breath-intake / the sweetly mathematical sound of Bach." Here art and science are united in the poet's vision as they are in much of her work. Part two of "Wedding Presents" imagines the human being who has developed even beyond the known harmonies of Bach. "Be bold, friend," it begins. Now "the goddesses are gone, and the chivalric ranks." The landscape of our world is beautiful in a new way. Here are "firm and beautiful machines":

> trees, where you sit, will crowd into a shade
> eclipsing Handel, shining electric powers
> of energy on polytechnic scenes.

There is a lovely strength in the new world which is "ill defined /

ready for the Columbus of the mind." The poet urges her friend: "open your thighs" to this strength and beauty. This is an unusual wedding poem, one which shows that in the poet's sensibilities personal love, sex, and hunger for beauty merge in an imaginative vision which includes art and science. Her "polytechnic scenes" are Auden's "new styles of architecture," deeply and permanently chosen.

Rukeyser had predecessors in her lyric style, women whose individual voices are distinct from hers but whose expression is more like hers than like Dickinson's, Brontë's or Rossetti's. Writing of these women poets of the late nineteenth and early twentieth century, Kenneth Rexroth says, "The best poetry by women in fact was written by feminists, revolutionaries, or lesbians." Unfortunately Rexroth does not mention a single name here, though he does go on to enumerate "the women poets who have survived in contemporary taste as specially feminine . . . subtle analysts of feminine sensitivity, psychology, and the disabilities of women in the erotic relationship." (Louise Bogan is among those he mentions.) Of Rukeyser's poetry Rexroth says, "if the social poems represent the fulfillment, in a more sophisticated age, of the Populist poets of the early years of the century, the later poems combine this concern with the enduring meanings of the feminine poets of those years raised to a new qualitative level." (Apparently Rexroth did not recognize the merging of personal—"feminine"—and social concerns in the early "social poems.")[32]

Lola Ridge (1883–1941) was one of the revolutionaries Rexroth was referring to. Her poetry deals with the city, the workers, and young idealistic revolutionaries. An ardent Communist (one critic calls her an "anarchist"), Ridge celebrated Russia in *Red Flag* (1927). *The Ghetto* (1918) celebrates the motley life on Hester and Grand Streets in New York City and concludes with a paean to the life that surges among the poor. The imagery is the kind Rukeyser often uses in describing human life.

> Electric currents of life,
> Throwing off thoughts like sparks,

32. Rexroth, *American Poetry*, 26, 124.

Glittering, disappearing,
Making unknown circuits,
Or out of spent particles stirring
Feeble contortions in old faiths
Passing before new.

Ridge also used scientific imagery to describe "Russian Women" (in *Red Flag.*)

Yet in you there is no peace,
but infinite collisions,
impact of charged atoms
in ceaseless vibration.
In you unimagined circuits,
in you uncoiled
passion electric—
the stroke swift
and the recoil as swift . . .
in you the identified power—
hysteria directed,
the world force.

Ridge's poems about labor leaders such as "Frank Little at Calvary" (in *The Ghetto*) remind one of Rukeyser's references to the living spirit of heroes who lived and died for the liberation of humanity. The way Ridge writes of Sacco and Vanzetti is familiar to the reader of "Theory of Flight":

Each had
That ancient singleness of heart
That Bruno knew and Galileo
And all the old discoverers
Who held to their course amid the veering winds
And kicked death off like a shoe,
The single aim, the pure intent,
The virgin purpose, sharp as love,
That neither love nor hate can move
Or swerve to any meaner bent. (from *Dance of Fire*, 1935)

But Ridge's poetry does not combine, as Rukeyser's does, personal exploration with social awareness. Ridge's poem "Submerged" tells how she wishes she could have been more exploring in her poetry and gone into the river Rukeyser refers to:

> I was afraid of the silence
> And the slipping toe-hold . . .
> Oh, could I now dive
> Into the unexplored deeps of me—
> Delve and bring up and give
> All that is submerged, encased, unfolded,
> That is yet the best. (from *The Ghetto*)

In her volume *Sun-up* (1920) Ridge in fact dives into those deeps, but in a startlingly contemporary exploration of the desires, fears, and dreams of childhood and the madness often entailed in probing them, there is no simultaneous awareness of a larger world as there is in Rukeyser. Ridge's personal exploration and her description of society are kept distinct.[33]

Lola Ridge is clearly in the tradition which produced Muriel Rukeyser. Rukeyser came to Ridge's social themes, the images of science and the city, the impulse to reveal the groping of childhood and youth and fused them in adaptations of the free-verse line of Whitman (and Eliot's and the cinema's movement of images) in a personal, inclusive poetry. Rukeyser's is a new kind of feminine lyricism, one which Denise Levertov and Adrienne Rich have also caused to flourish in the 1960s and 1970s.

Two women predecessors of Rukeyser were concerned to admit social themes into their poetry of personal revelation: Marya Zaturenska and Genevieve Taggard. The poems of Zaturenska and Rukeyser, apparently so different, are related attempts to fuse personal exploration and social awareness.[34] Zaturenska's poetry, as Untermeyer noted, was so restrained that "it misled the critics," who spoke of her work as "detached," "abstract," and "removed from the immediate world." Rukeyser herself, in a review of Zaturenska's

---

33. Lola Ridge, *Red Flag* (New York, 1927); Lola Ridge, *The Ghetto* (New York, 1918); Lola Ridge, *Dance of Fire* (New York, 1935); Lola Ridge, *Sun-up* (New York, 1920). Ridge was omitted from the Midcentury edition of Louis Untermeyer's seven-hundred-page anthology of modern American poetry, but she was included in the previous editions.

34. *Theory of Flight* is dedicated to Horace and Marya Gregory (among others), and *U.S. 1* is dedicated to Zaturenska. Zaturenska's second volume, *Cold Morning Sky* (1937), which won the Pulitzer Prize, is dedicated to Rukeyser.

third volume, says that Zaturenska's poetry had been misread. "The amazing and troubled images of the world" may be seen through "lyrics sealed in their transparency." Zaturenska uses familiar symbols such as "rose, bough, and moon," but we read "under them the contemporary stress."[35] The short symbolic lyrics on love, death, and nature in Zaturenska's first volume (*Threshold and Hearth*, 1934) bear no immediate resemblance to Rukeyser's poems; the persona is not struggling with a world whose values she is rejecting. She is in some sort of limbo in this volume. In "The Quiet House" she describes herself as one who has "lavendered away" her "agonies," discarding her passions. "I am alive and yet am not alive." She waits for "The word that shall loosen the storm and set the still house quaking." In "Symbols" she struggles with her poetic impulse and its expression, wishing for a newer idiom but at the same time asserting that more modern images can't reveal as much about human beings as can the "old symbols."

> Only by these old symbols do I move
> And by these ancient symbols do I die
> The spreading tree, the rock on the worn hill
> The moonbeam spent by love
>
> . . . .
> Oh why so still my song?
> Leave the eternal pastoral and fly
> To where the city's vast metallic eye
> Opens on visions carved of iron and steel
> Immaculate perfection that can feel
> No silent drop of blood beneath the stone.

Her next volume, *Cold Morning Sky* (dedicated to Rukeyser), speaks throughout of some sort of rebirth and new resolve. She has not discarded the old symbols in favor of hard, urban, scientific imagery. But there is now what Rukeyser called a "dark and intricate under-content" to the poems, and there is no "contemporary return to formalism" as in poets who use the old symbols and the traditional meters to insulate their vision against the moving, changing

35. Untermeyer (ed.), *Modern American Poetry*, 599; Muriel Rukeyser, review of Zaturenska's *The Listening Landscape*, in *Decision*, I (June, 1941), 81–83.

world.[36] In "The Lunar Tides" the face of the moon is "burning with war"; there is pain and terror abroad. In "The Virgin, the Doe, and the Leper" there is a "savage mountain," a "shower of blood," a stalking shadow. In "Nightpiece" there are references to "cloaked misery . . . with its fleshless hand," and to "the infested land." Rukeyser's "Night-Music" sequence in *U.S.1*, part of which is dedicated to Zaturenska, also makes use of natural imagery such as "savage branches" to render experience in the modern world. Those natural images are invariably mingled, however, with hard, urban ones like "factories bellow mutilation."

Nevertheless, as Rukeyser herself observed, the critics had misread Zaturenska's poetry when they echoed Marshall Schacht's review of *Cold Morning Sky*, where he said, "From the squawk of cities and the gnawing of the modern mind, she escapes to asylum and takes the veil."[37] Modern agonies gnaw at Zaturenska no less than at her contemporaries who express themselves in more modern imagery. The world has entered the "Quiet House" in *Cold Morning Sky*. There is no asylum for "outcasts from the age of steel," says the poet in "The Emigrés." She sees herself hiding "for fear behind old marble," but she is paralyzed by loneliness and unease and "sees no ancient solace near" in "the death-changed year."

> Oh, in a harsh
> Suspicious time
> Metallic angry, dark with war
> Disturbing every heritage
> That once made gold the poet's page
> To dream of pastoral days
>
> . . . .
> Brings but confusion.

In "The Respite" she cautions a younger poet who is now "Ophelia-garlanded with early flowers" (this may be Rukeyser) that she must also know

36. Rukeyser, review of *The Listening Landscape*.
37. Marshall Schacht, review of Zaturenska's *Cold Morning Sky*, in *Poetry*, LI (February, 1938), 266–67.

latitudes of silence vast and lonely
Gone is the season when the musical leaves
Measured their watery syllables on dry air
And the earth spoke in the brief speech of flowers.

Another predecessor and older contemporary of Rukeyser was
Genevieve Taggard who, born in 1894, began dealing with social
themes in her lyrics of the thirties. Taggard's poetry was essentially
traditional and highly personal, celebrating love and motherhood,
but poems even before 1935 reveal her growing social concern. She
too was published in *Proletarian Literature*, and her poetry of the
late thirties and early forties is increasingly revolutionary. Some
poems sound like echoes of "Theory of Flight" in their exhortation
to "Go / Rouse. Energy calls forth / Energy." [38] She, like Rukeyser,
published poetry in *New Masses*, but she continued her association
with that publication long after Rukeyser's work had ceased appear-
ing in its pages. Taggard's poems make little use of modern techniques. Her social poems are all in the style of her early "To an
American Workman Dying of Starvation." She seems to have taken
to heart the counsel of *New Masses* poetry critic Isidor Schneider to
shun the "snobbery" and "mysticism" of modern experimental poetry and concentrate on clear statements for the people. Her poems
do not fuse personal exploration and social themes.

But the revolt against the ideal of romantic love is seen in her
long poem, "Evening Love of Self," which reminds one of Rukeyser's
"In a Dark House." The woman speaker in the poem is describing
the stifling confinement of her life within a marriage. This is a startling poem, especially for 1934. The persona is a woman who has
hated married life and has reacted with "brutal response to the plain
facts about [her]," the absurd routine of household chores. She now
has "adult anger" over what her life has become and wills to change
it. "Evening Love of Self" seemed a kind of proclamation for Taggard. It was at this time that she began to write poems on social
themes. There is a poem about a middle-class American woman

38. Genevieve Taggard, "To Arm You for This Time," *Long View* (New York, 1942).

who can't sleep at night thinking of the poor and one on women strikers entitled, "At Last the Women Are Moving." Taggard became, in effect, a proletarian poet, abandoning her themes of self-revelation within the erotic relationship.

When Edna Millay turned to social themes her poetic gift could not accommodate them, and "the reviewers could not help deprecating the facile couplets and journalistic carelessness" of a book like *Make Bright the Arrows* (1940).[39] Her early attempts at poetry with social themes, such as her poem on Sacco and Vanzetti, "Justice Denied in Massachusetts," from *The Buck in the Snow* (1928), produce a variation on the weary-with-unrequited-love theme. When she hears of the final decision in the case of Sacco and Vanzetti she abandons hope in the struggle for justice.

> Forlorn, forlorn,
> Stands the blue hay-rack by the empty mow.
> And the petals drop to the ground,
> Leaving the tree unfruited.
>
> . . . .
>
> Let us sit here, sit still,
> Here in the sitting-room until we die.[40]

No woman poet made the successful fusion of personal and social themes in a modern prosody before Rukeyser.

39. Untermeyer (ed.), *Modern American Poetry*, 459.
40. Edna St. Vincent Millay, *The Buck in the Snow* (New York, 1928).

THREE

The Thirties

RELATIONSHIP is an important term throughout Rukeyser's work, through all her books of poems, her biographies, and her autobiographical novel. The poems of the thirties explore the relationship between generations, between ideological kindred, and between material fact and spiritual possibility. With the 1940s she plunged into the difficult details of the life and work of one of the most abstract scientists, Willard Gibbs, in pursuit of the relationship between pure imagination in science and in poetry. Later there would be two more biographies exploring the relationship between the living past and the present. But it has always been with the spirit of the poet as described by Emerson that she has taken on the responsibility of the poet. Emerson sought the poet who would reveal relationship. In "The Poet" he says, "Man, never so often deceived, still watches for the arrival of a brother who can hold him steady to a truth until he has made it his own. With what joy I begin to read a poem which I confide in as an inspiration! And now my chains are to be broken; I shall mount above these clouds and opaque airs in which I live— opaque, though they seem transparent—and from the heaven of truth I shall see and comprehend my relations." In *The Life of Poetry* Rukeyser says, "Those of us whose imaginations had been reached would not sell out: we would not stop at the images, or at 'sincerity,' at security, or at any one field. There are relationships, we said, to be explored; and in our weakness and limitation, in ignorance and several poverties and doubt and disgust, we thought of possibility."

Having considered at some length "Theory of Flight," in which

85

the poet weaves the themes of her lyrics into a mythic structure celebrating those chosen values of justice, freedom, love, and a belief in human potential, we can see the unity of *Theory of Flight* as a volume. Archibald MacLeish has said, "A book of poems is an attempt to come to terms with the experiences of a mortal life and it is almost always a whole thing—as whole in its way as a well-made novel." We have, with "Theory of Flight" in the center of the book, an extended credo springing organically from the briefer visions of the first section.[1]

Theory of Flight

The shorter poems of *Theory of Flight* such as "Notes for a Poem" reveal the poet's desire to apprehend the world more adequately than in Zaturenska's "old symbols"—which are nevertheless still valid for Rukeyser.

> Here are the long fields inviolate of thought,
> here are the planted fields raking the sky,
> signs in the earth   :
> water-cast shuttles of light flickering the underside of rock.
> These have been shown before; but the fields know new hands,
> the son's fingers grasp warmly at the father's hoe   ;
> there will be new ways of seeing these ancestral lands.

The poem enumerates in muscular lines of consonantal rhythms, using city as well as country imagery, the ways in which abundant "power is common" throughout the land. But there are ominous notes.

> "In town, the munitions plant has been poor since the war,
> And nothing but a war will make it rich again."
> Holy, holy, holy, sings the church next door.

In all the yield of the earth and of industry there is "unrelated strength." The conclusion of the poem affirms hope in imagination,

---

1. Archibald MacLeish, Introduction to *The Human Season: Selected Poems, 1926–1972* (Boston, 1972), vi.

scientific and artistic, to make a peaceful, human order of the world.

> (There must be the gearing of these facts
> into coördination, in a poem or numbers,
> rows of statistics, or the cool iambs.)
> The locked relationships which will be found
> are a design to build these factual timbers—
> a plough of thought to break this stubborn ground.

The two poems in "Place-Rituals" are on the theme of our relationship with ancestors and traditions. In "Tradition of this Acre" we find the same ambivalence about hallowed places and names as in "The Blood Is Justified" (above, p. 53), an ambivalence inevitable in a serious person who wants both to revere what is worthy in the past and to make it applicable to present realities. The poet says we approach our American heritage blindly in a "ritual of . . . habit," which will eventually become "repetitions in the lips of doom." But the companion poem, "Ritual of Blessing," counters this note. The poem describes an ancient religious ceremony of blessing the fields with "metal symbols precious to our dreams." The old blessings ("the feet of priests tracking the smooth earth"), though lovely, are insufficient. But there is hope in relationship:

> hands together in the fields, the born and unborn children,
> and the wish for new blessing and the given blessing blend,
> a glory clear in the man-tracks, in the blind
> seeking for warmth in the climates of the mind.

The old seeking of religion and the new seeking *can* blend, according to the poet, who does not spurn the warmth that traditional religion has afforded. "The feet of priests" are transformed into simple "man-tracks." For a poem by a revolutionary poet of the thirties, this shows unusual tolerance for traditional religion. One thinks by comparison of the last stanza of Spender's "The Landscape Near an Aerodrome":

> Then, as they land, they hear the tolling bell
> Reaching across the landscape of hysteria
> To where, larger than all the charcoaled batteries

> And imaged towers against that dying sky,
> Religion stands, the church blocking the sun.[2]

Rukeyser's poem displays her characteristic attitude throughout her work, an openness to seemingly incompatible values all "precious to our dreams." The inclusiveness of Whitman has helped her in this respect, she says, as has the Bible where God is in the thunder and also in the still small voice. There is little contempt and exclusion in her work, though there are traces of these in the early "revolutionary" poems. In a poem from *Breaking Open* she makes explicit what has been understood in all her books:

> Never to despise in myself what I have been taught
> to despise. Not to despise the other.
> Not to despise the *it*. To make this relation
> with the it : to know that I am it.

"Wooden Spring" again reveals the strong desire to find relationship. The first three stanzas describe the frustration of waiting for the flowering of a late spring; there is a great deal of "contemporary stress" behind the imagery of "frozen tight bulbs," and there is a trace of surrealism which will become more pronounced in her last volume of the thirties, *A Turning Wind*.

> The ghosts swim, lipless, eyeless, upward :
> the crazy hands point in five directions down :
> to the sea, the high ridge, the bush, the blade, the weak white
>   root :
> thumping at life in an agony of birth, abortive fruit.

The last three stanzas become explicit in connecting the natural imagery with the human situation and to the wish that a fruitful order come to the confused world and to the poet's perception of it.

> . . . there must be abstraction, where fields need not sprout,
>   waves pound,
> there must be silence where no rushing grasses sound,
> life in this lack of death, comfort on this wide ground.

Characterizing her early lyricism is the energetic impulse to mean-

2. Untermeyer (ed.), *Modern American Poetry*, 456.

ing, the struggle to make "this wide ground" of experience in a chaotic time yield the flower of a satisfying, relating idea, an "abstraction." In a poem such as "Wooden Spring" we have her impulse explained: her effort is like that of the "white root / thumping at life in an agony of birth," like all those who try to fit personal experience into a larger scheme.

"Sand-Quarry with Moving Figures" is the first of three poems in this section which tell of the poet's experience with the growing distance between generations. One notes the absence of bitterness which often characterizes such poems, particularly those of the thirties. The poet and her father, a builder, drove to a land-development project where he planned "rows of little houses." The young girl saw only "ruined marshlands," the "stubble and waste of black," and "his ugly villages." "Sand-Quarry" is one of the first references in poetry to the subdivision, that twentieth-century locus which has neither the city's nor the village's richness. The young girl did not care for the father's laughing promise of wealth ("We'll own the countryside"), and she shouted "No, Father, no" when he pointed out that the name painted on a marking stone was her name too. The ending is a surprise; one expects some kind of final sad rejection after the girl's shouted denial.

"No, Father, no!" He caught my hand as I cried,and smiling,
entered the pit, ran laughing down its side.

She has seen the worst her father could do to the land, she has denied his generation's values, but she is still lighthearted and hopeful enough to run laughing down the pit he has dug. Here is another insight into the poet's inclusive sensibility.

"Four in a Family" takes up the theme at what seems to be a later date. The father is now just that, "the father," no longer "Father"; "the mother" and "the sister" are also there, estranged by this impersonal designation. The father is no longer laughing. "He looked at me, / sorrowing, saying nothing, with his hard tired breath." Their faces are telling her, "This is your home . . . Stay." But she doesn't belong there or anywhere else yet. She does know that she is turning away from them; her state is a sad wondering, or perhaps just a stunned wondering, and a final ambiguous question captures very well the concern of youth in an economic crisis.

> Strange father, strange mother, who are you, who are you?
> Where have I come,
> how shall I prosper home?

Her last question is about her personal development and also about the family's material security; the dilemma is forcefully conveyed. (Rukeyser had to leave Vassar after her sophomore year because her father went bankrupt. He later disinherited her for her political views and "disobedience.")

The last poem in this section, "This House, This Country," expresses her decisive break with her family. Here the short lines with their syntactical ellipsis conveying a sense of urgent meaning remind one of Auden, for example his "1929." But the content of these urgent phrases, though superficially echoing Auden (travel, frontiers, fighting) is different in that it is incorporated, finally, into the affirmative statement of the poem. Where Auden resolves the time of "anxiety at night, / Shooting and barricade in street" in the private image of "the lolling bridegroom beautiful, there," Rukeyser sees the time of anxiety coming to a close as a result of the communal struggle with which she identifies.

> I crossed frontier
> the questions asked   the proofs shown   the name
> signed smiling   I reached knowledge of my home.
>
> I praised their matings
> and corner-meetings
> their streets the brightest I had yet walked down   :
>
> . . . .
>
> I have left forever
> house and maternal river
> given up sitting in that private tomb
> quitted that land   that house   that velvet room.
>
> Frontiers admitted me
> to a growing country
> I carry the proofs of my birth and my mind's reasons
> But reckon with their struggle and their seasons.

Unlike Auden's, Rukeyser's poem makes a statement about a commitment to social action and change, one which will not require, however, the submersion of personal identity.

The last section of *Theory of Flight* contains fourteen lyric poems which are more explicitly political than the earlier ones. "For Memory," in three parts, is an elegy by a young woman on a young woman friend.[3] The subject of the elegy, Ruth Lehman, of the well-known New York family, was at Vassar with Rukeyser, who recalled, "Ruth was meant to be extremely comfortably brought up, and she didn't want that. She wanted something stronger." A poet, she wanted to write about women in the labor movement, homosexual women, adventurous and rebellious women. She went from Vassar to work in shirt factories around Albany; she shined shoes in the Loop in Chicago (the newspapers carried a photograph of a Lehman in this demeaning position). Then she headed down the Mississippi to New Orleans where she got peritonitis and died. In Rukeyser's elegy, the dead young woman symbolizes the ideal bravery of her generation. She is an inspiration to her friends. Her death urges the poet to love more intensely. The poem has an eloquent simplicity and the eager generosity of youth.

> Stand to me in the dark
> Set your mouth on me for friends we did not know
> Be strong in love
> give strength to all we meet
> the loving   the kind   the proletarian strong
>
> . . . .
> This was my friend
>   forget the "my," speak out

"Study in a Late Subway" expresses a deep sympathy for the commuters, "tense and semi-crucified things." The poet and her friends ride the subway and sense the power that conveys them. Awareness of the energy at work in the mundane, in the routine, is a

---

3. The famous elegies in English (Milton's, Shelley's, Arnold's, Tennyson's) are by young men about young men.

constant source of hope to this urban poet. But she sees how that energy contrasts with the sapped human beings in its midst. She knows that the spirits of millions are not nourished, as hers is, by an awareness of the miracles of their technological civilization. The poet's resolve is to transmit the message of that energy and its implication for social change, for possibility.

> Speed welcomes us in explosions of night : here
> is wrath and fortitude and motion's burning :
> the world buries the directionless, until
> the heads are sprung in awareness or drowned in peace.
> Sleep will happen.   We must give them morning.

"Sundays, They Sleep Late" is a more explicit criticism of those like the lovers in "In a Dark House" who try to shut out the world. There are details, echoing Eliot, of sophisticated killing of time and the sense of purposelessness, of debility:

> the wind bled of vigor, the talk in the parlor
> of people pasturing on each other's minds, and sunset
> evolving in the air, a quiet change against the duller
> signs in pandemonium of day's gradual transit

But unlike Eliot, and unlike Auden too, Rukeyser has an answer to that sense of weariness: there are things to be done.

> There are these things to be remembered: the nine boys[4]
>   waiting,
> battle-fronts of the rising army with holes bitten by death,
> the man in the prison overland, and history beating
> out the recurrent facts of power, suppression, wrath.

Several poems in this section, including "Thousands of Days" and "The Surrounded," attest to the poet's own struggle with despair in a world of distorted values. She too has been "surrounded by shadows / more plausible than love." "Burlesque" and "Movie" are visions of the cheap reduction we have made of our desires and our ideals. "Movie" reflects Rukeyser's view of Hollywood and explains why, as a writer of titles and commentaries for Garrison

---

4. The "nine boys" are the Scottsboro boys.

Films, she worked with those makers of documentaries in the thirties who wanted to show America as it really was.

"Citation for Horace Gregory" explains what she believed poets in America must do. As always, they must give themselves wholly to the consuming work of poetry.

> These are our brave, these with their hands in on the work,
> hammering out beauty upon the painful stones
> turning their grave heads passionately finding
> truth and alone and each day subtly slain
> and each day born.

"Citation for Horace Gregory" flashes images of the contemporary world which the poet must not ignore but which must not distract from the work of poetry:

> The brass voice speaks in the street
> STRIKE STRIKE
>
> The nervous fingers continue elaborately
> drawing consciousness, examining, doing.

The poets who have done good work but are inadequate to this time are those like Eliot "who led us to the precipice / subtly and perfectly" and

> . . . there striking an attitude
> rigid and ageing on the penultimate step,
> the thoughtful man MacLeish who bent his head
> feeling the weight of the living; bent, and turned
> the grave important face round to the dead.

This poem was first published in *New Republic* in November, 1934; MacLeish's poetry up to that time was filled with a nostalgia for Europe where he had "exiled" himself in the twenties. Back in America he wrote *New Found Land* (1930) where he said, in "American Letter," "I am sick for home for the red roofs and the olives." That nostalgia was to vanish in the poetry of the later thirties and forties when MacLeish like Rukeyser focused on the worldwide struggle against fascism. But the view of the modern world MacLeish's poetry presented before 1936 was bleak. He felt, as Rukeyser put it, "the weight of the living"; he too grappled, for instance, with the significance of modern science to the modern personality in "Einstein" (from *Streets in the Moon*, 1929). As Signi Falk noted, MacLeish's "attempt to translate the laws of physics into poetic images" resulted in "a sense of loneliness and frustration, of man's inability to understand his relationship to the universe."[5] Though poets like MacLeish, Eliot, and Jeffers ("sick of a catapulting nightmare world") see no hope in the modernity of the modern world, Rukeyser says that Horace Gregory is different. He is "the brave unmedalled, who dares to shape his mind, / printed with dignity, to the machines of change." She urges young poets to follow him, for they are his heirs.

"Cats and a Cock," a six-page poem, is an intense, complex experience in which vivid descriptions of natural scenes alternate with passionate abstractions. The movement of the lines and the often bizarre imagery carry the reader along in sensuous thought to meanings which cannot be adequately paraphrased. Rukeyser's method in this poem is like that of certain shorter lyrics ("In a Dark House," "Wooden Spring," "Breathing Landscape") and foreshadows her longer poems such as the "Elegies" in which, as she explains in *The Life of Poetry*, images move in clusters and create a complex of meanings. "Our poems are not lyrics or one-emotion poems. . . . The poems which depend on several emotions, each carrying its images, move like a cluster travelling from one set of positions to another: the group ABCDE, say, moving to A′B′C′D′E′; a constellation. This gathering-together of elements so that they move together according to a newly visible system is becoming evident in all our sciences, and it is natural that it should be present in our writing" (LP, 17–18). Rukeyser's early statements about poetry are now taken for granted as describing contemporary poetry. But at the beginning of her career they were not widely accepted, and her poems were called "obscure."

5. Archibald MacLeish, *New Found Land* (Boston and New York, 1930); Archibald MacLeish, *Streets in the Moon* (Boston and New York, 1929); Signi L. Falk, *Archibald MacLeish* (New York, 1965), 42. MacLeish was one of the judges for the first Harriet Monroe Poetry Award, which Rukeyser won in June, 1941.

The poem is addressed to the writer and friend of the poet, Eleanor Clark (wife of Robert Penn Warren.) As the poem progresses the cats who stream up the hill are associated with picketers and the cock, slaughtered by the cats, is associated with the poet. The human goal, of course, is to reconcile the poets and the picketers, the artists and the partisans: "I pledge you death until / they fight and acquiesce, or one has died." The friend is urged to join in the social struggle of "conflicting graces moving to one end" and in the celebration of periodic human victories. Philip Blair Rice had high praise in 1936 for the next section of the poem:

> The latchpieces of consciousness unfasten.
> We are stroked out of dream and night and myth,
> and turning slowly to awareness, listen
> to the soft bronchial whisperings of death.
>
> Never forget in legendary darkness
> the ways of the hands' turning and the mouth's ways,
> wander in the fields of change and not remember
> a voice and many voices and the evening's burning.

"These lines convey thought," said Rice. "They are also 'pure poetry,' about as pure and as poetical as any lines that are being written today." [6] The thought in these lines and those following was central to the discussion of proletarian poetry in the thirties— what it should be, how much individual personality the artist must suppress in order to write such poetry. Here as elsewhere Rukeyser comes out strongly in favor of the artist's individuality, of the great variety of ways people can take "in the fields of change," of the great difference in voices. We must not forget, in making revolution, other human making:

> Turn and remember, this is the world made plain
> by chart and signal, instrument and name   :
> . . . .
> flier in advance, the cloud over his mouth   ;
> the inventor who produces the moment of proof   ;
> a sun and moon and other several stars   ;
> and those who know each other over wars.

6. Rice, "New Poet."

The phrase "moment of proof" is used four times as the poem moves toward its conclusion. Rukeyser will use the phrase again and again to signify a deep, complete awareness of relationship: "all values extended into the blood awake," she will say in another poem. The moment of proof here is the recognition that the "fearful antagonists" of poets and picketers can be reconciled in awareness.

> No hill can ever hold us, peak enlists peak,
> climax forces out climax, proud cock, cats streaming,
> poets and pickets contriving a valid country,
> : Mayday moment, forever provoking new
>   belief and blooming.

Reviewers were divided over the "proletarianism" of *Theory of Flight*. Geoffrey Stone in the *American Review* (which Samuel Eliot Morison called "the organ of an American fascist party") said her intellect "is a mechanical device which neatly sorts things into the categories of dialectical materialism." But Ruth Lechlitner in the leftist *Partisan Review and Anvil*, praising *Theory of Flight* as the most outstanding collection in ten years by a younger woman poet, said Rukeyser was not a "true revolutionary poet" because she "still drew on the romantic-lyric tradition and has not effected the transition from the 'I'-sympathizer type to the 'we' collectively working, emotionally unconfused poet." Lechlitner asserted that the true revolutionary poet has broken with the "romantic-personal, individual consciousness" and attained "collective, mass-identification with a universal consciousness." A poet sure of her thought and craft would not be guilty of "malfusion of romantic-metaphysical-mechanistic terms," in the seed-flower-fruit figure which Rukeyser applies to flight and to the processes of modern life. Eunice Clark in the leftist *Common Sense*, praising Rukeyser's "deep positive humanity," said she hadn't learned to speak simply yet and still suffered from the "aristocratic maladies of post-war poetry—snobbish erudition alternating with excursions into the incomprehensible sub-conscious." Writing about *Theory of Flight* and *U.S. 1* in the renamed *Partisan Review*, John Wheelwright also criticized her obscurity. "Confront communication," he said. "It devolves upon us to rediscover clarity. Revolutionary writing in the snob style does not reach a proper audience."[7]

Other reviewers who weren't necessarily concerned with the book's revolutionary quality said she used "blurred metaphors" where thought is not "reduced to sensuous terms." F. O. Matthiessen said her words were "too flowingly allusive and often leave a blurred effect." On the other hand reviewers appreciated the "open" quality of her poetry, its expansive and inclusive movement. Peter Munro Jack in the *New York Times Book Review* said the "sense of an opening and widening world gives her poems a definite and directive meaning." Kenneth Burke admired her work in the "regions of magic": blood, fire, the pit, the father. William Rose Benét said she "writes as a poet not a propagandist." His brother, Stephen Vincent Benét, said the same in his introduction to *Theory of Flight*. Philip Blair Rice concluded that her poems "are among the few so far written in behalf of the revolutionary cause which combine craftsmanship, restraint, and intellectual honesty." Such honesty meant for Rukeyser the complex fusion of social and personal elements, allowing unresolved conflicts into her poems, often through the very blurred, allusive lines Matthiessen found unsatisfying. *Theory of Flight* is her first and lasting commitment to a poetry of process which accepts no restrictions on its exploration and which invites other minds to their own creative expanding and inclusiveness. One thinks of Whitman's assertion, "I seek less to state or display any theme or thought, and more to bring you, reader, into the atmosphere of the theme or thought—there to pursue your own flight."[8]

---

7. Samuel Eliot Morison, *The Oxford History of the American People* (New York, 1965), 970; Geoffrey Stone, review of TF, in *American Review*, VII (April, 1936), 101; Ruth Lechlitner, review of TF, in *Partisan Review and Anvil*, III (March, 1936), 29–30; Clark, review of TF; John Wheelwright, review of *U.S.1*, in *Partisan Review*, IV (March, 1938), 54–56.

8. Rice, "New Poet"; F. O. Matthiessen, review of TF, in *Yale Review*, n.s. XXV (Spring, 1936), 604; P. M. Jack, review of TF, in *New York Times Book Review*, January 12, 1936, p. 15; Kenneth Burke, "Return After Flight"; W. R. Benét, review of TF in *Saturday Review*, December 7, 1935, p. 47; James E. Miller, Jr., Introduction to Walt Whitman, *Complete Poetry and Selected Prose* (Cambridge, Massachusetts, 1959), xl.

U.S. 1

There had not been anything in American literature like *U.S. 1* (1938). Two poems in the volume ("The Book of the Dead" and "Mediterranean") are based on investigative journeys, on literal fact; in these poems Rukeyser uses poetry to "extend the document," documents such as the reports of congressional committees and interviews with West Virginia miners. These poems are related to the documentary film, to reportage, and to the novel of social protest such as John Dos Passos' trilogy *U.S.A.* with its "camera eye" technique and its inclusion of newspaper headlines and "biographies" of outstanding figures. In this volume one also finds the polar opposite of these "documentary" poems: an allegory, "The Cruise." There is also a section of lyric poems which extend the themes and methods of the short poems in *Theory of Flight*. With this volume there is no question of Rukeyser's originality, and the poems demonstrate her early ability to write in a variety of styles. No poet had used prose documents this way before. And of the lyrics, Edna Lou Walton in the *New York Times Book Review* said that Rukeyser was writing in a new medium, almost in a new poetic language, because she was "trying to grasp a new scene and communicate new reactions to it." The state of the world and the quality of her vision caused Louis Untermeyer to claim, in the *Yale Review*, that the lyrics "could not have been written in any other day. . . . They could not have been written by anyone else but Miss Rukeyser." Willard Maas in *Poetry* said that some of her lyrics are "fine achievements which have not been duplicated. . . . by any other poet of the Thirties." [9]

"The Book of the Dead" is based on the poet's personal investigation of the survivors, the site, and the documents relating to an event which occurred in a valley in West Virginia in the early thirties. Two thousand men were digging a three-and-a-quarter-mile tunnel under a mountain from Gauley's Junction to Hawk's Nest

9. Edna Lou Walton, review of *U.S. 1*, in *New York Times Book Review*, March 27, 1938, p. 19; Louis Untermeyer, review of *U.S. 1*, in *Yale Review*, n.s. XXVII (Spring, 1938), 608; Willard Maas, "Lost Between Wars," *Poetry*, LII (May, 1938), 101–104.

in Fayette County so that a river could be diverted as part of a hydroelectric power project. When it was discovered that the rock through which they bored had a high content of valuable silica, the contracting company had the men drill the rock dry, to get more silica out faster. As *Time* magazine put it, many of the workers "died like ants in a flour bin" of silicosis, which is incurable, and which leads in effect to strangulation.[10] The workers and their families tried to get compensation, but an investigation before Congress was blocked, and lawyers charged the workers 50 percent of the meager compensation they finally received. In "The Book of the Dead" the poetic extension of the document makes the facts live in a larger dimension, connecting them, like the facts in "Theory of Flight," with the eternal dualities in the cosmos (essentially, power and annihilation) and with the poet's continuing elaboration of a reconciling vision. To the young poet the Gauley tragedy was a striking contradiction: men tapping a vast source of energy and being destroyed in the process. The social injustice of the situation is fascinating to the poet in its larger framework; "The Book of the Dead" is not principally the attack on capitalism reviewers such as John Wheelwright (*Partisan Review*) wished she had written.

The first section, "The Road," opens into the poem as it opens into the valley of the tragedy. In simple language and common rhythms and phrasing ("These are roads to take when you think of your country . . . reading the papers with morning inquiry . . . these roads will take you into your own country"[11]) the poet leads us into West Virginia. We hear an echo of "The Blood Is Justified": "By these roads shall we come upon our country." But now the phrasing is more direct, for the poet invites us to take that journey. The images of duality arise, but gradually, as part of the scenery.

> Gay blank rich faces wishing to add
> history to ballrooms, tradition to the first tee.

> The simple mountains, sheer, dark-graded with pine
> in the sudden weather, wet outbreak of spring

10. Review of *U.S.1*, in *Time*, March 28, 1938, p. 63.
11. Muriel Rukeyser, *U.S.1* (New York, 1938).

Part of her method in the poem is chosen here: "now the photographer unpacks camera and case, / surveying the deep country, follows discovery." [12] The photographer focuses on the major character in this drama, "the hard and stone-green river."

"West Virginia" begins with references to the discoverers of the seventeenth century—"Thomes Batts, Robert Fallam, / Thomas Wood, the Indian Perecute." Then the poet's own discovery of the "Indian fields," the "planted home," becomes indistinguishable from the old discoverers' until we gradually focus on the poet's discovery alone. She passes the site of the execution of John Brown; "the beaten land" from the strong spring rains is associated with the Civil War and with troops in Gauley Bridge. History and the poet's partly superimposed discovery are presented in long, loose lines. But the three last stanzas, giving the core of the poet's discovery, are in brief lines:

> But it was always the water
> the power flying deep
> green rivers cut the rock
> rapids boiled down,
> a scene of power.

The central fact in all this history is the power in nature. This theme will become dominant as the poem comes to its climax.

In "Statement: Philippa Allen," the facts of the tragedy emerge, as they would in a documentary film, in an interview with a social worker during a congressional hearing. The contractors, with thirty years' experience, knew the danger of dry drilling, yet they provided no safety devices for the men. In the sparest of dialogue, which sounds like the phrasing of an inquest but which, upon closer examination, is pared down to its essential rhythms, we learn that the tunnel was originally begun by the New Kanawha Power Company, subsidiary of Union Carbide and Carbon, which was licensed to divert water to a hydroelectric plant for public sale. But New Kanawha actually sold the power to another subsid-

12. Rukeyser went to West Virginia with her close friend, the photographer Nancy Naumburg.

iary of Union Carbide, the Electro-Metallurgical Company. (An act of the West Virginia State Legislature allowed that subsidiary to buy up New Kanawha.) Then when silica was discovered, the tunnel was dug wider, and Electro-Metallurgical shipped the substance to Alloy, West Virginia, and used it—without refining, it was so pure—for the electro-processing of steel. Thus the public was twice cheated of the resources of its land, and those men who toiled to develop the resources died of a horrible disease. The poetry in this section is in the masterful use of dialogue which limns the evil configuration of events.

"Gauley Bridge" begins, "Camera at the crossing sees the city" and proceeds to give the details as a camera would pick them up. It is smalltown America, rather dreary, people going about their business. In the last stanza the poet reproaches us for these thoughts:

> What do you want—a cliff over a city?
> A foreland, sloped to sea and overgrown with roses?
> These people live here.

This stanza seems addressed to those poets like MacLeish who could still write in 1933 of their nostalgia for red roofs and olive trees. Rukeyser seeks the possibility in human life where modern people must actually live it; she has no pastoral fantasies, no nostalgia for a more "lovely" world.

"The Face of the Dam: Vivian Jones" is a meditation on the facts of the tragedy by a man who drove a locomotive when the silica was being mined and shipped away. Up to now, we have received mostly the bare facts. Here the poet creates a human voice to respond to them. The movement of the poem is largely from the impersonal to the human to the particular subjectivity of the poet whose voice will emerge distinctly in a few pages. "Praise of the Committee" gives more facts, more ghastly as they arrive in greater detail. "The ambulance was going day and night, / White's undertaking business thriving and / his mother's cornfield put to a new use." "If the men had worn masks, their use would have involved /

time every hour to wash the sponge at mouth." This section is in long, loose lines of exposition, setting forth what the committee learns. Then in short-lined stanzas at the end the poet in her own full voice drives to the heart of the matter.

> These men breathe hard.
>
> . . . .
> One climbs the hill on canes.
> They have broken the hills and cracked the riches wide.
>
> . . . .
> Their hands touched mastery; now they
> demand an answer.

"Mearl Blankenship" is a monologue, his description of working in the tunnel and the choking he experiences now and his waiting for death. He is also waiting for some compensation for his family (he sued the company twice, but when the lawyers got a settlement they didn't pass it on to him). Such monologues as this one (and the following) prompted Untermeyer to call "The Book of the Dead" "a more passionate *Spoon River Anthology*." [13] "Absalom" is spoken by a mother who has lost three sons to silicosis and whose husband is dying of it. Here narrative lines ("I had three sons who worked with their father in the tunnel") are interrupted by rhythmic lyric lines in which individual maternal strength is connected with the universal power of regeneration.

> *I open out a way, they have covered my sky with crystal*
> *I come forth by day, I am born a second time,*
> *I force a way through, and I know the gate*
> *I shall journey over the earth among the living.*

As Rosenthal noted, "The mother's determination to make her youngest child's death count for something, to have him live again in her own work of struggle for a better life, is linked with the rebirth motif of the great religions, and specifically of the Egyptian religion" whose scripture is *The Book of the Dead*. Philip Blair Rice pointed out that the imaginative scheme of "The Book of the

---

13. Untermeyer, review of *U.S. 1*.

Dead" was that of Osiris' Way. The tunnel is the underworld, the mountain stream is the life-giving river, and the congressional inquiry is the judgment in the hall of truth. Rice noted that this scheme is suggested rather than presented; the poem is not overweighted with allegory. But Rosenthal is perceptive in identifying the persona in Rukeyser's poem with Isis not Osiris and with all the great female protagonists from mythological earth mothers to the strong modern women of Lawrence and Gorky.[14] Especially harrowing lines are spoken by the mother of an eighteen-year-old boy:

> Shirley was sick about three months.
> I would carry him from his bed to the table,
> from his bed to the porch, in my arms.
>
> . . . .
>
> He lay and said, "Mother, when I die,
> "I want you to have them open me up and
> "see if that dust killed me.
> "Try to get compensation. . . ."

Untermeyer said that he was emotionally and physically shaken by the combination of protest and prophecy in the poem. It ends with these lines, spoken by the mother:

> He shall not be diminished, never;
> I shall give a mouth to my son.

The next section, "The Disease," is a dialogue in which a doctor explains the course of the illness to a member of the investigating committee. The impersonal language of science conveys the horror of the disease as we follow the speaker to the window where he holds up x-rays and describes the fatal scarring of the victim's lungs. The rhythm of the questioning creates a refrain fraught with more doom than any medieval ballad.

> That is what happens, isn't it?
> A choking-off in the air cells?
> Yes.

14. Rosenthal, "The Longer Poems," 218; Philip Blair Rice, review of *U.S.1*, in *Nation*, March 19, 1938, p. 335.

> There is difficulty in breathing.
> Yes.
> > And a painful cough?
> Yes.
> > Does silicosis cause death?
> Yes, sir.

William Carlos Williams said in his review of *U.S. 1* that Rukeyser uses material such as X-ray reports "with something of the skill employed by Pound in the material of his *Cantos.* . . . She understands what words are for and how important it is not to twist them in order to make 'poetry' of them." Rosenthal noted that Rukeyser may have been the first poet to so fully integrate into a poem sections of a prose document such as the transcript of a committee hearing. She skillfully alters the language of the document so as to preserve much of the rhythm and the flavor of the actual situation.[15] The sections progress, with monologues by those who worked in the tunnel or came to investigate. The poet's voice is heard more and more, beginning in "The Cornfield," which describes the place where silicosis victims were furtively buried, five at a time.[16]

"Alloy" contains, in its description of the beautiful silicon-blanketed landscape, images such as the "disintegrated angel on these hills," which Rosenthal called in 1953 "one of the strongest images of perverted industrial mastery of nature in American poetry—comparable perhaps to the imagery in Crane's 'The Tunnel.'"[17] But unlike in Crane's looser poem, here the life-destroying yet miraculously creative contradictions arrive in a close contrapuntal rhythm within each stanza, or they play against each other in separate stanzas. The first stanza gives us the image of the classic gangster, "with his gun smoking and out," who "is not so / vicious as this commercial field, its hill of glass." The softness of the *l*'s in the

15. William Carlos Williams, review of *U.S. 1*, in *New Republic*, March 9, 1938, pp. 141–42; Rosenthal, "The Longer Poems," 216.

16. There is a jab at MacLeish in "Swear by the corn, / the found-land corn, those who like ritual."

17. Rosenthal, "The Longer Poems," 218.

last line of the first stanza (whose content is impersonal vicious-
ness and rapacity) is repeated in the second stanza whose imagery
is at first human and pastoral but then shifts again to its negation.

> Sloping as gracefully as thighs, the foothills
> narrow to this, clouds over every town
> finally indicate the stored destruction.

In the third stanza the contradictions arrive hard upon one another, in the contrast of liquid consonants against harsh plosives,
until in the last line there is a resolution in the smooth animal
movement of a machine.

> Crystalline hill: a blinded field of white
> murdering snow, seamed by convergent tracks;
> the travelling cranes reach for the silica.

Stanza after stanza the contradictions play against each other in
vivid imagery and appropriate sounds and rhythms. The play of *l*'s
against the harsher consonants is masterly, especially in the paradoxically soft-sounded "destructive" images: that of the very title,
"Alloy," and in lines like "Forced through this crucible, a million
men." The resolution of the poem is that above their death the precious silica dust rises "over the mills, / crystallized . . . beyond the
fierce corrosion," uniting with the durable strength of steel, for silica is used in the electroplating of steel. The "disintegrated angel"
thus acquires a new life in a new, strong form. Of course this new
life does not compensate for the death of those who worked in the
tunnel. But the fact remains that other lives and strengths are en-
hanced as a result of a marvelous technology which did not spare,
for the greed of its directors, those who gave it birth. The poem
contains the beauty and marvel of modern technology ("electric
furnaces produce this precious, this clean, / annealing the crystals
. . . perfected metal"), the horror of its perversion, and the implicit
cry that it be directed by caring human beings.

"Power" now conveys the landscape not as "murdering" but as
warming, even sexually exciting. Coming after the destructive
snow of "Alloy," these images of sun and river carry forward the

contrapuntal movement of the poem. In "Alloy" there were "the roaring flowers of the chimney-stacks." Here the "severe flame" of the furnaces becomes the "quick sun . . . yielding the sex up under all the skin" and the sun "a magnificent flower on the mouth." "Alloy" is filled with cursing, fear, poison; but the first stanza of "Power" has "gay . . . green designs," "miracle," "love," "grace," "marvel." Here is a bold example of the poetry of possibility as Rukeyser described it in *The Life of Poetry*: "Truth or reality, process or moment, gods or half-gods, are the terms for immortal necessities, which are not checks and balances, but phases, if you will, of essence—all to be fought for, realized, and sung" (LP, 68). The poet in "The Book of the Dead" is realizing and singing these phases, moving toward a resolution of "intolerable contradiction," as in "Theory of Flight."

The power plant is described in the second stanza in human, loving terms, as "the narrow-waisted towers" lifting "their protective network" like a "gymnast." These towers, bearing "god's generosity" are the necessary demiurges, giving "their voltage low enough for towns to handle." The whole system is humanized. Even "the power-house stands skin-white at the transmitters' side." At the beginning of the next stanza the poet reminds us that we have been taking roads into our country on journeys of spiritual as well as historical discovery. When we reach the power plant the poet makes it a symbol of our ordinary level of awareness:

> This is the midway between water and flame,
> this is the road to take when you think of your country,
> between the dam and the furnace, terminal.

Our ordinary level of awareness is a mediation and a compromise; we needn't dwell on unbearable terminal truths. We may focus on those aspects of the world which are hospitable to human life. The images of vibrant, organic life in the first two stanzas are extended in imagery of light, bright, gay colors (the control rooms are a rich green). But in our journey with the poet we must leave this tenuously balanced middle way of awareness.

With the designing engineer, Jones, quoting Milton and wanting "the men who work here to be happy," we plunge into the bowels of the plant, down past generators, on a spiral staircase into the blackness of the tunnel where men died. Images of cold, darkness, descent, and rigidity pile up ("Iron on iron resounds, / echoes along created gorges"). The imagery has prepared us for the conclusion, but it is still a shocking surprise.

> Down the reverberate channels of the hills
> the suns declare midnight, go down, cannot ascend,
> no ladder back; see this, your eyes can ride through steel,
> this is the river Death, diversion of power,
> the root of the tower and the tunnel's core,
> this is the end.

Has the poet abandoned the midway of awareness and sunk to midnight hopelessness? The conclusion of the poem is not negative, despite the arrival at death. As in much of Rukeyser's poetry, that conclusion contains elements which, in their relationship, point to possibility. There is the assertion, first of all, that human beings can see through or imagine beyond what they have wrought—the eyes of the imagination can pierce through steel. Therefore we can understand that we have harnessed power at the cost of human lives: the life-giving river has become the river of death. But it is still a source of strength. (The familiar concept of the fact of death providing a powerful impetus to live more fully is implied here too.) Nothing can gainsay these polar truths. "This is the end": a terminal of awareness. The depths in which we see these truths are nightmarish, the rungs on the ladder down to that vision "give, pliant, beneath the leaping heart." We needn't go that deep journey often, looking through steel to imagine that water. We may pause at "the midway between water and flame," at the powerplant in its bright, human landscape. We must remember, however, that there are those who relish the "after-night" where the presence of elemental forces is felt. Our guide, the engineer Jones, says, "This is the place. Away from this my life / I am indeed Adam unparadiz'd."

"Power" concluded, "this is the end." "The Dam" begins, "All power is saved, having no end." We are meant to hold these clusters of meaning in the mind as they reveal the fullness of reality. Some of the meanings the poet is allowing to expand into their constellations are these: in "Power" death is both finality and source of power; but in another sense, one cannot say that power has any source, any beginning or end—thus the first line of "The Dam." But that line is followed by

> Rises
> in the green season, in the sudden season
> the white the budded
> and the lost.

Thus more contradictions: power *does* have a beginning and an end. Assertion and counter-assertion, "phases of essence." In Rukeyser's poetry we are rarely permitted to rest at any phase.

There follows a description of the power of flowing water, "diverted water," "White brilliant function of the land's disease." As in "Alloy" we have power out of illness. As in "Absalom" a voice interrupts the natural description and associates the power of this river with the self-renewing, self-healing energy of the universe as it has been described in myth and religion.

> *I open out a way over the water*
> *I form a path between the Combatants:*
> *Grant that I sail down like a living bird,*
> *power over the fields and Pool of Fire.*
> *Phoenix, I sail over the phoenix world.*

After another page of description of water and dam, the poem encompasses the document at the appropriate point: a dialogue among members of the inquest further reveals the soullessness of the corporation's role in the tragedy. Then a line of stock quotation in newstype is incorporated into the poem. But the lines immediately resume their flowing description of the power of water.

> This is a perfect fluid, having no age nor hours,
> surviving scarless, unaltered, loving rest

The effect of the lines' movement and content is a healing, like the self-healing of a river. These obstructions (the machinations of commerce), these dead rocks in the path of flowing, live power are submerged in the watercourse. Even that murderous word—*glass*—(hear "hill of glass" from "Alloy") is redeemed: water is "willing to run forever to find its peace / in equal seas in currents of still glass." We have the core of the poetry of possibility in the last lines of "The Dam":

> Nothing is lost, even among the wars,
> imperfect flow, confusion of force.
> It will rise. These are the phases of its face.
> It knows its seasons, the waiting, the sudden.
> It changes. It does not die.

(At least one critic has remarked that Rukeyser begins another book even before she has completed the one she is working on. In "The Book of the Dead" we see her already dwelling on "phase," the phenomenon for which Willard Gibbs formulated the famous, widely applicable "phase rule.") The poem continues with two more "expository" sections in which we learn more about the course of silicosis and about its victims. We also learn that it is as easy to block a bill to prevent industrial silicosis as it is to cause that fatal blocking of blood supply to the air passageways. Blockage is the evil. After a stunning poetic re-creation of the document of the congressional subcommittee's findings, the penultimate section of the poem ends with reference to a risen ancestor who is a source of strength:

> dead John Brown's body walking from a tunnel
> to break the armored and concluded mind.

The final section, "The Book of the Dead," begins with a line that has become a refrain: "These roads will take you into your own country." The men dying of silicosis "fight off our dying, / cough in the theaters of the war." The tunnel workers, like the Republicans in Spain she will soon refer to, suffer to preserve the world we know. The poet says we cannot evade the meanings of their deaths: "The facts of war forced into actual grace." These deaths will become part of our "modern glory," which the poem goes on to describe in muscular three-line stanzas: the discovery of America, the casting off of Europe, the settling of the West, the contemporary struggles for freedom in

> the old Mediterranean
> flashing new signals from the hero hills
> near Barcelona, monuments and powers,
> parent defenses.

All these triumphs are "the extreme arisen / fountains of life" (in her "Lives" she will call them "risen images"), as are "unmade boundaries of acts and poems" and, paradoxically, "this fact and this disease." Again, as in "Power" and "Alloy," death is viewed as a source of energy.

In the second section the poem focuses on civilization's worn, ritual history: "all the shimmering names, / the spear, the castle, and the rose." (These "half-memories" were described in "Tradition of This Acre," in *Theory of Flight*.) But the deeper history of our country and its meanings are more a part of us.

> But planted in our flesh these valleys stand,
> everywhere we begin to know the illness,
> are forced up, and our times confirm us all.

The next two stanzas give an ancient reverberating image which encompasses the meanings of the poem, for, as Rosenthal observed, all opposites are included here.[18]

> In the museum life, centuries of ambition
> yielded at last a fertilizing image:
> the Carthaginian stone meaning a tall woman
>
> carries in her two hands the book and cradled dove,
> on her two thighs, wings folded from the waist
> cross to her feet, a pointed human crown.

Here is a powerful woman carved of stone, containing her power, wise and loving and a lover of peace, regal, in a position of accep-

---

18. Rosenthal, "Chief Poets of the American Depression," 495.

tance.[19] Here is an image other centuries created to express the ideals of civilization. But we cannot rest with this image. The next stanza continues, "This valley is given to us like a glory"; yet it is also a "blow falling full in face." This valley stuns us with its meanings, calling all of us in all our skills and creativity to "measure our times again" so that they too will have their "fertilizing image" as past centuries had their Carthaginian stone. (In "Breaking Open" she will say, "The whole thing . . . Must be re-imagined.")

In the third and last section the poet concludes her measuring of our times, whose burdens are borne by ordinary working men and women:

> These are our strength, who strike against history.
> These whose corrupt cells owe their new styles of weakness
> to our diseases;
>
> these carrying light for safety on their foreheads
> descended deeper for richer faults of ore,
> drilling their death.
>
> These touching radium and the luminous poison,
> carried their death on their lips and with their warning
> glow in their graves.
>
> These weave and their eyes water and rust away,
> these stand at wheels until their brains corrode,
> these farm and starve

Enlarging her meanings in "Theory of Flight" that in growth and change lie security, she says

> Defense is sight; widen the lens and see
> standing over the land myths of identity,
> new signals, processes

Speaking to artists, she urges that they be

> Voices to speak to us directly. As we move.
> As we enrich, growing in larger motion,
> this word, this power.

19. Rukeyser saw this statue in a photograph on a postcard she received from Rosenthal.

She will say in a lecture in 1940 (which was later incorporated into *The Life of Poetry*) that we need "voices to speak to us *as we move, directly*, insisting on full consciousness": acknowledgment of "mastery" and "discovery" on the one hand and of "frontiers and forests" on the other, and always the "fanatic cruel legend at our back" which is the history of our national wrongs. Yet to the victims of history she would offer the continuance of her voice which bears witness to their lives.

> Name and road,
> communication to these many men,
> as epilogue, seeds of unending love.

In acknowledging all the phases of essence, even in outrage she sings possibility.

This inclusiveness, this vision of possibility was not seen in the thirties for what it was. John Wheelwright in *Partisan Review* interpreted it as an imperfect attack on capitalism by an inexperienced socialist because "not one line of its thousand lines describes the wage system. . . . The poem attacks the excrescences of capitalism, not the system's inner nature." Wheelwright claimed that "a goodly number of poetry readers will say, 'We haven't the remotest idea why anyone but a dumb cluck worked there. It's a free country, isn't it?'" He concluded that Rukeyser's limited philosophy limits her poetry. Yet the greed at the root of the Gauley tragedy is everywhere manifest in the poem, and the captivity of the workers in this "free" country is described in very human terms in "Absalom." What Wheelwright couldn't see for his limited requirements of poetry was the larger intention and achievement of "The Book of the Dead," which is not only political narrative poetry but a poetry which traces the "immortal necessities" as they have worked in a certain human span in West Virginia.

At the other pole were the reviewers who felt Rukeyser's vision was not wide enough. Edna Lou Walton in the New York *Times* found the poem too prosaic. "This is reporting and not the imaginative vision." Willard Maas in *Poetry* also felt that Rukeyser ventured into fields "that have been more adequately explored and more tersely recorded by journalists." In "The Book of the Dead," which he felt was "modeled after leaflets," Rukeyser sounds like "Carrie Nation with a political hatchet on a Cook's tour." Both kinds of reviews are failures to see the poem for what it is, more than a political statement, more than reportage: it is, as P. B. Rice saw, "honest documentary writing" and myth making as well, of the sort that had not been attempted before in poetry and has not been duplicated since.[20]

The lyric poems in the middle section of *U.S.1* trace the pain and struggle of young adulthood in a world which is insensitive and resigned to a less than fully human life. As in the lyrics of *Theory of Flight* there is the desire to touch, to communicate. The world has become even less approachable, more rigid, "frozen solid," "maniac, catalept" ("A Flashing Cliff"). But there is the awareness, as in "Breathing Landscape" (TF), that love is "all rivers." Against the ice-bound, catalept world is asserted "the purified spirit" (in "Burning Bush") "training a flame upward along its vine" as it is educated to "bright horror." Rigidity is the theme again in "Girl at the Play," where "female paralysis" is brought on by the girl's resistance to a male's "powerful hand." But here art (theater) has the power to quicken her. In "Homage to Literature" it is poetry which quickens, which has "fixed this landscape" of "unbearable suns" rolling forever westward and annulling the image of a cripple's crutch thrown "as the headlights / streak down the torn street." In this poem "inimitable jazz" is set against "cannonadings," the "One Two Three" of hammers tearing up a street is offset by the rolling sunset, swamping the heartbeat. That sunset "repeats / sea beyond sea . . . Blake, Donne, Keats." The rhythms of the body, the universe, and art are poised against the rhythms of disease and destruction.

Another living image set against the rigidity of the world is that of "Eel": youth making its fluid, submarine way through an iron culture which encourages the young to throw off its sensitivity, its

20. John Wheelwright, review of *U.S.1*; Edna Lou Walton, review of *U.S.1*; Willard Maas, "Lost Between Wars"; Rice, review of *U.S.1*.

love, its rage, and accept "flippant defeat . . . a perfect husband, a promised income." The young wave "love's thin awkward plant among a crowd of salesmen." The poet has a sense of "ancestors . . . dead . . . parents busy somewhere"; there is doom in her perception of "Radio City, largest of riches, leaning / against the flaming cobalt, fatal as Belgium." The young compare their history lessons (Alexander, Euclid, "the violent empresses, Boone breaking through green country") to the heroism of what is now in the papers: Ann Burlak makes women "pound kettles / for drums, for a loud band!" These adolescents are restive during class, for "the street's outside." What they do not yet realize is that thousands like them see the times' disease and wish to eradicate it. The conclusion of the poem transforms the submarine eels into earth-striding creatures who are not alone in their perceptions and their goals:

> Parading upon a stage lit with immense firm flame.
> To change it. To mature. To find. To be these.

The poem is a universal expression of the restiveness and idealism of youth in the face of a materialist, war-focused culture. With a few changes in proper nouns, "Eel" could have been written by a young American poet of the sixties, in protest of the war in Vietnam and the society that fed it.

Certain poems in *U.S.1* focus on the sickness of the time as manifested in individual lives. "Panacea" recalls the theme of the need to touch. But here the speaker is herself ill (in previous poems the illness was in others), and she cannot find wholeness through another's touch. She seeks all other means to make herself well, believing "some force must be whole." Finally she finds at the window of the room: "This perseveres. / The sun, I say, sincere, the sun, the sun." It is the rhythm of her discovery—the music of it, as she would say—which is important here. That rhythm echoes the passage in "Theory of Flight": "Between murmur and murmur, birth and death, / is the earth's turning which follows the earth's turning." In *The Life of Poetry* she wrote of Whitman's rhythms: "Out of his own body, and its relation to itself and the sea, he drew his basic rhythms . . . the relation of our breathing to our heartbeat, and these measured against an ideal of water at the shore, not beginning nor ending, but endlessly drawing in" (LP, 80). This rhythm will recur in much of her prose and in all her poems of self-rediscovery, beginning with "Theory of Flight":

> "Body, return : I love you : soul, come home!
>
> . . . .
>
> unblind me, give me back myself, touch me now :
> slide, night, into the climates of the mind." (from "The Tunnel")

In "The Overthrow of One O'Clock at Night" from *The Speed of Darkness* the speaker is again at the window of her room and says, "trust in experience, the deep rhythms of your experience." Thus in the music of self-rediscovery, equilibrium is achieved in "Panacea."

"In Hades, Orpheus" focuses on the sick person who cannot return to the "all-green" world because she is "brimful of white / monotonous weakness." The illness is associated, in the imagery of the poem, with inflexibility. The figure in "The Drowning Young Man" also rigidly refuses to turn back to the world: "he has set his look" and in "the attractive water" he "is surrendered down." Peace is what he wants, not the struggle of the city. The surrender of the drowning young man contrasts with the determination of the young man in the poem on the facing page, "Boy with His Hair Cut Short," a poem of almost prosaic literalness which takes the reader by surprise, reminding one of the variety of Rukeyser's styles. The "camera eye" is at work again, as in many sections of "The Book of the Dead."

> Sunday shuts down on this twentieth-century evening.
> The L passes. Twilight and bulb define
> the brown room, the overstuffed plum sofa,
> the boy, and the girl's thin hands above his head.
> A neighbor radio sings stocks, news, serenade.

This young man is having his hair cut by his sister so he can continue to look for a job as he has been doing unsuccessfully for weeks. He has resolve, but the poet presents him as a victim: "He sits at the table, head down, the young clear neck exposed." His sister, too, is determined to be hopeful, "the blue vein, bright on her temple, pitifully beating." The poem is a classic portrait of the Depression, a Dorothea Lange in motion.

"More of a Corpse Than a Woman" recapitulates the themes of sickness and unresponsiveness. The tone is more revolutionary and more brash than any lyric since those in *Theory of Flight* such as "Movie." The poem originally appeared in *Partisan Review* and must have angered many of Rukeyser's contemporaries, "the dull girls with the educated minds and technical passions." [21] Rukeyser has included in her poetry every nuance of a vital sensibility's response to her time: this poem is in the bold strokes of feminist idealism and resolve.

> Give my regards to the well-protected woman,
> I knew the ice-cream girl, we went to school together.
> There's something to bury, people, when you begin to bury.
> When your women are ready and rich in their wish for the
>   world,
>> destroy the leaden heart,
>> we've a new race to start.

The poem owes its vehemence, doubtless, to the fact that Rukeyser discovered just before college that she "had been brought up as a protected, blindfolded daughter" who hardly realized that people lived below Fifty-Seventh Street (LP, 220).

The editing of *U.S.1* is very effective. Immediately after the simpler revolutionary strains of "More of a Corpse" we are given a series of subtle, rich, and strange lyrics which sing complex responses to the world. The three figures in "Three Negresses" appear in a compact fourteen-line poem whose themes of racial nightmare, beauty, hatred, and love are closely interwoven. "Formosa" sings fullness and certainty in images of sea and sky and in the rhythms of the coming of night on the shore and the coming in of the tide. In the basic rhythms of the universe, the last lines show the poet's recurrent achievement of equilibrium:

21. Rukeyser has not forgotten this type of young woman; she reappears in "Gradus Ad Parnassum" in *Breaking Open*.

midnight's an interval, darkness is promise, night's nothing,
nightmare is nothing, nothing but interval.

Eliminate all dreams: here, real: love come, high tide,
the risen, freehold moon, the fortunate island,
resting, blue-flooded, rests, delicately, the sea.

In the three lyrics which compose "Woman and Emblems" the poet touches on many of the themes of her past work but in the vivid shorthand of imagery. "Woman and Bird" describes a woman's wish to encompass the "sky, stranger, wilderness" of bird and the pain then of receiving the bird in her flesh where it is a mournful captive though the woman wishes intensely to fly. The lines are very short, the words simple, many of them harsh monosyllables intensified by alliteration. The poem expresses powerfully and succinctly the idealist's feeling of always falling short. "The Birthday" unfurls from "a spool of brightness," transforming images of birth and human career: "solemn crying," "flame crusading," "fighting-cock," a tree "casting seed"—all forces which "kill and engender." This is the imaged career of a poet of outrage and possibility. "Woman and Music" begins with a woman asking herself what has been her purpose in giving herself to art, to all the music of human making ("images, violins, dancers approaching"). She has turned from a vain self-concern to devotion to art ("laughing at a bone / . . . talking of ballet, flesh's impermanence"). The music of art has become her life: her life as poet is all her life. It is a powerful, chosen music:

dancing—and all the parks, walks, hours
descend in brilliant water past the eyes
pursuing and forgotten and subdued
to blinding music, the deliberate strings.

The last lyric in this central section of *U.S. 1*, "Outpost," is another vision of social change presented again in natural imagery. "Grave civilized man" sails out to sea, out past the "End of America," beyond familiar waters which teach us nothing but feed our "sickest / dread of strong icy seas, / disgust with sunlight." We must sail until the sad-faced, old life is out of sight. Though the images that have carried the argument to this point have been, if not predictable, somewhat traditional in their play about the motif of sailing into the unknown, the images which close the poem show the poet's commitment to "full consciousness," the refusal to simplify, the desire to be a voice which speaks to minds in their growing awareness of the changing world:

> here most civilized man,
> outpost survivor,
> the last and floating trace, streaming down every river
> into the sea whose foreign colors waver,
> hold to the end the images of violence
> on rising overwave and underwave,
> slave and slavedriver.

We sail to a newer world, but our old images are not easily drowned.

"The Cruise," a long narrative poem, is a political allegory. As with any allegory, to paraphrase its meanings is to render it dull and bald, but the poem itself is interesting and in many segments rich and exciting in its imagery and in the play of its themes. There are poweful descriptions of natural elements in a style recognizably Rukeyser's in its choice of arresting adjectives which give scenes a philosophical and moral dimension, a momentousness. As the ship pulls away from the dock

> Already, sea
> rose livid, boiling over the white expensive hull,
> imperious completely, undeniable.

For the most part scenes, dialogue, and action are presented in strong, spare language, very near to good prose, but intensified by its rhythms as are the expository passages of "The Book of the Dead."

The expensive ship, waved off by stockholders, represents society, which most people would leave to the management of a ruling class, provided enough fun and profit trickle down to the rest. The captain has orders "not to put in at any port / doubtful or dangerous." On the fourth day they pass an island; the passengers are eager for foreign cities, but the country is obviously at war. In a terse stanza we are given the radio's information: there is disaster back at home, planes falling, children dying, rumors of war, "strange clouds visible over the prairies, / blight on the wheat, dust in the middle air, unprecedented weather." Ships are ordered to make for port. They pass a city in flames. They go South in their pride, feeling safe: "we have machines." They are confident they will find a peaceful port. But the union man aboard urges the captain to land.

> "They must be fighting for something we know," he said,
> "I saw men advancing down those inspired hills,
>   guns and grenades are timed now against tyrants,
>   a wish to keep
>   us all alive! under its strictest grip
>   logical strength challenges conscience up."

(The contemporary reference is to the war against fascism in Spain: the feeling expressed was one shared by Rukeyser and many Americans.)

A poet aboard at first seems an escapist-hedonist esthete. He wants to land "in a port fit to receive us, / fleshly and bright, set in a frivolous growth, / giraffe plants, monster flowers." But though he calls the union man "a wandering motive" the poet has obviously reflected on responsibility himself: "If we are named . . . it is guilty generation." When it is realized that there is war in every city they pass, the poet says (prophetically for 1938), "That's our illness . . . the war our age must win." The poet is the most interesting character aboard because of his conflict: he understands what is happening on land but he will not allow himself to become preoccupied with that struggle. As the cruise progresses and the danger becomes more apparent, the poem turns surreal. The barmaid's baby is born and dies soon afterward: "Mother it said, enunciating distinctly, / refusing food." The poem then focuses on the poet, who is revealed to be a very complex man indeed; his "poetic" overtures to the blonde are ridiculous: "She smiled when he said, 'I praise the / marvel physical flowers upon your trellis skeleton, I welcome / from you, the discipline of every part.' He thought, Elaborate. . . ." But the interior monologue which follows shows the powerful sensual nature which is the ground of his imagination:

> I wait for the release, the explosive distorting act
> with the same fever that they wait for land;
> it fills the mind
> it is my port, lighthouse, coastal clew, token,
> suggesting harbors, a shore-image.
> The close-up in the mind, the head enlarging to fill
> the sky with its immense unique idea;
> Homer wrote Helen blind, the unfree are praising freedom,
> I know the exquisite taste of the sight of land.

Suddenly bells are heard, and they tip the poet's balance until he is deranged. He hears them as "perfected music I could never reach" in "our age broken like stone, all grace run out of grasp." Hearing "bells alive also under the sea," the poet dives overboard. We can't help thinking of Hart Crane here and of other contemporary suicidal poets whose natures couldn't absorb the violent shocks of our time.

Many on board including crew members then take the "rational" course of setting out on lifeboats in the direction of the bells. The captain calls them "criminal fools." The radio gives "no sound from the world" and the ship's supplies run out. Eventually the captain becomes insane with doubt, and the ship's engines go dead. The ship is lost in a yellow fog.

William Carlos Williams, praising *U.S. 1* on the whole, said that "The Cruise" was "an allegory too hastily written for my taste." He said he preferred the newspaper for "that sort of thing." But Kerker Quinn, who had complained about obscurity in other poems, had high praise for "The Cruise." He said of Rukeyser's images that they were "more clear-cut than any other poet's of this decade," that she had a much more complex perception of social ills than many social poets. "The Cruise" can't possibly please all tastes. But it is another example of the amazing variety of Rukeyser's styles. In 1940 Axton Clark said this variety resembled "the mutations of Stravinski's music or the 30-odd periods of Picasso" and called it "a symptom of the multiple spirit of our times." [22] In this poem she was obviously aiming at allegory's traditional simplicity. But in the poem we find also complexity and tension and often the challenge to participate in the creation of the image.

Witnessing the beginning of the fighting in Spain in 1936 made a profound and enduring impression on Rukeyser's life as a poet. Her writing since that time is in large part a record of her evolving vision of what the struggle begun in Spain has meant to civilization in our time and what it has meant in her personal life: Otto Boch, the German athlete whom she loved, was killed while fighting with the Loyalist forces. M. L. Rosenthal referred to "her sense of an essential bearing—if only one could close in on it—of social and international problems" on her personal experience "and therefore on her artistic concerns." To "close in on" the bearing that the world situation has had on her experience and on her poetry one need only take seriously her poems about Spain and her statements in *The Life of Poetry* and elsewhere about Spain: "that core of all our lives, / The long defeat that brings us what we know." [23]

Rukeyser went to Spain quite by accident. An editor of the Brittish *Life and Letters Today* who was to have gone to report the Anti-Fascist Olympics in Barcelona in the summer of 1936 had to attend a wedding, and Rukeyser accepted the assignment in his place. On the day she and the teams landed, the fighting broke out. It became so intense during the next five days that the Catalonian government ordered all foreigners evacuated, except those men who would fight and those women with nursing or childcare experience. Rukeyser wanted to stay. She says today she was intensely moved by the sight of "a real Popular Front: fierce people in an anarchist country" who were fighting for their freedom. But she had none of the experience that entitled her to stay, so she was evacuated to France along with a

22. Williams, review of *U.S. 1*; Quinn, review of *U.S. 1*; Axton Clark, review of *A Turning Wind*, in *New York Times Book Review*, April 7, 1940, p.2.

23. Rosenthal, *The New Poets*, 329; Muriel Rukeyser, "Neruda, the Wine," in *The Gates* (New York, 1977), 49.

group of five hundred people in a small boat. She describes her feelings on that boat sailing away from Spain in the introduction to *The Life of Poetry*; essentially she felt she was going into exile, for in Spain "everything we had heard, some of all we loved and feared, had begun to be acted out" by people who "in their purity and violence fought." She has said that she felt about Spain then, "Everything in the poetry of Shelley and Keats and Whitman was there."

In leaving Spain she knew that she had definite work to do. The foreigners who were being evacuated were told, "Now you have your responsibility. . . . Go home; tell your peoples what you have seen." Among the things Rukeyser saw were "the parts of our lives in a new arrangement." Someone asked her on that boat, "And poetry—among all this—where is there a place for poetry?" She says that in answering his question, "Then I began to say what I believe." She saw acted out in Spain the "exterminating wish," the violent forces of repression and by contrast the fierce assertion of freedom. She had investigated destructive forces before, but never had she seen them so nakedly exposed. In West Virginia men licensed by the state killed other men with silica, slowly. In Spain there was blood on the walls. She began to seek a place for poetry in such a world; she would not evade these realities. In 1974 she wrote that a friend was surprised to see her moved by the televised Olympics because they reminded her of the events in Spain in the thirties. Rukeyser remarked, "Not to let our lives be shredded, sports away from politics, poetry away from anything. Anything away from anything." [24] In 1968 she published "Segre Song":

> Your song where you lie long dead on the shore of a Spanish
> river—
> your song moves under the earth and through time,
> through air—
> your song I sing to the sun as we move
> and to the cities. . . .(SD, 46)

And in 1973 she published, in *Breaking Open*, many poems about

24. Muriel Rukeyser, "We Came for Games," *Esquire*, LXXXII (October, 1974), 192–94.

resisting authoritarianism. In joining with resisters of the Vietnam War, she felt, "It is something like the breaking open of my youth" (BO, 132). The climax of that original "breaking open" was Spain. Spain was the beginning of working out and saying what she believed about the role of the poet in the twentieth century. Spain meant she could never withdraw into an ironic distance. She would always be writing from the core of that struggle which began in Spain. There the violence was unleashed; she recognized its counterpart in herself and she has since acknowledged the complex need to resist violence and repression and still be nonviolent. She has recorded her struggles, calling herself in *Breaking Open* "a violent woman in the violent day" who resolves, "I will try to be nonviolent."

The poem "Mediterranean," her thoughts as she sailed away from Spain, harbors the seeds of her following volumes. There is the awareness of war and suffering, the rush of love for the brave fighters, the sense that they are fighting our war by resisting repression. Otto Boch is described in one stanza; "this man, dock, war" she knows will be "a latent image" in much of her future poetry. There is the acknowledgment that witnessing the start of a brave struggle has made her life more real and shown her truths of love, war, and peace she might never have known:

> If we had not seen fighting,
> if we had not looked there
> > the plane flew low
> > the plaster ripped by shots
> > the peasant's house
> if we had stayed in our world
> between the table and the desk
> between the town and the suburb
> slowly disintegration
> male and female

As the poem progresses in the ship's growing distance from Spain, the images of the poet's understanding become more compelling to her: "the picture of that war enlarging clarified / as the boat perseveres away, always enlarging, / becoming clear." She takes her responsibility and, characteristically, she repeats a phrase used in "The Cruise":

> The clouds upon the water-barrier pass,
> the boat may turn to land; the shapes endure,
> rise up into our eyes, to bind
> us back; an accident of time
> set it upon us, exile burns it in.
> *Once the fanatic image shown,*
> *enemy to enemy,*
> *past and historic peace wear thin;*
> *we see Europe break like stone,*
> *hypocrite sovereignties go down*
> *before this war the age must win.*

"This war the age must win" is the repeated phrase. She is not afraid to use a good line again and again. "The phrase in a different position is new," she said in an interview where she noted that a phrase's recurrence is her way of going beyong rhyme to create "a time-binding . . . a physical binding, a musical binding." [25] In "The Cruise" the phrase is spoken by the suicidal poet; it is repeated by the voice of the resolved poet in "Mediterranean." The reader who has come through both voyages sees that the assertion is transformed in its passage from a context of weakness and unacceptance into a context of strength and affirmation.

Reviewers vaguely complained about the "obscurity" of certain poems in *U.S. 1*. Kerker Quinn said that obscurity was the result of the poet's "omitting transitions between far-flung images and dissociated ideas." Such practice, he said, makes whole poems indecipherable. Omitting transitions is, of course, now widely accepted in poetry; the contemporary reader does not expect to find what Marvin Bell has called the "paths of perception" clearly blazed in a poem. But even Virginia Terris complained in her article in 1974 that the poems contain "eternally obscure passages." [26] Rukeyser has

25. "Craft Interview with Muriel Rukeyser" in Packard (ed.), *The Craft of Poetry*, 163.
26. Kerker Quinn, review of *U.S. 1*, in *New York Herald Tribune Books*, February 20, 1938, p. 12; Terris, "Muriel Rukeyser: A Retrospective."

said that when someone says a poem is obscure, nothing has been said about the poem. In *The Life of Poetry* she has written a good deal which can help a reader receive her poems more fully. Throughout the book she insists that a poem is not to be read or analyzed as a static object obeying fixed rules (those of logic, for instance, which cannot deal with the emotional progression of the poem.) A poem cannot be reached "if criticism is projected by the critic's lack, if a dry perfectionism is substituted for the creative life." (LP, 14) This perfectionism is, among other things, the "habit of expecting units (words, images, arguments) in which, originating from certain premises, the conclusion is inevitable. The treatment of correspondence (metaphor, analogy) [by the perfectionist] is always that of a two-part equilibrium in which the parts are self-contained." But, she says, we must "dismiss every static pronouncement and every verdict which treats poetry as static" (LP, 177).

Rukeyser's poetics are influenced not by the New Critics but by her understanding of modern science. In reference to her biographic and poetic treatment of Willard Gibbs, she draws this comparison between science and poetry: "Truth is, according to Gibbs, not a stream that flows from a source, but an agreement of components. In a poem, these components are, not the words or images, but the relations between the words and images. Truth is an accord that actually makes the whole 'simpler than its parts,' as he was fond of saying. Originality is important before the accord is reached; it is the most vivid of the means in a poem, and the daring of the images allows the reader to put off his emotional burden of association with single words, allows him to come fresh to memory and to discovery" (LP, 178). Thus the equilibrium of a poem is not the two-part equilibrium of a static system which can be neatly analyzed. It is the accord of a complex, moving system, the tension and attraction of whose components make any balance momentary: in Frost's famous phrase, "a momentary stay against confusion." But it is not even so much a "stay" as in Frost's poems for it suggests, in its passionate arrival, that the reader must begin again at the beginning. Rukeyser returns again and again to the motion of a poem, an element not stressed by the New Critics. When she says that the passion and intensity of a great poem are not in "the start, the image, the crystallization" but "fly through and over" (LP, 182), she anticipates Charles Olson's "Projective Verse," an essay said to have broken ground for the new poetry of postmodernism. "ONE PERCEPTION MUST IMMEDIATELY AND DIRECTLY LEAD TO A FURTHER PERCEPTION . . . get on with it, keep moving, keep in, speed, the nerves, their speed, the perceptions, theirs, the acts, the split second acts, the whole business, keep it moving as fast as you can, citizen. And if you also set up as a poet, USE USE USE the process at all points, in any given poem always, always one perception must must must MOVE, INSTANTER, ON ANOTHER! So there we are, fast, there's the dogma." Rukeyser said it another way in her review of Frost's *Collected Poems* in 1939 (above, p. 64): he cannot show the speed of the modern imagination in its seizing hold and letting go fast.[27]

Also useful to the reception of her poems are her comparisons of poetry and the movies.

> Now films and visual sequences may be put together smoothly with all the links filled in, or according to other rhythms, in which one sequence will approach a main meaning, to be cut off by another sequence—about different people, in different circumstances, say,—so that the third sequence will be reinforced, made to change and grow because of what has gone before.
>
> Much of modern poetry moves in terms of quick, rhythmic juxtapositions. Our contemporary journalism still uses more even linkage. Each method prepares you for the climaxes of the poem. If you can be flexible of mind, remembering movies you have liked, and being aware of their richness and suspense and the dense texture of their realities, you are approaching what may have seemed to you the most broken of modern poetry. (LP, 17)

In *The Film Sense* (acknowledged in the bibliography of *The Life of Poetry*) Eisenstein explained that in montage separate film shots (representations) are juxtaposed so that the result (an image) is not the sum of one and one but a creation in which the viewer is re-

27. Charles Olson, "Projective Verse," *The New American Poetry*, ed. Donald M. Allen (New York, 1960), 387–88. The essay first appeared in *Poetry New York*, III, 1950.

quired to participate. The image "is not fixed or ready-made, but arises—is born." The spectator experiences the "dynamic process of the emergence and assembly of the image just as it was experienced by the author." [28] Rukeyser, throughout *The Life of Poetry*, speaks of a poem's requiring the total, active participation of the reader who receives the images arriving in "linkage and collision." Finally, she has written statements such as the following which, if accepted through the experiencing of her poetry, make the charge of obscurity meaningless. "The symbols are never finished; they continue to grow; perhaps that is their power. We know that the poetic strategy, if one may call it that, consists in leading the memory of an unknown witness, by means of rhythm and meaning and image and coursing sound and always-unfinished symbol, until in a blaze of discovery and love, the poem is taken" (LP, 200).

A Turning Wind

A Turning Wind is more difficult than any poetry Rukeyser had written before. Finished on September 1, 1939, on the eve of Hitler's taking Poland and England and France's declaring war on Germany, the book reflects the harrowing time of its composition. Robert Lowell is reported to have said of Auden, "He's made the period immortal, of waiting for the war." [29] But Auden's work from 1936, the beginning of the Spanish War, through 1940 represents another kind of waiting than that recorded in *U.S.1, A Turning Wind,* and *The Soul and Body of John Brown.* Auden's poems often reveal a haunting, ironic detachment from the course of events. And his stance, in the form his poetry takes and in his philosophy, is increasingly restrained. In the dedicatory poem to *On This Island* (1937) he writes:

> Since the external disorder and extravagant lies
> The baroque frontiers, the surrealist police;

28. Sergei Eisenstein, *The Film Sense* (New York, 1942), 31–32.
29. Alan Levy, "In the Autumn of the Age of Anxiety," *New York Times Magazine*, August 8, 1971, p. 41.

What can truth treasure, or heart bless,
But a narrow strictness?

In the volumes that cover the period of the Spanish War and the events leading to World War II, Auden wrote mostly in traditional forms. For example, the *Letters from Iceland* (1937), what Auden called "my conversational song," are witty, quasi-eighteenth-century epistles in rhymed seven-line stanzas. Though Auden's poem "Spain, 1937" has as its refrain, "Today the struggle," his later writing does not indicate that the events in Spain gave him as they gave Rukeyser a new sense of mission as a poet. In fact, as Spender writes in *The 30's and After*, "Auden . . . edited out of his work what might be termed The Thirties' Connection." Spender says that "perhaps Auden came to view most of his poetry written at this time" as "an aberration." [30]

In 1940 Auden returned to Anglicanism. Rukeyser too waited for the war by seeking traditional "sources of power," "our inheritance, part of our common property" (see the introduction to *A Turning Wind*). In a sense both poets sought strength outside themselves and their private visions, a universal framework in which to continue to write of their personal experience in a troubled time. Auden's return to the church seems related to the formalism and discursiveness that came to characterize his later poetry. Rukeyser's personality, her general bearings, and her decision to use "studies in symbolism" and "studies in individual lives" led to a freer, more complex poetry than in her previous volumes. *A Turning Wind* takes its title from ancient spiral symbolism in which, as Donald Mackenzie says, "the spiral gusts or whirlwinds . . . were 'life-givers' which caused the birth of the year." Rukeyser quotes Jacob Boehme's interpretation of that symbolism at the beginning of her book: "for the forms of nature are awakened, and are as a turning wheel, and so they carry their spirit the wind." Clearly the title is positive—and complex. [31]

30. W. H. Auden, *On This Island* (New York, 1937); W. H. Auden, *Letters from Iceland* (London, 1937); Stephen Spender, *The 30's and After* (New York, 1978), 234, 10.
31. Muriel Rukeyser, *A Turning Wind* (New York, 1939). Mackenzie is quoted in the foreword, p. xii.

Adding to the complexity of the poems was her growing conviction that for poetry to be of use to people in times of crisis it had to be free to reflect all the meanings of the crisis. "Always we need the audacity to speak for more freedom, more imagination, more poetry with all its meanings. As we go deeper into conflict, we shall find ourselves more constrained, the repressive codes will turn to iron. More and more we shall need to be free in our beliefs, as we come to our forms" (LP, 28). More than ever is her poetry a movement of the great clusters of images of modern life. More than ever must the reader respond fully to participate in the emergence of the poem's meaning. These poems are not the tight, finished universes of formalist verse. We must allow ourselves to be led "by means of rhythms and meaning and image and coursing sound and always-unfinished symbol, until in a blaze of discovery and love, the poem is taken" (LP, 200).

The need to salvage in personal vision the ideals damaged in Spain is in the very first stanza of "First Elegy. Rotten Lake."

> As I went down to Rotten Lake I remembered
> the wrecked season, haunted by plans of salvage,
> snow, the closed door, footsteps and resurrections,
> machinery of sorrow.

In "September 1, 1939," Auden, "beleaguered by . . . Negation and despair" felt that the liberal ideals of the thirties were merely "the clever hopes . . . of a low dishonest decade." But the elegies (later dedicated to Otto Boch, who fought and died defending the Spanish Republic), detail not only the pain and loss of that decade but the "untamable need" of the speaker to continue pursuing the idealistic "wish" that had informed those years.[32] As "First Elegy" progresses we see that the wish is for love, wholeness, a sense of continuity with her personal past. "The future depended on my unfinished spirit"; the quest in the elegies is for the finishing. Frankly autobiographical, the first elegy details the young poet's journey toward the wholeness she felt most strongly in Spain.

> When you have left the river you proceed alone;

32. W. H. Auden, "September 1, 1939," *The Collected Poetry of W. H. Auden* (New York, 1945), 57–59.

> all love is likely to be illicit; and few
> friends to command the soul; they are too feeble.
> Rejecting the subtle and contemplative minds
> as being too thin in the bone; and the gross thighs
> and unevocative hands fail also. But the poet
> and his wife, those who say Survive, remain;
> and those two who were with me on the ship
> leading me to the sum of the years, in Spain.[33]

The poem focuses on that "untamable need" for wholeness in the poet and in all humankind and shows how that need may be "converted" instead of defeated by its very intensity. We are presented with "the forms of nature" (Boehme) awake and intensely wishing: "the lines at the employment bureau," "the tense students at their examinations," fearful and stern lovers. But all of these "needing makes clumsy and robs them of their wish." The power in these intense forms is being thwarted by a "failure of the imagination." The poet calls up the power of her own imagination to create a vision of fulfillment. "I prophesy the meeting by the water / of these desires." In several nightmarish stanzas she gives us images of her own thwarted wish, but then she asserts that the wish itself is a promise of its fulfillment (recalling the image in "Theory of Flight" of "Elohim intermittent with the soul"):

> and cry I want! I want! rising among the world
> to gain my converted wish, the amazing desire
> that keeps me alive, though the face be still, be still,
> the slow dilated heart know nothing but lack,
> now I begin again the private rising,
> the ride to survival of that consuming bird
> beating, up from dead lakes, ascents of fire.

"Second Elegy" gives a name to this time: "The Age of Magicians." As Rosenthal pointed out, Rukeyser is in this poem recalling the Bible's distinction between the two antagonistic mysticisms of

---

33. "The poet and his wife" are Horace Gregory and Marya Zaturenska; Gregory published *Chorus for Survival* in 1935. George and Betty Marshall, to whom *A Turning Wind* is dedicated, were on the ship to Europe with Rukeyser; George worked on the Committee for Constitutional Rights in the thirties and during the war.

miracle and magic. Miracle, associated with the prophet, is the power for good because it "consists in the discovery of that which is actual—in the total awareness of reality by mind and senses." [34] But magic is a simplistic perversion, a "trance of doom", a denial of the wholeness of reality. The prophet (and we must remember that the poet in the "First Elegy" identified herself, in the power of her imagination, with the prophet), seeing the wholeness of reality or at least believing in it, necessarily weeps in this age.

> The aim of magicians is inward pleasure.
> The prophet lives by faith and not by sight,
> Being a visionary, he is divided.

The magician who comes to rule the world simplifies, denies freedom, truncates reality, "brings up his children by . . . / the march-step, the staircase at night, the long cannon. / The children grow in authority." In his desire to rule, the magician is "against the unity of light." But the prophet fights to realize this unity, to deny none of it.

> The index of prophecy is light
> and steeped therein
> the world with all its signatures visible.

We recognize Rukeyser's description of the function of poetry in these statements about the prophet. From *The Life of Poetry*: "Poetry may be seen . . . as an image of the kind of fullness that can best meet the evening, the hostile imagination—which restricts, denies, and proclaims death." The hope for wholeness and strength in this age is to hold its giant clusters of meaning and relationship in the mind, as the vision of poetry allows us to do.

> This is the vision in the age of magicians:
> it stands at immense barriers, before mountains:
> 'I came to you in the form of a line of men,
>
> . . . .
>
> And when you saw the table of diplomats,
> the newsreel of ministers, the paycut slip,
> the crushed child's head, clean steel, factories

34. Rosenthal, "Chief Poets of the American Depression," 556–57.

.   .   .   .

You never inquired into these meanings.
If you had done this, you would have been restored.'

The poet affirms her hope in this vision, though "armies of magicians filled the streets." Speaking to "the people," she says, though "all this is because of you / . . . all this is avenged by you." Merging the image of the poet / prophet with that of enduring imaginative humankind, she exhorts:

Your index light, your voice the voice,
your tree half green and half burning,
half dead half bright,
your cairns, your beacons, your tree in green and flames,
unbending smoke in the sky, planes' noise, the darkness,
magic to fight. Much to restore, now know. Now be
Seer son of Sight, Hearer, of Ear, at last.

The third elegy entitled "The Fear of Form," details more ways in which reality is truncated and meanings evaded in our time. If the magicians are those who rule by exclusion, those who fear form are artists and critics who guard their officially sanctioned art from unsophisticated laymen.

Tyranny of method! the outrageous smile
seals the museum, pours a mob skidding
up to the formal staircase, stopped, mouths open.
And do they stare? They do.
At what? A sunset?

A tyrannic and exclusive art, however, is inadequate to this age.

But the car full of Communists put out hands and guns,
blew 1-2-3 on the horn before the
surrealist house, a spiral in Cataluña.

New combinations: set out materials now,
combine them again! . . .

The events of our time are surreal; we need a new artistic method to render them. The poet believes that this new method is not completely new but involves "new combinations." The modern "surrealist house" is an ancient "spiral." Here Rukeyser gives us images for the prose argument she sketched in the introductory note to the volume: "New methods, the staring circle given again / force, a phoenix of power."

The second part of this elegy restates these themes in a fierce attack on the "chorus of bootblacks, printers, collectors of shit" who make up the tyrannic contemporary art world. The attack is delivered by a man "walking, wearing the world" who can see no meaning to the "dislocated wish" and whining terrors of certain artists. Rosenthal says Rukeyser identified this man as a type of ideal artist—specifically Charles Biederman, the American abstract artist who built the monuments in Minnesota referred to later in the poem. (The lines about the sphere, later in the poem, also refer to Biederman and are explained in *The Life of Poetry*: a scientist improved the structural design of the cyclotron at the suggestion of the artist Biederman.) "The usable present starts my calendar," says this ideal artist. He summons the exemplary "memorable ghosts" of the great moderns like Picasso. But the ideal artist sees that now the art we need is wholly of our time and our country:

> by God a pure high monument
> white yellow and red
> up against Minnesota.

The rest of the poem, in clusters of images, presents the attitude ("flame, fusion, defiance") which the poet says must guard and the materials ("the sphere, the circle, and the cluster") which she says must guide an art which is adequate to our time. Thus, repeating a line from "Second Elegy," we will have in art "the world with all its signatures visible." Repeating two more lines from the beginning of this elegy the poet affirms in the conclusion that those who come to museums should see in art not the "tyranny of method," which is the fear of new forms, but "Our needs, our violences / . . . Contortion of body and spirit. / To fuse it straight." People coming to an adequate art should have a vision of the artist growing, struggling toward adequate forms. Thus people will see imagination at work, and they will see the passion in their own lives reflected in art. Rukeyser was well ahead of her time in her view of form in poetry. She anticipates the statements not only of Olson but of the San Francisco Renaissance poets, specifically Robert Duncan. Duncan wrote in 1953, "After Freud, we are aware that unwittingly we achieve our form. It is, whatever our mastery, the inevitable use we make of the speech that betrays to ourselves and to our hunters the spore of what we are becoming. I study what I write as I study out any mystery. A poem, mine or anothers, is an occult document, a body awaiting vivisection, analysis, X-rays."[35]

"Fourth Elegy. The Refugees" begins by focusing again on the artist, this time seen as a child who wants to be a writer for our time.

> I want to write for my race. But what race will you speak,
> being American? I want to write for the living.
> But the young grow more around us every day.
> They show new faces, they come from far. . . .

The problem in wanting to write for the living in a time of great turmoil is that one must find a language of growth and process. The difficulties involved in writing for our time mean that "many are cast out, become artists at rejection," for it is easier to conceal, to reject, than to grow, to encompass, to include. "The age of the masked and the alone begins . . . a loss shall learning suffer / before the circle of this sun be done."

But there is hope for those artist-refugees who have rejected trying to make the contemporary world intelligible.

> It is the children's voyage must be done
> before the refugees come home again.

Artists must become as little children and learn again what children know in themselves, the undeniable urge to form in the growth of their bodies and spirits.

> They are the children. They have their games.
> They made a circle on a map of time,

35. Robert Duncan, "Pages from a Notebook," in *The New American Poetry*, ed. Donald M. Allen (New York, 1960), 400.

skipping they entered it, laughing lifted the agate.
I will get you an orange cat, and a pig called Tangerine.
The gladness-bird beats wings against an opaque glass.
There is a white bird in the top of the tree.
They leave their games, and pass.

The poetry here becomes increasingly broken, the harsh images related only in their violence: it is the image of the stunned child in all of us facing our brutal world. But gradually there emerges the image of the potential of the child in all of us passing the barriers, "coming to strange countries" and realizing, "I like this city. This is a peaceful city." The hope is in the inclusive children in all of us. "They fuse a dead world straight." In the poet's vision, personal and artistic maturity is the restoring of the urge to growth of childhood:

free of the ferryman Nostalgia, who stares at the backward
    shore.
Growing free of the old in their slow growth of death,
they hold the flaming apples of the spring.

The children are not free of danger and their guides are few. But they (all who "issue survivors from the surf of the age") will endure.

Free to be very hungry and very lonely.
And in the countries of the mind, Cut off at the knee. Cut off
at the armpit. Cut off at the throat.
Free to reclaim the world and sow a legend,
to make the adjustments never made,
repair the promises broken and the promise kept.
They blame our lives, lie on our wishes with their eyes our own,
to say and to remember and avenge. A lullaby for a believing
    child.

The growth of the refugee children is presented in terms of a voyage, as the whole process of the "unfinished spirit" in the elegies is initially presented as a voyage in "First Elegy." In "Fifth Elegy: A Turning Wind" the voyage continues, still identified as growth, and associated with the notion of form as "a function of time" (a concept illustrated by the scientist D'Arcy Wentworth Thompson in his classic On Growth and Form, discussed in The Life of Poetry).

> Knowing the shape of the country. Knowing the midway travels
> of migrant fanatics, living that life
> . . . .
> Shape that exists not as permanent quality, but varies with
> even the movement of bone.
> Even in skeletons, it depends on the choices of action.

The individual's growth and form-finding through the process
of experience is then associated with the United States' urge to its
own form:

> torn off from sympathy with the past and planted,
> a primitive streak prefiguring the west, an ideal
> which had to be modified for stability
> to make it work.

In the spare language of scientific explanation, whose poetic rhythms
Rukeyser discovers here as in "Theory of Flight," the growth of the
country is then associated with biological growth, whose parallel
meanings in the human realm are familiar to her readers.

> There are these major divisions: for those attached to the sea-
> floor,
> a fan at freedom, flexible, wavering, designed to catch food
> from all directions. For the sedentary, for those who crouch and
> look, radial symmetry,
> spokes to all margins for support. For those who want
> movement,
> this is achieved through bilateral symmetry only,
> a spine and straight attack, all muscles working,
> up and alive.

The second section of the elegy focuses on the human race's
"years of roads, and centuries of need" in images of seeking, of admitting one's wish, of the "one gesture: rejecting of backdrops." Always during the human voyage there is the recurrent realization of
the satisfaction, even the fulfillment of the moment in process:

> this shape, this meaning that promises seasonal joy.
> Whose form is unquietness and yet the seeker of rest,
> whose travelling hunger has range enough, its root
> grips through the world.

The United States as a country seeking its form comes into focus again in this description of human voyaging.

> The austere fire-world of night: Gary or Bethlehem,
> in sacred stacks of flame—or stainless morning,
> anti-sunlight of lakes' reflection, matchlight on face,
> the thorny light of fireworks
>
> lighting a way for the shape, this country of celebrations
> deep in a passage of rebirth. . . .

Lifegiving images of whirling wind and winding lights proceed to some of the most remarkable descriptions of our country in literature. T. C. Wilson said of *A Turning Wind*, "Her evocations of the American landscape are as beautiful as any I have ever read." [36]

> Butte and pavilion
> vanish into a larger scape, morning vaults all those hills
> rising on ranges
> that stand gigantic on the roots of the world,
> where points expand in pleasure of raw sweeping
> gestures of joy, whose winds sweep down like stairs,
> and the felled forests
> on hurricane ridges show a second growth.

The climax builds in images of landscape and spiral symbolism, and all the poet's hopeful themes ring their changes again.

> Charts of the country of all vision, imperishable
> stars of our old dream: process, which having neither
> sorrow nor joy
> remains as promise, the embryo in the fire.
> The tilted cities of America, fields of metal,
> the seamless wheatfields, the current of cities running
> below our wings
> promise that knowledge of systems which may bless.

We recognize here a new term for her concern with "relationship"—the term is "systems," and, characteristically, this seed will grow in another poem, "Gibbs."

The last six lines of the elegy bring it to a full circle which re-

36. D'Arcy Wentworth Thompson, *On Growth as Form* (Cambridge, 1917); Wilson, review of TW.

flects "First Elegy" in its phrases about the dead lake rising and the converted wish. It is "knowledge of systems" that

> May permit knowledge of self, a lover's wish of conversion
> until the time when the dead lake rises in light,
> the shape is organized in travelling space,
> this hope of travel, to find the place again,
> rest in the triumph of the reconceived,
> lie down again together face to face.

"Fourth Elegy" is here again resolved, for it is the knowledge of the shape of the country which permits self-knowledge; "the shape" of the self so earnestly sought emerges during the voyage, is "organized in travelling space." Such a knowledge—of systems and of the self—negates the simplification and exclusion of the magicians in "Second Elegy." And the poet here foresees as well "the triumph of the reconceived"—the goal of art envisioned in "Third Elegy." The last line's image ("lie down again together face to face") dispels that of the sapping fatigue of voyagers "too tired to / turn to each other" described in the first two stanzas of this "Fifth Elegy."

The five elegies thus move in their striking complex of images (a fullness which satisfyingly reflects the complexity of our time) to an equilibrium which is convincing in its arrival and which invites the reader to go around once more, for such is the passion in momentum of these poems.

John Malcolm Brinnin in *Poetry* (1943) had high praise for the elegies and their "wild beautiful language," saying that in the face of the "general impotence" which resulted from the split among partisans of the left in the late thirties Rukeyser "achieved her finest sequence of poems." The elegies "show an integration of method, a fibre of belief, a philosophical authority superior to all that has gone before." Brinnin admired their range, the expansion of her powers, and their fusion. "Almost always she is consciously reconstructing a faith that will match that of her adolescence." The sequence, said Brinnin, is her "unsentimental insight into a failing world in order to survive its terrors with dignity." Although he acknowledged the poet's powerfully voiced need and faith, M. L. Rosenthal felt the reader is "driven just a little too fast" by the "inescapable rhetorical pressure" in the elegies.[37]

Several reviewers complained of the obscurity of the elegies. C. A. Millspaugh in *Kenyon Review*, who referred to her as an "indifferent scholar" for her "free handed forays into historiography" in citing Burke and Mackenzie in her introductory note, objected to what he called "the haphazard operations of her verse," her "illogical juxtaposition of images and abstractions." But it is Millspaugh who displays an "indifferent scholarship" when he objects that the elegies are not elegiac but are "compositions of indiscriminate tone." Rukeyser offered this note from the *Encyclopaedia Britannica*, eleventh edition, when she reprinted the elegies in the collection *Waterlily Fire*: "When the elegy appears, in surviving Greek literature, we find it dedicated, not to death, but to war and love."

Millspaugh's contention that Rukeyser's references to Mackenzie and to Burke to explain her use of symbols and to locate the source of some of her ideas is "sophistry" and insufficiently rigorous scholarship shows the narrow concept of scholarship which was beginning to gain ascendance.[38] Lines from the fourth elegy anticipate responses like Millspaugh's: "The age of the masked and the alone begins . . . a loss shall learning suffer / before the circle of this sun be done." The concept of specialization, which forbids scholars' crossing into fields other than their own and apparently denies the scholarship of the poet who tries to make ideas live in another medium, is one which will plague Rukeyser throughout her career. Archibald MacLeish attacked this notion of specialization and aloof scholarship in *The Irresponsibles* (1940), wherein he urged scholars to do just what Rukeyser has tried to do in much of her work. MacLeish put it in terms of defending culture; his book appeared at a time when he felt Americans should realize what they would be defending in fighting fascism. Rukeyser's aim in *A Turning Wind* is

37. John Malcolm Brinnin, "Muriel Rukeyser: The Social Poet and the Problem of Communication," *Poetry*, LXI (January, 1943), 554–75; Rosenthal, "The Longer Poems," 223–25.
38. C. A. Millspaugh, review of TW, in *Kenyon Review*, II (1940), 359–63.

not primarily to "defend culture," but her impulse to use our "sources of power" as part of our "techniques of living" parallels MacLeish's idea that scholars should make our cultural heritage live in the present. She also refused to be confined to "any one field" but explored the relationships in the workings of the imagination in many fields.

Another reviewer who complained about the obscurity of the elegies was the poet Ruth Lechlitner, who said that the poems suffer from "an unrelieved bombardment of fragmentary phrases and half-sentences, sometimes packed with abstractions, sometimes overburdened with physical imagery." She found in them "an indiscriminate scrambling of tenses and inexactness of pronominal references." Lechlitner urged Rukeyser to return to the "clarity and simplicity" of "The Book of the Dead." We can recognize in Lechlitner's detailing of the offenses of obscurity those techniques of a poetry which requires creativity of the reader, techniques which parallel the building of the film image as described by Eisenstein. Louis Untermeyer answered Lechlitner's and other reviewers' charges of obscurity in the elegies. Writing in the *Saturday Review* in 1940 he hailed Rukeyser's struggle against the contemporary "stifling of the spirit of free inquiry, the deadening of pure imagination in a period that demands only the immediate and the practical." He reminded reviewers that one must read a poem more than once to get beyond surface music and outer meaning. Of the poems in *A Turning Wind* he said, "The strength of her conviction and the power of its communication/are/ equally obvious. Integrity is perceived even before it is understood; the meaning, sometimes muffled by her very rush of words, declares itself finally and fully."[39]

In the introductory note to *A Turning Wind* Rukeyser begins to refer to the fear of symbols and the fear of poetry in our culture; she alludes to them in "Third Elegy" with its description of the tyranny of the restricted imagination. She elaborates her perception of these fears in *The Life of Poetry*. We have seen how her concept of poetry strikes at the roots of these fears by insisting that poetry invites the

39. Ruth Lechlitner, review of TW, in *New York Herald Tribune Books*, January 7, 1940, p. 10; Untermeyer, "The Language of Muriel Rukeyser."

full response which negates the fear of disclosure, the fear of the full exercise of the relating power of the imagination. We have seen how her poetry is an invitation to an expansion of the self, to a human meeting place, a touching.

In the prefatory note we are told that the second section of *A Turning Wind* (entitled "Moment of Proof"—that recurrent phrase which binds poems and volumes) "turns about these fears": the fear of symbols and of poetry. The first poem in this section, "Reading Time: 1 Minute 26 Seconds," is a definition of this fear. (The title is an ironic echo of the magazine *Liberty*, which printed for readers an estimate of how long it would take to read particular pieces.) The fear of poetry is defined in the poem by images as examples of an intense stimulus followed by an unsettling "moment of proof":

> The fear of poetry is the
> fear: mystery and fury of a midnight street
> of windows whose low voluptuous voice
> issues, and after that there is no peace.

The fear of poetry is the fear of this moment which proves the intensity of the stimulus. Beyond other intense stimuli here enumerated (the shot bullet, the look of love), the poem itself remains potentially a continual cause of that "moment of proof": "That climax when the brain acknowledges the world, / all values extended into the blood awake." People fear this climax as they fear all intense emotion, recognition, and disclosure.

The "o" sounds in the poem alternating with the open "e," "a," "i," and "y" sounds carry the meaning through in a music that is like the concentrating and releasing of a spiral.

> That round waiting moment in the
> theatre: curtain rises, dies into the ceiling

The last stanzas intensify the concentration toward the crucial meaning of the poem.

> Love touches so, that months after the look of
> blue stare of love, the footbeat on the heart
> is translated into the pure cry of birds
>
> . . . .

> They fear it. They turn away, hand up palm out
> fending off moment of proof, the straight look, poem.
> The prolonged wound-consciousness after the bullet's shot.
> The prolonged love after the look is dead,
> the yellow joy after the song of the sun,
> aftermath proof, extended radiance.

The last lines release the meaning in the final unraveling of the bright spool.

In "Song, the Brain-Coral" the coral is a symbol of changeless love; it is a quintessential "unfinished symbol" because the poet in the last lines arrives at the impenetrability of all things, even of her intense love for which she seeks a symbol. The white coral is only the appearance of the all-colored world, not that brilliant world itself.

> Lie still, love, while the many physical worlds stream
> passionate by,
> in dreams of the exterior intricate rainbow world,
> dreaming the still white intricate stone of the world,
> —bring you brain-coral,
> a world's white seeming.

Poetry, like the brain-coral, is the temporary reflection of the "intricate rainbow world"; it is the "seeming" which is the best the imagination can do when confronted with many intensities.

"Otherworld," a sequence of three poems, is recognizably autobiographical, containing images and phrases from the poet's previous volume. These bind the sequence to her continuing journey and her continuing reflection on that journey. "Landing at Liverpool," the first poem of the sequence, begins in the same mood as "Outpost" from *U.S.1* and echoes its phrasing:

> This was the journey. Out of adolescence.
> Past Anticosti, Labrador, past Belle Isle,
> end of America.

The final poem of the sequence, repeating the title "Otherworld," begins with a phrase from "Landing at Liverpool": "Coming among the living." Another phrase, a few lines later, "coming among the dead," is also from "Liverpool." There is much binding in the first lines as phrases from the first poem of the sequence are repeated: "feeling earth slip under / standing among innumerable nets." The binding emphasizes the motif of the journey. This is so momentous to the poet it is first described as "the dream-journey," for she crosses ocean-divides of realization as she crosses the Channel and travels south on the train. Now she is in "Paris the fluent city running by like film," which contains the arresting, ominous image of "the straddled tower, the arch framing a gas-mask poster." Her train plunges southward until she reaches

> a country of cave-drawn mutilated hands
> of water painted with the color of light
>> where the world ends as the wheels stop turning
>> people begin to live by their belief.

She has arrived at the place—Spain—where the world is in its crisis and where people cannot ignore the crucial issues of the time. The poet–traveler is now referred to as "the initiate" undergoing "a rite of passage." She sees at the end of her voyage war and love. By the light of that love (which "identifies armies") she is taken

> into a room where all the chairs fall down
> and all the walls decay and all the world stands bare
> until the world is a field of the Spanish War.

In this binding we hear echoes of her poem "In a Dark House" from *Theory of Flight* in which the walls of a private house fall and the world is revealed to a pair of isolated lovers. Here she conveys in powerful, echoing imagery that through her love for the Loyalist fighters in Spain (and for one fighter especially) she sees that Spain's struggle for freedom is the world's.

Here in Spain is being publicly enacted all that she has experienced in her personal relationships; here are the eternal forces unchained which she wrote of in her first poems of social concern:

> seas of the sky cruised by anonymous planes
> subjective myth becomes a province, a city

>whose wish goes to the front with its final desire
>monomanias come   their diaries   their days
>the burning capitals.

Witnessing the staging of one's subjective myth can be devastating, especially if one has prophesied victory for the forces of liberation and these do not actually triumph. Then indeed the world seems to turn into the dreadful sea (hear the echo, in these last lines, of the first stanza, the sea-journey, of "Landing at Liverpool"):

>when the bricks of the last street are
>up in a tall wave breaking
>when cartwheels are targets are words are
>   eyes
>the bullring wheels in flame
>the circles fire at the bleeding trees
>the world slips under the footbeat of the living
>everybody knows who won the war.

The spiral symbolism in these last lines is an ironic association with the powers of death, not of life: the firing circle is, of course, a gun.

Similarly, the spiral symbolism which begins in the very title of this volume is echoed ironically in the next poem's title, "Nuns in the Wind." The first stanza shows the poet indelibly marked by the defeat of her ideals in Spain.

>As I came out of the New York Public Library
>
>· · · · · · · · · · · · · ·
>the street was assaulted by a covey of nuns
>going directly toward the physics textbooks.
>Tragic fiascos shadowed that whole spring.

The nuns remind her of the Catholic Church's support of Franco; that those on the side of darkness and repression are heading for the science textbooks is sharply ironic to the poet.[40] The poem connects the poet's distressed personal life with the chaotic state of the world in images of frustration and loss. Nevertheless, the poet expresses her characteristic hope in the processes of time and experience:

40. Rosenthal, "Chief Poets of the American Depression," 573.

If the wind would rise, those black throbbing umbrellas
fly downstreet, the flapping robes unfolding,
my dream would be over, poisons cannot linger
when the wind rises . . .

It is a time of waiting for inevitable world war. The poet waits, her
life reflecting the world's disorder.

All that year, the classical declaration of war was lacking.
There was a lot of lechery and disorder.
And I am queen on that island.

Her wish to come through this time is very strong, but so is her self-
doubt: "Now make believe you can help yourself alone." The poem's
ending is a somewhat bitterly affirmative recognition that "cities"
will "shake in the wind" of time and change.

In unabatedly surreal imagery, "For Fun" elaborates the theme
of waiting for war:

wigs
on the meat at the butchers', murderers
eating their last meal under the Arch of Peace.

The Floating Man is back (he first appeared in "Lover as Fox" in
U.S.1) and he has taken on new overtones of personal guilt:

It was long before the troops entered the city
that I looked up and saw the Floating Man.
Explain yourself I cried at the last. I am
the angel waste, your need which is your guilt,
answered, affliction and a fascist death.

The poet's personal distress and need kept her from speaking more
forcefully what she learned in Spain: "Everything spoke : flames,
city, glass, but I / had heavy mystery thrown against the heart."[41]

"Correspondences," a sequence of four poems, is dense with im-

41. Rukeyser says that for many years she felt guilty about not finding a way to get
back to Spain. "After all," she says, "I got to California." She tried to go as a reporter for
Time, but Whittaker Chambers, then an editor, wouldn't send her because he said she "had
no angle" to report. "I knew I didn't have the story," she says. "I wanted to go and get the
story." In her regret at not having gone back to Spain, she often felt she hadn't been brave
enough to find a way.

ages of waiting for war, actual war, spreading war. "Democritus Laughed" attacks the "soldier laughter" of those who reduce all human striving to materialist terms, "who grin with reason" and reduce the "war on starve" and the "war on love" to the same blind operation of forces. There is a certain kind of detached laughter which is not strengthening, says the poet, but which undermines the best efforts of human beings. This laughter will be described in the last poem of the sequence.

"Tree of Days," in four-line tetrameters with fairly regular rhyme, focuses on the tree of war, which has been growing "dense and strong" from the winter of the poet's birth. "1/26/39" elaborates in four spare stanzas with the last line a refrain the theme that "When Barcelona fell, the darkened glass / turned on the world an immense ruinous gaze."

The long first movement of "Correspondences," the last and title poem of the sequence, takes up the theme begun in "Democritus Laughed":

> Laughter takes up the slack,
> changes the fact, narrowing it to nothing,
> hardly a thing but silence on a stage.

Rosenthal noted that to Rukeyser as to MacLeish in *Panic* (1937), irony is "the whipped man's speech," a self-defeating attitude in times of crisis. The way in which the artist responds to crisis is very important, for it is the artist's role "to indicate . . . the valid sources of power" available to people.[42] Here Rukeyser criticizes an ironic contemporary writer who did not look deep enough into the human situation:

> we saw the novelist, pimp of character,
> develop the age so it be understood
> to read like his book, a city of the dead.[43]

The poem closes with a final warning about irony.

> Humor, saliva of terror, will not save the day

42. Rosenthal, "Chief Poets of the American Depression," 580.
43. These lines reflect her review of Faulkner's *Dr. Martino and Other Stories* for *New Masses*. See page 62 herein.

or even one moment when the cities are
high in a boneyard where clowns ride up and down

The earnestness of this poet was born in a period of horrors and waiting for horrors; having faced these realities as few poets did, breaking open her personal history to show its reflection of the age, she could hardly be expected to develop the ironic sensibility of poets who did not so passionately identify their personal hopes with the struggle that began in Spain.

"Noguchi," also about waiting for war, proceeds appropriately with a play on open sounds. The theme is awareness, and the recurrent phrase is "Open now and obey": become responsive to the signals of the time. The title itself has an open vowel, and each line ends with an open sound, as in the first stanza:

Since very soon it is required of you.
Even here, on this bed, your face turned up and away,
a strong statue's face turning up and away,
the spangled eye staring live and away.
And the call comes: Open and now obey.

The accumulation of these sounds and the visual impact of so many o's on the page here again produce a spiral, this time rising to an expression of hope:

but effort of light comes, overflow morning
. . . Love, we'll stay awake until it's healed
until the time is brought to a fair hour,
obey the heart that calls to prove alive
a love, an age, all soldiers home again,
the growing time a child up and alive,
until the world is done.

The scientist Noguchi as a baby was scalded and was saved by his mother's constant, attentive care. The hope in this poem springs from the belief in constant "effort," in human striving and its counterpart in the forces of life and light in the universe. Such hope and belief were voiced in the "Preamble" to "Theory of Flight." The next three poems will continue to focus on human effort and the "effort" of light.

In "Seventh Avenue," almost a companion piece to "Noguchi,"

there is "not enough effort in the sky for morning." The poem describes "two o'clock night-walkers" who are cripples (the poet seems to include herself) because they can see nothing as it is, not even themselves. They wait "for trial to prove their innocence / with one straight simple look," but what can they do besides wait? The times are murky, ambiguous. The landscape to "the third layer back is always phantom." The poem ends with the wish for "the look to set this avenue in its colors," but here is the world at its darkest: "wounds, mysteries, fables, kings / in a kingdom of cripples."

"The Shortest Way Home" is a resolution of the previous poem, taking up the theme of "Noguchi" and many other poems in these volumes: effort can be made, light can come after darkness. The first stanza presents a cluster of meanings which play on dualities: light-dark, desert-city, arid-fertile. The poem goes further than the previous two in that the impulse toward awakening, toward light and healing, is here an actual exploration. The poet describes a journey through her vast country in which she finds directive and life-giving "relics of ancestors":

> tourist, we hunt the past as the farmer hunts rain,
> as the manic depressive in tired hunt for equilibrium
> hunts sleep, swarm up the totems for a view,
> see older beds outcropping, dipping seaward and blue.

Finally the traveler is rewarded with a vision of the continuity of the country "through Black, Marl, Salt, to coast-land, vein to vein." The last stanza recalls by contrast the insomniac cripples of "Seventh Avenue" in their phantom landscape:

> Pathologies of lightnings turn to prose,
> broken and jarring forms to peace.
> A fugue of landscapes resolved, the hunt
> levelled on equilibrium, that totemic head seeing
> a natural sleep, a place for people and peace.

She has seen ravaged human beings, but she has also seen, with the help of ancestors, the continuity of life and wholeness.

Lest we rest at this "peace," this "equilibrium," the next poem, "Palos Verdes Cliffs," sets the clusters of meaning in motion again.

THE THIRTIES / 149

The poet is standing on a cliff and surveying the land to the sea. She is aware that the still, brilliant "overheated landscape" is creating an illusion in her sight and in her mind, the "produced illusion" of "absolute calm." She knows the world is otherwise.

In "Paper Anniversary" the poet returns to the theme of responsiveness. The scene is the crowded concert hall the night of the stock market crash. The audience cannot respond to Mozart ("water-leap, season of coolness, / talisman of relief") or to Brahms ("season of fruit"):

> they could not meet it with love; they were lost with their
> fortunes.
> In that hall was no love where love was often felt
> reaching for music, or for the listener beside.

The economic crisis creates a rift between generations (the young can still joyfully respond to the music) and reveals how little the older generation experienced and learned from their concert-going. The market crashed, "ending all music for the evening-dress audience," for all but the young to whom "the night is joy, and the music was joy alive, / alive is joy."

The next poem, "From the Duck-Pond to the Carousel," is the joyful young urban poet's celebration of life which continues strong and glad. That ancient repetition, spring, comes for her as "a phonograph record of a windy morning," and her vision of life-giving recurrences is filled with circles and with risings and fallings: the pond, the carousel, "wound-up lovers fidgeting balloons," a little girl tossing up crumbs which, as they fall, are met by reaching white "Quacks." The poem is an abundance of o's—to the very end where "O mister with the attractive moustache" meets a "Mademoiselle." What else can they say but "Hello, hello"? There is a note of reservation in the poem: "O you pastoral lighting what are you getting away with?" But it is a wholehearted and light-hearted avowal of joy, a tribute to the poet's gift for play, even in bleak times.

"The Victims, a Play for the Home" continues the theme of the search for liberation, for a larger world. A player ("female or male") on a stage in a "traditional" role is in a familiar room with the exits, "a window and a door, both shut." The player opens the window, "letting the dark shine down," a dark which is like the night of "In a Dark House"—the dark outside symbolizing the fullness of the world which the house shuts out. There is the sense that individual life is bound by traditional roles, that one is gaped at by crowds ("an immense vaudeville of a century") who wait to see what one will do next, and how, if ever, one will get out of that room. The player is shown confused by all possibilities of rescue: letters from friends saying "We Need. / Come out and help us" and the crippling influence of parents who "lowered resistance" in their children. By act four the player is despondent, the chief cause being the inadequacy of parents like those described in "Paper Anniversary," adults unable to be responsive because they are preoccupied with material concerns. The player contemplates and discards the idea of suicide.

The stanza describing the fifth act begins by removing the possibility of rescue by any "champion angel"—any established religious or cultural program—for if that angel appear, "it is a statue." What will happen to the player? "The end's prepared. / This victim must come to death as the shade goes down." Yet in a typical gathering of strength (the "access of power" of "Theory of Flight") the poem reverses its downward spiral and asserts those values which Rukeyser has affirmed before. The player shouts to the audience:

> "Not everything that happens happens in the street!
> You are souls riding me, and I'm to be your ghost—
> I have more in me than that! Ticket-taker, their money back!
> I know a way to start." Laughs, and slams out the door.

Here is the poet's credo in this difficult time: she is free within herself; she asserts the possibility of personal growth and personal human achievement which can have reverberations in society. She will not agree with those who maintain that the personal is an anachronism in our time. The whole poem is an answer to reviewers of her early work such as Ruth Lechlitner who said Rukeyser was not a true revolutionary poet because she had not broken with the "romantic-personal individual consciousness."[44]

"Speech for the Assistant," from the play *Houdini*, is dedicated to Marya Zaturenska and plays, in surrealistic imagery, on the theme of isolation, especially that of the poet in an age of madness just before world catastrophe. The imagery of the isolation of each person is relentlessly horrible:

> a windowpane, two stains where eyes should stammer;
> the head in the barber-chair, nothing behind it but hands;
> ghost, boat-burial, a headless coat on the dancing clothesline.
> A shouting single dream of alone,
> or the islanded paranoiac insisting
> my dear dear dear dear dear dear dear
> my dear my dear dear.

The poet is pictured as a bird, more alone than anyone. The poet is open, sees secrecy as "criminal," and suffers the loneliness of the vulnerable who will not withdraw into impersonality. The poet says that she has not lost sight of herself, even in this time of loneliness, anonymity, and fear. And she says that only those who have suffered the times responsively, opening themselves to the meanings of the times, are real to her.

> Only those passed through madness have any sense for us,
> whose eyes say I have seen, whose mouths read I have been
> there.
> . . . .
> When song is insecure, again
> the solo lark goes mad for song.

The ending is rich with the meanings that have traveled through the poem. "Lark" is an appropriate reference to the poet in a poem dedicated to Zaturenska; but that traditional symbol is placed in a harsh, modern context. The sense, at the end of the poem, is of the poet making a great effort to continue her vocation in a time when it has been called into question. "Goes mad for" expresses that intense desire; of course the phrase also connotes the danger of per-

44. Lechlitner, review of TF.

sonal disintegration caused by the stress of the age so vividly described in the poem.

In "Judith," the last poem of this section, the strengths and determinations of the previous poems of struggle and resolve converge in the image of "a dark woman at a telephone." She is a modern reincarnation of the powerful, noble, and dedicated biblical figure who penetrates the enemy camp and murders Holofernes. The theme of the journey recurs, this time as the journey of the dark woman away from her broken country on a crucial mission. That the dark woman is the reincarnation of a strong ancestress is emphasized by a striking parallel with the natural world. (The irregular rhyme is characteristic of the entire poem.)

> At the green sources of the Amazon
> a bird develops, who repeats his race
> whole in a lifetime; hatched with primitive claws
> he grows and can absorb them and is grown
> to a green prime of feathers. This is known.
> A woman sitting at a telephone
> repeats her race, hopes for the trap's defence.
> Defenders rumored nothing but skeleton.
> Applause of news. Suicides reaching for
> ritual certainty in their last impatience.

Here is the unfinished symbol cluster: the developing bird of the Amazon, the daring woman repeating her race, and these juxtaposed and contrasted with the suicide who must have immediate, fatal certainty. As in "Theory of Flight" and in other poems, Rukeyser sets hope in *process* against the death wish.

In this poem the wandering children in "Fourth Elegy" are recalled as those whom the dark woman will try to save on her mission: they "cannot obtain" now, for they are surrounded by the dragons of the times (suppression of feeling, isolation, rant). The children are faced with "the hand / palm placing out"—recalling those who turned away from the "moment of proof" in "Reading Time," "hand up palm out." The hope is in "the newborn, the youngest in the world" who will be "a new twisting wind . . . all winds / to cancel this, rejuvenating rain / to wash it away, forces to fight it down." The dark woman is to merge somehow with "this twisting wind," this life force; she is "answered by silence and cruelest dragon-silence," but she is ready to set out.

The next section of the volume, "Lives," refers, as Rukeyser says in the introductory note, to "individual creative energy." For the reader coming to the "Lives" after "Judith," it is as though the strength of that modern repetition of the race is extended in several brilliant incarnations of strength, creativity, and wholeness. "Lives" is proof that "Not everything that happens happens in the street" (as she wrote in "The Victim") and proof of the esthetic beliefs of "Third Elegy": form is the full, intense manifestation of the developing individual.

"Lives" is the record of a search, like that recorded by Paul Rosenfeld in *Port of New York* (1924), for "an America where it was good to be." Rukeyser says in her note that the five people in the "Lives" are "Americans—New Englanders—whose value to our generation is very great and partly unacknowledged." Four subjects of these first five "Lives" were Americans whose personal achievements broke through the obsession with practicality and with material and mechanical accumulation which characterized the Gilded Age. The other was a Communist organizer in the thirties. Other concerns of those who sought ancestors are evident in "Lives." First there is the concern, also expressed in "Theory of Flight" and *The Life of Poetry*, that we must choose our traditions and decide what values, what compelling images to pass on to our posterity. Citing the example of Van Wyck Brooks, Waldo Frank in *Our America* expressed this concern in terms of "creation." Frank sought the ideal America as opposed to the America manifest in the world of business or the academy. "We go forth all to seek America. And in the seeking we create her. In the quality of our search shall be the nature of the America that we create." [45]

Frank discusses the painter Albert Pinkham Ryder, the subject of one of Rukeyser's "Lives," in *Our America*. There is a chapter

45. Paul Rosenfeld, *Port of New York: Essays on Fourteen American Moderns* (New York, 1924), v; Waldo Frank, *Our America* (New York, 1919), 9–10.

on Ryder in Rosenfeld's *Port of New York* as well. Rukeyser says she is indebted to him for her information on the painter. In Rosenfeld's search for the meaning of America and for a sense of belonging here, he uses terms Rukeyser will later emphasize in her discussion of the role of poetry. Poetry, she believes, should discover to people the passion they possess for the full extension of their capacity to respond and to see relationship. Rosenfeld also wrote of the passion for relationship. "It was the towers of Manhattan one wanted to see suddenly garlanded with loveliness. One wanted life for them and for oneself together . . . to come into relation with the things and the people . . . in the form of one's utmost self." Artists evoked this sense of relationship for Rosenfeld. It was given "to a dozen or more of artists to find the values again here on the soil, to restate ideas of work and growth and love, and run the flag of mature developed life once more to the masthead." In the intensity of their individual creation, using American materials, these artists became "worth-givers" and helped their countrymen to a sense of intensity, "the commencement of a religious sense," one which enabled them "to come into relationship with one another and with the places in which they dwell." [46]

The sense of intensity, almost a religious sense, which the creative inspire through their work and their lives is the theme of one of Spender's best-known lyrics, "I Think Continually of Those." Spender, like Rukeyser, though much more briefly and without specific detail, sang of the personal inspiration he received from creative human beings, those who never allowed "gradually to smother / with noise and fog the flowering of the spirit," those "who wore at their hearts the fire's center." [47] Clearly, in times when the spirit feels it will be crushed by materialism, repression, and brutality, artists and intellectuals turn to the example of other creative people whose personal growth was achieved despite aridity, hardship, neglect, and often abuse. Frank, Rosenfeld, Spender, and

46. Rosenfeld, *Port of New York*, 294–95.
47. Stephen Spender, "I Think Continually of Those," in Untermeyer (ed.), *Modern American Poetry*, 458–59. (Originally in *Poems*, 1933).

Rukeyser so turned in the twenties and thirties. Rukeyser has continued through the seventies to write her "Lives," to celebrate "individual creative energy" in many fields.

To understand the uniqueness of her spirit and vision in continuing her series of "Lives" (and in embodying their vision in poem after poem), one has only to compare them to the view of the creative individual expressed by Rukeyser's exact contemporary, the poet Delmore Schwartz. Born in the same month and year as Rukeyser, in the same city, growing up under the same clouds of war and economic disease, he responded in radically different ways to the stimuli of the times. His poem "Let Us Consider Where the Great Men Are" (from the play *Shenandoah*, 1941) typifies the sense of alienation permeating his poetry, a sense that became the hallmark of postwar poetry. When Schwartz considers great creative genius he concludes that it must necessarily flourish in exile. The poem begins, "Let us consider where the great men are / Who will obsess the child when he can read." This statement is followed by a list of the creative in exile: Joyce teaching school in Trieste, Eliot working in a bank, Pound expatriated, Rilke and Yeats in isolation, and so forth. Schwartz's conclusion is that art is principally an index of the agony of the gifted. The creative spirit, to Schwartz and to other postwar poets who felt the same alienation, is doomed to a painful solipsism.

> All over Europe these exiles find in art
> What exile is: art becomes exile too,
> A secret and a code studied in secret,
> Declaring the agony of modern life:
> This child will learn of life from these great men,
> He will participate in their solitude,
> And maybe in the end, on such a night
> As this, return to the starting-point, his name,
> Showing himself as such, among his friends.

Robert Lowell also, in *Life Studies*, 1959, describes modern writers rejected and ultimately destroyed by their culture.[48]

48. Delmore Schwartz, "Let Us Consider Where The Great Men Are," in Untermeyer

It is different with Rukeyser. The poem which begins the section of *A Turning Wind* called "Lives" has no title; there are four stanzas of ten lines each, with irregular but recurrent rhyme. The lines are of irregular length, mostly long and following the rhythms of the poet's thought. The thought itself is an elaboration in images of the intense life of the creative spirit; in its life and light we may all live.

> The risen image shines, its force escapes, we are all named.
> Now that the threads are held; now that the footcuts hold
> where these intent finders of tumult climbed
> in music or mathematical intensity,
> and paint, or fire, or order, found and held,
> their achieved spirits gleam. In the dark perfect sky
> a hand is risen firm under its crackling globe of flame.
> Against the stare it floats, over our agony of street,
> repeated eyes, disclosures and closures of walls,
> glimpses of centuries until the shining fails.

In these lines there is binding to the "stare" of those who skidded up to the sealed museum in "Third Elegy"; here they are not denied the vision of the creative spirit. "Our agony of street" is an echo of "The Victims," where the player says he knows another place to grow beside the street (the marketplace or the public world.) Those agonizing for self-fulfillment may stare at the "risen image" of "achieved spirits" and take heart to develop their own.

The second stanza begins, "The faces are normal," again emphasizing that the life of the creative spirit is recognizably human, not aberrant or grotesque. But upon these normal faces shines "the super-human light" of their own intense effort. The rest of the stanza describes that enormous effort, and the last lines are a binding to those poems which have connected human striving with the arrival of dawn-light, from "Theory of Flight" on. The faces of these creative people "hold pitiless under street-flares colors of

---

(ed.), *Modern American Poetry*, 653 – 54; Robert Lowell, *Life Studies and For the Union Dead* (New York, 1967); see especially "Ford Madox Ford," "For George Santayana," "To Delmore Schwartz," and "Words for Hart Crane."

night, react, / remain in a passion of daybreak effort when the day arrives." The risen image of these creative spirits is to us an "ease" in our "tormented cities" where there are "women / with brilliant carriage and averted face / proving a paranoiac rule tricking to death its children." The women are the concealers of feeling, the suspicious evaders, the "masked and alone" of the elegies; they make refugees of their children. But the last stanza affirms the energizing power of the creative spirits who will be described in the series of "Lives."

> But there are more in the scheme: the many born
> charging our latest moment with their wave,
> a shaking sphere whose center names us all as core,
> risen among the timid and the torn
> toward the sun-cities which the brain has known
> whose moment of proof races through time to live.

Again the binding phrase "moment of proof" asserts the irrepressible awareness that comes after one has been open to a creative stimulus. The capacity to respond to the energy of creative genius and thus to participate in it is, as Rukeyser has often said, a source of human strength and human relation. In *The Life of Poetry* she says that "the work that a poem does is a transfer of human energy . . . consciousness, the capacity to make change in existing conditions." Thus, far from being doomed to exile, the creative spirit is in potential relation with countless human beings of many generations.[49]

The first of the "Lives" is about the American scientist Willard Gibbs, the subject of Rukeyser's 465-page biography (1942), which she has called a footnote to the poem. The poem itself is some 115 lines long, in spare language appropriate to the severely disciplined personal and professional style of Gibbs. He was a scientist who wanted to grasp the whole, to gain an understanding of systems. As

---

49. Charles Olson will write in his "Projective Verse," 1950: "A poem is energy transferred from where the poet got it . . . by way of the poem itself to, all the way over to, the reader. Okay. Then the poem itself must, at all points, be a high energy-construct and, at all points, an energy-discharge."

such he applied himself to the contemplation of the whole; he made no experiments in an age of experiment, trusting his intuition that "the whole is simpler than any of its parts." By trusting the operation of his mind as it contemplated systems, he discovered laws of matter, "deduction from deduction."

> Austerity, continence, veracity, the full truth flowing
> not out from the beginning and the base,
> but from accords of components whose end is truth.
> Thought resting on these laws enough becomes
> an image of the world, restraint among
> breaks manacles, breaks the known life before
> Gibbs' pale and steady eyes.

It is not difficult to see the appeal of Gibbs to Rukeyser. In some ways he was her opposite: she made many "experiments," in Alabama, in Spain, in West Virginia. She immersed herself in particulars in her effort to achieve a vision of the whole, or "relationship." Where Gibbs "withdrew" (the word is almost a refrain in the poem) to contemplate systems, the poet plunged into their phases. But, though there are differences in the ways Gibbs and Rukeyser approached the world, she says of Gibbs, "He knew the composite / many-dimensioned spirit, the phases of its face." The same can be said of her poetry, which also seeks to realize the "many-dimensioned spirit" in its phases: the fullness she allows her perceptions to follow. She says in *The Life of Poetry* that "art and nature are imitations, not of each other, but of the same third thing—both images of the real, the spectral and vivid reality that employs all means" (LP, 24). The way to approach a knowledge of this third thing, this many-dimensioned spirit, is to know its phases, in their systems, their relationships. She writes poems in the light of the conviction by which Gibbs worked and which she explicitly applied to poetry in *The Life of Poetry*: that the full truth is not something which emerges from one still point or base "but from accords of components whose end is truth."

"Gibbs" begins in her characteristic way of plunging into the stream of images and meanings (those "components" whose accord is truth) which the subject generates.

It was much later in his life he rose
in the professors' room, the frail bones rising
among that fume of mathematical meaning,
symbols, the language of symbols, literature . . . threw
air, simple life, in the dead lungs of their meeting,
said, "Mathematics *is* a language."

Here in the first stanza a great theme of Gibbs's life, and of Rukeyser's, is sounded: relationship, the vital similarities between living things, in this case between the living (moving, growing) symbols of mathematics and of language. For convenience we separate disciplines, fields of study. But a great imagination, in science or the arts, will eventually assert the similarities of disciplines.

The poem proceeds with images of New Haven at the beginning of the Civil War and Gibbs's place in this scene. The paradox emerges of the similarity between Gibbs and Whitman, both seeking a vision of the whole, each in his own way.

Condense, he is thinking. Concentrate, restrict.
This is the state permits the whole to stand,
the whole which is simpler than any of its parts.
And the mortars fired, the tent-lines, lines of trains,
earthworks, breastworks of war, field-hospitals,
Whitman forever saying, "Identify."
Gibbs saying "I wish to know systems."

There is an attempt in the poem to give scientific thought its sensuous terms, its correspondences in the familiar world in which Gibbs lived and, the poet assumes, from which he got scientific ideas. Just as the scientist gets ideas from his daily living and as people make statues of mathematical diagrams (one such statue was made of one of Gibbs's diagrams—of water—by the English scientist Clerk Maxwell), the poet makes poetry out of scientific ideas. Here again is the embodied transcendental conviction that "the spectral and vivid reality" is translatable into various "languages": those of nature, mathematics, solid geometry, poetry.

. . . driving
his sister's coach in the city, knowing the
rose of direction loosing its petals down

atoms and galaxies. Diffusion's absolute.
Phases of matter! The shouldering horses pass
turnings (snow, water, steam) echoing platted curves,
statues of diagrams, the forms of schemes
to stand white on a table, real as phase,
or as the mountainous summer curves when he
under New Hampshire lay while shouldering night
came down upon him then with all its stars.
Gearing that power-spire to the wide air.
Exacting symbols of rediscovered worlds.[50]

The rest of the poem presents more of Gibbs's thought in poetic
images and concludes with the triumph of this intense, persistent
man who

rose and dared
sever waterspouts, bring the great changing world
time makes more random, into its unity.

Rukeyser had few precedents in her attempt to give us the poetic
equivalent of scientific imagining. She herself in her biography of
Gibbs and in *The Life of Poetry* cites the obscure and maligned
nineteenth-century poet James Gates Percival as one who dealt with
science in poetry. Archibald MacLeish in "Einstein" (1929) imagined the scientist grappling with problems. But as Hyatt Waggoner
pointed out, the poem shows that science gave MacLeish no hope; a
brave man had to carry on *despite* the findings of science.[51] Gibbs is
for Rukeyser the symbol of the self-reliant imagination discovering
truths of relation that "create the creative," enabling others to pursue their own productive work.

"Ryder" is an evocation in rhythm, sound, and image of the
mystic, rude, and original canvases of Albert Pinkham Ryder and of
his personal life, which was as unconventional as his art. The first
stanza's long lines have the movement of the sea, which was the
chief influence on Ryder; they come toward the meaning of this
man, withdraw, and surge in again as the poet closes in on her
subject.

50. Rukeyser admits that the phrase "In livery" is inaccurate in describing Gibbs "driving / his sister's coach in the city."
51. Hyatt Waggoner, *The Heel of Elohim: Science and Values in Modern American Poetry* (Norman, Oklahoma, 1950), vii.

> Call himself unbegun, for the sea made him; assemblages of
> waters gave him his color.
> But not the sea; coast-line, coast-water, rising sfumato from
> smoke-holes of the sea,
> pitching onto the black rock of the ocean-edge. But not the
> coast line,
> the Atlantic coast, flinging him headlong from its rigors
> into his art.
> Great salt swept boldface captain, big-boned New Englander
> drowning deep
> among the mysteries of the painful western adventure, circling
> in unappeased circles into America.

The poem describes Ryder's canvases, the room in which he
worked, his personal behavior, his aesthetics, showing how integrated (in its storms) was his life. But unlike Gibbs, whose knowledge and imagination yoked disparate "fields" and produced theories
which enabled succeeding generations of scientists to make new discoveries, Ryder was tragically solitary in his genius,

> master of meaning and never mastering means,
> wasteful and slow, without tradition. He shortens
> the life of his paintings in their friable colors
> by ignorance, by storms.

Nevertheless, despite the technical deficiencies which caused many
of his paintings to deteriorate, his vision, like Gibbs's theories, sur-
vives. He turned from formal painting to his own turbulent, abstract style of expressing the complex forces which he saw in the
American landscape and in the American experience. His example is
liberating.

> Refusing the dead life
> like a nest of tables whose next is always smaller
> refined and congruent, slashes American sky
> by derelict lightning, turning all landscape into
> sublunar ocean.

Ryder's belief in his own vision, his rejection of dead formalism,
had a great appeal to Rukeyser. In imagining Ryder, his experience,
and his work, the poet uses those symbols which she has associated

with life and rebirth throughout the volume: the moon, circles, many o sounds, the whirlpool. The poem ends:

> His head that was moon the center of the storm.
> His boulders that were eyes washed by the drift of ocean.

Rosenthal quotes from "Ryder" in asserting that its phrases describe much of Rukeyser's own work: "He believes with his eye . . . [seeing] mystic reconciliations, feeling the world enlarge / and never complete itself."

In writing about essayist and poet John Jay Chapman, Rukeyser chose again to celebrate an original spirit larger than his time. The theme in his life, as the poem brings out in its first lines, is his turning

> to punishment as we all return, in agonized initiation proving
>   America,
> a country returning to moments of conversion, in agony
>   supporting its changes, receiving
> the past, the clews of instinct, and the rich return:
> conviction in our people's face, all in pain.

The poem proceeds to set up the contrasts in Chapman's life: he is the young, handsome man dancing in Boston in a roomful of "marvellous skirts." Yet in this comfortable, well-lit setting he is drawn (the emphasis, appropriate in this volume, is on his *turning*) to darkness, mystery, "to a sibyl-minded woman," to Dante, and to the irrational act of giving a blow to a rival's head and then going home to put his own hand in the fire. Chapman's way of coming alive and into contact with reality in a too-comfortable world is to seek and know darkness and pain. He will say later, "The one time in my life I lived was twenty days of pain."

The poem explores Chapman's growth from this first knowledge of life in pain, then in his reflection on the meaning of his act of choosing pain, then in his going into public life and his attempt to know men "at the center of systems" (here is an unmistakable binding with "Gibbs"). Without telling us exactly what Chapman does in his life the poet gives us the feeling of his growth:

> the crisis comes,
> air seethes, and all the bushes flicker up,
> memories parasite in the life underground
> irrupt with convulsions and the speech of fire.
> At the focus, the cool life is insufficient.

We are given the barest of detail: his first wife dies, and "his spirit's legs are broken." His second wife "holds him while he becomes / incredible to himself," hard as "fulgurite fused by lightning." But then his son dies

> and he heals, he is born again,
> fed on his agonies, wanting again

> his gritty taste of truth.

From this time he is alive again, among "those who are many-born." He keeps himself alive through discomfort and pain. "He fights for the acute senses, terror, passion, and need. / 'I make it a policy to say nothing I will not regret.'"

But personal rebirth is not indefinitely possible, says the poet. Chapman, who sought intense life through pain, becomes "upholstered deep / in Harvard Club armchairs—a monument to Zero." The poem concludes with images of Chapman, who "carried flame," flaring out; yet there is an integrity even in his "selling out," and the "vortex" image connects Chapman's "modes of life" with the turning wind and with Gibbs's "phases of matter." The poet concludes that Chapman's last phases were

> simple and imperceptible transitions
> in countries of transition giving other lives
> the long remorseless logic of their love.

Ann Burlak, like Gibbs, Ryder, Chapman, and Ives, is a profoundly influential force in other lives, but hers is the most direct influence portrayed in this sequence. A Communist and labor organizer in the thirties, she is presented in the poem as a great speaker who can describe and illuminate the lives of a listening crowd and give voice to unspoken dreams. The poem is dense with the details of workers' lives, as in a proletarian novel. Burlak speaks too of social injustice and the penalties of those who resist it:

> the premature birth brought on by tear-gas,
> the charge leaving its gun slow-motion, finding those
> who sit at windows knowing what they see

The poem's detail is periodically subsumed into the larger vision of *A Turning Wind* and connected with other poems which describe life-bringing recurrences:

> She knows the field of faces at her feet,
> remembrances of childhood, likenesses of parents,
> a system of looms in constellation whirled,
> disasters dancing.

Here in the center of a sequence on lives of illustrious achievement is a striking passage in celebration of unknown heroes:

> She speaks to the ten greatest American women:
> The anonymous farmer's wife, the anonymous clubbed picket,
> the anonymous Negro woman who held off the guns,
> the anonymous prisoner, anonymous cotton-picker

Everywhere in the anonymity is the figure of the circle, the spiral, the return:

> their moments over the dishes, speaks them now,
> wrecks with the whole necessity of the past
> behind the debris, behind the ordinary
> smell of coffee, the ravelling clean wash,
> the turning to bed, undone among savage night
> planning and unplanning seasons of happiness
> broken in dreams or in the jaundiced morning
> over a tub or over a loom or over
> the tired face of death.

Horrors accumulate in the poem—beatings, strikes, the stupidly insensitive words of the well-to-do, the suffering of children. But the conclusion of the poem echoes the hopeful prophecies of "The Book of the Dead."

> Suddenly perceives
> the world will never daily prove her words,

but her words live, they issue from this life.
She scatters clews. She speaks from all these faces
and from the center of a system of lives
who speak the desire of worlds moving unmade
saying, "Who owns the world?" and waiting for the cry.

"Ives" begins appropriately with a piling up of "incongruous" detail like the detail of Charles Ives's music, which has been described as excruciatingly difficult because of its packing in of musical images, its requiring different tempi for different instruments, and its use of the "cluster chord." When the reader has reached this point in the sequence of "Lives," if not before, there comes the satisfying realization that Rukeyser's verse in describing her subjects has been beautifully adapted to each one. The verse at the beginning of "Ives" is suited to his dense style, just as the spare lines of "Gibbs" are appropriate in describing the imagination of the scientist and the long, rolling lines of "Ryder" are suitable for the artist obsessed with the sea and with reworking his canvases over and over. The phrasing of "Ann Burlak" contains much parallelism, as would that of a masterful orator. It is difficult to "say" the opening lines of "Ives," in the mind or aloud, just as it is difficult to play an Ives composition. Ives scoffed at people's need of facile, harmonious sounds.

Knowing the voices of the country, gathering
voices of other harvests, farm-hands who gather in
sources of music on the blueberry hills,
the village band, lines at the schoolhouse singing—
lit cheeks and lips over the blown-glass lamps
in the broad houses, along the pebble beach,
or up the baldface mountain's granite sky

The second part of the first stanza becomes smoother, as there is sweetness of melody in passages of Ives's music. But on the whole, in that music, there is what the poet calls "uncompromising sound"; and in her verse there is the close-packed imagery which follows Ives's bidding:

Call off your wit and write

> for silent implicated men, a crabbed line
> of intercepted music with the world between.
> Networks of songs. . . .

The images of "Ives" play on his compositions; the poet focuses on the *Concord* Sonata and its meanings for the artist. Ives, like Ryder, shunned dead, formal traditions. He was inspired by the men of Concord: Hawthorne, Emerson, Alcott, Thoreau, who, in Ives's rendition of their spirit,

> Raise us an instrument
> limitless, without the scarecrow keyboard
> can give repose and fame to successful pianists
> playing to camouflage dullness.

In the stanza which begins the closing movement of "Ives" the poet changes her rhythm and speaks to us directly, as teacher.

> This is Charles Ives.
> Gold-lettered insurance windows frame his day.
> He is eclectic, he sorts tunes like potatoes
> for better next-year crops, catching the variable
> wildest improvisations, his clusters of meaning
> railing against the fake sonorities, "sadness
> "of a bathtub when the water is being let out,"
> knowing the local hope knocking in any blood.
> "Today we do not choose to die or to dance,
> "but to live and walk."

There is no mistaking her admiration, nor the affinity between her own work and that of the musician who composed "clusters of meaning," nor the echo, in Ives's work, of Gibbs's—and her own—belief that truth is an accord of myriad components. Like Rukeyser's Whitmanesque ideal for poetry, Ives "gathers the known world total into music . . . naming the instruments we all must hold."

Thus ends the volume, *A Turning Wind*. The book as a whole is a manifestation of the poet's struggle to compose the meanings not only of her immediate present and personal past but of the strengths of our common past as they live in the present and prophesy the future. The book is strong proof that the poet's sensibilities are tuned

to far more than contemporary concerns. She is convincingly jubi-
lant about human achievement, despite the global failures of the decade. One cannot agree with Rosenthal that "the general mood of
the poems in this book is despair rather than the heroics of the earlier volumes." [52] Nor can one accept his contention that the poet's
"message" is that if there is any hope it is in the biographies of those
whose achievements have transcended the destructiveness of our
civilization. The hope, for the poet, is not in their biographies,
which are dead letters, but in our living imaginations which can
take clues from theirs and which can hold the instruments they have
named.

Rukeyser's perception of the failure of what Auden called "a low
dishonest decade" is only one of the realizations in these complex
poems. Though her hopes fell with the dashing of hopes for an im-
minent world-wide rejection of fascism, she still maintained faith in
the ideals represented by the subjects of her "Lives." These creative
individuals embodied the American tradition she spoke of in a lecture given at Vassar in the fall of 1940: "the violent axiom-breaking
gesture of the imagination that takes its sides, chooses its own tradition, and gets to work, facing what it must face. . . . Our poetry is
that. Founded on the breaking of axioms; and our sciences, our inventions. It is a tradition of the audacious spirit, of the imagination
that asserts itself against the world, life, and death and all the dead
wars." The editors' statement in the issue of *Twice-a-Year*, where
Rukeyser's lecture was published, notes that the contributors to that
issue of the journal all "stress the identity of the traditional-creative
and the living-creative spirit of any time." John Malcolm Brinnin
wrote in 1943 that Rukeyser "is the most distinguished /of those
poets who/ have undergone the disappointments and tortured doubts
of the last decade and yet succeeded in enlarging both their strength
of purpose and the scope of their poetry." [53]

52. Rosenthal, "Chief Poets of the American Depression," 588.
53. Muriel Rukeyser, "The Fear of Poetry," *Twice-a-Year*, VII (Fall–Winter, 1941), 21–
22; this was later incorporated into *The Life of Poetry*; Brinnin, "Muriel Rukeyser: The Social Poet and the Problem of Communication," 555.

The last poem Rukeyser published before the United States entered the war was "The Soul and Body of John Brown." [54] The poem is permeated with the hope amid darkness of its epigraph from the prophet Joel, insistent in its headlong rhythm: "Multitudes, multitudes in the valley of decision." In the Old Testament, Joel proclaims: "For the day of the Lord is near in the valley of decision" (Joel 3:14). The message is a prophecy of blessing on the innocent and destruction of those who persecuted the Lord's people. The mood of the poem is that of a spirit, identified with a nation, plunging toward the embrace of a decisive truth, as the strong voices of its tradition (John Brown's revolutionary values) demand to be heard. The "decision" in Joel is the Lord's; but there is an emphasis in the poem, pointed in its repeated invocation to the prophet Ezekiel, that the decision is also each person's responsibility. The decision is to awaken, to bring our dreams, forebodings, and ideals into full consciousness.

> His life is in the body of the living.
> When they hanged him the first time, his image leaped
> into the blackened air. His grave was the floating faces
> of the crowd, and he refusing them release
> rose open-eyed in autumn, a fanatic
> beacon of fierceness leaping to meet them there,
> match the white prophets of the storm,
> the streaming meteors of the war.
> Dreaming Ezekiel, threaten me alive!

John Brown is like the subjects of "Lives" in that Brown's image is also a "risen image," a source of strength which may inspire other human beings to personal growth. But this poem had even more contemporary relevance than "Lives" in that the driving wish the poet saw as necessary to Americans in 1940 was embodied in Brown: freedom. In this poem, however, the focus is not on examples of inspiring creative originality but on a life whose intensity of desire—for freedom—*must be reborn* in our lives. It is appropriate that the section from which the epigraph from Joel is taken is

54. A first version of the poem appeared in *Poetry*, LVI (June, 1940), 115–20; later it was published in *Beast in View*.

considered a messianic prophecy and that the seasonal movement in the poem is from "October's fruition-fire" through winter and spring to "summernoon." Brown is pictured in the poem as one who took upon himself the guilt of an age, who was martyred, and who is then continually reborn in the awakened spirits of his countrymen.

> Brown wanted freedom. Could not him-
> self be free
> until more grace reached a corroded world. Our guilt his
> own.
> Under the hooded century drops the trap—
>
> . . . .
> Brown sees his tree
> grow in the land to leap these mountains.
> Not mountains, but men and women sleeping.
>
> O my scene! my mother!
> America who offers many births.

These "many births" arrive in the poem in images of Brown asking "more miracles" of the people, asking for freedom, deliverance for those locked (as in the poems of *A Turning Wind*) in "symptoms of ice." Brown comes like "Spring: the great hieroglyph: the mighty, whose first hour / collects the winter invalids."

With the coming of spring, the second half of the poem is decidedly hopeful of such freedom and deliverance: Brown is resurrected in people believing their own dreams and sharing them with others.

> They more and more, secretly, tell their dreams.
> They listen oftener for certain words, look deeper
> in faces for features of one remembered image.
>
> . . . .
> Death was its method. It will surpass its
> furious birth when it is known again.

In the earlier version of the poem, which appeared in *Poetry* in 1940, the word "papers" in the line "Whether he weaken searching for power in papers" was "pamphlets." Rukeyser made the political reference more universal in her final version of the poem. The meaning, less pointed, nevertheless remains: to search for power in factionalism is weakness. Rukeyser did keep the line "stopgap slogans of a thin season's offering" to designate an inadequate vision of world events. The immortal Brown calls for what the poet herself wanted in the period of waiting for war, a period when some artists felt they had to censor their expression or narrow their focus (Auden choosing "a narrow strictness").

> Lost in the face of a child,
> lost in the factory repetitions, lost
> on the steel plateaus, in a ghost distorted.
> Calling More Life. In all the harm calling.

In the exhorting rhythms of "Theory of Flight," the last stanza of the poem echoes Rukeyser's imagery of walls going down. This final stanza contains the fullness of perspective she has been demanding of poetry, the encompassed contradictions of blessing and curse found in this nation and its values. For there is danger in promise, in possibility. And the life-giving sun, it must be remembered, is like Brown: a relentless fanatic.

> More life, challenging
> this hatred, this Hallelloo—risk it upon yourselves.
> Free all the dangers of promise, clear the image
> of freedom for the body of the world.
> After the tree is fallen and has become the land,
> when the hand in the earth declined rises and touches and
> after the walls go down and all the faces turn,
> the diamond shoals of eyes demanding life
> deep in the prophet eyes, a wish to be again
> threatened alive, in agonies of decision
> part of our nation of our fanatic sun.

Untermeyer said of this poem in 1940, "It is, perhaps, Miss Rukeyser's most important work up to date, for it embodies not only her credo and reveals her style at its richest, but it serves as a manifesto for her generation. . . . In a steadily mounting chorus of contrasted voices, the poem proceeds to its affirmative climax. . . . In the midst of desperate remedies and clamoring negatives, she affirms the life of people and the life of poetry—the life of the spirit giving all processes and inventions, the creative life which is the double answer to living slavery and to the wish for quick escape, comforting death."[55]

Rukeyser's professional associations during the late thirties and early forties show her affirmative spirit. In the spring of 1935 she became associate editor of *New Theatre*, the periodical of the Theater Union, a producing unit "dedicated to dramatizing the life of the working man." The union resisted the Communist party's attempt to direct its policies, calling itself "a united front theater." Encompassing "the full spectrum of radical opinion," the union often released this statement to the press: "We produce plays that deal boldly with the deep-going social conflicts, the economic, emotional, and cultural problems that confront the majority of the people." As would be expected, Rukeyser also worked with groups such as the Theater Committee for the Defense of the Spanish Republic, which produced a radical play on the Spanish Civil War. She did other work to help tell Spain's story to the world such as translating for the anthology of antifascist Spanish poems, *And Spain Sings*.[56]

Rukeyser began to publish in *Decision* with its first issue, January, 1941, and she became associate editor in July, 1941. The editorial in the first issue sounds like Rukeyser in *The Life of Poetry*: Ours is the decision to examine what we want not to lose to totalitarianism, to examine and explore "the ideal of a *new humanism*." The magazine would be "a new forum for the creative spirit," not an ivory tower but a place where many traditions and concepts would be analyzed. The magazine would not seek answers but would display the tolerant, mutual search for the right attitudes for our times. "The fact that we venture, just now, on the foundation of a literary

---

55. Untermeyer, "The Language of Muriel Rukeyser," 13.
56. Malcolm Goldstein, *The Political Stage: American Drama and Theater of the Great Depression* (New York, 1974), 58–59, 178; M. J. Benardete and Rolfe Humphries (eds.), *And Spain Sings: Fifty Loyalist Ballads Adapted by American Poets* (New York, 1937).

periodical—a review of Free Culture—is in itself a gesture of protest and a gesture of hope."[57]

Decision did not survive into the war, but *Twice-a-Year* did. Beginning its publication in 1938 it ran through fifteen volumes, to 1947; Rukeyser's work appeared there frequently. The magazine was dedicated to the photographer Alfred Stieglitz, who said, "To show the moment to itself is to liberate the moment." Calling itself "a Journal of Literature, the Arts, and Civil Liberties," *Twice-a-Year* spoke for the belief that artists and intellectuals can influence the course of events by working freely. Editors' statements continually emphasized that there would be no propagandizing in their pages for any point of view. Rather the editors would publish a wide spectrum of response to world events by those who had participated in them. In the third issue, for instance, they published André Malraux, who worked in Spain for the Loyalists, and Evan Thomas, the absolute pacifist. They also regularly published texts from the past which they felt were applicable to contemporary problems. Thus Thoreau, Rilke, and Randolph Bourne's letters from the First World War appeared in the same issue as one of Rukeyser's "Elegies."

In a period when intolerance and cynicism ran high, *Twice-a-Year* was remarkable for its tolerance and idealism. The true anti–Nazi attitude, said the editors, is "mutual respect . . . for the essential interdependence of the contributions of all" in their individual temperament and conscience. The artist creates the freedom to create and thus must be free. "The artist sees the infinite all-embracing conflicts implicit in life and the tragic impossibility of resolving them. . . . He proceeds as with a faith that the resolution of all irreconcilables is nevertheless miraculously possible." The editors saw themselves as "part of the force attempting to keep alive the music, the fulfillment of the world."[58] The pages of *Twice-a-Year* were a most appropriate place for Rukeyser's work in its striving for the fullest expression of human concerns.

---

57. "Issues at Stake," *Decision*, I (January, 1941), 6–8.
58. "Editors' Statement," *Twice-a-Year*, VIII-IX (1942), 11–21.

Myra Rukeyser and Muriel at age one

At Yaddo, Saratoga Springs, 1934

Top row: John Duke, Arthur Berger, unknown, Martin Craig, unknown, James T. Farrell, Joseph D. Martini, Alexander Godin Standing near pot: Irving Fineman, Muriel Rukeyser Seated on bench: Dorothy Farrell, Roy Harris, Walter Quirt, Jean Liberte, Elizabeth Ames, Eugene Jaffe, Ann Rivington, John Cheever On pillows: Louis Hechenbleikner, Kristl Hechenbleikner, unknown

At Yaddo, 1938

Back row (against grill): Hubert Skidmore, Kenneth Fearing, Fred R. Miller, unknown, Wallace Stegner, unknown, Joseph Vogel, Charles Naginsky, Henry Roth Front row: Leonard Ehrlich, Muriel Parker, Marjorie Peabody Waite, Mary Barnard, Rebecca Pitts, Muriel Rukeyser, Edna Guck, unknown, Helen Margaret, Elizabeth Ames, Mrs. Willard Thorp, Susie Fuchs (Mrs. Daniel Fuchs), Daniel Fuchs, Willard Thorp

A photograph by Imogen Cunningham
IMOGEN CUNNINGHAM TRUST,
SAN FRANCISCO, CALIFORNIA

Bollingen Poetry Prize Committee, 1954

This group, assembled at Yale on January 9, 1955, chose Miss Leonie
Adams and Miss Louise Bogan as co-winners of the Bollingen Poetry Prize.
Committee members are Wallace Stevens, Randall Jarrell, Allen Tate, Mari-
anne Moore, and Muriel Rukeyser. COURTESY YALE UNIVERSITY

In front of Monet's Waterlilies, Museum of Modern Art, 1963

With son Bill in San Francisco, 1947

With grandson Jacob, Berkeley, 1976

At Papitos, Cyprus, 1974

A tree planting for peace, Central Park, New York City, 1975

In support of poet Kim Chi-Ha. Westgate Prison, Seoul, Korea, 1975

PHOTOGRAPH BY ROY WHANG, ASIA ECONOMIC NEWS

With the president of Sarah Lawrence College, Charles R. DeCarlo, at a writers' conference on December 9, 1978, "A Day in Honor of Muriel Rukeyser."

At Sarah Lawrence College, December of 1978

VASSAR QUARTERLY / DIXIE SHERIDAN

FOUR

The Forties

THE SPIRIT of American poetry in the forties may be approached through the titles of its celebrated volumes: Lowell's *Lord Weary's Castle*, Jarrell's *Losses*, Berryman's *The Dispossessed*. Participants in a *Partisan Review* symposium entitled "The State of American Writing, 1948" discussed the poetry of the decade and tried to explain why and how it differed from that of the thirties. Berryman said that the forties were the decade of survival, of political, even moral paralysis. He said that the bracing views of European existentialism had little effect on the arts in America and that the chief cultural phenomenon, the desertion of Marxism by intellectuals, had probably been replaced by nihilism. Robert Gorham Davis explained that writers of the thirties "caught an organic, dynamic, historical sense of literature in society and of the poet as hero, that went back through Marx to the Romantic theorists, especially in Germany, to Herder, Fichte, Hegel, and the rediscoverers of Vico." But in the forties theories of art and the function of the artist were sharply different. Davis characterized these theories as aloof "academic attitudes" which grew out of a reaction against Marxism after the Moscow trials and the Ribbentrop-Molotov pact and were formed in "the political vacuum in which the war was fought" and then in the "flight from history after the atom bombing" and the photographs of the concentration camps. Writers, who in increasing numbers were becoming affiliated with expanding universities, stressed ambiguity and irony in their work and in the works they taught, rather than literature's historical, social, and psychological character.[1]

1. "The State of American Writing, 1948," *Partisan Review*, XV (August, 1948), 855-94.

Winfield Townley Scott noticed the "academic" tendency even in 1941, in his review of *Five Young American Poets* (Berryman, Jarrell, W. R. Moses, G. M. O'Donnell, and Mary Barnard). Scott felt that the critical allegiances of the young men—to Eliot, Blackmur, Winters, and Tate—were producing the "chill" of "the academic and the special" on their poetry. Scott saw the young poets reacting to the romanticism and "crudeness" of Whitman, Emerson, Dickinson, and Robinson. But the effect, Scott said, was that you leave a poem by Berryman remembering the method; it is a pseudo-classicism reacting against poetry of social consciousness. Though the latter has often been dull and speechifying, said Scott, at least "its best work has warmth, humor, vigor, great possibility, and offers within its still sprawling confines all the roots of America's most potent poetic traditions which the reactionary would either ignore or deny."[2]

Indeed the forties saw the triumph of the New Criticism or analytical criticism in prestigious literary quarterlies such as the *Kenyon Review* and the *Sewanee Review* and in colleges and universities. Following Eliot, the New Critics denied that "human life and morality can be decisively improved through social and economic changes." They manifested "a distrust of science, industrialism, and the idea of social progress," especially as that idea is embodied in Marxism and liberal democracy. Literature, to these critics, has to avoid the romantic pitfalls, in form and content, which characterized writing from Shelley to Whitman to the proletarians. Above all, they maintained, "irony is a constant characteristic of poetry of the highest order."[3]

Rukeyser had seen the forties coming. Recall her poetic images for them in *A Turning Wind* and her insistence in the lectures that formed the basis of *The Life of Poetry* on a poetry of full response and possibility. Her work in the forties and fifties flaunted standards then in vogue and she wrote in her own vein with such spirited determination that she left herself wide open to the attacks of the literary establishment. It appears she almost invited them, putting her

2. Winfield T. Scott, "The Dry Reaction," *Poetry*, LVIII (1941), 86–90.
3. Walter Sutton, *Modern American Criticism* (Englewood Cliffs, N.J., 1963), Chap. 5.

own work on the line, in the dauntless spirit of the thirties.

Her work of the forties and fifties is actually an organic, inevitable extension of her rich production of the thirties, of the vision and resolve born in Alabama, West Virginia, and Spain. As F. O. Matthiessen wrote in 1944 in his defense of Rukeyser against her *Partisan Review* critics (see below, p. 180), "Her writing shows her to have been throughout the past decade a convinced anti-fascist and radical democrat."[4] Neither Auden nor Lowell nor Berryman nor Roethke nor Blackmur nor Tate nor Winters had confronted the world of the thirties as she had and delivered it in anything like the agonized yet hopeful imaginative vision of *U.S.1*.

Moreover she bore into the era of the New Criticism and the ironic stance her vivid apprehension of the century's earlier large-scale muffling of reality: in a statement in *The War Poets*, Oscar Williams' anthology of 1945, she wrote, "For myself, war has been in my writing since I began. The first public day that I remember was the False Armistice of 1918." She explained in this statement as she had done before, both in prose and in poetry, that her task as a poet in this time was to keep alive and make more people aware of the meanings that were being fought for on the battlefield. The war, she said, "has not been in much of our poetry because the meanings of this war have been lost; and through this the fashion in writing is aversion, wit, or easy mysticism and easy despair. . . .We confess by this war that we did not react to fascism as it arrived. But now the fact that it might be a war against fascist ideas has slipped away." Against fascist ideas, she wished to assert "the force that works for creation and freedom . . . a way in which peoples can work together for a wide creative life. I believe that poetry is a part of that, of the means which is peace, and of the living changing goal."[5] Unlike most American poets, she still held, in the forties, to the notion of the poet as hero, as one who could alter consciousness.

Rukeyser's view of poetry explains the remarkable thrust of her work to the present. "The war for those concerned with life, the

---

4. Matthiessen, "The Rukeyser Imbroglio (cont'd)," 217–18.
5. Muriel Rukeyser, "War and Poetry," in Oscar Williams (ed.), *The War Poets* (New York, 1945), 25–26.

truth which is open to all, is still ahead. It is a struggle in which poetry also lives and fights." The notion of poetry as a "fight" is not common today and was not part of the New Critical vocabulary. The fight for her as a poet is to keep all the meanings alive, to keep Emersonian possibility plausible, not to surrender to any of the narrower visions of the world, even when the horrors of Auschwitz and Hiroshima made the world seem less redeemable than ever in artistic vision, even when Korea and Vietnam entered the history of this bloody century. From *The Speed of Darkness* (1968) there is "Poem," which looks backward and looks ahead, and shows that her attitudes of the forties were deeply held, developing resolves:

> I lived in the first century of world wars.
> Most mornings I would be more or less insane,
> The newspapers would arrive with their careless stories,
>
> . . . .
>
> Slowly I would get to pen and paper,
> Make my poems for others unseen and unborn.
> In the day I would be reminded of those men and women
> Brave, setting up signals across vast distances,
> Considering a nameless way of living, of almost
>   unimagined values.
> As the lights darkened, as the lights of night brightened,
> We would try to imagine them, try to find each other.
> To construct peace, to make love. . . .[6]

In the introduction to one of his anthologies of the forties (*New Poems*, 1943), Oscar Williams described the role and the fate of the poet in wartime in a way that perfectly summarized Rukeyser's work and its reception. "In wartime it is not the function of the poet to go into uniform, but to resolve and state, as precisely and freshly as he can, the emotional experience of being alive and suffering before, during, and after the eruption. Though he never go near a military camp he receives the wounds, and gives warning long before the first bomb wails. The poets of this generation functioned, before the movement of armies, as prophets great and tormented as any be-

6. Muriel Rukeyser, *The Speed of Darkness* (New York, 1968).

fore them. And like all prophets, they were rejected by society."[7] Ru-keyser's prophetic work of the thirties, waiting for war, and her "fighting," tormented work of the forties received more than its share of official rejection from well-known critics in established journals. It was in 1948, for example, that Randall Jarrell felt free to imply in the pages of the *Nation* that her work was outmoded.[8] That no substantial study of Rukeyser's work was undertaken until 1975 was also a form of rejection. In the forties Rukeyser published prose and poetry that reflected her struggle to grow in a world at war. Happily, she was able to record the coming of a peace, both to the world and to her own life, despite great personal trauma in the birth of her child.

Wake Island

Wake Island was Rukeyser's first response to United States involve-ment in World War II. The ninety-four-line poem was published in 1942 as a pamphlet with a sturdy purple cover, selling for fifty cents. It was described on the cover as "the first poem of major im-portance to be written about the war." William Rose Benét in the *Saturday Review* described it accurately as "Not too elliptical . . . for the average reader—who, after all, should allow his or her mind to do a *little* work on what it reads."[9] For one following Rukeyser's work, *Wake Island* is more. It is the explicit binding of images which shows that the poet saw the fight in Spain and the fight in the Pacific as part of the same struggle and that she was working to make its meanings live for her readers. The courageous defense of Wake Island by a small garrison of Marines is described in the first line of the poem as "Proof of America" and later in the poem as a "wish, in that moment of proof, [for] more life for the world." "America," to those who come to *Wake Island* from *A Turning*

7. Oscar Williams, *New Poems* (New York, 1943), vi–vii.
8. Randall Jarrell, *Poetry and the Age*. This review of *The Green Wave* originally ap-peared in *Nation*, May 8, 1948, pp. 512–13.
9. Muriel Rukeyser, *Wake Island* (Garden City, N.Y., 1942); William Rose Benét, re-view of *Wake Island* in *Saturday Review*, August 29, 1942, p. 14.

Wind, is axiom-breaking: it is Chapman's "proving America . . . in agonized initiation," choosing agonizing changes. "America" is the fullness and freedom of Charles Ives and Albert Pinkham Ryder, the single-minded achievement of Willard Gibbs and of all the anonymous women who have kept the world turning daily and nightly. "America" is the "risen image" of heroes like John Brown who call for more freedom, more life. The poem develops meanings which Rukeyser, working in the poster division of the Office of War Information, knew must be continually presented to people. In an article in the *New Republic* entitled "Words and Images" she explained, "These are images which need to be built up over a period of time, as an image is built up in a poem. . . .As a whole country, we need the images and words which will strengthen our lives, for war and for peace . . . [images] that continually set before us the clarity and belief which strengthen us, and the tradition and future we fight for." [10]

The "images and words" of *Wake Island* progress to the statement that "the world is one world." "We know the world is one; we name it Freedom." Here the poet achieves the clarity she feels is needed in such a poem; she has cast off for this mode the "heavy mystery thrown against the heart" of the poems of *A Turning Wind*. In this "public" poem she assumes the mission she was given on the boat on her way home from Spain. She is connecting antifascist struggles everywhere, insisting that we must fight

> until the war's first weapon is liberty,
> and there is no slaveholder and no slave,
> not even in the mind.

It is a free world the poet is concerned with in this poem; her lines are not nationalistic. As it happens, Americans are "fighting to prove us whole." As it happens, "Wake was built for a link." That link must now hold, for the world's sake.

It is easy to disparage and dismiss a poem like *Wake Island,* as Louise Bogan did in the *New Yorker*, saying of Rukeyser, "She has

10. Muriel Rukeyser, "Words and Images," *New Republic*, August 2, 1943, p. 141.

sincerely taken as her thesis that the stand on Wake was a fight for freedom throughout the world. But how damply she represents this conviction! With what rhetorical hollowness and limpness! We are right back in the parlor, with the oil lamp, the antimacassars, and the volume of Owen Meredith on the centre table. I still think that the poetry of this war will be written in the field and that it will sound far more simple and moving than anything Miss Rukeyser has produced in this volume." [11] Though *Wake Island* is not simple, it lacks the complexity, including the complexity of tone, one has come to expect in modern poetry. But one can, if one wishes, see what the poem was designed to evoke (especially for one who had read Rukeyser before): a pattern of meanings comprehensible to the average American encouraging him or her to make the link between Wake Island and the concepts of one struggling world and humankind's chief weapon in its struggle to evolve—freedom.

Weldon Kees's review of *Wake Island* in the *Partisan Review* is entitled "Miss Rukeyser's Marine Poem." The review is as follows: "There's one thing you can say about Muriel: she's not lazy." *Partisan Review* then printed, in its issue of September–October, 1943, an unsigned piece on Rukeyser with the baldly sexist title, "Grandeur and Misery of a Poster Girl." It would be difficult to find a comment with more malice and distortion on any modern writer in a major publication. In 1941 Morton Dauwen Zabel had attacked MacLeish in a two-part article in the *Partisan Review* entitled "The Poet on Capitol Hill." Here MacLeish was accused, as Rukeyser later would be, of "bandwagon-jumping," "verbal ineptitude and moral hogwash," and "oracular vapidity" for his zealous pronouncements on the role of literature in world crisis. But Zabel's article, largely because of its length and its documentation, is not the slap in the face of the unsigned piece on Rukeyser. The substance of the attack is that her various political statements had all been "indignant" but "fashionable." As the editors explain in a subsequent piece, *Wake Island* was proof that her "poetic equipment was avail-

---

11. Louise Bogan, review of WI, *New Yorker*, October 31, 1942, p. 68.

able, on short notice, for any patriotic emergency. *Wake Island*, with its apostrophes to the Marines and spectacular Americanism, was scarcely an organic development from her earlier work." They called it "a symptom of the backsliding so common among writers today and their irresponsible exploitation of political motives and ideas for purposes of literary aggrandizement." [12]

The original piece in the *Partisan Review* is replete with innuendos, personal abuse, and sexism. Rukeyser gave the lectures that were the basis of *The Life of Poetry* to "Vassar girls. Here she was revealed in a new role: that of a big-league representative of the 'creative spirit,' speaking her piece with all the unctuousness and culture-*schmerz* of a junior theologian of poetics." Her belief that the meanings of the war had to be exhibited in popular art (posters) was trivialized and denigrated in the *Partisan Review*'s interpretation to mean that "she argues that a poet with a poster can win the war, bringing to mind the dapper ghost of James J. Walker, a famous song-writer, who remarked, when a question of the censorship of books arose, 'I never heard of a girl who was ruined by a book!' " The piece continues, "As Ring Lardner used to say, there is a limit to games and to fun, and to quote once more: 'Fun is fun, but a girl can't keep laughing all the time.' " [13]

The *Partisan Review* printed eloquent replies to their piece by

---

12. Weldon Kees, review of WI, *Partisan Review*, IX (November–December, 1942), 540; "Grandeur and Misery of a Poster Girl," *Partisan Review*, X (September–October, 1943), 471–73. (This piece was initialed "R.S.P.," which many readers assumed stood for the Editors: Philip Rahv, William Phillips, and Delmore Schwartz; Morton Dauwen Zabel, "The Poet on Capitol Hill," *Partisan Review*, VIII (January, 1941), 1–17.

13. According to Rukeyser, the *Partisan Review* came down so hard on her because she refused their offer to be poetry editor. One of her first assignments would have been to do in print to proletarian poet Sol Funaroff what the *Partisan Review* subsequently did to her. William Phillips declined to discuss the journal's treatment of Rukeyser when I wrote to him in 1976. Dwight Macdonald, who had resigned from the editorial board ("by mutual agreement, for political reasons") before the "Poster Girl" piece appeared, explains that the journal's attack on Rukeyser was more brutal than that on MacLeish because "MR was more one of us (and family quarrels have always been the bitterest) as against the older, officially established MacLeish. . . . I'd hazard that Delmore [Schwartz] wrote it in the main—the witty, trenchant, allusive style is typical—with political input from Rahv and Phillips [the piece is signed "R.S.P."]. . . . You must admit it's a witty, and elevated, title—Delmore MUST have thought it up." (From a letter to the author from Dwight Macdonald).

Rebecca Pitts and F. O. Matthiessen. Pitts's reply said, "No matter what her faults are, as a writer . . . they spring from an intuition of the relationships between orders of intellectual, emotional, and social experience which have been kept separate too long. And this is what people are looking for—this effort to link—this concern, precisely, with 'meanings.' " But the *Partisan Review* replied, this time in a piece signed "The Editors" (Philip Rahv, William Phillips, Delmore Schwartz), that *Wake Island* and *Willard Gibbs* "are obvious examples of that neo–American inspirational literature which is the product not of a healthy national consciousness but of intellectual demoralization." Though one may find in the politics of the *Partisan Review*'s position a valid alternative to Rukeyser's beliefs expressed in her writing, the tone and innuendos of the journal's attack remain deplorable.[14]

Willard Gibbs

Willard Gibbs (1942) is one of the few books by Rukeyser that can still be picked up at a secondhand bookstore. Mine, costing $1.50, came with its dustjacket, on which is printed, in large type, "This book, like all books, is a symbol of the liberty and the freedom for which we fight. You as a reader of books, can do your share in the desperate battle to protect those liberties—BUY WAR BONDS . . . become a true soldier of Democracy." We are unaccustomed to this ardor, genuine for millions in 1942. Similarly, we are unaccustomed to the ardor with which Rukeyser begins her book and to her admission in the acknowledgment that she wrote the book because she "needed to read it." [15] Rukeyser approaches the subject of Gibbs as she approaches a poem, saying in the "Author's Note" that she "welcomes any addition to the significant life and impact of Willard Gibbs . . . from anyone who can add further truth to his image as it enlarges on our scene." It is the developing image the poet is pas-

14. Pitts, "The Rukeyser Imbroglio," 125–29; Matthiessen, "The Rukeyser Imbroglio (cont'd)," 217–18.
15. Muriel Rukeyser, *Willard Gibbs* (Garden City, N.Y., 1942).

sionately interested in, the accord of myriad components, not the still point of truth. There is no still point. "This is not an authorized biography," she begins.

Rukeyser writes because during war we look "for deeper sources, for the sources of power that can bring a fuller life to a desperate time." "Willard Gibbs is such a source of power. Living in the Middle Period of the American people—from the point at which we stand—doing his work in silence, in isolation, in the years of rejection directly after the Civil War, when abstract work was wanted least of all, when the cry was for application and invention and the tools that would expand the growing fortunes of the diamond boys, his wish was for systems. He lived closer than any inventor, any poet, any scientific worker in pure imagination to the life of the inventive and organizing spirit in America" (WG, 2). We are unaccustomed to the prose which begins Chapter 1. It is a prose which suggests the mythic forces among which we live, to which we ourselves contribute in what we usually consider our routine lives.

Whatever has happened, whatever is going to happen in the world, it is the living moment that contains the sum of the excitement, this moment in which we touch life and all the energy of the past and future. Here is all the developing greatness of the dream of the world, the pure flash of momentary imagination, the vision of life lived outside of triumph or defeat, in continual triumph and defeat, in the present, alive. All the crafts of subtlety, all the effort, all the loneliness and death, the thin and blazing threads of reason, the spill of blessing, the passion behind these silences—all the invention turns to one end: the fertilizing of the moment, so that there may be more life. Spring, and the years, and the wars, and the ideas rejected, the swarming and anonymous people rejected, and the slow climb of thought to be more whole, the few accepted flames of truth in a darkness of battle and further rejection and further battle. We know the darkness of the past, we have a conscious body of knowledge—and under it, the black country of a lost and wasted and anonymous world, an early America of knowledge; jungle-land, wasteful as nature, prodigal.

This glorification of the moment comes as a shock to contemporary readers in our environment of shopping malls, brilliantly drab technologies, and zoned neighborhoods. Grand sweeps of thought are anomalous in our scene. They may even embarrass us, just as passages of *Walden* might embarrass us if they were cited by a journalist in describing a contemporary situation.

Willard Gibbs is not an easy book to read. Its prose strives to keep in motion, as in Rukeyser's most complex poems, the myriad components of imaginatively apprehended truth. In writing about Gibbs Rukeyser writes, for example, about how his philologist father's goals illuminate his own, how the work of many men of imagination, working in New Haven at the time of his father's maturity, constitute the life of imagination at that time. The biography of Gibbs is composed as a series of biography clusters and of clusters of event. Henry Adams, William James, and Willard Gibbs go to Europe, they return, and their efforts and achievements constitute a discernible "event" to Rukeyser's imagination; ordinary prose can't render this event as she apprehends it.

The book is evidence of the young poet's great synthesizing ability, for instance in her account of the background of the development of the science of thermodynamics (pages 148–50). On the other hand there are passages in the book which can only be called history as flash: in one page the story of Robert Mayer, who first formulated the law of the conservation of energy, is given in its personal determination, pathos, and triumph. It is the outline of a novel, narrated with intensity; history in film flashes. Joseph Wood Krutch, in fact, described this facet of her style—which he disliked—as "various sketches of bits of American political, industrial, and social history, presented almost in the fashion of Mr. Dos Passos's 'newsreels' and dubiously related to the subject." In reading *Willard Gibbs* one must often use one's imagination to connect these vivid sketches to the ongoing exposition, just as the viewer of certain vital films, said Eisenstein, must actively create the whole film image. Eisenstein and Rukeyser believed that in a vital work the image "is not fixed or ready-made, but arises, is born." Thus the viewer or reader, actively drawn into the work, experiences "an emotionally exciting and moving story as distinguished from a logical exposition of facts." [16]

Many readers are unwilling to exert the effort that Rukeyser's prose demands. Many readers can't put by the irritation caused by a series of paragraphs that can't be displayed in a conventional outline. As we shall see, even the most sympathetic reviewers found "grave fault" with Rukeyser's prose style. A teacher of composition might want to edit some passages and put in topic sentences, but as Untermeyer reminds one about the elegies: "The meaning declares itself finally and fully." A reader of *Willard Gibbs* must admit the validity of a prose that moves like poetry and has poetic coherence.

Rukeyser's passionate prose transmits her deep conviction, one shared by MacLeish at the time and by Lewis Mumford in the 1920s, that art, specifically poetry, should help people develop the kind of vision they need in a dark time, a time when there are few images to satisfy the spirit's need for meaning. Here is MacLeish in 1938: "We live in a time of crisis . . . of the heart. . . . The failure is a failure of desire . . . a failure of the spirit: a failure of the spirit to imagine. . . . This failure of the spirit is a failure from which only poetry can deliver us. . . . For what is lacking in the crisis of our time is only this: this image. . . . The poet may bring the mind of this nation one step nearer to an understanding of its will and one step nearer to an imagination of the world in which it can believe and which, believing, it can bring about." In *A History of American Poetry*, Horace Gregory and Marya Zaturenska aptly note that *Willard Gibbs* is like Lewis Mumford's *Herman Melville* (1929). Both books seek to view the imaginative life in the light of the human spirit's continual search for a larger meaning, which the goals of society, manifest in daily living, do not supply. Here is Mumford: "Whatever Melville's life was, his art in *Moby Dick* exhibits that integration and synthesis which we seek. Through his art, he escaped the barren destiny of his living; he embraced Life; and we who now follow where his lonely courage led him embrace it, too. This em-

16. Joseph Wood Krutch, review of *Willard Gibbs*, in *Nation*, January 16, 1943, p. 97; Eisenstein, *The Film Sense*, 31, 34.

brace was a fertile one; and in each generation it will bring forth its own progeny. The day of Herman Melville's vision is now in the beginning. It hangs like a cloud over the horizon at dawn; and as the sun rises, it will become more radiant, and more a part of the living day." [17]

This study is concerned primarily with Rukeyser's poetry and will take her at her word when she says *Willard Gibbs* is "a footnote to the poem." [18] I see the biography as an attempt to achieve that "access of power" ("Theory of Flight") in personal vision which enabled her to develop as a poet of positive utterance and faith through a period in American life when most poets were unable to maintain such faith. The "power" was the power of transformation, as she has said, "moving past one phase of one's own life . . . and moving past impossibilities." Gibbs's work on the changing phases of matter gave the poet "a language of transformation," which she translated into poetic language and apprehended as humanly significant. Of the meaning of transformation she has said, "That meaning is a religious meaning." Thus in writing the biography of Gibbs that she needed to read, she created a source of power. She was also able to convincingly display for readers her imagination's apprehension of this source of power: this is what *Willard Gibbs* is—a manifestation of the poet's imagination successfully combining and contemplating those elements in the image of Gibbs which were most inspiring to her. (But only a superficial reader would call the book "inspirational literature.") In sum, Rukeyser undertook *Willard Gibbs* for the sake of her poetry.

It is by a long road of presumption that I come to Willard Gibbs. When one is a woman, when one is writing poems, when one is drawn through a passion to know people today and the web in which they, suffering, find themselves, to learn the people, to dissect the web, one deals with the processes themselves. To know the processes and the machines of pro-

---

17. Archibald MacLeish, "In Challenge Not Defense," *Poetry* (July, 1938), 212–19, quoted in Zabel, "The Poet on Capitol Hill"; Lewis Mumford, *Herman Melville* (New York, 1929), 368.
18. "Craft Interview with Muriel Rukeyser," 169.

cess: plane and dynamo, gun and dam. To see and declare the full disaster that the people have brought on themselves by letting these processes slip out of the control of the people. To look for the sources of energy, sources that will enable us to find the strength for the leaps that must be made. To find sources, in our own people, in the living people. And to be able to trace the gifts made to us to two roots: the infinite anonymous bodies of the dead, and the unique few who, out of great wealth of spirit, were able to make their own gifts. Of these few, some have been lost through waste and its carelessness. This carelessness is complicated and specialized. It is a main symptom of the disease of our schools, which let the *kinds* of knowledge fall away from each other, and waste knowledge and time, and people. All our training plays into this; our arts do; and our government. It is a disease of organization, it makes more waste and war. (WG, 12)

Rukeyser persuades us, and herself, of the mastery of Gibbs's imagination in formulating such theories as the Phase Rule. That a human being was able by intense effort to achieve this "immense landmark of imagination" which unveils fundamental relationships of systems in nature is sheer joy to the poet. That Gibbs also saw science as communication ("Mathematics *is* a language," he said) is delight to Rukeyser who said, "Facing and communicating, that will be our life, in the world and in poetry" (LP, 40). Gibbs's view of the free imagination was utterly compelling to the poet and strong support for her own beliefs. Likewise, a powerful influence on Gibbs was Karl Pearson, who in *The Grammar of Science* (1892) refuted the arguments of scientists like Gibbs's old teacher in Berlin, Du Bois-Reymond, who claimed, "These ideas of force and matter and the complexities they bred were all abstractions" and to be ignored (WG, 297). Like Galileo, Pearson asked, "Who is willing to set limits to the human intellect? . . . We are to learn these languages [of abstract science]; to understand that material science is coextensive with our whole life, and the whole physical and mental life of the universe. . . .But beyond the formal process of reasoning fixed by these facts and their sequences, there is an element in our being which is not satisfied, except by the free imagination. Even here, scientists have shown more imagination, says Pearson, and used their gifts more beneficially, than any other group in this generation, even than the poets." Rukeyser says, "These must have been strokes to the heart of Gibbs," as they obviously were to hers.

Gibbs was the paragon of the unspecialized imagination, an ideal the poet holds supreme in our time. In Gibbs's day, the last quarter of the nineteenth century,

The expert was advancing as technical knowledge rose in value. . . .He was, most often, a skilled detail-worker who was highly conservative—reactionary, indeed—because there was nothing in his training to let him see where, in society, his own skills became mixed with all other knowledge. The professors of literature were turning out little critics, with appetites as broad as hairlines for democracy; the economists were turning out disciples in economics; and the technical schools beginning to flourish were turning out a new man in the world—highly surfaced, confident only of the limited knowledge he recognized in himself and was aware that his colleagues recognized, and almost without earned opinions about anything else. (WG, 316)

Rukeyser believed Brooks Adams spoke of the need in the Gilded Age as in our own: " 'Apparently modern society, if it is to cohere . . . must have a high order of generalizing mind—a mind which can grasp a multitude of complex relations' " (WG, 317). Such was the mind of Gibbs.

It is fascinating to note how Gibbs's method is similar to the poet's. Rukeyser found this description of the scientist's method in a preface to a French translation of Gibbs's great paper, "The Equilibrium of Heterogeneous Substances": "His method, like that of Newton, Fresnel, and Ampère, consists in starting with a small number of first principles or hypotheses, and searching out all the necessary consequences of those principles, without ever introducing in the course of the reasoning any new hypotheses or relaxing the rigor of the reasoning" (WG, 324). This method parallels what Cyril Stanley Smith sees as Rukeyser's work in *Willard Gibbs* and *The Traces of Thomas Hariot*, "starting off from a factual scrap of information and extending it imaginatively." [19] In the poet's "searching

19. Quotations from Cyril Stanley Smith of M.I.T. are from a letter to the author dated April 6, 1976.

out all the necessary consequences" there prevail not the rules of logic but the demands of imagination; these are no less rigorous for the poet intensely seeking relationship.

Rukeyser saw Gibbs's gifts "as those of the poet and discoverer ... the type and emblem of the imagination in America. . . . The highest level, that level of our thought at which Gibbs stands, looks to the past with re-affirmation and to the future with foreboding. Such foreboding is not the dark gaze, but the creation of images which speak for the future *as it arrives*, with the speed of the poet, and not the attendance on the fact of the reporter" (WG, 434–35).

Thus Rukeyser saw Gibbs as a type to emulate, and her book is replete with explorations of what Gibbs means to the life of the imagination, to the artist, today. This aspect of Gibbs I believe is most important to her and to the nature of the book. But *Willard Gibbs* is other things as well. Rukeyser's was the first biography of this scientist who is recognized as one of the ten most influential physical scientists of the eighteenth and nineteenth centuries. It contains, as reviewers said, a "brilliant account of the life" of Gibbs, admirably detailed explanations of his theories and their usefulness to industry in the years since his death (these are sometimes difficult for the layman to follow), and "a significant and sensitive interpretation of Gibbs's connection with his times." This connection—along with her style—stamps the book a biography by a poet. Eduard Färber writing in *Isis* (the distinguished journal of history of science) said that Rukeyser "gives a general impression of the contents of 'The Equilibrium of Heterogeneous Substances' and the later 'Statistical Mechanics' with remarkable skill. But others could have done this as well. On the other hand, how many are there who could have seen the relationship between 'the line of divines and theologians behind him' and the character of his work, who else could have written, 'Father and son deal with two facets of one theme: words as symbols, symbols as words, and the system in which they live'?"[20]

20. Bernard Jaffe (author of *Outposts of Science*), review of WG, in *New York Herald Tribune Books*, November 22, 1942, p. 4; Eduard Färber, review of WG, in *Isis*, XXXIV (Summer, 1943), 414–15.

A chapter which typifies her poetic approach to Gibbs's connection with his times is entitled "Three Masters: Melville, Whitman, Gibbs." Joseph Wood Krutch said of this chapter, "A climax of absurdity seems to me to be reached in . . . "Three Masters" . . . in which . . . we seem to be asked to see the relation between the Second Law of Thermodynamics and the White Whale." [21] In this chapter Rukeyser shows the parallels in the imaginative tasks of Gibbs, Melville, and Whitman. All three were unrecognized by society in their time. Yet in a fragmented age in which industry and invention leaped forward chaotically, all three men succeeded in apprehending vast systems. For Melville it was a system, a cosmos of conflicting energies, with "the two equilibrated principles, freedom and evil" (WG, 353). For Whitman it was the "ensemble"—the whole, inclusive, catalogued sweep of his society. Rukeyser says Whitman's meaning for ensemble is "closely related to Gibbs's 'Let us imagine a great number of independent systems, identical in nature, but differing in phase, that is, in their condition with respect to configuration and velocity' " (WG, 359). All three men had "unprecedented faith in a veiled future that was the core of their re-affirmation" (WG, 361). Rukeyser shows Whitman, Gibbs, and Melville as believers in the possibility of satisfying meaning emerging from an apparent chaos. "The single faces of Whitman's people, the faces of principle in Melville, the stars seen as the molecules of a great bubble of gas according to Gibbs, the furnaces pouring metal—these are linked" (WG, 368). The chapter does not yield its theme as readily as my description would indicate, nor is that theme quite so simple. Complicating the theme are the many pathways Rukeyser's prose takes in approaching it. One can outline this chapter only in the most general way.

Nevertheless the meaning declares itself. Surprisingly, that meaning was lost on the humanist Krutch, largely because he so disliked her style, which he called "rhapsody" and "mystical rhetoric." The meaning was also lost on a number of reviewers in academic and scientific journals. Ralph Gabriel in the *American Historical Re-*

---

21. Krutch, review of WG.

view said that she should have mentioned more of Gibbs's contemporaries: "The book, when the American background is considered, is a dazzling façade concealing a lack of substance within. . . . Why the author omitted from the list of Gibbs's great creative contemporaries Winslow Homer, John La Farge, and Louis Sullivan is unexplained: They are no more irrelevant than Melville and Whitman." But the very point Rukeyser makes in her reference to the historical context of Gibbs's work is that those whom we now recognize as having achieved the greatest triumphs in the arts and sciences were not recognized in their day by society at large. Gibbs, Whitman, and Melville worked on levels of imagination which were not appreciated by their contemporaries; Homer, Sullivan, and La Farge were successful popular artists whose achievements, though admirable, are simply not on the same level as those of the "Three Masters." Gabriel nonetheless praises Rukeyser for taking up the subject of Gibbs and chiding students of history for ignoring him. "She has swept their alibis aside by reminding them of the ultimate unity in the creative imagination of science and the humanities." [22]

A reviewer in the *Journal of Chemical Education*, praising *Willard Gibbs* for its "intimate and detailed picture of the life of two generations of professors at Yale in the 19th century," nevertheless added, "Readers who are accustomed to technical accuracy and complete sentences will not enjoy Miss Rukeyser's repetitious style, fragmentary sentences, and round-robin chapters." The reviewer also complained of "extraneous material" in the book. Charles A. Kraus, writing in the *Journal of the American Chemical Society*, wrote that since Gibbs left few writings and dealt with science in one of its most abstract forms, it is "not surprising that Miss Rukeyser has produced a biography that will fail of commendation from many of the scientific fraternity." Her style, he said, "borders on the cryptic"; she includes much useful and interesting material, but this is interspersed with irrelevant material. (Kraus doesn't specify.) Missing Rukeyser's central theme, Kraus continues, "Science is as

22. Ralph Gabriel, review of WG, in *American Historical Review*, XLVIII (July, 1943), 750.

little interested in applications as is poetry or art—perhaps even less so. . . . Miss Rukeyser, in interpreting Gibbs' work from the point of view of its practical application misleads the reader into thinking that the value of Gibbs' contributions to science is to be measured by the material benefits that may have accrued to industry as a result of their practical applications. Nothing could be further from the truth. Miss Rukeyser has failed to realize that science, while it deals with material things, is the product of the mind seeking the truth without regard to any possible material benefits." But this is exactly what the poet found so great in the withdrawn, singleminded scientist! Her account of the applications of Gibbs's theories is only one part of her book.

Kraus makes some mention, as do other reviewers in scientific journals, of the technical inaccuracies in *Willard Gibbs*. Yet the inaccuracies in the 465-page biography are remarkably few. One error is funny: Rukeyser in commenting on the incredibly difficult notebooks Gibbs kept in Berlin confuses the physicist Beer with the beverage. Kraus comments, "One minor error . . . brings to light the fundamental weakness underlying the whole of the present biography, namely, the lack of familiarity on the part of the author with the subject with which she is dealing." Kraus's conclusion is most unscientific, for the error, he admits, is minor. But his attitude is most revealing: no matter how hard a poet labors to become familiar with the work of a difficult scientist—and her book is proof of this labor—she will never succeed in achieving enough "familiarity" to make valid statements. For "familiarity," to Kraus, is the dialect one learns in achieving membership in what he called "the scientific fraternity." [23] Reading the judgments of *Willard Gibbs* by scientific

23. Elbert C. Weaver, review of WG, in *Journal of Chemical Education*, XX (1943), 259–60; Charles A. Kraus, review of WG, in *Journal of the American Chemical Society*, LXV (December, 1943), 2475–76; Rukeyser had hoped that Albert Einstein would write a preface to her book. She wrote him asking that he lend his name to her effort to make Gibbs known to a time that needed the story of his achievement. Einstein saw only the negative prospects of Rukeyser's undertaking. Without reading her book, he refused, answering:

In my view there is but one way to bring a great scientist to the attention of the larger public: it is to discuss and explain, in language which will be generally understood, the problems and the solutions which have characterized his life-work. This can and academic reviewers makes one marvel all the more at Rukeyser's sheer courage in undertaking the book. "Courage" is a word she disallows in discussions of her biographies, however. "They became obsessive hunts," she has said. She wrote them because she needed to explore, to relate.

John Johnston in *Chemical and Engineering News* described the book as Van-Wyck-Brooks-like in its portraits of Gibbs's contemporaries. But the reviewer said there is no reason to believe Gibbs's thinking was in any way influenced by these contemporaries, so he advised "judicious skipping," especially in the first fifth of the book, by readers willing to distinguish factual from imaginative truth. Johnston found many pages in *Willard Gibbs* unrelated to Gibbs and his achievements. The inability of some readers to see Rukeyser's effort at linking imaginative achievements is proof of her point that our education has made us narrow and specialized.[24]

In 1952 Lynde Phelps Wheeler published a biography authorized by Gibbs's surviving family who, Wheeler says in the preface, "were concerned about the scarcity of available biographical material of a personal nature, and about the use which had been made in recently published biographies of such as did exist." The book also boasted the authorization of publication by Yale University on the occasion of its 250th anniversary. Wheeler was a former pupil of Gibbs as well as a former professor of physics at Yale. The indirect reference from his preface and one other reference in the body of the book are all the mention Wheeler makes of Rukeyser's groundbreaking work. Her name appears only in a footnote and in the index. The remark in Wheeler's text incorrectly states that she contrasted the "sparkling clarity" of Maxwell's style to that of

---

only be done by someone who has a fundamental grasp of the material. . . . Otherwise, the result is a banal hero-worship, based on emotion and not on insight. I have learned by my own experience how hateful and ridiculous it is, when a serious man, absorbed in important endeavours, is ignorantly lionized.
(The letter from Einstein is from the Rukeyser correspondence in the Berg Collection of the New York Public Library.)

24. John Johnston, review of WG, in *Chemical and Engineering News*, XXI (March 10, 1943), 342.

Gibbs, "a comparison which seems to me to reveal a fundamental ignorance of the styles of both masters." [25] (Rukeyser's comment about Maxwell's "clarity" is not part of a comparison of the styles of the two scientists. Throughout her book, in fact, she praises the beautiful austerity of Gibbs's formulations.) Fundamental ignorance: that, according to Wheeler, is all he need note of Rukeyser's pioneering study that opened the paths for understanding of the still too slightly known Willard Gibbs, but, alas, Wheeler's attitude is again proof that knowledge has been compartmentalized.

Cyril Stanley Smith has offered an overview of the reaction of scientists to *Willard Gibbs*.

You ask about scientists' views on *Willard Gibbs*. Frankly, most of them think that it is not the biography of a scientist. For all of its studies of incoming and outreaching influences, it fails to catch the intellectual experience of the scientist in finding and clarifying his problems and it doesn't distinguish between the moments of insight and the hard work of verification and transmission. On the whole, though I have often argued in favor of the book, I think these criticisms are justified. It does not reflect what scientists like to think a scientist's life should be, or the aspects of which they are the most proud and which they most value in their peers. . . . But Muriel Rukeyser was the first to study both Gibbs and Harriot in depth and she deserves great credit for seeing their significance. It takes the imagination of a scientist or a poet to see this at first. . . . Her work needs to be supplemented by more critical biographies . . . with emphasis placed upon their work as scientists and on the demonstrable influence of their ideas. Both men should be *far* better known than they are.[26]

Martin J. Klein of Yale in the *Dictionary of Scientific Biography* calls Rukeyser's book a "popularly written biography, valuable for period background and a poet's insight." [27]

The *Partisan Review* in its "Poster Girl" piece saw neither humanistic nor scientific value in Rukeyser's book, but among those who were moved by the spirit of the book and fascinated by its in-

25. Lynde Phelps Wheeler, *Josiah Willard Gibbs* (New Haven, 1952), Preface, 5, 95; review of *Josiah Willard Gibbs* in New York *Herald Tribune*, March 25, 1951, p. 13.
26. From the letter of Cyril Stanley Smith to the author.
27. Martin J. Klein, "Willard Gibbs," *Dictionary of Scientific Biography* (New York, 1970–76).

sights were F. S. C. Northrop, who wrote, "There is hope for our culture. At least one humanist believes that it is necessary to understand the scientist." He praised Rukeyser's attempt to try to heal the eighteenth-century separation between natural science and values. He concluded that her book prepares the way for the integration of natural philosophy and moral philosophy, aesthetics and mathematical physics "essential if the technological forces released by modern science are to be brought again under the control of man's humane ideals." John Chamberlain in the New York *Times* found the book impressive "on its five or six levels": "a cultural history of America, an essay on the historical impact of energy, a study of the nature of freedom, a history of old New Haven, and a biography of a scientist." Waldemar Kaempffert also in the New York *Times* found it "excellent biography" and John G. Kirkwood in the *Yale Review* found it "brilliant and significant biography." Henry Nash Smith in the *New England Quarterly* said "Miss Rukeyser's method . . . seizes upon the only form of expression that is at all likely to prove able to impose unity on such varied materials as Melville's tragic sense and the physicist's concern with mathematical descriptions of the habits of matter." Smith said, however, that her effort is "only partially successful" because she doesn't really explain Gibbs's thought, which ultimately has to be "taken on faith"—on the testimony of scientists who can really understand his "austere language." But descriptions of Gibbs's thought are apparently inadequate, as are paraphrases of poems. Northrop said, "One has only to read the many accounts of Gibbs's work written in ordinary language by scientists . . . to realize that they talk about Gibbs's achievements rather than convey precisely what they are." And Jonathan Leonard, reviewing Wheeler's book in the New York *Times* said, "Mr. Wheeler tries manfully to explain Gibbs's theories to the reader, but he does not succeed very well. The subject is too difficult, too mathematical, too remote from the layman's experience." [28]

28. F. S. C. Northrop, "A Poet Discovers the Mathematical Physicist," review of WG, in *Saturday Review*, December 5, 1942, p. 10; John Chamberlain, review of WG, in New York *Times*, November 24, 1942, p. 23; Waldemar Kaempffert, review of WG, in *New York*

Henry Nash Smith complained about the unsatisfactoriness of the book as a whole due to the "cosmic emotion which tempts her to strain language beyond ordinary limits of expository prose. The effect aimed at would have been described in an earlier age as sublimity—and sublimity has always been notoriously dangerous." *Time* also found the book "frequently verging on the apocalyptical in language" and "perfervid," though a wonderful "*Moby Dick* of a book in intention and intimations, touching on 'the sum of things.' " Alfred Kazin in the *New Republic* caught Rukeyser's spirit and in a piece entitled "Another Ancestor" called the book a "long and sometimes agonized hymn . . . an effort at the recovery of one of the most extraordinary achievements . . . of the human imagination . . . recovery of our American pride, of still another phase of our growing American self-knowledge and celebration." Kazin also saw in *Willard Gibbs* "a study in our contemporary sense of loss. . . . Living under the star of the disintegrators and the specialists, the little men with their half knowledge [we seek the] comprehensive men, the structural men, and the consecrated men" of the past with their "joy of fulfillment." And Kazin aptly characterized Rukeyser's prose: "It is this overpowering sense of Gibbs's greatness, and of a proper homage before it, that gives Miss Rukeyser's book so passionate and disturbed a life of its own. We have entered into a sphere in which only Carlyle's swooning language before heroes and Carlyle's exultation in them, seem enough for us." [29]

Clifton Fadiman in the *New Yorker* said, "At times she ascends into a mystical heaven where her syntax and your correspondent desert her simultaneously, but for the most part she writes with extraordinary brilliance and passion." Fadiman concluded, "If the Pulitzer Prize Committee judges overlook it, they may comfort themselves with the assurance that they are firmly in that tradition

Times Book Review, December 13, 1942, p. 3; John G. Kirkwood, review of WG, in *Yale Review*, n.s. XXXII (Spring, 1943), 579; Henry Nash Smith, review of WG, in *New England Quarterly*, XVI (September, 1943), 525; Jonathan Leonard, review of *Josiah Willard Gibbs*, in *New York Times Book Review*, April 8, 1951, p. 6.

29. Smith, review of WG; review of WG in *Time*, January 4, 1943, p. 90; Alfred Kazin, "Another Ancestor," *New Republic*, December 7, 1942, p. 752.

of our higher learning which for so many years overlooked the greatest intellect of our country's history, the towering one of Willard Gibbs." Bernard Jaffe said that "her poetic sensitivity expresses itself at times in thoughts not easy to comprehend." But Jaffe found "no harm" in this, quoting the scientist and musician J. W. N. Sullivan: "'It is the scientific man, not the poet, who is the dweller in dreamland.'" Jaffe said that her linkage of Gibbs with his great contemporaries will add to our understanding of the cultural history of America as did Vernon Parrington's seminal *Main Currents in American Thought*.[30]

Philip Blair Rice in the *Kenyon Review* deplored those reviews of the book which were superficially negative, trivial, and malicious: "Both before and after writing this book, Miss Rukeyser has received for her intrepidity a number of slaps on the wrist—and even, from a particularly malicious reviewer, one in the face." Rice found that "within the limitations of one who is not a physicist and who was not granted access to all the personal documents, she has done a thorough as well as an honest job." Rice complained of "the inflatedness [of the style] for which Van Wyck Brooks has set the recent mode in writing about an expansive age. Miss Rukeyser's categories are sometimes fuzzy and her conclusions oracular." But Rice concluded that Rukeyser "is almost unique among our poets in her intellectual inquisitiveness . . . *Willard Gibbs* shows her desire to see all around the objects of her interest." Rice reminds us that she went to aviation school before publishing *Theory of Flight* and she made a firsthand investigation of the scene for *U.S.1*. Eunice Clark in *Common Sense* also saw *Willard Gibbs* in the light of all of Rukeyser's books: "the drive of all her work—to absorb in her own mind America's full spiritual ancestry—flowers in this life of Gibbs." Clark found a "wealth of poetry and scholarship" in the book. She said, "The academic scientists will doubtless ignore it or attack it as

30. Clifton Fadiman, review of WG, in *New Yorker*, November 7, 1942, p. 67; Bernard Jaffe, review of WG.

an essay on Gibbs," but she found it a "successful effort to bring Gibbs to the lay consciousness."[31]

In 1949 in an article in *Physics Today* Rukeyser explained again why she undertook a book on Gibbs. This explanation constitutes a defense of her work against the criticism of those who said that her book lacked proper credentials or proceeded in an improper style.

It is because he dealt in law and in relationships that one may come to him from any point of interest, however inadequate one's background be. I came to him through poetry, without any of the proper training, feeling that in this time, full of its silence in spite of the weight of paper and the weight of words poured on us every day, full of its barriers set up between the peoples of the world and any two people—in this time our sources are to be reached. It seems to me that if we are in any way free, we are also free in relation to the past, and that we may to some extent choose our tradition. . . .We see that the barriers which have been erected between 'field' and 'field,' between people and people, are artificial. If we believe in the unity of man, if we believe in the unity of nature, if we believe in the unity of knowledge, then we believe also in the unity of imagination.

The method of science approaches the method of poetry. As Epicurus and Lucretius, scientist and poet of the sum of things, match each other, the workers in systems—in poetry and in science—approach and touch. Poets and scientists give themselves closely to the creation and description of systems. To the poet, his own nature is his chief instrument; the nature of the physical scientist is apart, he deals with a world of law in which there is no understanding. The world of the poet, however, is the scientist's world. Their claim on systems is the same claim. And as the Englishman, looking for explosives, came to Gibbs; as the American, looking for democracy, came to Gibbs; as many, looking for the nature of relationship came, I came; first through a poem, and later to an inquiry into the life of this quiet man, living without spectacle and without experiment, making discoveries.[32]

The first critical article on *Willard Gibbs* and *The Traces of Thomas Hariot* together, "Muriel Rukeyser: The Poet as Scientific

31. Philip Blair Rice, review of WG, in *Kenyon Review*, V (1943), 310–12; Eunice Clark, review of WG, in *Common Sense* XII (January, 1943), 461.
32 . Muriel Rukeyser, "Josiah Willard Gibbs," *Physics Today*, II (February, 1949), 7–8.

Biographer" by Professor Clive Bush of Warwick University, appeared in 1977. Bush praises Rukeyser's life work in the "tradition of creative risk and axiom-breaking" and points out that "in recent years these possibilities [of transcending specialization] have come strikingly to the front as the volume of inter-disciplinary work grows. In such collections of essays as Kepes' *Structure in Art and Science* (1965) and in Gene Youngblood's *Expanded Cinema* (1970), the Korsybskian vision of non-Aristotelian structure and the rejection of dialectic and lineality are taken for granted." Bush's article concludes:

> Robert Duncan's claim for himself, "I am not an occultist or a mystic but a poet, a maker up of things," describes exactly Muriel Rukeyser's own achievement. Her connections are made with the exactness of poetic making. These two works, spanning a writing career of many years are the result of a characteristically American devotion to experimentation, with judgements repeatedly risked and inheritances continuously questioned. Purely as an academic achievement these two books are outstanding, but they are in fact creative works of art in their own right. What Paul Metcalf said of his own work of creative history, *Genoa* (1965) applies here and it explains the direction the greatest American art has had from the beginning: "The reach is from Homer to a recent newspaper—the time-flow broken, the elements handled separately, impinging directly on one another: history emphatic in its bearing upon the only time it may have bearing, *the present.* . . . Again, history is available to us both as genealogy, and in 'free use': in the grab bag of history, we may (and do) select our own ancestors." With Willard Gibbs and Thomas Hariot, Muriel Rukeyser has made her own ancestors and in so doing created a highly original American art.[33]

Beast in View

The "beast" in Rukeyser's fourth book of poems, *Beast in View* (1944), is her deepest self, which she also calls in this volume her "myth" or the vital pattern of her being. That myth is fluid—the "language of water," which is the language of transformation she

33. Clive Bush, "Muriel Rukeyser: The Poet as Scientific Biographer," *Spanner* 11, II (July, 1977).

learned in a new way from Gibbs (she knew it before—we see it in the transformations, the "moving past impossibilities" of the elegies and "Theory of Flight.")[34] In *Beast in View* more than ever transformation is in the movement of her verse and in its imagery. The myth of herself—that beast—is that movement. The image of the beast appears in "First Elegy" as "the black-haired beast with my eyes walking beside me" and as "what must be stood beside and straightly seen" (TW, 15–16). She has sought to assume this beast before, to make "it" one with herself. Until she does, she is not whole. Thus in this collection the voyage of the unfinished spirit (a voyage of transformation) of the elegies continues not only in the three new elegies printed here but in the other poems as well. The poems in this volume pursue the realization of *A Turning Wind* that her personal struggles mirror those of the world in the middle of the twentieth century. Therefore in seeking to reach herself, her "beast," she will know that tormented world even better and she will know too what are its desires and its possibilities of deliverance. There are poems in this volume which again re-imagine the experience of Spain and what that country's struggle meant to the history of our own conflicts and losses. There are poems which present again the tortured images of the defeat of social ideals. And there are visions of transformation and fulfillment.

Rukeyser' book is notably different in scope, content, and style from the book of poems which received the Pulitzer Prize for poetry published in 1944, *V-Letter* by Karl Shapiro.[35] In the introduction to that volume Shapiro says, "Certainly our contemporary man should feel divested of the stock attitudes of the last generation, the stance of the political intellectual, the proletarian, the expert, the salesman, the world-traveler, the pundit-poet." Rukeyser could not divest herself of what Shapiro calls these "stances" because she was in fact an intellectual of the broadest order (*Willard Gibbs*), a radical democrat (associated with the "proletarians"), a world traveler who had vividly recorded her response to the United States, England, Spain,

34. "Craft Interview with Muriel Rukeyser," 170.
35. Karl Shapiro, *V-Letter and Other Poems* (New York, 1944).

and Mexico, and a teacher-poet who freely and passionately offered her insights into what she held to be the function of poetry in her time. Significantly, all these profoundly chosen human positions can only be "stances" and "stock attitudes" to Shapiro.

Beast in View begins with "One Soldier," a poem placed before the table of contents. The poem sets the theme of the volume.

> When I think of him, midnight
> Opens about me, and I am more alone;
> But then the poems flower from the bone.—
>
> You came to me bearing the truth in your two hands;
> I sit and look down at my hand like an astonished
> Fortune-teller, seeing the mortal flesh.
>
> Your wish was strong the first day of the war
> For it had been strong before, and then we knew
> All that I had to be, you had to do.
>
> Once when you stood before me, kisses rose
> About my lips; poems at my lips rise,
> Your live belief fills midnight and my eyes.

Beast in View is a phase of her lifelong response to the love she knew in Spain (for Otto Boch) and to the personal and social ideals consecrated by that love. The poems that follow "One Soldier" are struggles to allow that "live belief" to "flower" into poems to light the midnight of war and loss with hope and with prophecy of transformation and deliverance. ("The Soul and Body of John Brown," that great transformation, is in this volume.) The poet's hopes and ideals are larger than life, than individual lives, for she identifies with the struggle of humankind.

Compare the hopes and wishes expressed by Shapiro in the last two stanzas of "V-Letter":

> Give me the free and poor inheritance
>   Of our own kind, not furniture
> Of education, nor the prophet's pose,
> The general cause of words, the hero's stance,
> The ambitions incommensurable with flesh,
>   But the drab makings of a room
> Where sometimes in the afternoon of thought

> The brief and blinding flash
> May light the enormous chambers of your will
> And show the gracious Parthenon that time
>   Is ever measured by.
>
> As groceries in a pantry gleam and smile
>   Because they are important weights
> Bought with the metal minutes of your pay,
> So do these hours stand in solid rows,
> The dowry for a use in common life
>   I love you first because your years
> Lead to my matter-of-fact and simple death
>   Or to our open marriage,
> And I pray nothing for my safety back,
> Not even luck, because our love is whole
>   Whether I live or fail.

In Shapiro's moving and beautiful lines we have the characteristically private poetry of the forties, the reduced hopes, the concentration on the immediate, nuclear relationship. (Recall the walls falling down around isolated lovers in Rukeyser's poetry of the thirties.) We have in Shapiro's lines, too, an explicit rejection of those ideals that Rukeyser and other poets celebrated in poetry called "proletarian" or, in disparagement, "neo-American inspirational," poetry such as "Theory of Flight," or "Gibbs," "Ryder," and "Ives": Shapiro wants no heroic ambitions, "ambitions incommensurable with flesh."

In *Beast in View* Rukeyser published a ten-poem sequence entitled "Letter to the Front." The first poem of the sequence describes poetry as prophecy and insists that the war is being fought for meanings that are muffled in ordinary life and finally lost even to the fighting men.

> Women and poets see the truth arrive.
> Then it is acted out,
> The lives are lost, and all the newsboys shout.
>
> . . . .
>
> All the strong agonized men
> Wear the hard clothes of war,
> Try to remember what they are fighting for.

> But in dark weeping helpless moments of peace
> Women and poets believe and resist forever:
> The blind inventor finds the underground river.

Throughout the sequence there is strong belief in goodness and peace, and there is the poet's prophecy, that is, her imagining of transformation and peace, "our dear wish." In the fourth poem of the sequence, a villanelle, she gives us an account of her witnessing the first day of fighting in Spain, "the soul's country." In a binding to the poems of *U.S.1*, she calls the struggle in Spain "The war this age must win in love and fighting." The poem that follows, the fifth in the sequence, is a dream-vision of "all the people at all the rails," lifting their hands "in a gesture of belief."

The seventh poem, a sonnet, is a striking acceptance of the meanings of the war and an affirmation, as in "Theory of Flight," that deep yearnings of the human spirit shall be fulfilled. The poem has been included in the Reform Jewish prayerbook, *The Service of the Heart*:

> To be a Jew in the twentieth century
> Is to be offered a gift. If you refuse,
> Wishing to be invisible, you choose
> Death of the spirit, the stone insanity.
> Accepting, take full life. Full agonies:
> Your evening deep in labyrinthine blood
> Of those who resist, fail, and resist: and God
> Reduced to a hostage among hostages.
>
> The gift is torment. Not alone the still
> Torture, isolation; or torture of the flesh.
> That may come also. But the accepting wish,
> The whole and fertile spirit as guarantee
> For every human freedom, suffering to be free,
> Daring to live for the impossible.

Rukeyser can say "Daring to live for the impossible"; Shapiro, one recalls, wants no "ambitions incommensurable with flesh." Rosenthal argued in his article of 1953 that Rukeyser's affirmations were like those of "many poets [who] are under a similar compulsion to force resolution by willful assertion." [36] The poet's positive statements in these poems are indeed "willful assertions," but in Rukeyser's poetic vision she finds the seeds of possibility in the darkest human situations, and she asserts that possibility. Whether the poems "satisfy" a reader in a disenchanted time is, I suspect, dependent on the reader's temperament, on how much of Rukeyser's poetry that reader has experienced, and on how much the reader is willing to admit that such a poetry is genuine in a period when most poetic sensibilities are tuned just the opposite from Rukeyser's. I think her poetry of the forties can be better received for what it is now that the new critical standards, with their emphasis on irony, are no longer unchallenged. For example, Robert Merideth, in a 1976 article on the poet John Beecher in the *American Poetry Review*, contrasts his "public, powerfully prophetic" poetry with the "self-destructive and diminishing ironies" of other contemporary poets.[37]

In the eighth poem of the sequence the poet deplores, as she has in other poems and in prose, these diminishing ironies, the narrowing of human goals, the cynical avoidance of the larger meanings of the war, as in the man

> who said of our time which has only its freedom,
> "I will not ever say 'for a free world,'
> 'A better world,' or whatever it is;
> A man fights to win a war,
> To hang on to what is his—"

Such words and motives are inadequate to Rukeyser. "The man of strong belief," she feels, is not enough supported and valued in our time.

"Letter to the Front," like many poems in *Beast in View*, develops a theme which is rare in modern poetry, a theme which feminists of the sixties and seventies rediscovered and popularized. In the first poem of the sequence "women and poets," those whose vi-

---

36. Rosenthal, "The Longer Poems," 226.
37. Robert Merideth, "Homage to a Subversive: Notes Toward Explaining John Beecher," *American Poetry Review*, V (May–June, 1976), 45–46.

sion is uncorrupted by the "male" goals of success and power, can allow themselves "dark weeping helpless moments of peace." Then they see the truth that men, trying to be hard and strong, cannot see. There is pity and love in the poem for "the strong agonized men" who must fight even though they have never been allowed the luxury of knowing the "underground river" of their emotions. In the ninth poem soldiers coming home are faced with the old requirement of hardness, of suppression; this requirement is more difficult than ever, for the soldiers have experienced what women and poets know:

> Among all the waste there are the intense stories
> And tellers of stories. One saw a peasant die.
> One guarded a soldier through disease. And one
> Saw all the women look at each other in hope.
> And came back, saying, "All things must be known."
>
> They come home to the rat-faced investigator
> Who sneers and asks, "Who is your favorite poet?"
> Voices of scissors and grinders asking their questions:
> "How did you ever happen to be against fascism?"
> And they remember the general's white hair,
> The food-administrator, alone and full of tears.

The soldiers come home and find women and children who understand more than the men who run the country.

> The cities and women cry in a frightful voice,
> "I care not who makes the laws, let me make the sons."
> But look at their eyes, like drinking animals'
> Full of assurance and flowing with reward.
> The seeds of answering are in their voice.
> The spirit lives, against the time's disease.
> You little children, come down out of your mothers
> And tell us about peace.

The poet changes rhythm now, praising her own sex, but cautioning too in an ancient sing-song that the strain placed on womanhood by war and the suppression of the meanings of the war are destructive.

> I hear the singing of the lives of women,
> The clear mystery, the offering and pride.

But here also the orange lights of a bar, and an
Old biddy singing inside:
    Rain and tomorrow more
    They say there will be rain
    They lean together and tell
    The sorrow of the loin.

The last poem of the sequence affirms the healing that women
may offer the world.

Surely it is time for the true grace of women
Emerging, in their lives' colors, from the rooms, from the
    harvests,
From the delicate prisons, to speak their promises.
The spirit's dreaming delight and the fluid senses'
Involvement in the world. Surely the day's beginning
In midnight, in time of war, flickers upon the wind.

She has a vision of "the future shining / In far countries" and suddenly flashing now, "at home," in womanhood—"In music freeing
a new myth among the male / Steep landscapes." The new myth, the
diffusion of women's vision, is the earth saying to "traditional
man,"

. . . "Come here, come to me.
Here are your children." Not as traditional man
But love's great insight—"your children and your song."

This letter to the front, then, is the poet's strong prophetic imagining
of a new ground of world peace and love: the androgynous spirit.
Adrienne Rich will write of it in her poetry of the seventies. For
Rich, "a world masculinity made / [is] unfit for women or men."
That world suppresses relationship, the awareness of the larger effects of individual success and power, the spill of sympathy for fellow human beings. That world insists that men be hard. It is not
that Rukeyser or Rich wants an unreasoning world. In *Toward a
Recognition of Androgyny*, Carolyn Heilbrun argued that "the fusion within the Bloomsbury group, perhaps for the first time, of
'masculinity' and 'femininity' made possible the ascendancy of reason

which excludes violence but not passion." [38] So would the world Rukeyser imagines in "Letter to the Front," a world in which men and women can allow their "spirit's dreaming delight." The poet "sends" this letter to those fighting, "for a beginning," for as she says in her concluding lines, after having envisioned a world where "the true grace of women" transforms "traditional man": "Nothing has been begun." This poem, "offered in time of war," is a beginning.

R. P. Blackmur, a respected New Critic, said in a review of *Beast in View* and other volumes that "Miss Rukeyser is confused about sex. . . . It may be thrown out for what it is worth that sex seems to be the source of what organization there is in Miss Rukeyser's poems, but that until she decides whether sex is predominantly a force or a sentiment, her poems and her readers' response to them will be left at a loss." [39] For Rukeyser sex is a force, one which may be used to expand the personality and to touch others; it may also be constricted to ends of pleasure and violence alone: "hard" men become blind sexual and social aggressors. Sex, to the poet, is thus a force which is directed according to one's attitude or "sentiment." To say that sex is either a force *or* a sentiment is to fail to see the possibility of androgyny (or of any direction or education of the force of sex) and therefore the vision of much of Rukeyser's poetry in *Beast in View* and in her later volumes. Blackmur saw sex as "the source of what organization there is" in Rukeyser's poems; he felt her poems to be essentially loose and disorganized. It is unfortunate that he did not pursue his notion of sex (physical rhythm, impulse to union) as organizing form.

Although many New Critics found Whitman completely "amorphous" and thus weak, Rukeyser praised Whitman's line and found in him the essence of poetry: "His readers reacted violently from the beginning to his writing about sex—and of course it is not writing *about* sex, it is that physical rhythms are the base of every clear

38. See Adrienne Rich, "The Stranger," "Merced," in *Diving into the Wreck* (New York, 1973); Carolyn G. Heilbrun, *Toward a Recognition of Androgyny* (New York, 1973), 126.

39. R. P. Blackmur, *Language as Gesture* (New York, 1952), 360–62. This review of *Beast in View* originally appeared in *Kenyon Review*, VII (1945), 339. Blackmur is apparently referring to Henry Adams' distinction between sex as "force" and "sentiment" in "The Dynamo and the Virgin," Chapter 25 of *The Education of Henry Adams*. According to Adams, only Walt Whitman among American artists "had ever insisted on the power of sex. . . . All the rest had used sex for sentiment, never for force."

line. . . . He remembered his body as other poets of his time remembered English verse. . . . He cannot be imitated . . . but what is always possible is to go deeper into one's own sources, the body and the ancient religious poetry, and go on with the work he began" (LP, 75–82). To Blackmur, the "escaping" of the strength of physical rhythms into poetry (along with what the reader senses as the poet's whole personality's corresponding impulse to union) is not as strong as the chosen control of traditional prosodic form. But one can admit both kinds of strength. Physical rhythms are the perfect rhythms for a philosophy of possibility and a poetic method which values "recurrence" and "binding."

In one of her most famous poems, "Ajanta," named after the caves of India, she journeys into herself and finds a place where in the midst of the frustrations, annihilations, and disconnections of war she experiences a sense of the unity of life and particularly of her own life in its transformations. When she reaches this place in herself, "this cave where the myth enters the heart again," she possesses the world at its most fulfilling, in a union which transcends the sexual but which can best be rendered in physical rhythms and images.

> The space of these walls is the body's living space;
> Tear open your ribs and breathe the color of time
> Where nothing leads away, the world comes forward
> In flaming sequences.
>
> . . . .
> The spaces of the body
> Are suddenly limitless, and riding flesh
> Shapes constellations over the golden breast,
> Confusion of scents and illuminated touch—
> Monster touch, the throat printed with brightness,
> Wide outlined gesture where the bodies ride.
> Bells, and the spirit flashing. The religious bells,
> Bronze under the sunlight like breasts ringing,
> Bronze in the closed air, the memory of walls,
> Great sensual shoulders in the web of time.

In the poem, as in the rhythms of life, the poet knows frustration again, after this vision of fulfillment. It is the frustration of love interrupted by death; she remembers the love she lost in the war. Unlike in other poems, the loss of that love is now more vivid to her

than the love itself. That loss makes physical desire absurd and re-
pulsive to her.

> You touched my life.
> My life reaches the skin, moves under your smile,
> And your throat and your shoulders and your face and your
>   thighs
> Flash.
>   I am haunted by interrupted acts,
> Introspective as a leper, enchanted
> By a repulsive clew,
> A gross and fugitive movement of the limbs.
> Is this the love that shook the lights to flame?
> Sheeted avenues thrash in the wind,
> Torn streets, the savage parks.
> I am plunged deep. Must find the midnight cave.

She does find her way to the cave again, to her inmost self, even to
the androgynous vision.

> The shoulders turn and every gift is made.
> No shadows fall. There is no source of distortion.
> In our world, a tree casts the shadow of a woman,
> A man the shadow of a phallus, a hand raised
> The shadow of the whip.
> Here everything is itself,
> Here all may stand
> On summer earth.

This is perhaps her most successful imagining of human fulfillment
since the passages in "Theory of Flight," whose analogies are the
flight of the spirit.

The poems which follow "Ajanta" in this first section of *Beast in
View* are a record of the gains and losses in the poet's pursuit of her
beast, of the vision of fulfillment which comes from self-possession,
as in "Ajanta." "Mortal Girl" is a version of the myth of the mortal
woman ravished by a god. This girl's desire, in her contact with the
god, is not for divinity but for a more intense human life. If she
wishes to know the superhuman, it is only to be more herself. There
are poems in *Beast in View* which, individually, do not arrive at
resolution or hope: "Madboy's Song," "The Minotaur," and "Holy
Family." But most of the poems in the first section progress through

images of horror and loss to a realization of the speaker's own strength and hope in human beings in their brave mortal struggles. Typical of this progress is the short poem "Who in One Lifetime," dated 1941:

> Who in one lifetime sees all causes lost,
> Herself dismayed and helpless, cities down,
> Love made monotonous fear and the sad-faced
> Inexorable armies and the falling plane,
> Has sickness, sickness. Introspective and whole,
> She knows how several madnesses are born,
> Seeing the integrated never fighting well,
> The flesh too vulnerable, the eyes tear-torn.
>
> She finds a pre-surrender on all sides:
> Treaty before the war, ritual impatience turn
> The camps of ambush to chambers of imagery.
> She holds belief in the world, she stays and hides
> Life in her own defeat, stands, though her whole world
> burn,
> A childless goddess of fertility.

It is rare to find a contemporary poet referring to herself as "whole" and "integrated." But essentially, so has Rukeyser been, though she has had to struggle for this wholeness because, as a fully responsive poet, she has been vulnerable, the eyes of her spirit "tear-torn."

In "Wreath of Women" the poet is again a praising, grateful goddess, "Mrs. Walpurga" who "moves / Among her fountains." Here Rukeyser acknowledges the personal inspiration of courageous women who refused "interminable girlhood" and chose "composite lives." Though the poem refers to "three such women," Rukeyser says she had four in mind: Rebecca Pitts, Carson McCullers, Marion Greenwood, and Katherine Anne Porter.

> Women who in my time
> Move toward a wider giving
> Than warm kitchen offering
> And warm steady living
> Know million ignorance
> Or petty village shame,
> And come to acknowledge the world
> As a world of common blame.

> Beyond the men of letters,
> Of business and of death,
> They draw a rarer breath,
> Have no career but choice.
> Choice is their image; they
> Choose the myth they obey.
>
> . . . .
>
> From three such women I
> Accepted gifts of life

The poet feels linked to these women in an "unbreakable wreath," and she offers its meanings to the reader.

> Old sorrows, old beginnings,
> Matured a summer wreath.
> I offer it to you.

The line length and the statement of "Gift Poem" resemble Auden's "September 1, 1939." Compare Auden's "I sit in one of the dives / On Fifty-second Street / Uncertain and afraid / As the clever hopes expire / Of a low dishonest decade" to the beginning of "Gift Poem":

> The year in its cold beginning
> Promises more than cold;
> The old contrary rhyming
> Will never again hold—
> The great moon in its timing
> Making the empty sky
> A continent of light
> Creates fine bombing weather
> Assures a safer flight

But Rukeyser breaks this rhythm with longer lines, and her statements, though abstract, are not cerebral like Auden's "Exiled Thucydides knew / All that a speech can say / About Democracy." Her developing theme in "Gift Poem" is that the horrors of this time cause a response in her that is more than "the mild ways of grief." The resolution of the poem affirms that a passionate response to the times will bring us through them. Rukeyser is more successful when she uses the longer line of the elegies or the short, broken rhythms of

"Breaking Open." Auden can frame an abstract statement almost epigrammatically; hers is a different gift, a poetic energy which requires something like the pulsing line she admires in Whitman.

The six poems on Mexico, beginning with "Chapultepec Park—I" focus again in rhythm and content on "the body's forms." In "Chapultepec Park—II" the speaker tells what draws her to Mexico City:

> The city of the heart
> Is like this city. Its names commemorate
> Beliefs and lovers, books and the body's forms.

"A Game of Ball" extends the forms of the body to those forms in which people play and thus learn to live gracefully and fearlessly in a terrifying world.

> But over the field flash all the colors of summer,
> The battle flickers in play, a game like sacrifice.
> The sun rides over, the moon and all her stars.
> Whatever is ready to eat us, we have found
> This place where the gods play out the games of the sky
> And bandy life and death across a summer ground.

"Gold Leaf" affirms that the real beauty of the world is not its decoration—"a mask of gold."

> You must go deeper to find the pure dark way
>
> . . . .
>
> Pain and the desperate music of the poor.
> The true darkness. A naked human door.

"All Souls" is the culmination of the poet's emphasis, in *Beast in View*, on the joy which is the mortal body. The scene is a graveyard in Mexico on All Souls' Day; families sit on the graves of their loved ones and eat the "feast of our mortality." In this culture there is no evasion of the meaning of death, as there is in our Halloween; therefore people share a heightened sense of life in the Mexican graveyards on All Souls' Day:

> The drink of flowers and fire in the sun,
> The child in pink holding her sugar skull—

> This appetite raving on death's high holiday:
> Love of the dead, fierce love of the alive.
> We eat the feast of our mortality,
> Drink fiery joy, and death sinks down with day.

Nevertheless the poet, in her holiday in this land which exults in the body and the senses, knows she has her work to do and she laments in the last poem on Mexico, "Evening Plaza, San Miguel":

> No one will know who in a strange land
> Has never stood while night came down
> In shadows of roses, a cloud of tree-drawn birds,
> And said, "I must go home."

"Beast in View" is the last poem in this first section, after the sensuous poems on Mexico and before "Letter to the Front." Here the poet, no longer on holiday, fixes the realization, in regular four-line stanzas and regular rhyme, that her task is to find herself, her form, as she said was Whitman's and every poet's task. "To discover his nature as a poet and to make his nature by knowing it is the task before every poet" (LP, 76). She knows her form will be determined by the love she has known which is still in her life "a vivid fountain." She knows her "myth" is her deepest self and that she does not hunt something apart from her own body's knowledge or her own transformations.

> I hunted and became the followed,
> Through many lives fleeing the last me,
> And changing fought down a far road
> Through time to myself as I will be.

In the elegies printed in *Beast in View* (six through nine) the poet is still seeking, as in the first five, the vision of wholeness she knew in her youth, especially in Spain. In these new elegies the search is described as a search for her own form which will reflect the world's. "Sixth Elegy; River Elegy" (dated Summer, 1940) begins with a turbulence of destructive images in which we recognize the dreadful events and forebodings of that time when totalitarian forces were building momentum in Europe. The poet, in all this, seeks the hopeful vision.

In burning summer I saw a season of betrayal,
the world fell away, and wasteful climbing green
covered the breaking of bodies, covered our hearts.
Unreal in the burning, many-motioned life
Lay like a sea, but fevers found my grief.
I turned in that year to retrieve the stainless river,
the lost, the flowing line of escaped music.

She sees that the state of the world and of men's spirits is reflected in
her own desolation; she sinks with others in her despondence. But
then she rises and can speak what she believes.

Let me tell you what I have meant all along:
Meaning of poetry and personal love,
a world of peace and freedom, man's need recognized,
and all the agonies that will begin that world.

It is the suffering mortal heart, again, that is the source of hope and
meaning, that floats the swimmer. The suffering heart calls to the
imagination to redeem the world.

Terror, war, terror, black blood and wasted love.
The most terrible country, in the heads of men.
This is the war imagination made;
it must be strong enough to make a peace.

. . . .
Only the meanings can remain alive

. . . .
There is no solution. There is no happiness.
Only the range must be taken, a way be found to use
the inmost frenzy and the outer doom.

Here she characteristically recognizes the full range of terrors of this
time; she will evade nothing. But she can still envision transformation and fulfillment in wresting form out of defeat.

Years of judgment! Century screaming for
the flowing, the life, the intellectual leap
of waters over a world grown old and wild,
a broken crying for seasonal change until
O God my love in time the waste become
the sure magnificent music of the defeated heart.

The poet says the defeated heart can make this "sure magnificent music" in dream, in imagination. The seventh elegy is the "Dream-Singing Elegy." Dreaming is "the bursting heart of wish." The abandoned heart can find strength in itself. Finally the dreaming of individuals serves to unite people, as in "The Soul and Body of John Brown."

> In the summer, dreaming was common to all of us,
> the drumbeat hope, the bursting heart of wish,
> music to bind us as the visions streamed
> and midnight brightened to belief.
> In the morning we told our dreams.
> They all were the same dream.

The vision at the end of this elegy is of a united humankind. "Eighth Elegy; Children's Elegy" describes the struggle for transformation in terms of the struggle of children orphaned in wartime to adjust to the world and to find love there. Like adults who suffer the defeat of their ideals in war, orphans have the same task:

> The children of the defeated, sparrow-poor and starved,
> create, create, must make their world again.
>
> . . . .
>
> "I search to learn the way out of childhood;
> I need to fight. I wish, I wish for home."

In the second part of the elegy the poet describes her own coming to consciousness, in childhood, of a war-torn world. She also became conscious, at the same time, of the power of love:

> Peace is asleep, war's lost. It is love.
> I wanted to die. The masked and the alone
> seemed the whole world, and all the gods at war,
> and all the people dead and depraved. Today
> the constellation and the music! Love.

At the end the poet reminds us that the images she creates are a reflection of the world and of others' experience of the world. She sees her "entire life as a procession of images" which are symbolic and are a human meeting place.

> You who seeking yourself arrive at these lines,

> look once, and you see the world,
> look twice and you see your self.

In "Ninth Elegy; The Antagonists," she writes of "a gallery of lives / fighting within me, and all unreconciled." This conflict in herself, she says, is the conflict of America, and we can learn from the country how to resolve our personal dualities. In powerful, driving verse the poet describes the conflicts, the diversities of America—in its physical shape, in the temperaments and goals of its leaders. In America, form develops out of conflict.

> The forms of incompleteness in our land
> pass from the eastern and western mountains where
> the seas meet the dark islands, where the light
> glitters white series on the snowlands, pours its wine
> of lenient evening to the center. Green
> on shadows of Indiana, level yellow miles . . .
> The prairie emblems and the slopes of the sky
> and desert stars enlarging in the frost
> redeem us like our love and will not die.
> All origins are here, and in this range
> the changing spirit can make itself again,
>
> . . . .
>
> and form developing
> American out of conflict.

In the bicentennial year, Anthony Lewis wrote a piece for the *New York Times Magazine* called "We Have Really Seen the Future and It Works." In it he reminded readers that the characteristic element in the American system is conflict. The framers of the Constitution intended to promote conflict within the powers of government, a "creative disorder" that would call up all of men's best energies at compromise (always with respect for the individual) and that would preclude autocracy.[40] In "The Antagonists," Rukeyser also sees the creative function of conflict, that it is a characteristically American phenomenon, that the intense individual can achieve self-fulfillment in attempts at reconciliation. "Create the creative, many-born! / And

40. Anthony Lewis, "We Have Really Seen the Future and It Works," *New York Times Magazine*, July 4, 1976, pp. 24–27.

use your love, unreconciled." As Americans, bound to defend liberty, we are plunged into the conflicts born of this war; but even now the creative spirit can grow. Thus Rukeyser's hopeful vision in this dark time springs from a deep insight into the nature of the free system in which we live, from a poetic contemplation of the physical face of America, and from that philosophical belief in dialectical growth through conflict first expressed in "Theory of Flight." In Rukeyser's very first poems, conflict is presented as a possible source of renewal. So is conflict seen in *Beast in View*, only here the agony of conflict has become more keenly identified with the poet's own life, with that "beast" which is alive and suffering in her "raw desire" for transformation, wholeness, and peace.

Several reviewers said they did not see this "beast" in any vivid way in *Beast in View*. The reviewer in the New York *Times* called Rukeyser's a public poetry (as opposed to Shapiro's private poetry). "She most conscientiously convolutes her imagery. . . . Miss Rukeyser remains curiously anonymous and her coils entangle and trip us up. They do not unwind to lead us anywhere." Ruth Lechlitner called *Beast in View* "a poetry of confusion in a confused world—a poetry which submits to that confusion—falls back upon the nonrational: the myth, the dream, the supernatural." Lechlitner said the poems are best when dealing with factual events "or experiences common to the majority of men and women today. Then she becomes positive, clear, coherent" as in "Letter to the Front," "The Soul and Body of John Brown," and "Ninth Elegy." This reviewer found invalid Rukeyser's attempt to view the public world in terms of the personal world but called *Beast in View* Rukeyser's most significant book in its attempt to resolve and affirm.[41]

Louise Bogan, complaining that Rukeyser made no attempt to rise above her time in *Beast in View*, said "I wish she'd write more clearly. Often I can't understand what she's talking about." F. W. Dupee, in the same review in which he praised the imagery of Rob-

41. F. C. Flint, review of BV, in *New York Times Book Review*, September 3, 1944, p. 4; Ruth Lechlitner, review of BV, in *New York Herald Tribune Book Review*, December 31, 1944, p. 4.

ert Penn Warren's *Selected Poems*, disparaged Rukeyser's. Dupee said that though Warren's stone and bone imagery doesn't always rise to poetic symbolism, it is "an exciting evidence of a genuine personal obsession. The images that clutter up the later verse of Muriel Rukeyser do not justify themselves even on grounds of a neurotic urgency. . . . [In *Beast in View*] I can discover no passion apart from a desire to publish more poetry. The titles and the 'myths' are her own and are very nice. The more essential materials of language, rhythm, and image are out of the stockroom. . . . On view is not a live beast but a dead pigeon."[42]

Oscar Williams called *Beast in View* her best book and "Ajanta" her finest poem. Noting that she sought form in the rest of the poems, in lyrics, sonnets, and elegies, Williams said that her folklore and imagery "strain these forms without allowing them properly to shape a complete poem." He found that her general fault is an overabundance of material. "In the midst of one poem she habitually begins another, and though practicing a perpetual literary sleight-of-hand, sometimes manages to cover a hatrack of form with a mammoth smothering wool comforter of vocabulary."[43] Rukeyser's struggle to allow form to grow from an abundance of observation and reflection is the hallmark of her poetry, as is the binding, which Williams called her beginning one poem in the midst of another. This "growth as form" (see the title of D'Arcy Wentworth Thompson's volume), a display of the artist's transformations, is Rukeyser's method, one she defended in her third and fifth elegies, one which parallels that of Whitman, and one which, as she learned from Gibbs, is the essence of the multiphasic universe.

The Green Wave

The Green Wave was published in 1948 to wide critical acclaim. If Rukeyser sought in *Beast in View* the transformations that would

---

42. Louise Bogan, review of BV, 91; F. W. Dupee, review of BV, in *Nation*, November 25, 1944, p. 662.
43. Oscar Williams, review of BV, in *New Republic*, October 23, 1944, p. 534.

win her a vision of wholeness and peace, she succeeded brilliantly. In this volume her "dear wish" has been realized. Here there is no more pursuit. She and the myth of transformation are one. She is borne by the surging wave of being. The epigraph says it well:

> Let poems and bodies love and be given to air,
> Earth having us real in her seasons, our fire and savor;
> And, reader, love well, imagine forward, for
> All of the testaments are in your favor.

Now, after her wish in the sixth and seventh elegies that the defeated heart make the magnificent music of dream, the heart does—in "Water Night":

> Sources and entrances, they lie no more,
> Now darkly keep, now flow now bright
>
> Until all wandering end, a hand
> Shine, and the leadings homeward of delight
>
> Seem to begin my deepest sleep
> To make a lake of dream.[44]

As with Thoreau returning from the village after dark, it is the night which has allowed the poet of *The Green Wave* to dream. The volume is full of the imagery of darkness, which paradoxically yields the blinding light of revelation. In "Gold Leaf" in *Beast in View* she expressed her realization that "Pain and the desperate music of the poor" are "the true darkness. A naked human door." In "All Souls" she went through that naked door and saw that we may "eat the feast of our mortality." She has learned to plunge eagerly into dark realizations because she knows that this is where she may find the seeds of light. In "Darkness Music" in *Beast in View* she saw the "wavering dawn" even in her "black altitudes." *The Green Wave*'s rich imagery of the dark is the first flowering of the gifts of darkness in this poet's work. "Eyes of Night-Time" shows a lush, sensuous awareness of those creatures that see in the night, the utter beauty of nature looking through the blackness, almost ecstatic wonder that human beings may also see in the night of the earth and

---

44. Muriel Rukeyser, *The Green Wave* (Garden City, New York, 1948).

of the spirit. As Francis B. McCarthy noted in his New York *Times* review, Rukeyser observes nature in a new way, offering minute detail:

> . . . spangles in the cat's, air in the moth's eye shine,
> mosaic of the fly, ruby-eyed beetle, the eyes that never weep,
> the horned toad sitting and its tear of blood,
> fighters and prisoners in the forest, people
> aware in this almost total dark
>
> . . . .
>
> And in our bodies the eyes of the dead and the living
> giving us gifts at hand, the glitter of all their eyes.

Passages like these are surely what prompted McCarthy to say of *The Green Wave*, "Every lyric has overtones of social meaning."[45]

Another poem which shows the poet's concentrated powers of observation and her newest, most versatile rhythms is "A Charm for Cantinflas." As in "Eyes of Night-Time" the poem makes larger statements on the human situation while piling up its rich physical detail.

> After the lights and after the rumba and after the bourbon
>   and after the beer
> and after the drums and after the samba and after the
>   ice cream and not long after
> failure, loss, despair, and loss and despair
> *There* was the laughter and there was Cantinflas at last
>   and his polka
>
> . . . .
>
> and on this stage always the clown of our living
> gives us our sunlight and our incantation
> as sun does, laughing, shining, reciting dawn, noon, and down,
> making all delight and healing all ills
> like faraway words on jars, the labels in Protopapas' window:
> marshmallow, myrtle, peppermint, pumpkin, sesame, sesame,
>   squills.

"Easter Eve 1945" is a resurrection poem, a coming through the darkness again. In the poem the speaker is actually walking at

---

45. Francis B. McCarthy, review of GW, in *New York Times Book Review*, March 14, 1948, p. 6.

night, seeing that "Lit by their energies, secretly, all things shine /
Nothing can black that glow of life." Recalling "All Souls' Day" she
says, "Now I name / death our black honor and feast of possibility."
In flowing lines and rhythms that recall the elegies the poem moves
to the fierce commitment to life of the last lines: "What fire survive
forever / myself is for my time."

"This Place in the Ways" situates the poet in the Dantesque
dark. The poet Richard Eberhart called it "an almost perfect lyric—
fine balance, restraint giving onto austerity." [46] Indeed before this she
has written no poem so spare and lucid which nevertheless is brim-
ming with passion. Here is the dark in which the light of mystery reveals itself.

> Having come to this place
> I set out once again
> on the dark and marvelous way
> from where I began:
> belief in the love of the world,
> woman, spirit, and man.
>
> Having failed in all things
> I enter a new age
> seeing the old ways as toys,
> the houses of a stage
> painted and long forgot;
> and I find love and rage.
>
> Rage for the world as it is
> but for what it may be
> more love now than last year
> and always less self-pity
> since I know in a clearer light
> the strength of the mystery.
>
> And at this place in the ways
> I wait for song.
> My poem-hand still, on the paper,
> all night long.
> Poems in throat and hand, asleep,
> and my storm beating strong!

46. Richard Eberhart, "Art and *Zeitgeist*," 173–76.

The poems are fluid with images of water and darkness and with fluid consonants. Poem after poem establishes the sense of flowing peace, fulfillment. From "Song, from 'Mr. Amazeen on the River' ":

> The hour of voices on the water and oars
> Speaking of blue, speaking of time.
> His colors, colors of deepness will arrive,
> Island-sleep, keel-sleep, cloud-controlling evening.
> They say to me at last "I am your home."

The flowing is strong enough to bear away the worst disasters, the most unyielding sense of personal inadequacy. From "Clouds, Airs, Carried Me Away":

> Deep now in your great eyes, and in my gross
> flesh—heavy as ever, woman of mud—
> shine sunset, sunrise and the advancing stars.
> But past all loss
> and all forbidding a thing is understood.
>
> Orpheus in hell remembered rivers
> and a music rose
> full of all human voices;
> all words you wish are in that living sound.

The theme of darkness yielding light constantly recurs; the poet is reborn in her dark night. One particularly flowing but brief poem (which has the spirit of haiku) is a flash of insight into the marvelous cosmos and the silliness of human anxiety. This is a new mode for the poet, and she is very good at it already.

> Salamander
> Red leaf. And beside it, a red leaf alive
> flickers, the eyes set wide in the leaf head,
> small broad chest, a little taper of flame for tail
> moving a little among the leaves like fear.
>
> Flickering red in the wet week of rain
> while a bird falls safely through his mile of air.

"His Head is Full of Faces," dedicated to the artist Bernard Perlin, is on the theme of continual resistance to fascism; here the poet reminds us again that often the resistance is made by others, for our sake. In this book of flowing, we are reminded that suffering flows too, generation after generation.

> Now
> he has become one given his life by those
> fighting in Greece forever under a star
> and now he knows how many wars there are.

"Mrs. Walpurga"—goddess of springs—takes its title from the name the poet gave herself in "Wreath of Women" in *Beast in View*. The lines and rhythms of this poem are longer, for "Mrs. Walpurga" is the full embodiment of the gift the three women made the poet in "Wreath of Women." It is the gift of the poet's own streaming life.

> These are her endless years, woman and child, in dream
> molded and wet, a bowl growing on a wheel,
> not mud, not bowl, not clay, but this *becoming*,
> winter and split of darkness, years of wish.

In this poem the flowing, the transformations, are not all happy. The images for a cosmos in perpetual movement are often tortured, a "surrealistic Freudian fantasia," in Francis McCarthy's words. But the last images flow to peace:

> the river braids and unfolds in mingling song;
> and here is the rain of summer from the moon,
> relenting, wet, and giving life at last,
> and Mrs. Walpurga and we may wake.

Wet is a numinous word for the poet in "Mrs. Walpurga," and it will appear most notably in *The Orgy* (1965).

"A Certain Music" is convincing assertion that since the poet has known the "music" of complete love, it does not really matter that this love is now withheld from her. "Now it has become me, now it is nerve, song, gut." This poet is incapable of expressing the kind of loss for which contemporary poetry is famous, for she makes what she loves a part of her. When asked once why her lines do not mourn the past she said, "I have it. It's inside me." She doesn't let her vision stop at loss; she searches the dark for a clue. When she recognizes a destructive tendency she focuses on her great need to dissolve it. From "The Motive of All of It":

> this
> Must be given back to life again,
> Made superhuman, made human, out of pain
> Turned to the personal, the pure release.

Even "Foghorn in Horror," with its brilliantly effective refrain ("Blu-aa! Blu-aa! Ao . . . ") which renders the loss and fear of the poem so vividly, is not without its ray of hope. In the first stanza the poet by the harbor sees "black clothes only and white clothes with the fog running in / and all their shadows." But in the last stanza, having admitted "Thirty years, and my full strength, and all I touch has failed," she sees "the black clothes on the line are beautiful, the sky drifting away. / The white clothes of the fog beyond me, beautiful, and the shadows." For this poet there is no human situation without its beauty.

The most striking poems in the first section of *The Green Wave* are those whose theme involves childhood, often the poet's own. *Green* is the adjective that fills these poems, with its myriad overtones of life, youth, and hope. "Green Limits" tells in spare lines of her aunts' walking her into the surf when she was a child. She had the helpless feeling of a small child in the rushing ocean. But she knew she could "dive and be saved"; she knew she would be safe if only they would let her ride the waves. The last stanza applies the lesson:

> My limits stand inside me
> forever like that wave
> on which I ride at last
> over and under me.

Paradoxically, though now she is a prisoner of flowing being, she has in fact no limits, for she has learned to flow with it. In "Summer, the Sacramento," the lush green flows and the colors of maturing flow and blend in the poet's satisfying acceptance of the process of her life and death. Rosenthal, reviewing *The Green Wave* in the New York *Herald Tribune* said, "Passionately she affirms her relation to the physical universe."[47]

47. M. L. Rosenthal, review of GW, 4.

> Under me islands lie green, planted with green feathers,
> green growing, shadowy grown, gathering streams of the green
> trees.
> . . . .
> Flows to the flower-haunted sea, naming and singing, under my
> eyes
> coursing, the day of the world. And the time of my spirit
> streams
> before me, slow autumn colors, the cars of a long train;
> earth-red, earth-orange, leaf, rust, twilight of earth

Poem after poem celebrates her realization that she is fulfilling herself simply by being her own intense self. She knows her "beast" now. There is no more puzzling or seeking.

> Then I saw what the calling was :   it was the road I traveled,
> the clear
> time and these colors of orchards
> . . . .
> I came into my clear being; uncalled, alive, and sure.
> Nothing was speaking to me, but I offered and all was well.
> And then I arrived at the powerful green hill.

As a young girl she exhorted, in "Theory of Flight": "Believe that we bloom upon this stalk of time"; now, in her thirties, the poet actually knows that blooming. In the face of the blank unmeaning of the cosmos, that "nothing," she has learned to make the simple offering of herself. She can look back on her childhood and adolescence and realize that time did indeed grow for her "richer and richer." From "Crayon House":

> Roads are in all I know :   weapon and refugee,
> color of thunder calling   Leave this room,
> Get out of this house. Even then, joy began,
> went seeking through the green world, wild and no longer wild,
> always beginning again. Steady giving and green decision,
> and the beginning was real. The drawing of a child.

"Speech of the Mother," from the play *The Middle of the Air* is spoken by a strong woman recalling the years since the poet's birth:

"Chaos began us, war in my own time, war in my children's time." [48]
The language is simple, the vision is whole and simple:

> A woman moving in my own house among my daughters,
> I remember their hands when they were little, and smoothing
> their shining hair. They change. And one will have her child.
>   The year passes. Around me chaos grows.
> And darkly
> our time renews itself.
>
> . . . .
>   among the accusations all things glow.

Rukeyser's poems about motherhood and children are rare in contemporary poetry. They are as exciting as the actualities they deal with: pregnancy, birth, mothering. The reader of contemporary poetry knows the "motherhood" poems of Sylvia Plath and Anne Sexton. These women in several memorable poems detail the horror of bearing and caring for children when one has effectively lost belief in the value of living. Rukeyser's poems about motherhood and children, as would be expected, are quite different.

In a review of the poet Charlotte Marletto's *Jewel of Our Longing* Rukeyser laments the lack of poems of birth or pregnancy in world literature.[49] At the time she wrote this review and the poems in *The Green Wave* it was true, as she said, that not many women readers of *Poetry* had seen a birth or were conscious while giving birth. Rukeyser's "Nine Poems for the Unborn Child" are remarkable for their dwelling on a theme which was shrouded in silence during those years when women placed their pregnancies entirely in the hands of their obstetricians and were "knocked out" routinely during their deliveries. In her review Rukeyser writes of the "anatomical fallacy" in Marletto's poems "which are written in an overdecorated 'modern' idiom with all its errors." She explains, "Lips are rivers fingering; there is 'lip-sculptured foam / bright-braceleted once more by sun.' The traps are all illustrated here: we have the

---

48. This play was produced by Hallie Flanagan in Iowa City in 1945.
49. Muriel Rukeyser, "A Simple Theme," *Poetry*, LXXIV (July, 1949), 236–39.

'cervix hall,' 'cerebral hall,' 'orgastic waves,' 'cephalic shores,' and the wild line, 'shocking his schizospheres together.' But there are moments in broken phrases, when Charlotte Marletto forgets the details of anatomy and sentiment, and says, 'Flesh my intercessor,' and speaks of the totem of sense and the apocryphal animals." Clearly, what Rukeyser wants in poems of pregnancy and birth is the strong sense of "the green wave," a religious sense. Pregnancy and birth were to Rukeyser an experienced proof of her identification with the power of the cosmos. Francis McCarthy in his review of *The Green Wave* said the poet "triumphantly embraces a mysticism of individual mortality and collective immortality." "Nine Poems" are indeed mystical but also warm and simple celebrations of perhaps the most mysterious event that a human body and spirit can experience.

The nine poems trace in a most "unmodern" and "undecorated" idiom, in sweeping phrasing which is religious in its implications, the progress of a woman from "the childless years alone without a home" to the point where she may say, in the ninth poem,

> Praise that the homeless may in their bodies be
> A house that time makes, where the future moves
> In his dark lake.

When she is told that she is pregnant, she writes, "And in my flesh at last I saw." (Hear the biblical "And in my flesh shall I see God.") The poet does not fear for her child, though legally he will have no father:

> —I have known fatherless children, the searching, walk
> The world, look at all faces for their father's life.
> Their choice is death or the world. And they do choose.
> Earn their brave set of bone, the seeking marvelous look
> Of those who lose and use and know their lives.

In the third poem of the sequence the poet feels herself, in her pregnancy, in the surging green wave of being.

> We earthly are aware of transformation;
> Miraculously, life, from the old despair.
> The wave of smooth water approaches on the sea-

Surface

. . . .
now high above
Me, the scroll, froth, foam of the overfall.

The fourth poem of the sequence develops the flowing, water imagery. The flowing turns from a physical to a spiritual sense of transformation:

Now the ideas all change to animals
Loping and gay, now all the images
Transform to leaves, now all these screens of leaves
Are flowing into rivers

. . . .
The waves are changing . . .
. . . they become waves of light

. . . .
Now I am light and nothing more.

In her review of Marletto's book Rukeyser writes of "the body
of pregnancy, which seems almost unspecialized, as one thinks one's
body in infancy might have been, seeing with the whole body, tast-
ing with the whole body." The fifth poem in the sequence presents
this unspecialized body experiencing life, seeing the splendid processes of the single human life in its immense blank context.

Eating sleep, eating sunlight, eating meat,
Lying in the sun to stare
At deliverance, the rapid cloud,
Gull-wing opposing sun-bright wind,
I see the born who dare
Walk on green, walk against blue,
Move in the nightlong flare
Of love on darkness . . .

The sixth poem confronts death in phrasing that binds this
poem to others which have dealt with the sacrifice of Otto Boch in
Spain; now his sacrifice for life ("advancing, / His hands full of
guns") becomes hers. She becomes the ship of deliverance she saw in
the second poem of "Letter to the Front"; her hands make the gesture of the lifted hands of the fifth poem of that sequence. The doctors ask her to choose who shall live, if there must be a choice
between her life and the baby's.

> Laughter I learned
> In that moment, laughter and choice of life.
> I saw an immense ship trembling on the water
> Lift by a gesture of hands. I saw a child. I saw
> A red room, the eyes, the hands, the hands and eyes.

The last three poems of the sequence address the child directly, now that she has chosen life for the child rather than her own. It is as though her choice has made the child a more real person to her. Choice, a theme begun in the second poem when she spoke of the choice fatherless children must make, becomes a central theme at the end of the sequence. In the seventh poem the world is presented as an arena of constant choice.

> World where again Judas, the little child,
> May grow and choose. You will enter the world.

The eighth poem celebrates the relationship which is the result of her choice:

> you hold me in your flesh
> Including me where nothing has included
> Until I said : I will include . . .

The ninth and last poem of the sequence is the poet of *A Turning Wind's* paean to birthing. Here a woman who is also an artist and a passionate seeker of social evolution, who has witnessed the social failure of war and narrowing ideals, knows the joy of participating in the immense recurrent process which bears more life, new life, possibility.

> Rider of dream, the body as an image
> Alone in crisis. I have seen the wind,
> Its tall cloud standing on a pillar of air,
> The toe of the whirlwind turning on the ground.
>
> . . . .
>
> Praise that the homeless may in their bodies be
> A house that time makes, where the future moves
> In his dark lake. Praise that the cities of men,
> The fields of men, may at all moments choose.
> Lose, use, and live. And at this daylight, praise
> To the grace of the world and time that I may hope
> To live, to write, to see my human child.

In her working papers at the Berg Collection, there is an unfinished poem whose first title was "Over the Cradle." This title is crossed out and "The Only Child" is written above it.

> I thought of the far country: for this man this belief,
> I said, I would give my life, but there is no
> > giving of life
> Except this giving
>
> . . . .
> > there is no giving of life
> except the giving of life

She saw that giving life to and nurturing a child was for her the true giving of life for Spain, for the ideals Spain represented.

In "Tenth Elegy. Elegy in Joy" the voyager who began at "Rotten Lake" in the "First Elegy" is now "beyond my lake." She has reached

> The sea at last, where all the waters lead.
> And all the wars to this peace.

The images of this last elegy flow toward fulfillment, and in a striking phrase the poet reiterates a theme of her first long sequence, "Theory of Flight":

> Now burning and unbegun, I sing earth with its war,
> And God the future, and the wish of man.

Here is the ultimate counterstatement to the theme of the lost Eden.

Many lines bind this elegy to previous elegies and other poems. There is "fusing a dead world straight," from "Third Elegy," here applied to the struggle of war. Later we see the familiar terms of "Second Elegy":

> Now there are no maps and no magicians.
> No prophets but the young prophet, the sense of the world.

The last phrase occurred in "Private Life of the Sphinx." "And all things glow" recalls "Easter Eve 1945" and "Speech of the Mother." One brief stanza recalls several elegies:

> All this, they say to us, because of you.
> Much to begin. Now be your green, your burning,
> bear also our joy, come to our meeting-place

and in the triumph of the reconceived
lie down at last together face to face. (83)

Besides recalling poems in past volumes, the phrases and images of
the conclusion of "Tenth Elegy" anticipate poems yet to come. One
derives much more satisfaction from Rukeyser's poems if one reads
several volumes. Her work indeed demands to be experienced in its
continuum. It will be recalled that she said, "The phrase in a different position is new, as has been pointed out by many poets. But I
think I use this as other poets use rhyme. It's a time-binding thing, a
physical binding, musical binding, like the recurrence of the heartbeat and the breathing and all the involuntary motions as well. But
in a poem I care very much about the physical reinforcement, the
structure in recurrence." [50] Here is the conclusion of the tenth elegy:

The word of nourishment passes through the women,
soldiers and orchards rooted in constellations,
white towers, eyes of children:
saying in time of war What shall we feed?
I cannot say the end.

Nourish beginnings, let us nourish beginnings.
Not all things are blest, but the
seeds of all things are blest.
The blessing is in the seed.

. . . .

Love that gives us ourselves, in the world known to all
new techniques for the healing of a wound,
and the unknown world. One life, or the faring stars.

We hear in the first lines of this conclusion the call to women in
"Letter to the Front"; we see the tower in West Virginia transmitting
energy in "The Book of the Dead"; we remember all the seeking
children of all the poems. The imagery of seed and beginnings occurred in the last poem of "Theory of Flight": "We bear the bursting
seeds of our return . . . we cry beginnings." "What shall we feed?"
anticipates a poem published in *Breaking Open* (1973), "Wherever":
"Whatever we stand against / We will stand feeding and seeding."

50. "Craft Interview with Muriel Rukeyser," 163.

"One life" will become the title of her book on Wendell Willkie. To the attentive reader this binding is immensely satisfying.

The Green Wave contains translations of six poems by Octavio Paz. In the foreword to her translation of the *Selected Poems of Octavio Paz* (1963), Rukeyser wrote of what drew her in the forties to Paz's poems. She admired "his early lyrics, with their speed, their transparencies, their couples lying together, all couples, all opposites." She saw that in the title of his first book, *Condición de nube*, Paz, like Gibbs, like herself, had been considering "phase" (this is Rukeyser's translation of *Condición*) and he "was beginning to express the sense of transformation which I have been valuing in my writing, in all writing." Rukeyser felt a kinship with Paz's emergence "out of his student frenzy, out of the fighting grief, the grief buried of the civil war in Spain . . . and to the great world of these transformed." Paz was able as she was to salvage his ideals; he worked for them as a diplomat and journalist. "He moves as the poet who has spoken as much as anyone in his time for the assertion of hope and the assertion of despair, in a war to the death of both, in a war that will kill all images and then, with a movement that is of necessity religious, transform all images." In a quotation from Ramon Xirau which could be applied to Rukeyser's own work, she notes, "Paz seems to have set out in search of the most desperate experience in order to emerge from it with at least a grain of hope." [51]

The six poems translated in *The Green Wave* are very brief. They all go in simple language to the paradoxical heart of things; they all assert the irrepressible urge to life of the intense person, the poet's "unreal life of truth" ("Poet's Epitaph"), the seeker of relationship's belief that it is always possible.

> Two bodies face to face
> are at times two roots
> and night is the earth.
>
> . . . .
> Two bodies face to face

51. Octavio Paz, *Selected Poems of Octavio Paz*, trans. Muriel Rukeyser (Bloomington, Indiana, 1963), 8, 10.

> are two stars falling down
> in an empty sky.

After the Paz translations there are nine translations of Polynesian "rari" or "love chants" from the Marquesas. Rukeyser says, "These songs are like the songs that Melville heard" (GW, 55). In bluntly erotic images these brief poems celebrate the force of sexual love as it is reflected in the lush tropical world of pandanus trees, ripe fruit, burning sun. Virginia Terris in her article on Rukeyser in the *American Poetry Review* (1974) says, "As is evidenced in her early work there is precious little sexual frankness or even interest." [52] Recalling the poems of passion (including physical passion) in volumes from *Theory of Flight* through *Beast in View* and coming to these translations of "rari" which she published in her thirty-fifth year, one must disagree with Terris. It seems to me Rukeyser has always been frank in asserting physical need; her images become more important than her statements on this subject, even than her rhythms, as the poetry grows from "Say Yes" to the "flaming sequences" of "Ajanta." But the need has always been evident. Terris is right in noting that Rukeyser's language when writing about sex becomes more personal and explicit in the later volumes—I think beginning with *Beast in View*. Nevertheless Rukeyser simply evolves the theme begun in *Theory of Flight*: sexual love as touching, meeting, growing, as emblem of personal and social expansion. The "rari" in *The Green Wave* are as simple, frank, and exuberant as any primitive songs. They are astonishing in a volume of American poetry, especially of the forties.

> Come, gardenia of Tahiti,
> Strike with the rice-white weapon,
> Into heaven twist and turn
> The circumcised end—
> Raise the blue flower!

The Green Wave drew praise from most reviewers. But the *New Yorker* reviewer said Rukeyser "grows more subjective as time goes

52. Terris, "Muriel Rukeyser: A Retrospective," 13.

on. . . . /She is/ still a devotee of loose, erratic, and disjunctive rhetoric, and since her gift is in no way lyrical, her writing is increasingly complicated and heavy-handed." Randall Jarrell had an absurdly grotesque vision of Rukeyser in *The Green Wave* as "the Common Woman of our century, a siren photographed in a sequin bathing suit . . . /bringing/ sex to the deserving poor." He admitted to "trudging through the book full of uneasy delight" but objected to her "random melodramatic hand" and to her choice of "unfortunate models and standards"—"the horrible advertising-agency idealism of Corwin or Fast or MacLeish or the National Association of Manufacturers." Jarrell called her an orator, not a poet, "woolyheaded and oracularly emotional." He said the poems in *The Green Wave* are "improvisations, easy reworkings of the automatic images of a rhetorical-emotional trance-state in which everything slides into everything else." He said there was too much dream, not enough "common logic" and "everyday unchanging fact" in her poems.[53]

Jarrell's phrasing for his objections is revealing. His "uneasy delight" sounds like the language of guilt in what Terris calls "the dark selves of the spirit and the body" as opposed to the demands of logic and fact. Terris points out that Rukeyser has the "animal awareness" of Whitman (which is associated, as in Whitman, with a spiritual awareness). It is "the sense of the wholeness of life, of man's belonging to the entire tissue of living things and, as such, animal, and, as animal, healthy and life-loving." Terris continues, "In her revolt against the tyranny of intellectualism as distinguished from physicality in Western thought, Rukeyser's poetry has dealt with unconscious and irrational elements. . . . But the mythic modes are both more numerous and far-reaching than her subrational ones." These modes, says Terris, show Rukeyser's "discontent with the structured intellect. Coming out of the mythic mode is the incantatory voice which many of the mid-century poets have discovered and that is expressive of the search for unity with the nature of being. The incantatory is nothing new for Rukeyser. It has been her

53. Unsigned review (containing Bogan's terminology) of GW in *New Yorker*, May 8, 1948, p. 115; Jarrell, review of GW.

natural voice for years." Jarrell, and other critics, each for his or her own reasons, have objected to Rukeyser's voice, often calling it "oracular," as if by describing it as such they have automatically discredited it. Critics have assumed that we cannot have an incantatory poetry in our time, one which does not value logic and fact preeminently. But this is merely their assumption. Many readers have been moved by Rukeyser's natural voice; many readers have not wished her more ironic or less preoccupied with the unconscious and the idealistic. Jarrell's objection to Rukeyser's voice was basically a political and philosophical objection. He said the reader goes through "this strange, moral, sexual wish-fantasy for which he is to be awarded, somehow, a gold star by the Perfect State." He saw her poetry as a continuation of the aberrant proletarianism of the thirties. Jarrell, poet, respected critic, and professor of English, could simply not appreciate, as Terris implies, "the character and significance of the body of her work." Terris read Jarrell on Rukeyser and did not question his judgments until she herself read a good deal of Rukeyser and saw that "an almost complete re-assessment was in order." [54]

Several reviewers of *The Green Wave* were more appreciative than Jarrell. Richard Eberhart saw that Rukeyser had "maintained a consistent attitude through a number of years and books. Hers is a rich nature expressing itself in doctrinal verse: the doctrine is of a positive and elemental nature. She has spoken for large concepts like love, freedom, and peace." Eberhart answers the objections of critics who have found her "formless" or "illogical." "She has not operated as a perfectionist of language or of linguistic subtleties; she has not performed in the interests of intellectualism or ideation only; she has not attempted the erection for their own sake of examples of aesthetic perfection." Nevertheless, Eberhart said that he preferred, in *The Green Wave*, those poems which show "a change toward impersonality and aesthetic inviolability" such as "This Place in the Ways" and "Nine Poems." Terris has said that "the variety of themes and modes of expression" in Rukeyser's work are "staggering."

54. Terris, "Muriel Rukeyser: A Retrospective," 14–15.

What Eberhart saw in 1948 as "a change toward impersonality" was simply a variation, in several poems. Rukeyser would continue to be both impersonal and more starkly personal than ever.

James R. Caldwell in the *Saturday Review* found that in *The Green Wave* the "hurry of masses . . . [the] agitation of great waves of image and rich concept beat . . . on the margins of fear and pain." He admired the fact that Rukeyser had no rigid commitment to a single level of perception. Anne Freemantle in *Commonweal* found soaring verse, despite the burden of meaning. M. L. Rosenthal noted admiringly that she "eschewed the reach for an artificial myth, or tradition . . . or . . . approved . . . formulas including 'the Pure and Absolute Horror of it All.'" He saw her taking up "her old theme of universal love, never pausing as Auden does to deride his own former simplicity but changing, enriching the context without rejecting her past." He found the poems "strong, convincing," and he called them "healing affirmations." Of her technique Rosenthal concluded, "Even in her intelligently functional verse patterns, Muriel Rukeyser avoids the retreat to formalism and pushes forward along the path of meaningful experimentation." He found "Elegy in Joy" provided the key to her values and technique: "Nourish beginnings, let us nourish beginnings."[55]

Not turning her back on her past is Rukeyser's rare characteristic as a poet writing in the postwar period. Auden turned his back. So did Lowell, who served five months in prison as a conscientious objector in World War II (he had tried to enlist twice in 1943 but was rejected; when he was drafted he refused to serve because he said the country was out of danger and he could not participate in the bombing of civilians). In "Memories of West Street and Lepke" in *Life Studies* (1960), Lowell ironically, almost apologetically muses on his youthful ardor and simplicity:

> These are the tranquillized *Fifties*
> and I am forty. Ought I to regret my seedtime?

55. James Caldwell, review of GW, in *Saturday Review*, March 20, 1948, p. 16; Anne Freemantle, review of GW, in *Commonweal*, XLVIII (August 13, 1948), 430; Rosenthal, review of GW.

> I was a fire-breathing Catholic C.O.,
> and made my manic statement,
> telling off the state and president
>
> . . . .
>
> I was so out of things, I'd never heard
> of the Jehovah's Witnesses.

In "Man and Wife" from *Life Studies* Lowell describes himself as "tamed by *Miltown*." But Rukeyser can say, of her youth and young adulthood, on the one hand, "all I touch has failed," and on the other, "Steady giving and green decision, / and the beginning was real." She can use the word "seedtime" without irony, for in her later work her early ideals and vision were not tranquilized.[56]

Orpheus

Orpheus was published in 1949, with a drawing by Picasso.[57] The poem begins a moment after the murder of Orpheus by the Thracian women. The first long section is powerful description of the women fleeing the dismembered corpse.

> The mountaintop stands in silence a minute after the murder.
> The women are furies racing down the slope
>
> . . . .
>
> Scattered, there lit, in black and golden blood:
> his hand, a foot, a flat breast, phallus, a foot,
> shoulder and sloping back and lyre and murdered head.

Here the poet of *The Green Wave* who has just assumed her beast, "come into" her own body, expresses loss not in terms of *journeying to find* (as in the elegies) but in terms of physical mutilation. (Loss as mutilation figures in some of the imagery of "Second Elegy.") The next sections focus on the parts of Orpheus crying to be reunited and finally achieving their wish. The poem is a fine example of the kind of poetry Rukeyser has been writing, especially in the elegies, the kind of poetry she said she found in Paz, who

---

56. Untermeyer, *Modern American Poetry*, 692–93; Robert Lowell, *Life Studies*.
57. Muriel Rukeyser, *Orpheus* (San Francisco, 1949).

sought hope in the most desperate experiences. In *The Life of Poetry* she writes, "I cannot say what poetry is; I know that our sufferings and our concentrated joy, our states of plunging far and dark and turning to come back to the world—so that the moment of intense turning seems still and universal—all are here, in a music like the music of our time, like the hero and like the anonymous forgotten" (LP, 184). *Orpheus* is such a plunging and a turning, and an actual, achieved return.

The second section of the poem is philosophical argument in imagery.

> Scattered.   The fool of things.   For here is Orpheus,
> without his origin   :   the body, mother of self,
> the earliest self, the mother of permanence.
> He is sensation and matter, all forms and no form.
> He is the pieces of Orpheus and he is chaos.
>
> All myths are within the body when it is most whole,
> all positions being referred to flesh in unity—
> slow changes of form, the child and growing man
> as friends have seen him, altered by absences and years.

Terris disapproved of Rukeyser's introducing "intellectualized and abstract summary" into poems of concrete image. Rosenthal, praising the dramatic opening of the poem, said he found that in the second section, "an intensive vision has been balanced off by a theoretical statement" which he, too, felt weakens the poem. But this alternation of image and theoretical statement or abstract summary has it precedents, notably in Whitman.[58]

Rukeyser's passages of "theory" are less diffuse, more spare and intense than Whitman's, however. To call them, as Terris does, "unwarranted" is to say that a poetic vision is not permitted to alternate between concrete, intensely beheld phenomena and an intense, imagistic contemplation of their meanings. But if we take the speaking voice as the element which holds the poem together—

58. Terris, "Muriel Rukeyser: A Retrospective," 15; Rosenthal, "The Longer Poems," 228–29; see Whitman's "By Blue Ontario's Shore," for example.

as we do in Whitman—then we must accept the different modes in which that voice chooses to speak. Rukeyser's poetry, except for the "documentary" parts of "The Book of the Dead," has been lyrical, autobiographical. She is the persona, the consciousness, of the poems. She has said many times that to write a poem is to work on the self; in many of her poems we see that self beholding phenomena and then thinking, in images, about them. She wrote, in "The Poem as Mask" from *The Speed of Darkness*:

> When I wrote of the women in their dances and wildness,
>   it was a mask,
> on their mountain, god-hunting, singing, in orgy,
> it was a mask; when I wrote of the god,
> fragmented, exiled from himself, his life, the love gone
>   down with song,
> it was myself, split open, unable to speak, in exile from
>   myself.

But we knew this already. The celebration of the body in *Orpheus* that Rosenthal found a weak "theoretical statement" ("All myths are within the body when it is most whole") is spoken by the persona whose experience we have followed in *The Green Wave* where she said, "Praise that the homeless may in their bodies be / A house that time makes." With time, and love, and risk, the pieces of Orpheus come together into his body again as the consciousness in the poem beholds, reports, and formulates the meanings of possibility.

In the second movement of the second section, the wounds speak, each part of Orpheus crying to be touched and loved; but there is no response to this crying. There is hope in a "turn," and intense yearning, and the characteristic urging, "Let the wounds change." It is this great wish which brings about the impossible:

> . . . now they need be whole.
> And the pieces of the body cannot be.
> They do not even know they need be whole.
> Only the wounds in their endless crying.
> Now they know.

The wounds go from not knowing to knowing (remembering) their need in a flash. Rosenthal comments, "The object . . . remains to make desire become reality in the course of a single poem despite the shadow; and . . . the demand on the reader is too great for this purpose." [59] I think it is very helpful to read *Orpheus* in the light of all of her poems of intense wish, beginning with "Theory of Flight," where she said that intense desire implies its fulfillment, that "Elohim" is "intermittent with the soul." In many poems after her first long sequence she reiterated her vision of "the insistence . . . strong, the wish converted" of the first elegy. And of course the poems of *A Turning Wind* are filled with the imagery of effort.

The following section of *Orpheus* begins,

> Touch me! Love me! Speak to me!
> One effort and one risk.
> The hand is risen. It braces itself, it flattens,
> and the third finger touches the lyre.

The risk is to create, to make poetry, though one is dismembered. It is the singing, the poetry which then effects the healing, the coming together of the torn body and spirit. In the poem the hand of Orpheus "with a sowing gesture / throws the lyre upward." (In this "sowing gesture," hear all the "feeding and seeding" lines in Rukeyser's work, the urging to "nourish beginnings.") Orpheus at this point can't actually sing; but he flings the instrument up to the sky and the strings sing as they go, "Eurydice." They sing, that is, the most intense love of the poet, and its name does the healing. Slowly the pieces of his body come together. What makes him complete, finally, are his wounds "losing self-pity" and changing into mouths of song. As Rukeyser related in *The Life of Poetry*, a friend suggested to her that "the god must include his murderers if murder is part of his life."

> Now the body is whole; but it is covered with murder.
> A mist of blood and fire shines over the body,
> shining up the mountain, a rose of form.

59. Rosenthal, "The Longer Poems," 229.

> And now the wounds losing self-pity change,
> they are mouths, they are the many mouths of music.
> And now they disappear. He is made whole.
> The mist dissolves into the body of song.

Orpheus perceives his complete form, including his murder, and assumes it. The "rose of form" is the inclusiveness of his life. That rose is like the "rose of direction" that Gibbs knew as he drove about the city and pondered his systems. Another striking echo of "Gibbs" then appears in *Orpheus* when the god becomes whole: "His life is simpler than the sum of its parts. / The arrangement is the life. It is the song." Orpheus is completely identified with the entire process of his life: he is "growth as form." He could be the hero of the elegies; of course, he *is*.

Orpheus then becomes an inclusive singer like Whitman, as Rukeyser strives to be. First we have a description of what the poet sings: the process of recurrence, the possibility, the fullness. Then in conclusion we are given the actual song of Orpheus:

> Voices and days, the exile of our music
> and the dividing airs are gathered home.
> The hour of light and birth at last appears
> among the alone, in prisons of scattering.
> Seeming of promise, the shining of new stars,
> the stars of the real over the body of love.
> The cloud, the mountain, and the cities risen.
> Solving the wars of the dead, and offering dream
> making and morning. Days and voices, sing
> creation not yet come.

The final song, and much of *Orpheus*, is not a poetry of precise observation and minute detail, though there are passages of rich observation and detail in the poem too, as in "A Charm for Cantinflas." Rukeyser composes, in *Orpheus*, a structure of recurrent, suggestive, numinous words: *clouds, winds, fire, blood, wounds*. This is what Eberhart calls her "primordial and torrential" poetry which displays "massive awareness of large phases of existence" and "splendors of passionate realization." As one observes in every volume, Rukeyser displays an amazing variety of styles which in-

clude the rich concrete style she uses in describing physical landscape, the spare style she uses when referring to science and
technology, and the incisive, imagistic style with which she frames
philosophical and aesthetic concepts. Perhaps Terris was referring
to a poem like *Orpheus* when she wrote that Rukeyser "overuses
certain words, such as 'singing' and 'waking,' to such a degree that
the reader becomes inoculated against them." This may be true for
certain readers. One must realize, however, that the "music" of
Rukeyser's "primordial" poetry—like that of *Orpheus*—depends
on the recurrence of these words and on what she has called their
"unfinished" resonances (LP, 194–202). This recurrence is like
that of ancient or primitive poetry or chanting (like that of the *rari*
in *The Green Wave*.) This is a valid mode for poetry; we late-twen-
tieth-century readers with our limiting predilection for the tangi-
ble, preferably brand-named concrete, often cannot enter into the
spirit of other kinds of writing. For many of us the magic of words
cannot be revived. Reviewers who praised *Orpheus* said, like David
Daiches, that it is a fine poem, "rich in echoing meanings without
becoming clotted or obscure." He found in the poem the skillful
"suggestion of the parts coming together into an incommunicable
complex whole."[60]

Elegies

In 1949 Rukeyser also published all ten elegies together for the
first time. There are some minor variants in punctuation and
phrasing in this volume and, regrettably, some careless proofread-
ing that blurs the meaning of certain phrases (in the ninth elegy
"the second Adams' fever" becomes "the second Adam's fever.")
But it is good to have the elegies in their continuum. When Rosenthal reviewed this book in the *New Republic*, he praised the symbolic fusion of fragmented, often contradictory motifs of modern

---

60. Richard Eberhart, review of *The Speed of Darkness*, in *New York Times Book Review*, June 23, 1968, p. 24; Terris, "Muriel Rukeyser: A Retrospective," 15; David Daiches,
review of *Orpheus*, in *New York Herald Tribune Book Review*, June 25, 1950, p. 8.

life toward which much of our poetry strives. He called *Elegies* "a principled and moving—if sometimes hysterical—effort to grasp the special meaning of our moment in history." But in his article of 1953 he said that publishing all the elegies together shifted "the whole focus from a struggle for faith to the positive assertion that the faith will become reality. The elegies, now, begin in deep depression and end in triumphant joy. . . . In outward form the sequence has [a] pattern intended to be the earned result of a bitter effort to deal with harsh reality. . . . But the tendency of the sixth to tenth elegies is to oppose just a little too glibly—though often most magnetically—the sense of betrayal in these latter years against the certainty of final victory on all emotional fronts."[61]

Louise Bogan in the *New Yorker* noted that in *Orpheus* and *Elegies* Rukeyser tries to trace the spiritual journey from chaos toward order and from despair toward joy. "But she does this so incoherently, so superficially, and so imitatively (. . . her titles and even, partially, her form approximate those of Rilke's last great works) that we cannot credit her with much knowledge, either of herself or of her world." Moving on to other volumes by Peter Viereck and Emma Swan, Bogan continued, "The younger generation is by no means totally lacking in sincerity and variety." At this point in following Bogan's judgments of Rukeyser's developing body of work one wonders why Bogan didn't simply refrain from mentioning Rukeyser's books in the *New Yorker* column, for the comments Bogan made through the years all insist that Rukeyser isn't worth reading.

Bogan's friend Rolfe Humphries gave Rukeyser's *Orpheus* and *Elegies* the following review in the *Nation*: "The indefatigable Muriel Rukeyser has appeared lately with *two* volumes—an 'Orpheus' . . . and 'Elegies'. Of the comparisons which Miss Rukeyser invites with these titles, the less said the better. *Schloss Duino, soll leben!* " One does not expect so trivializing a review from Humphries, poet and translator of the classics, later professor at Am-

61. Muriel Rukeyser, *Elegies* (Norfolk, Connecticut, 1949); M. L. Rosenthal, review of *Elegies*, in *New Republic*, February 6, 1950, p. 21; Rosenthal, "The Longer Poems," 226.

herst College and judge in the National Book Awards. Humphries'
dislike for Rukeyser's work dated from her association with the
Gregorys, whom he disliked. He wrote to Bogan in 1938, "Comrade Louisa Boganova! . . . Down with . . . Gregoryites, Zatyruen-
skayaites [sic]." In 1963, when he was a judge for the National
Book Awards, he wrote to Bogan, "You never told me what you
thought about Bill Stafford. At least we did not give it to Anne
Sexton, nor, as some reviewer predicted, Rukeyser." In the *Kenyon
Review* in 1941 Rukeyser generously reviewed Humphries' translation of Lorca—along with two other translations—, saying it is
"the cleanest and most successful of the three because it avoids the
dangers of literalism and of the injection of his own personality."
Rolfe Humphries' formal poetry is quite unlike Rukeyser's; and
she said in her review that "his own poetry is as far away from
Lorca's as can be imagined, I suppose." But she made no disparag-
ing remarks about Humphries' work, so unlike her own. Rukeyser's sympathies have always seemed much broader than her critics'.[62]

James R. Caldwell reviewed *Orpheus, Elegies,* and *The Life of
Poetry,* which also appeared in 1949, in the *Saturday Review.* "In
a time of shrinking poets and shrinking critics here, at any rate, is
one capable in both poetry and criticism, who expands and embraces. In a generation of artists all angry rejecters of this murderous world she rejects only arty rejection." Of the poems and prose,
Caldwell said, "Pervading the whole is the ideal for poetry and for
life of full consciousness, free of inhibition, contempt, and neurotic coldness." He aptly quotes Rukeyser: " 'This is the country in
which all activity is creative and true and . . . the only treason is di-
sowning.' Miss Rukeyser disowns little or nothing." Though Caldwell, like other reviewers of Rukeyser's prose, has reservations
about her "oracular" style and the energies and ideals straining at

62. Louise Bogan, review of *Orpheus* and *Elegies,* in *New Yorker,* May 20, 1950, p.
114; Rolfe Humphries, review of *Orpheus* and *Elegies,* in *Nation,* January 28, 1950, p. 94.
I quote from the private correspondence of Rolfe Humphries to Louise Bogan. These letters
are at the Frost Library at Amherst College and are dated 1938 and October 12, 1963. Permission to quote from them is gratefully acknowledged. Muriel Rukeyser, "Lorca in English," *Kenyon Review,* III (1941), 123–27.

the form, he finds her poetic and prose style "the natural result of the poet's passionate sense of movement as essence, a condition of that 'climate of excitement and revelation' which is for her the climate of the universe. . . . She discovers, at any rate, and I think especially for youth, invigoration and a brilliant hope." [63]

Charles J. Rolo in the *Atlantic* admired the way in which "respectfully but scorchingly Miss Rukeyser assails the exponents of the 'New Criticism' who hold that poetry is words." But Rolo said *The Life of Poetry* is marred by its "non-prose style that blurs the argument with ecstasy, that suggests an emotional shorthand, and presents other discouragements. It is certainly 'intelligible.' But the receptiveness it calls for, and the strain it imposes on the receptive reader, unfortunately limit its appeal." One recalls that Rukeyser praised Gibbs for not condescending to simplify; clearly, she is convinced that her "non-prose style" is the fullest way to render her complex of ideas and emotions. David Daiches said of *The Life of Poetry* that it revealed "one of the most undoctrinaire of contemporary minds." He found it a passionate, lively, personal book. "The argument is sometimes spasmodic but is always conducted with a fine fervor; it is the testimony of a poet to the reality and force of poetry in life . . . a richly stimulating document . . . that teems with ideas and excitement." [64]

Rukeyser's next published book was *Selected Poems* (1951), a disappointing collection to one seriously interested in Rukeyser's poetry. Poems are savagely truncated, and they appear in the volume in no particular chronological order, so that though one has some sense of the great variety of her styles, one can't trace the development of her themes and methods. I. L. Salomon, in a review characteristic of the fifties entitled "From Union Square to Parnassus," praised the "mythopoetic" direction her poetry took in "Ajanta" and *Orpheus*. Salomon saw her reaching toward what he

63. James R. Caldwell, review of *Orpheus, Elegies,* and *The Life of Poetry*, in *Saturday Review*, March 11, 1950, p. 26.

64. Charles J. Rolo, review of LP, in *Atlantic*, CLXXXV, March, 1950, p. 81; David Daiches, review of LP, 8.

called "pure poetry," away from "her social protest experimenta-
tions, now carefully expunged from this edition." They are not expunged, of course; they are abridged. The lines of social protest
from "Theory of Flight" and other poems remain. (And Rukeyser
will write poems of protest through the 1970s.) But Salomon felt
Rukeyser had created a volume to fit the current "Parnassian"
standards. He said her longer poems had been excised for this volume because "it is apparent Miss Rukeyser had over-written her
long poems." This is not apparent to a reader today who finds in
the *Selected Poems* that the magnificent "Preamble" from "Theory
of Flight" is cut down to eleven lines, "The Gyroscope" is completely omitted, etc. Rukeyser is a poet of Whitmanian volume and
cumulative effect. Her poems shouldn't be abridged.

Louise Bogan reviewed *Selected Poems* in the *New Yorker* in
her characteristic fashion. Not surprisingly, Bogan found little
development of technique or idea apparent in the volume; had the
reviewer read Rukeyser's other volumes carefully she would have
seen that *Selected Poems* unfortunately was not put together to
show Rukeyser's development or her great integrity. Bogan further
displayed her inattentiveness in this description of Rukeyser's poetry: "Her early work was filled with the gloomy humanitarianism
of its time." "Theory of Flight" gloomy? [65]

As if in answer to Bogan and Salomon, Richard Eberhart in the
New York *Times* wrote, "One's time is a variable phrase. Muriel
Rukeyser's time may achieve indefinite extension. . . . Her insight
as an artist . . . has overcome partisan spirit. The depth of her understanding is what makes her poetry ring true." Eberhart saw that
there were too many cut poems in the volume, but he said, "Studied either historically or for immediate pleasure, this swift-moving
and rich volume shows Muriel Rukeyser's grasp on the essential,
her practice of positive speech." [66]

65. I. L. Salomon, "From Union Square to Parnassus," review of *Selected Poems*, in *Poetry*, LXXX (April, 1952), 52–57; Louise Bogan, review of SP, in *New Yorker*, November
3, 1951, pp. 150–51.
66. Richard Eberhart, review of SP, 30.

Looking back over the work Rukeyser published after *The Green Wave* (1948), one sees that only *Orpheus* was completely new. *The Life of Poetry* was composed of lectures she had given since the early forties, and the elegies, of course, had all been published before. From 1948 Rukeyser was raising her young son, without a father. She will allude to the first of these difficult years, and to their effect on her development as a poet, in "The Gates" (1976).

FIVE

The Fifties

One Life

Rukeyser describes *One Life*, whose central subject is Wendell Willkie, as "a story and a song." Its title is from the epigraph, taken from Coleridge: "Everything has a life of its own . . . we are all one life." Willkie's life, to Rukeyser, had its distinct essence, but in its contradictions and process it was very much like that of many Americans. "He is real; he is a myth; we can see our lifetime through him." Rukeyser, trained as a film editor, writes of Willkie's life as a procession of images moving into the present. "When I began to write this book, the people and the images moving through the story had begun to open up the present for me, and my childhood, and a great deal that I knew and imagined about our bonds with the world." The hero as image, his life as a series of images that reflect our lives: these are familiar terms to the reader of Rukeyser. She will use them when writing of Hariot. She has used them in a brief talk on Thoreau, whose life she saw as "the effort of a person . . . to make something that can flash again and again with an integral moment in its flashing." She seeks another ancestor in Willkie, the same way she sought ancestors in the thirties and early forties; and again she calls up "risen images" as she did then, to have them flash into this moment.[1]

Willkie is a hero in "his way of finding himself and finding the world. At the same time." The hero is his process of apprehension, the slow unraveling of his sense of himself and thus of the world.

1. Rukeyser, *One Life*, xiii; Muriel Rukeyser, "Thoreau and Poetry," in W. R. Harding et al., *Henry David Thoreau: Studies and Commentaries* (Rutherford, N.J., 1972), 103 – 16.

What Willkie achieved, what Paul, the young German refugee here described, achieved, and what we all need to achieve is "an image of the world" which is full and satisfying. We will have it when we have the full, sequential image of ourselves (our "beast"). Willkie is thus a hero of perception, of imagination.

As with *U.S.1*, there is nothing like *One Life* in American literature. Charles J. Rolo in the *Atlantic* alluded to its documentary techniques which resemble the "camera eye" and "newsreel" of Dos Passos's *U.S.A.*: news flashes, excerpts of conversations and court proceedings, richly detailed scenic descriptions, anecdotes—and interspersed through all this, poems. Richard Eberhart called her style "an individualistic method of composition. It is a medley of news reports, historical scenes, poetic cross-references, dream inferences, realistic depictions and subjective truths summoned across a large canvas to appraise the deep American idealism of the hero. It is like some new kind of extended, extensive, rapid-fire telegram recreating the turbulence of the world in Willkie's time." Rolo praised it as a new form: "The new biographical form she has created—its effects recall those ancient forms, the epic and the ballad—is well suited to her purpose. It eloquently dramatizes what is characteristically American in her subject's experience and brings into poetic relief the universal values which are at stake."[2]

Paul Engle in the New York *Times*, referring to the original form Rukeyser evolved to write of an American original, said, "The facts . . . are here, but the author does not so much relate them as sing them. . . . The book breathes and quarrels and proudly believes." One recalls Benét's description of *Theory of Flight*: "When you hold the book in your hands you hold a living thing." That is a good description of the kind of reading experience that *One Life* affords the person who takes it up and tries to take it in. The book is alive in a way few books are. The first passages (they are not paragraphs—they are blocks of sentences separated by asterisks, massings of scene, anecdote, and speculation) bring the young Willkie and his Indiana boomtown environment to life and

2. Charles J. Rolo, review of *One Life*, in *Atlantic*, CXCIX (May, 1957), 82; Richard Eberhart, review of OL, in *New York Herald Tribune Book Review*, April 28, 1957, p. 4.

prefigure the whole development of the man. To the reader of Rukeyser these passages in their keynotes also reach into all her work and show the poet alive not in a new way but in a new flowering. It is not true, as Virginia Terris says, that "much of the book is . . . weak because it departs from the source of strength Rukeyser has discovered in the intense, the personal, self." For her intense, personal self is here in the poems entering into the spirit of Willkie, which she recognizes as her own spirit: "we are all one life." The book is alive in the contradictions and veerings of life. The prose passages are the tamer ones; the poetry, sounding her characteristic themes of process and possibility, is often headlong and maddening in the "wildness" which she posits as her central theme on page two.[3]

Wildness: for Wendell Willkie? Yes, as for Thoreau. The surprise of this notion strikes at the very beginning of her book. She will write in "Thoreau and Poetry" that "wildness" is Thoreau's central theme and that it means to him a reaching out beyond the safe, the secure, the suburban, the predictable. Thoreau's famous statement on wildness, which she quotes in her essay, is germane to *One Life*: "We need to witness our limits transgressed and see some light pasturing freely where ours never wander. In wildness is the preservation of the world. Every tree sends its fibers forth in search of the wild." Willkie sent his fibers forth; he was born and bred in a town that encouraged him to.

A boom town, breathing a flame of its own. The excitements: the certainty of wildness, of the next morning with everything expanded a little, the factories coming in to build, the map of the town staked out like a gambling table; these fields might as well be green baize. Schoolteacher turned lawyer, Willkie's father is now a real-estate man, Herman Willkie, called Hellfire; his strong children all six born and changing fast, the town darkening. The brick and stacks, smoking and darkening. The whole thing riding fast, riding high. The crest of the boom. That speed and taste and blood, that makes you want somehow to match it, to live breakneck from then on. (OL, 2)

But the opening chapters trace the contradictions in Elwood,

3. Paul Engle, review of OL, in *New York Times Book Review*, April 14, 1957, p. 16; Terris, "Muriel Rukeyser: A Retrospective," 11.

Indiana, and thus Willkie's growth in an atmosphere where oppositions were palpable. "Tin mill, glass works, saloons, whorehouses. The towers of fire always from the open wells of gas. Turn out the street lights by day? In Elwood? No one turns them out, says the boy. It's just as cheap to let them burn. All burning; all wide open. Forty saloons and forty bawdy houses. A law? There's a law forbidding flares. But there are people around here—13,000 of them—and they figure a man can do what he likes with his own property." And the opposite. "It is a strict town, too, with the force of its contradictions. These children are forbidden to play cards. The house is very silent on Sundays. Quiet up the stairs, quiet on the next floor. Up the attic stairs there is a small sound, then the little stiff slapping noise. Sitting in a circle on the floor, holding the Sunday-school cards overlapping in fans of pale acid color, there they are. All the children, and Wen speaking up: I'll just take that trick with my little Jesus" (OL, 3). Early in life Willkie learned to pass through contradictions.

The theme is sounded at the beginning of the book that the awareness and feelings of a child can mirror those of adults in his time. When Willkie was a child, William Jennings Bryan visited his parents, and their discussions "rang and rang, rang in the small boy's head" and made the boy sense the great ideas and forces of the larger world. "A child can go through the course of all the meanings and knowings," says the poet. (There will be two other children in the book whose awareness of the world will mirror that of adults—Willkie's and ours.) Growing up, Willkie will become one who enjoys adversaries, debate, pushing beyond the accepted in thought: wildness. He will become a college radical. Rukeyser praises the radicalism of youth, its urge to growth (hear the elegies):

College radicals, a term meaning, in the United States, the young who have not surrendered.

    Many surrender early everywhere, forgetting their birth.

    Forgetting the origin in bravery and full relationship. The surrender is made easy. There is a foam of rewards; you may float along stag lines, festivals and ball games, like the songs. Before they know it, they are surrendered—the spectacular boys, the long adventurous girls, talented, shining. All are surrendered, and then pretending coldness, or pretending they are used to the world. Walling themselves in, from their first adolescence. Beginning at puberty to forget. They begin when they are troubled by what they suppose they should be feeling. The wound is there; the consciousness, which is variety, which is the need for growth and form as well as their perception, the consciousness has begun its own corruption. The rites of change become a memory of jungle, and these—the next people, the most beautiful—have forgotten animal and plant and mud, and nebula; they know only the floors of their own forgetting.

The icicles and the assassins have begun. (OL, 14)

If this passage, like several in the book, is overwritten, one must remember that it appeared in the late fifties when the college generation was calling itself "silent." Even then Rukeyser protested against such silence and withdrawal. Rukeyser had taught the young in 1954 at Sarah Lawrence, and she would teach again there beginning in 1958; at that time the Westchester County American Legion criticized the college for hiring what they called "a celebrated Leftist" in Rukeyser, one who had been affiliated with several "radical" organizations.[4] *One Life* contains passages of radical protest against the stifling attitudes of the fifties.

After this passage on youthful radicalism there are rich passages describing the comfort and abundance of middle-class life in Indiana "urging all people to be warm and easy. Be happy and conform, like Indiana where everybody seems to." But Willkie has his urge to growth and wildness. At his graduation from law school he makes, before an audience which includes a row of justices of the Supreme Court of Indiana, what his college president will call the "most radical speech I ever heard." There is a wildness in Willkie which the poet says is stifled in all of us, beginning in adolescence. "Better take what comes: the life run through and folded, run through and folded, folded again, that they all want for you. Their calculating looks. Pretty well tamed, they are figuring" (OL,

4. New York *Times*, November 14, 1958, p. 11.

27). But Willkie's urge to wildness can't be stifled. He parachutes from an airplane wing on a bet, and there is a poem about his gesture's integral place in his life. The poem, "Willkie—Stopless Falling Through Air," is a recognizable offshoot of *The Green Wave* and restates its themes as well as those of *Theory of Flight*.

> For the first time today
> I see for the first time
> Throwing myself away
> Into the flood of change.
>
> Falling, meet the dark flame
> Over America,
> There is a lie in the curse
> Of the fall of man.
>
> I know the shaking doom
> With doom the only sure.
> Earth rushing up at my eyes
> With the speed of fear.
>
> Possibility. (OL, 30)

In a poem immediately following this one we are given the core of the book: "If you see your life as a procession of images / You will know you have not forgotten a single meaning." Willkie's life, in this book, is a procession of images which he himself recognizes in revelations which allow him to grow. He can see the integrity of his developing life, and he can accept its development, move beyond old positions, pass beyond temporary contradictions.

A successful lawyer, Willkie goes to work for the power business in New York. In Part Two, "Tree of Rivers," we enter into Willkie's (and the poet's) fascination with the power of modern technology (here the TVA) and of the forces of nature that technology harnesses for human use. This section is, like those which sang power in *U.S.1* and *Theory of Flight*, an imaginative exploration of the meanings of modern technology. We are given its negative side and reminded of the crystal killer in West Virginia; but we are also given technology's meanings of renewal. A woman whose baby was born just after she learned of her husband's death of silicosis says that she welcomes the coming of massive technology to her native valley and her displacement.

> I didn't know how I'd get through. The birth
> Was so much leaving and putting away myself and starting
>   again
> Another birthing seems easy and right.
> When the man talks about The Valley, he tells me
> What I have thought and kept secret, telling it open and plain.
> (OL, 48)

The poet, and Willkie who is placed in this scene, see technology not only as a help in practical human life but also as an emblem of our relationship with the forces of the cosmos.

> —You had a bad time of it last year, he said.
> —Twisted the door off, spilled mud ankle deep in.
> But down in the cove they had real trouble, where the houses
>   float by
> . . . .
> Next year it'll be built. There! she says, pointing down.
> . . . .
> A stroke of lightning is laid across the river
> Stopping the rush, the rapids, the windflowing leaves.
> Law blazing across the river.
> . . . .
> Not leaves, not lightning, not that greatness of rivers.
> The woman who sees herself in her lifetime, moving,
> The man at work who uses the valleys
> And still sustains the valleys.
> The water-spiral turns the fire
> That breaks upon the miles of air,
> Leaps through the furnaces of change
> To make and make. From those steel pools
> The healing of earth is given a man. (OL, 48–49)

Words of Roosevelt are quoted to extend the vision of technology as human relation, binding *"earth to earth and man to man"*: *"It is clear that the Muscle Shoals development is but a small part of the potential usefulness of the entire Tennessee River. Such use, if envisioned in its entirety, transcends mere power development"*

(OL, 53). From this document the poet continues to build her imaginative vision:

> Now in the unity of all vision, unity of the land, the forests
>   and water,
> See nature, the nation, as a web of lives
> On the earth together, full of their potencies.
> The total unity, reached past images,
> Reaching past the naming of religions.
> We reach to create. That is our central meaning,
> Suggestion of art and altar in all our passwords,
> For the meaning of "mirror of nature," the meaning of "image
>   of God"
> Is a simple fiery meaning: man is to create.
> Making, singing, bring the potential to day. (OL, 54)

Over twenty years after her first insight into the human meanings of modern technology, this poet continues to explore them; her positive vision intensifies. Singing the praises of twentieth-century human skills is extraordinary in contemporary poetry where one most often finds revulsion for the machine and a yearning to return to a simpler life.

Willkie, fascinated by power, cannot conceive of government management of natural power. He fights the TVA and its chairman, David Lilienthal. Willkie can't understand why a man like Lilienthal doesn't seek his rewards (money and power) in private industry, where they would be greater; Willkie calls government ownership "red revolution" and "socialism." But in this section of the book we are shown the man coming slowly to certain realizations, losing his rigid patterns of thought, passing through the apparent contradictons of private industry versus governmental control.

There is another way to see the fight. It involves an entire way of seeing, in which you acknowledge fully that you are dealing with the lives of people in relation to a valley. Not one river, but many rivers streaming together; not the tree of rivers, but the land and itself and the future time.

. . . .

Is the purpose of the Valley project to make a system of relation between people and a valley—their environment—beyond any idea of the state? Unless the state is allowed to be a growing system of relation. Unless we think in this way. (OL, 75)

Willkie sees that this new way of thinking is integral to his life, which in its various phases sought ways of living and thinking beyond the accepted. His thinking grows from his youthful radicalism, his early wildness.

In this section we are given the parallel growth in realization of four-year-old Paul, a German refugee whose father is missing. The poet reminds us at the beginning of his story that "In a song, in a clear look, the heat and blood of history may come, through a child, to us all." Paul's teacher says, "His creations are real. / His agonies / Are curiously related to the trouble of the people of the world" (OL, 85). Rukeyser's vision here is rare and remarkable: to include the experiences of a child in the story of the growth of a prominent man—this is to accord the child a dignity and importance he has not known since the poems of Blake. Paul, believing his father will never be found, creates for himself an older personality; he calls himself "Timmy Torin," who is nine and who can take care of himself. By imagining, Paul can cope with loss; he can be at home in the world. Thus Paul's growth is like Willkie's, like ours. This vision is often rendered cumulatively and effectively by the poet, but too often the lines of poetry run to vagueness. One wishes Rukeyser hadn't written so much here, or had pruned more carefully.

In Part Three we are given Willkie the candidate for president. He campaigns emphasizing that "the heart of the American system is the control of power." We are shown in this very entertaining section just what power, especially political power, means in America—the "amorphous America" for which, as Philip Booth noted in his review, "Miss Rukeyser, too, risks so greatly." We are told that Anne McCormick says that "Willkie . . . means the big, anxious, fluctuating world of the middle class." Then follows a question and answer page satirizing this class's statistics, questionnaires, categories, and stigmas placed on us for our beliefs. The passages of poetry focus on the mean accommodations that create political power. We are reminded of the capacity of human beings for the full range of experience, from the heroic to the loathsomely self-serving. We are given the heroic struggle for survival of pioneers and its debased version in the modern American political system.

> They trade their partisans. That is their method of choice.
> When they say survival, they do not mean living under the avalanche.
> They do not recognize the existence of the avalanche.
> They mean how to set up shop in the arroyo,
> And show a profit after the first six months.(OL, 107)

Philip Booth said that "few readers will ever come closer to politics than in those sections of the book that focus directly on the Republican Convention of 1940, and on that last prewar campaign." We are even given the astrologist Bertha Stuckey's reading of Willkie: it is full of misspellings and malapropisms, but it is uncannily accurate. The book builds its vision on these strange, diverse elements of American life. Booth said, "The bookmaking is beautiful. . . . episodic, dissonant, fragmented, and explosive—as Willkie's life was and as his country still is." [5]

Part Four, on Willkie's campaign, contains marvelous descriptions of that whirlwind American phenomenon and what must be among the best descriptions of the American industrial landscape south and west of Chicago. She gives us the feel of this countryside from the relentless campaign train, though the poet's rendering of primordial forces is overwrought. Here is Rukeyser risking greatly, in Philip Booth's words. Her voice reaches for the intensity which she feels is the true climate of the world, not the climate of American poetry or American life in the fifties, to be sure, but a "climate of excitement and revelation." She fails repeatedly, but the risk and the successes, one feels, are worth it. As Philip Booth said, "This is perhaps the most ambitious attempt since *Let Us Now Praise Famous Men* to define a segment of America, and for that it deserves any reader's praise."

5. Philip Booth, review of OL, in *Saturday Review*, August 3, 1957, p. 12.

But some readers like Murray Kempton in the New York *Post* didn't even try to receive the book. In his review he gave no evidence of having read it, saying, "The scheme, the structure, the lyric sense, the imagery of the entire performance seem to me on a level below argument. You merely fall back from it." Nevertheless he took the opportunity to deride *One Life*, and we see in his attack the poet's penalty for making herself vulnerable, allowing her vision its full expression, her voice its risking.[6]

Halfway through *One Life* we have Willkie losing the presidential election, going to Florida, and experiencing a deep work going on in himself in terms of images. "What? he thinks. Really hard work! Far under, essays he has never known. He hears the women's voices diminishing near him. They suppose he is asleep. He is not. It is a work of images, like mourning or falling in love. A mask is off and the mirrors will not again show him that stare. The work is difficult and bare. Very slow" (OL, 146). At the end of this episode of recovering from defeat, he can say, "For I am born, I believe myself again. . . . Now I speak only the words I can believe, throwing away the rigid corroded terms of hatred. The sly resonant pity." Since he found himself through images he will also find the world that way. The next chapter is called "A Coast of Images," and in it we have Willkie deciding to go to England to see the war for himself. Before leaving he hears Roosevelt's inaugural speech: "Democracy is the structure of the limitless civilization; its capacity is infinite process toward a developing fullness—the fullness of human life. . . . A people . . . must go on knowing itself, understanding the hopes and needs of its neighbors. The neighbors of the mind are all those that live and have lived in the world" (OL, 157–58). (Rukeyser seems to have shared both Roosevelt's vision and his terms for it.) These words of his old opponent will take root in Willkie's consciousness. The images which he beholds in brave, invasion-threatened England join with Roosevelt's words and what Willkie recognizes as his own meanings, the images of his personal life. On the jetty at Dover he achieves a new vision of

6. Murray Kempton, review of OL, in New York *Post*, April 14, 1957.

the oneness of the world, a vision which is the natural consequence of that procession of images he has been "seeing" all along. When he leaves England this onetime apologist of the rights of business speaks of the need to defend "human rights and Freedom"; his vision has expanded. "I now newborn. Protest prepareth me" (OL, 190).

In Part Seven, "A Proving Flight" (a brief, seven-page section), Willkie has the realization of the persona of "Theory of Flight": "One way to meet threat is with a leap of growth. To become oneself at the next level, and declare." In Part Eight, "Open System," he begins to act in accordance with his leap of realization that the world is one world. The press and the politicians don't believe in mythic transformations, in rebirths, so they see Willkie's statements as "opportunism." But the reader can see Willkie as the poet does. The refugee Paul is introduced into the story again, a child whose irrepressible urge to growth is the life force's best witness.

> A child riding the stormy mane of noon
> Sang to me past the cloud of the world:
> Are you born? Are you born?
> The form of this hope is the law of all things,
> Our foaming sun is the toy of that force.
> Touch us alive, developing light! Today,
> Revealed over the mountains, every living eyes.
>
> . . . .
>
> The song of a child; the song of the cloud of the world,
> Born, born, born. Cloud become real,
>   and change,
> The starry form of love. (OL, 207)

Here the poet achieves an even more humanly satisfying vision of the life force, of process and change: it is love. Both Willkie and Paul are "touch[ed] . . . alive" by that "developing light."

Paul changes and grows; one of his phases is violent rejection, a mythic refusal. But he returns, too, like a hero in myth.

For a while, for a short while, it was full cruelty. Assailed he was, with danger over his life-space. Fretful he was, restless and stern, the artificial boasting king. Loud and unreal to himself, with all his conflict packed for him to carry, and the admiring, the pity of the adults, out of reach.

But at the moment at which the grownups would have stopped it, at the moment when the five-year-olds would have turned on Paul, it was as if he remembered. He was on his journey, he was moving toward his world. The long exchange with Miss Lorence—her cheek bent over him as he lay himself down, her short soft questions, the open feeling of her answers, came back to him like Eden. It had always been there. And his own people, the five-year-olds! He remembered the other life: communication.

He turned back to his own group with his whole life in his act of choice. (OL, 216)

Then Paul meets Willkie (this episode is not based on fact), and the man sees his relationship to Paul: Willkie's people also came from Germany. Through a procession of images out of his own past, images which have moved from the beginning of this book, Willkie realizes his connection with the child and our responsibilities to all living things.

When Willkie returns from England he is a champion of civil liberties, agreeing to defend an American Communist whose citizenship is threatened. "Of all the times when civil liberties should be defended, it is now," he says (OL, 228). Willkie learned this principle of the need to defend civil liberties, especially when the country is being threatened from without, in a vivid scene he witnessed in the House of Commons. A Labour member strongly denounced the government's suppression of the London *Daily Worker*. What Willkie learned transfigured him, and the process is described in mythic terms, in a phrase from "Second Elegy." "He felt split by a stroke, a tree half green, half burning. . . . There are many kinds of homecoming. . . . It was the most dramatic example of democracy at work that anyone could wish to see" (OL, 179). But Willkie falls from grace and vision and "in the grip of the appetite for power" says mindless, chauvinistic things to crowds. He grows, and he speaks in his real voice again: "We cannot, he says, seal ourselves against the world" (OL, 230–33).

Willkie accepts the world, even in its denial of him, even in his party's turning from him, "in their frigidities against him." The great realization for Willkie is that the world can be accepted *in one's own image* of it. The poem concluding this section is an Emersonian celebration of the self as creator of the universe. In the poem we hear "Crayon House" from *The Green Wave*:

> Everything here is real and of our joy.
> The rivers are real, they come bringing their colors,
> The lives flow through us too in meaning, in form
> Which is meaning and motion. Nothing here is unreal.
> The beginning is giving; and the land is wide.
> Daring of voices and faces, the moment being in flow,
> Our selves being now, we and our word alive.
>
> Throw away the code   :   there is no success or failure,
> You will move through success and you will never fail,
>
> . . . .
>
> The songs of your lifetime sing and say and relate:
> You are the beginning, as you are the end.
> The song is song, it sings, and it is real.(OL, 237–38)

In Part Ten Willkie journeys to Russia and China. The Chinese give him the three words of his Chinese name: "Powerful, You, Foundation—which mean in English, strengthen your inner self." Willkie is now saying what he deeply believes.

Not elected; never elected; he has never had anything like the power he imagined. With no status except the status given by a moment before a microphone to which he brings his lifetime. No weight, like the moment in love when the body lets go of substance. A gathering of splendors like memory. He looks at the instrument, complex black and silver giving him possibility, his voice. He speaks to whoever will listen to him—a world of listening, as if he were speaking to one woman who gave him words. Or one man, a life to a life.
Toward world unity, he says. (OL, 276)

The press criticizes his statements, saying, "Mr. Marco Polo Willkie has already caused more embarrassment to the Allies than any man abroad."

Charles J. Rolo in the *Atlantic* found that Rukeyser idealized Willkie too much in this section. We do not learn, Rolo says, that Willkie was "monumentally hoodwinked by Stalin," that some of

Willkie's statements on one-worldism were foolish. These criticisms would perhaps be justified if this were another kind of book, one whose method is what Rolo wants—"searching analysis" rather than story and song. (Rukeyser herself said in the foreword that she didn't think she was writing biography.) Rolo might have the same comments about *Walden*: "Miss Rukeyser has been carried away by fuzzy thinking and idealization. Her book must be taken as a celebration of a man's conversion to what Miss Rukeyser believes to be the Light. And as such *One Life* belongs, for better and for worse, in the upper echelons of inspirational literature." Alas, in this age of "searching analysis" and drastically reduced hopes, we cannot even admit the wisdom of idealism which has not yet found its means. Perhaps that is why we have few prophets of anything but doom.

In the last sections of the book Willkie fades in and out of his real voice as he admits or refuses to admit growth and change. We are given the poetry of the "Lives" and of "The Soul and Body of John Brown" again, as Willkie becomes a "risen image" reflecting our lives and hopes. Just before his series of fatal heart attacks Willkie has become a real poet of possibility, of inclusiveness: "Our thinking and planning in the future must be global. . . . I maintain that if you look deep enough into the heart of your enemy, there you will see your twin brother. I have faith in the fact that nothing is static. . . . There is no conflict among the hopes of peoples" (OL, 289–91). The poetry of process at the end of the book is splendid, but as before one wearies of the description of the physical world offered as parallel to the progress of consciousness. I believe the song is simply too long, though the poet's performance is vigorous and often dazzling. To those who come to *One Life* with an open spirit, it is, as Eberhart said, "a life-confronting and a life-giving book."

Body of Waking

Kenneth Rexroth's magnificent review of *Body of Waking* in the New York *Times* dove to the heart of the book as he found in the poems Rukeyser's characteristic themes and modes. He wrote of the "primary virtue" of her poetry: "a kind of mood, an instinctive organic awareness." He described the "peasant quality" of her "sense of the processes of life all interconnected and spreading illimitably away." He noted that the "sonority" of her poetry, the "soft rumble and murmur of consonants . . . imparts naturally and beyond all argument that sense of at-homeness in the world that modern man so conspicuously lacks." In the poems of *Body of Waking* which are in the line of "Ajanta" and *Orpheus* he found "a kind of implicitly philosophical poetry, a species of unassuming, objectively presented but lucid and profound 'wisdom literature.' The meanings of life are not analyzed and explicated, they are responded to and embodied. Pre-eminently these poems are responses rather than reactions." He found "the art of peacefulness" in the poems, and he concluded thus:

> *Body of Waking*—it is a very good title, because that is just what the poems are about, the organism, filled and complete, rising out of dream to continuously widening and deepening levels of realization. This book does not differ from the poet's others except for the years. It is the work of a more mature, a wiser woman.
>
> At the beginning she was something of a child prodigy, but there is nothing at all prodigious about her work today. The promises are fulfilled, the facilities are all accomplishments now. There is no message, no rhetoric, there are no answers, and yet, there is the awareness of that which only knows all the answers—"body of waking." [7]

The poems strike one by the sense of fulfillment, so rare in contemporary poetry. It is not self-satisfaction or smugness, and it everywhere admits the particular terrors of the modern world. But Rukeyser's is a vision of the immense riches of the world and the mountain of possibility the human race could scale if it chose to. Here is a poet's urging to growth, to flight, an intense affirmation lit with the energy of undeniable conviction and embodied in constellated associations.

The amazing variety of the poet's style is evident in this vol-

7. Kenneth Rexroth, review of *Body of Waking*, in *New York Times Book Review*, October 19, 1958, p. 46.

ume, for besides the "theoretical" poems like those from the Willkie book there are those in which Winfield Townley Scott found "a lyric, personal change," poems which he compared to "A Charm for Cantinflas" in *The Green Wave*. Most often in her work the concrete and the theoretical have been mingled in individual poems, as in *Orpheus*, or the theoretical has been given free rein, as in many poems in *One Life*. We have not often had, before *Body of Waking*, poems predominantly concrete, except in those "social" poems from *Theory of Flight* like "Boy with His Hair Cut Short" and the "documentary" poems of *U.S.1*. But in this volume poems like "Pouring Milk Away" and "Born in December" anticipate the brief, concrete, direct lyrics of *Breaking Open*.

> Pouring Milk Away
> Here, again. A smell of dying in the milk-pale carton,
> And nothing then but pour the milk away.
> More of the small and killed, the child's, wasted,
> Little white arch of the drink and taste of day.
> Spoiled, gone and forgotten; thrown away.
>
> Day after day I do what I condemned in countries.
> Look, the horror, the waste of food and bone.
> You will know why when you have lived alone.[8]

Similarly, "Suite for Lord Timothy Dexter," another in the sequence of "Lives," anticipates in its short, choppy lines and homely humor the pungent poems in *Breaking Open*. "Dexter" is the only one of the "Lives" that is funny—in a Blakean way. Dexter was, as *The Columbia Encyclopedia* says bluntly, an "American merchant and eccentric" of the eighteenth century. In his "wildness" and illiteracy, his "clap of mockery," his childlike belief in himself and in God, he said and did profoundly original things while amassing a fortune. Dexter was an original like Ives, Ryder, Gibbs, and Chapman, but in the poem he doesn't take himself as seriously as they did; Rukeyser's poem about Dexter is entertaining. At least one reviewer thought she was referring to herself in her creation of the

---

8. Muriel Rukeyser, *Body of Waking* (New York, 1958).

unorthodox Dexter.[9] ("Dexter" is the first of the "Lives" containing passages written in the first person.) If so, she certainly answered her reviewers lightheartedly:

> How can I speak to them today? What can I know,
> What can I show so that we see ourselves?
> Voices of stinted singing in the towns,
> Voices of wildness and fear of wilderness.
> The rhythm, the root. Gathering in
> Sources of music and the wild sea-rose.[10]
> Sea-music and the sea building its waters,
> The weathervane beast. My song.
>
> Whenever I say what I mean
> They mock me and call me mad.
> They slip my meaning—
>
> .   .   .   .
>
> I speak in images so they may know
> My gold spread-eagle on the cupalow.

Some of Dexter's ideas about "Cadameys and Collegeys" (and the "hell on earth" caused him by his son-in-law, "mad with learning, as poor as a snake, / As proud as Lucifer") must have tickled the poet who was attacked for her scholarship, in one way or another, all her life. And in Dexter's belief that the world is one creature, Rukeyser met her own profound conviction. The concept is central to the thought of Giordano Bruno, a hero of "Theory of Flight" and *The Traces of Thomas Hariot* where Bruno's *De Immenso* is discussed.

In addition to the style of certain poems in *Body of Waking* which flourishes in the poems of *Breaking Open*, the 1958 volume begins a new phase in the procession of images in Rukeyser's work, one that reaches a climax in *Breaking Open*. The image of "breaking open" first appears here, in the poem "Mother Garden's Round." Death has come to the poet's garden, her "Mother Garden," her sensed world of being. It is the death of love and per-

---

9. Louis Simpson, review of *Waterlily Fire*, in *Hudson Review*, XVI (Spring, 1963), 130.
10. Yes, these phrases have been met before, in "Ives."

haps, as another poem in this volume suggests, the death of the poet's mother as well. The pain of absence fills the poem. In order to relieve her soul of the specter of death and absence the poet contemplates the turning season:

> Something is dancing on leafdrift, dancing across the graves:
> A child is watching while the world breaks open.
> Garden my green may grow.

The last line becomes the refrain of the poem and is recognized as a prayer by the end of the poem when she says, "We wish to be born again." The image of the world breaking open resonates with several other striking images in the volume: "the maimed triumphant middle of my way" and the heart as "tearflesh beckoner" ("A Birth"); the milkweed saying to the distraught poet who has witnessed a bitter quarrel, "Never mind, never mind. All splits open. There is new inside" ("After Their Quarrel"); the tree which "stood blasted open" but nevertheless bore a fertile crown of apples ("Tree"). These images grow out of the poet's experience of giving birth. Her vision of the hope in process and possibility is now embodied in imagery more organic than ever. Now there is not just seed: now there is seed bursting its pod. "We bear the bursting seeds of our return," she said in "Theory of Flight." Now she *is* the bursting seed. It is the physical bursting that is focused on; she will say it explicitly in "Poem as Mask" (from *The Speed of Darkness*): "Myself split open in sleep."

In the development of Rukeyser's poetry we can actually see embodied the experience of motherhood. It has given this poet her great procession of concrete images that reach in their associations into the spirit, into possibility. In the first section of *The Green Wave* she wrote as a woman who had not yet given birth; there she spoke of a renaissance of spirit, of being reborn in a sense of self-discovery, self-acceptance ("This Place in the Ways," "Crayon House.") She spoke of having found her myth, her "beast," in her identification with flowing being ("Green Limits.") Her images in that volume were powerful and vibrant with their green associations—beginnings, hopes. But in *Body of Waking* she writes as a woman who has given birth; as she said in the second poem of "Nine Poems," "And in my flesh at last I saw." The bursting body is now the unmistakable generator of Rukeyser's imagery, the body that has survived crisis. She had written of surviving the crises of collapsed political and social ideals; she had written of surviving the death of a lover; she had composed a poetry of physical rhythm with images growing out of delight in the mortal body. But only in *Body of Waking* can she write of surviving a physical crisis that brought new life out of great peril. "Fountains of images" rise from that experience. One has to say it was the perfect "proving" experience for a poet of her persuasion. Now she can say she is "newborn" with giving birth. Now she can see her life as a procession of images leading to this fertile moment, and nothing wasted.

> Lit by a birth, I defend dark beginnings,
> Waste that is never waste, most-human giving,
> Declared and clear as the mortal body of grace.

In choosing to bear a child, in accepting the immense vulnerability of that condition, she accepted the world in a way that transcends the merely philosophical. From the beginning, in *Theory of Flight*, she had accepted the world intellectually and emotionally; she had not rebelled against the given of mortal existence, as Eliot rebelled, turning to an unearthly justification for daily life. But in giving birth she accepted the process of the world in her own flesh. Her poems body forth that acceptance from then on. (More and more her poems identify her self with her sexual, often her generative, body: "Too secret are the entrances / To my stretched hiding-place," she writes in a poem about leaving a cold lover to find herself.) The ultimate compliment she pays the analyst Frances G. Wickes on her eightieth birthday is to say, "Deep in the waking, her life builds in light / The vision of the body of the soul" (BW, 48). Accepting the body as ordinary given, we usually speak of having a vision of the mysterious soul. Now Rukeyser situates the mystery in the body as well. The lines also suggest that the body as well as the soul enjoys its vision. In "On the Death of Her Mother" the poet laments her mother's negative personality: "All those years, Mother, your arms were full of absence." Her mother refused the body of the world: "all the running of arrows could never not once find / Anything but your panic among all that substance." But the daughter has found the substance, the body of the world and of the soul. In her flesh she has seen.

> Starflash on water; the embryo in the foam.
> Dives through my body in the waking bright,
> Watchmen of birth; I see.

The translations from Paz in this volume are also celebrations of the substance of the world which is more lovely and mysterious than we recognize: "The insects then were jewels who were alive." Paz and Rukeyser have come to a vision of the ineffability of substance, of body.

> The world arrives
> Burning its name the names that clothe the world
> Nothing remains but an enormous sound
> Tower of glass that shelters birds of glass
> Invisible birds
> Made of a substance identical with light

If giving birth was obviously the source of much of Rukeyser's imagery from *Body of Waking* on, the experience of nursing an infant also gave rise to a complex of images. "Night Feeding" is the central poem about this experience. In the poem she describes being awakened by an infant at night; the child's cry starts milk flowing from the breasts. Because the mother's body responds even if she is weary, nervous, rebellious, or ill, it is a most vivid instance of the kind of adequate response Rukeyser wrote of in "Theory of Flight":

> go travelling to balance need with answer
> . . . .
> food to the mouth, tools to the body
> . . . .
> go answering   answering   FLY.

In "Night Feeding" the poet, obviously leading the harassed life of a nursing mother complicated by the absence of a father and filled with private difficulty and "green pain" (she learned after her delivery that she had had a hysterectomy), knows the satisfaction of feeling her body work. She knows then its affinity with the nourishing powers of the cosmos:

> woke to the burning song and the tree burning blind,
> despair of our days and the calm milk-giver who
> knows sleep, knows growth, the sex of fire and grass,
> renewal of all waters and the time of the stars

Her old themes are here, in her body which is nourishing a new life; here is the satisfaction of "answering   answering." In the darkness of the night and the mystery of her bodily functions she finds the light of her growing belief. Here is the darkness of *The Green Wave* actually felt in the body.

> Shadows grew in my veins, my bright belief,
> my head of dreams deeper than night and sleep.
> Voices of all black animals crying to drink,
> cries of all birth arise, simple as we,
> found in the leaves, in clouds and dark, in dream,
> deep as this hour, ready again to sleep.

The dark of the miraculously natural, nourishing, developing functions of the body is celebrated in poem after poem. In "A Birth" there is "the smile of darkness on my song and my son," and in "Rite," a celebration of the poet's first menses (is there another such poem in Western literature?), she refers to herself and to her sister as "two dark sisters [who] laughed and sang."

It is probable that nursing gave rise to the images in the following lines that focus on the world as food, on the poet as one consumed:

> Childhood in tide-pools where all things are food.
> Behind us the shores emerged and fed on tide.
> We fed on summer, the round flowers in our hands
> From the snowball bush entered us, and prisoner wings,
> And shells in spirals, all food. ("Children, the Sandbar, That
>   Summer")

From an untitled poem:

> Make and be eaten, the poet says,
> Lie in the arms of nightlong fire,
> To celebrate the waking, wake.
>
> . . . .
>
> Only and finally declare
>
> . . . .
>
> The body of waking and the skill
> To make your body such a shape
> That all the eyes of hope shall stare.(BW, 24)

These lines recall the stare of the mob hungry for artistic vision in the "Third Elegy," those who skidded up to the formal staircase of the sealed museum. Here is also the stare of those in the "agony of street" who need the "risen image" of the poet's "Lives." Now the hunger is described in physical terms and its appeasement will involve the body. In *Body of Waking* artistic vision is recognized as springing from the body—like the child, like milk.

Opposed to the certainty of the body and its births and nourishing, opposed to the calm of the spirit that has learned from the body its "bright belief," one finds in this volume the "century of absence in the valley of confusion": the cold-war world, the nineteen fifties. Several poems in the book are stark reminders that the poet's hopeful vision persists in a grim time. In "Body of Waking" nations are "separate wards in the same hospital." Here are the hatred, vengefulness, and suspicion of East and West after World War II:

> Revenge which spikes the cross and splits the star
> Withers the crescent. The world circles among
> The solitude of Spain, the solitude of Stalingrad,
> Solitude in the hills of loess and the caves of Africa,
> And now your solitude, New York, who raised yourself
>   above.

The poet calls upon her countrymen to wake from the slumber of material prosperity and recognize the needs of all peoples and their own spiritual needs.

> Does the fat belly know its heart is broken?
>
> . . . .
>
> Much later, after you speak of the weapon birds
> And the spies in your milk and the little split children
> Bleeding models of cars; you told their fortunes
> According to a harvest of slot-machines;
> According to the obscene pattern of bombers.
>
> . . . .
>
> What do you do then? Weep for the generations?
> You change your life. No. You begin again
> Going on from the moment in which you stand today.

But the poet believes that the energy spent in suspicion and in isolating and arming ourselves can be redirected:

> The force that split the spirit could found a city,
> That held the split could shine the lights of science.
> This rigid energy could still break and run dancing
> Over the rockies and smokies of all lives.

The same wish for redirection of knowledge and energy is expressed in "Hero Speech," a recognizable offspring of "Theory of
Flight":

> And in an age at war,
> Dead power, the lying opposites, the great cities fighting in the
>   air,
> We think of flying, the flying of all dreams,
> The ancient reaching for the chance to return changed—

In "Body of Waking" the poet sees her vision in the elegies embodied in

> the young, talking together of growth and form,
> Arrived once more at the terms.
>
> . . . .
>
> Seeking continually developing light.

There are no specific answers to the times here; there is simply
celebration of generous, accepting, peaceful lives.

> Growing to feed each other, lover, mother of gesture
> To turn against fear and withholden reach,

The movement at the center of all things
Making a stillness never a refusal.

The times refused F. O. Matthiessen, who is honored in this volume in a poem about his suicide in 1950. "This was a terrible period for all of us," says Rukeyser. Matthiessen had been attacked and vilified by reviewers of his travel diary, *From the Heart of Europe*, in which he showed, as Malcolm Cowley wrote, a spirit of internationalism which sought to break cold-war barriers. Matthiessen was a scholar who stressed communication, who wanted to participate fully in the life of the community. *Time* magazine referred to him in 1948 as "a bald, mild-mannered little bachelor who thinks the job of U. S. intellectuals is to 'rediscover and rearticulate' the need for Socialism." *Time* called him "naive" and said, "Seldom has the gullibility and wishful thinking of pinkish academic intellectuals been so perfectly exposed as in this little book," his travel diary. This scholar who in Cowley's words had been "inspired by the early work of Van Wyck Brooks and Lewis Mumford [to] join in their search for a usable tradition in American literature," this sensitive intellectual who like Rukeyser sought the most humane and progressive elements in our heritage, was deeply depressed in April, 1950. He left this note before he jumped to his death from a hotel window in Boston: "How much the state of the world has to do with my state of mind, I do not know. But as a Christian and a Socialist, believing in international peace, I find myself terribly oppressed by the present tensions." He was forty-eight years old.[11]

Rukeyser's poem on Matthiessen emphasizes the terrors of the times (described in "Body of Waking") which he could not survive.

F. O. M.

the death of Matthiessen
It was much stronger than they said. Noisier.
Everything in it more colored. Wilder.

11. Malcolm Cowley, "Matty for One," *New Republic*, April 24, 1950, p. 21; *Time*, September 20, 1948, pp. 112–14; *Time*, April 10, 1950, pp. 40–43.

> More at the center calm.
> Everything was more violent than ever they said,
> Who tried to guard us from suicide and life.
> We in our wars were more than they had told us.
> Now that descent figures stand about the horizon,
> I have begun to see the living faces,
> The storm, the morning, all more than they ever said.
> Of the new dead, that friend who died today,
> Angel of suicides, gather him in now.
> Defend us from doing what he had to do
> Who threw himself away.

Rukeyser saw Matthiessen's pain the way she saw everything, and still does: in a social, often a cosmic context. There is more to a life of struggle than she can ever say, the poem insists. There are the great, undefinable aspirations of the idealist. Her poem on Matthiessen reflects her feeling that a life is more than any poet can tell, because

> No one ever walking this our only earth, various, very
>   clouded,
> in our forests, in all the valleys of our early dreams,
> No one has ever for long seen any thing in full, not live
> As any one river or man has run his changes, child
> Of the swarms and sowings. (BW, 116)

Robert Lowell, coming out of the forties as the leading poet of the antiheroic tradition of Shapiro's "V-Letter," also wrote a poem on Matthiessen's suicide. A comparison of these treatments highlights Rukeyser's difference from most of her contemporaries. Lowell's poem has the brilliant ironic pathos characteristic of the literature of our times when every reverberating gesture is reduced to its small, private, often shameful motive.

> Who knows whom he might have killed,
> falling bald there like a shell. I'm scared
> to hit this street, or stand like Stonewall Jackson
> spitting on the superhighways.
> . . . .
> Mattie, his Yale *Skull and Bones* on the dresser, torn
> between the homosexual's terrible love

for forms, and his anarchic love of man . . .
then dies, unique as the many, lies frozen meat,
fast colors lost to lust and prosecution.[12]

In "The Loan," Rukeyser, singing the consolation of love and idealism, addresses one who is being persecuted by the times, as was Matthiessen. The person, having "accepted curse of a false sun" is depressed by "nightmare judgments of innocence and guilt" and has assumed "private self-given torment." The poet takes upon herself another's pain of accusation.

> The wound reaches its opposite, shines on my face, a flower
> Bright among violence, the passion that is peace.
> We have promises to make:
> We saw that in each other's eyes.
> Not to accept the curse, but wake,
> Never to act in formal innocence.
> It was not the maze of the time
> But possibility we felt
> In full gaze as we began to wake.

These poems with references to the McCarthy years, the cold-war years, are filled with the suffering of one aware of spirit-splitting isolation and suspicion. The world of *Body of Waking* is very far from Willkie's and the poet's vision of one world.

In November, 1978, Rukeyser received her dossier from the Department of Justice. In that document she found proof that her earlier fears of being under surveillance had been well founded. Her 118-page dossier—parts of which are heavily inked out and some pages of which are missing—shows that the F.B.I. gathered information about her and her family beginning in the thirties. "They knew more about the circumstances of my father's bankruptcy than I did," she says. Beginning in the forties, if not sooner, her phone was tapped and both letters she wrote and letters she received were opened or acquired and examined. The F.B.I. knew, for instance, the contents of a letter she wrote in the early forties inquiring whether Otto Boch was still alive. They also knew the

12. Robert Lowell, *Notebook* (New York, 1971), 172.

contents of a letter from her mother. In most instances they noted that the material of her phone conversations and her correspondence was of no interest. The principal informants for the F.B.I. were Eugene Lyons and Louis Budenz, two well-known active anticommunists who maintained she was a concealed communist. Rukeyser has always denied this.

But despite the chilling atmosphere she lived and worked in, the poems that flowered in the darkest of those years, the poems of *Body of Waking*, embody her vision of waking and oneness. The vision may be expressed quite simply, as in "Born in December":

> They reckon by the wheel of the year. Our birth's before.
> From the dark birthday to the young year's first stay
> We are the ones who wait and look for ways:
> Ways of beginning, ways to be born, ways for
> Solvings, turnings, wakings; we are always
> A little younger than they think we are.

Often the hopeful vision emerges from a concrete situation, as in "Divining Water" with its effective central metaphor:

> While the old man held his branch and walked toward water
> Walked to that moment where the branch dives down
>
> . . . .
>
> Diving of prayer leaping to find deep under
> Reason and rock the cold sweet-driven springs

But in the long final section of *Body of Waking* the hopeful poetry is not always built from concrete situations. The poems flow, singing "the meaning of rivers" and "change deep in the form of things." Poem after poem sings the union of person with cosmos, person with her own childhood: "You know the murmurs. They come from your own throat. / You are the bridges to the city and the blazing food-plant green" (BW, 85). In magnificent song the poet gives us "the meanings as they move," her first themes in new contexts. "Powerplant," for example, is like "The Dam" in *U.S.1*, deriving the meanings of spiritual growth from a technological phenomenon, even religious meanings from the industrial landscape. "We know the light incarnate, we have seen / At last that the flashing is our old light, and flesh." That is what "light incarnate" (Christ, God) is: ourselves freshly recognized, assumed, functioning. The power which starts with water in the physical plant "coils, sheathes, transforms itself turning, into light." So can we turn to light. (The image has recurred in several poems now. Recall "Now I am light and nothing more" in the fourth of the "Nine Poems" and her translation of Paz's "substance identical with light.") Light is power is love. The equations are not neat; they flow associatively. They work. The meaning of linked renewals is conveyed in this poetry. One must acknowledge and follow the flow of it, let the imagination "seize hold and let go fast." The poetry doesn't always work; sometimes the reader needs a slower procession of images, more explicit linkings, more concreteness, but it rewards attentiveness; and giving over one's full consciousness to the poetry is what it requires.

What strikes the reader who has followed the poet's developing themes is that in *Body of Waking* she has had personal proof of the renewal she has been singing since *Theory of Flight*. She has had a child. And she recognizes that she has been able to imagine wholeness, peace, and love in a time of fragmentation, war, hatred, accusation. Events in her lifetime are bearing out her early vision. In a rich coincidence, the geographical area in which the Scottsboro trials were held in the thirties, where she was detained in a station house and contracted typhoid ("Where Sheriff Fever / Ordered me to trial"), was flooded in the TVA project. Here is renewal and power:

> Psalms awake and asleep, remember the manmade
> Lake where those barren treecrowns rode.
> Where air of curses hung, keel of my calm
> Rides our created tide. (BW, 94)

Reviewing *Body of Waking* in *Yale Review*, Thom Gunn wrote, "I doubt if Muriel Rukeyser . . . has any idea of what she is saying," and he complained about "vague emoting" and "a certain fashionable disjointedness" in her poetry. But other reviewers were enthusiastic. In *The Nation*, Rosenthal praised the book, saying Rukeyser's mind is wider-ranging than Roethke's and that she uses her intelligence more actively in her poetry. There is nothing in Roethke, said Rosenthal, "to match the general awareness of a whole world's interlocking meanings." He praised her "controlled, inward calm" and her "remarkable lyric ease and musicality, perfectly obvious to anyone who paid attention." But the music, he felt, was often obscured by "endlessly involuted strugglings toward self–identification." W. T. Scott praised her "steady, solid accomplishment."

To my utter agreement, Miss Rukeyser is one of those who has never written as though she thought poetry "a game." Her first poems of more than twenty years ago antedate that currently fashionable, chi-chi attitude (which apparently requires a religious background), and from the first she has barged ahead, dedicated to the proposition that for her the poetry is in the meaning. . . .The energies of deep conviction have often failed to lift the verse beyond journalism or above speech-making. . . . Yet rarely has she failed to be rewarding in the heavily pregnant line . . . for example, in this new collection—"Where there is giving needing no forgiving."

Philip Booth said, "It is true that her statements can become burdened by rhetoric, but she risks statement in a way which few poets do." He found in *Body of Waking* "a maturity of vision which is beyond paraphrase." [13]

13. Thom Gunn, review of BW, in *Yale Review*, n.s. XLVIII (December, 1958), 299; M. L. Rosenthal, review of BW, in *Nation*, March 21, 1959, pp. 259–60; W. T. Scott, review of BW, in *Saturday Review*, January 3, 1959, p. 14; Philip Booth, review of BW, in *Christian Science Monitor*, December 24, 1958.

SIX

The Sixties

Waterlily Fire

In *Waterlily Fire*, a collection from all Rukeyser's volumes from 1935 to 1962, one may trace the unfurling themes and images through the years. The new poems expand the meanings; their cadences display a sureness and naturalness that are the result of decades of crafting. Richard Eberhart stated in his review, "The strength of her conviction coupled with her integrated conception of the world probably makes for the originality of her style, which is uncompromising in its difference from that of other poets and is always fresh, vibrant, profound." Several reviewers have tried to describe Rukeyser's mature style, one which does not call particular attention to itself. Stephen Stepanchev said, "She is not technically deft; her poetry is not a poetry of word, rhythm, and formal tensions." But Hayden Carruth distinguished two kinds of Rukeyser poem. In the first he found "force, directness, affection for the separate word, tension, knowledge of cadence and syntax as components of meaning rather than vicissitudes of fabrication"—the elements Stepanchev found lacking in her poetry. Carruth found her "characteristic poem . . . busy, rather long, full of intellectual machinery. . . . The effect is like that of an impasto, colors heaped upon one another until the surface is thick and lightless." Carruth praised the "absolute honesty" in the prayerlike quality of all the poems. Geof Hewitt, writing in Rosalie Murphy's *Contemporary Poets of the English Language* (1970), admired the simplicity of a poem from *The Speed of Darkness*: "What gimmicks of 'style' has the poet employed? One knows only that the poem is bound by a natural rhythm, and seems to relate a part of the poet's experience."

If one has read a good deal of Rukeyser, from the earliest poems on, one recognizes the strong voice in its modulations, the central themes in their progress through the years. The authority of this poetry stems from the "absolute honesty" Carruth sensed. Her work is various, but of a piece. The new poems in *Waterlily Fire* are fresh apprehensions of a lifetime vision rendered in natural rhythms and images more and more associated with the creative body.[1]

That vision is luminous and bold in certain poems like "The Speaking Tree," where the fruitful world is now described in simple, mythic terms.

> The trunk of the speaking tree looks like a tree-trunk
> Until you look again. Then people and animals
> Are ripening on the branches
>
> . . . .
>
> Snakes, fishes. Now the ripe people fall and run,
> Three of them in their shore-dance, flames that stand
> Where reeds are creatures and the foam is flame.

"To Enter That Rhythm Where the Self Is Lost" is the poem she had wanted to see written; it is finally what she has meant all along. (See "A Birth" in *Body of Waking*: "Nothing I wrote is what I must see written.") Several new poems in this volume strike the reader as climactic in this way. In "To Enter" writing poetry, making love, and giving birth (physically and in all beginnings) are seen as types of creation in which the self is completely merged with the power of the cosmos. "Use yourselves. Be. Fly," she wrote in "Theory of Flight." In this brief poem which is beyond paraphrase, which plunges rhythmically toward its meanings, Rukeyser has embodied the essence of her vision.

> To enter that rhythm where the self is lost,
>   where breathing : heartbeat : and the subtle music

1. Muriel Rukeyser, *Waterlily Fire: Poems 1935–1962* (New York, 1962); Richard Eberhart, review of *Waterlily Fire*, in *New York Times Book Review*, September 9, 1962, p. 9; Stepanchev, review of WF; Hayden Carruth, review of WF, in *Poetry*, CI (February, 1963), 358–60; Geof Hewitt, "Muriel Rukeyser," in Rosalie Murphy (ed.), *Contemporary Poets of the English Language* (New York, 1970), 946–49.

of their relation make our dance, and hasten
us to the moment when all things become
magic, another possibility.
That blind moment, midnight, when all sight
begins, and the dance itself is all our breath,
and we ourselves the moment of life and death.
Blinded;   but given now another saving,
the self as vision, at all times perceiving,
all arts all senses being languages,
delivered of will, being transformed in truth—
for life's sake surrendering moment and images,
writing the poem;   in love making;   bringing to birth.

"The Way Out" from "Akiba," another poem in her sequence of "Lives," is "Music of passage" and "Music of those who have walked out of slavery," and its meanings are those of loosening bonds, casting off shackles, discovering the immensity of freedom. The music comes from the alliteration, the assonance, the repetition of words; the music comes also from the moving and enlarging meanings. As she wrote in her couplet "The Sixth Night: Waking" in *Body of Waking*, "That first green night of their dreaming, asleep beneath the Tree, / God said, 'Let meanings move,' and there was poetry." In "Akiba" the meanings move in this visionary way. She is still singing the heroism of those in "Theory of Flight" who pioneered by rebelling. She is still singing the bridging of oppositions:

the walkers
who walked through the opposites, from I to opened Thou,
city and cleave of the sea. Those at flaming Nauvoo,
the ice on the great river : the escaping Negroes,
swamp and wild city;   the shivering children of Paris
and the glass black hearses;   those on the Long March:
all those who together are the frontier, forehead of man.
Where the wilderness enters, the world, the song of the
   world.

The images in the poem are familiar to the reader of Rukeyser; they reverberate in their new contexts: "A child watching / while the sea breaks open. This night. The way in." The last stanza rephrases her concerns in the "Lives," her great admiration for the work of Gibbs, who tried to understand more than partial truths: immense systems. This last rich stanza is the poet's statement going far beyond Gibbs's "Mathematics *is* a language." The final lines recall the thrust of her *Elegies*.

> In a time of building statues of the stars
> valuing certain partial ferocious skills
> while past us the chill and immense wilderness
> spreads its one-color wings until we know
> rock, water, flame, cloud, or the floor of the sea,
> the world is a sign, a way of speaking. To find.
> What shall we find? Energies, rhythms, a journey.
> Ways to discover. The song of the way in.

"For a Mexican Painter" continues developing an ever-present theme, since her experience of giving birth:

> Carlos, your art is embryos,
> These eyes are shaping in the dark
>
> . . . .
> Toward the requirement of light
>
> . . . .
> Deep in the hieratic blood
> Toward sleep toward dream the process goes,
> Toward waking move the sex, the heart,
> The self as woman man and rose.

These themes are familiar; the language, now, is utterly pure and basic.

> A Song of Another Tribe
>
> Guilt   said the bony man [2]
>   Do you feel guilt
>   At your desires?
>   No   I said   my guilt comes when
>   My desires find no way.
>   Country of sand and claws;
>   I wait for my rescuer.
>   No one will venture there.

2. He is Eric Berne.

The music, again, is in the repetition of words, in the assonance, in the movement of meanings (including those associated with the journey in the elegies) to statements which ring final and true. As in *Orpheus*, it is finally her poetry making that rescues her; she is her own rescuer.

> O let my singing bring me
> To that place
> Where live waters
> Rise and go.

"Waterlily Fire" is, as poet May Swenson noted in *The Nation*, the "crown piece" of this collection. The poem, in five parts, deals with the destruction by fire of Monet's *Waterlilies* at the Museum of Modern Art in 1958, the poet's life in Manhattan, a protest of nuclear war, the destructiveness and the creativity of science, and the "procession of images" which is a person's life. All these themes are related in a most satisfying way; images recur from previous poems in startling new contexts. One has to say again that the more one reads of this poet the more rewarding individual poems become: for her work has indeed been "stages of the theatre of the journey." She has apprehended and expressed her life as "the long strip of our many / Shapes, as we range shifting through time." The movement of these images, these meanings in this poem is faster than ever before. The poem has a palpable speed. The phrase "whatever can come . . . can come to me" is a refrain of enlarging meanings. "Waterlily Fire" displays, as Swenson said of Rukeyser's characteristic poems, an artistic method involving "the big canvas, the broad stroke, love of primary color and primary emotion. . . . Her vision is never small, seldom introverted. Her consciousness of *others* around her, of being but one member of a great writhing body of humanity surging out of the past, filling the present, groping passionately toward the future, is a generating force in her work."[3]

3. May Swenson, review of *Waterlily Fire*, in *Nation*, February 23, 1963, pp. 164–66.

The opening description of the poet walking toward the museum and seeing it on fire is realistic and mythic all at once. The poet peers into the flaming moment and sees her life and times illumined.

> Saw down the bright noon street the crooked faces
> Among the tall daylight in the city of change.
> The scene has walls   stone   glass   all my gone life
> One wall a web through which the moment walks
> And I am open, and the opened hour
> The world as water-garden   lying behind it.
>
> . . . .
>
> Whatever can happen in a city of stone,
> Whatever can come to a wall can come to this wall.
>
> I walk in the river of crisis toward the real,
> I pass guards, finding the center of my fear
> And you, Dick, endlessly my friend during storm.
>
> The arm of flame striking through the wall of form.

The last line frames hope and despair in most effective sound and image. It is hope as well as despair to the reader of Rukeyser because one remembers the truth in wildness beyond all walls in her poems and the creativity of flame, as in the "flame, fusion, and defiance" of "Third Elegy." (Later in the poem, flame is associated with awakening.) Characteristically Rukeyser has plunged past the guards who would have kept her from the most dangerous, most terrifying sight. She has beheld the most frightful vision: one of civilization's crowning achievements in flames. This indeed can come to all art in our time. But she finds in this moment the seed of hope.

The next section of the poem is a movement expanding the hopeful theme in the poet's associating herself, like Whitman, with Manhattan, "the change city." "Born of this river and this rock island, I relate / The changes." In spare, skillful lines the poet establishes her oneness—deeper, really, than mere association—with the historical Manhattan:

> I was the island without bridges, the child down

            whose blazing
Eye the men of plumes and bone raced their canoes and fire

As the poem progresses, the city grows and changes and so does
the girl: "I am a city with bridges and tunnels." She loves the city
as she loves the change which is the essence of human life; she
loves the city as it grows. Here is a glimpse into a childhood scene
like those which obviously gave rise to the poet's fascination with
technology.

    Hearing the sounds of building
                            the syllables of wrecking
    A young girl watching
                        the man throwing red hot rivets
    Coals in a bucket of change
    How can you love a city that will not stay?[4]
    I love you
    like a man of life in change.

    The poet senses in her life the entire life of the city, past and
present, rich and impoverished, lovely and brutal.

            And my poor,
    Stirring among our dreams,
    Poor of my own spirit, and tribes, hope of towers
    And lives, looking out through my eyes.
    The city the growing body of our hate and love,
    The root of the soul, and war in its black doorways.

    . . . .
    Among a city of light, the stone that grows.

We are back at the burning museum at the end of this section,
which closes with the binding line: "I walk past the guards into my
city of change."
    The journey of the elegies is described again in the third section
of this poem, but now the sexual body is more explicitly involved
in the progress of the spirit:

    Waiting and walking and the play of the body
    Silver body with its bosses and places

4. Somerset Maugham asked her this question.

> One by one touched awakened into into
> Touched and turned one by one into   flame

Flame now symbolizes not destruction but heightened life. The stages of the journey advance to a striking final scene:

> Over the scene of the land dug away to nothing and many
> Seen to a stripped horizon carrying barrows of earth
> A hod of earth taken and emptied and thrown away
> Repeated farther than sight. The voice saying slowly
>
> But it is hell.   I heard my own voice in the words
> Or it could be a foundation   And after the words
> My chance came.   To enter.   The theatres of the world.

The scene recalls the poet's journey to West Virginia in the thirties, to the silicon-coated landscape and the despairing people who were paradoxically laying a foundation of power.

The next brief section offers the phrases of a poem in *Theory of Flight*, "Effort at Speech Between Two People." But now the phrases make a much larger statement on her central theme of communication.

> Fragile
> I think of the image brought into my room
> Of the sage and the thin young man who flickers and asks.
> He is asking about the moment when the Buddha
> Offers the lotus, a flower held out as declaration.
> "Isn't that fragile?" he asks. The sage answers:
> "I speak to you. You speak to me. Is that fragile?"

The last section, "The Long Body," builds on the image of the island child become the island woman now bound with bridges to others. "Whatever can come to a city can come to this city" from the second section now becomes "Whatever can come to a woman can come to me," as she depicts herself among a group of protestors of nuclear weapons.

> We are the living island,
> We the flesh of this island, being lived,
> Whoever knows us is part of us today.
>
> Whatever can happen to anyone can happen to me.

The concluding lines of the poem celebrate again the rose from out of the rottenness, the embryo from the dark, the endless communication of the languages of life.

Hayden Carruth said in his review of *Waterlily Fire* in *Poetry*, "Make no mistake, these poems are deeply felt; prayers, I should say quite desperate prayers, for the things which the poet needs but cannot command—peace and justice. For this reason they are intrinsically, connately a part of our ethical crisis, and as such ought to win the prior respect and endorsement of all of us, whatever esthetic considerations may arise later on." Though Carruth recognized "good poetry" in Rukeyser's volumes, he was uncertain as to the merits of many of her poems. "Although I have known Miss Rukeyser's poems for a long time, I shall need to know them much longer still before I can decide whether or not they are, taken as a whole, really good. Possibly I will never decide. Must one stuff every book one reads into a category?" But it is not necessary to categorize to recognize the integrated vision of her work and to say she has rendered that vision convincingly and movingly. On the whole the poems are skillful in their momentum, which is achieved through sound, rhythm, and repetition, especially in the enlarging of meanings as her hallmark phrases recur in new contexts. The new poems in *Waterlily Fire* manifestly feed on the spirit and skills of the poems that came before and blossom in a more intense, deceptively simpler style. For it is not simpler, of course, to the attentive reader of the collection who allows the meanings of the new poems to reverberate. The style, in image, sound, and rhythm, is a rich condensation, an "access of power."

The Orgy

The Orgy (1965), like *Willard Gibbs* and *One Life* (and the later *The Traces of Thomas Hariot*), is a book that cannot be categorized. On that basis it drew the censure of several critics. Bernard Bergonzi in *The New York Review of Books* wrote,

It is a book whose ambiguous status makes me very uncertain about how to handle it. . . . The reason why is to be found at the very beginning, in the discreet little note that reads: "The goat is real; Puck Fair is real; the orgy is real. All the characters and the acts of this book, however, are—of course—a free fantasy on the event." In other words, it should not be regarded as an autobiography, since a good deal of it is "free fantasy," and it isn't a novel, since most of what Miss Rukeyser writes about is "real." This, assuredly, is playing both ends against the middle in fine style. In fact, the "real" parts are the best.

Bergonzi found too much emphasis on "the subjective reverberations of the event in her narrator." He also objected to "some of her more ambitious stylistic flights," saying that rather less 'free fantasy' and rather more humility before the concrete event would have made *The Orgy* a better book." Again, we have the reviewer wishing he were reviewing another book, not the one before him. He wants either a novel or a straight autobiographical narrative whose "concrete" events are conveyed as travelogue and memoir. But Rukeyser in *The Orgy* was again breaking forms and asserting the volatileness of the so-called "concrete event."

The reviewer for *Choice* (*Books for College Libraries*) also complained, "Whatever *The Orgy* may be, it is not a novel. A patchwork of poetic impressions, it lacks structure, characterization, and direction. It neither coheres nor rings true. The emotions of the narrator seem artificially Lawrentian—self-induced, fuzzy, and diffused. Not recommended." (Rukeyser has said she has often wondered why reviewers and booksellers will not admit a category called "Book.")

P. Mortimer in the *New Statesman*, referring to the excerpts in the notes to *The Orgy* "from Margaret Murray and John Millington Synge respectively, which explain Puck Fair in reasonably lucid and concise terms," asserted that Rukeyser "was being unfair to herself when she included them in her book." Of the narrator's meditations on the significance of the fair to her personal life and feelings, Mortimer said, "Mrs. Rukeyser seems determined to convince her readers that she is not only a poet but a very sexy lady as well, which proves to be a double embarrassment—both the writing and the writer protest too much." One recalls Rukeyser's statements in *The Life of Poetry* about the contemporary fear of emotional disclosure. Even in 1965 her frank avowals of sexual and psychological need seemed gauche to reviewers. Ronald Hingley in the *Spectator* said, "If you fancy . . . evocative prose with lots of priapic philosophising by an American poetess, then this is your dish of broth." [5]

Denis Johnston, however, wrote appreciatively of *The Orgy* in *The Nation*, recognizing that "one gets from this lively, and in many ways delightful, book a more vivid picture of the writer than of Puck Fair." He saw the essential poetry of the book, calling it "both exciting and intriguing. It is written in an unusual style that might, perhaps, be described as verse, under the disguise of free prose, rather than the more usual prose in the form of free verse. This method has many of the allusive qualities of poetry, together with its concomitant disregard for continuity, and some occasional doubts as to who or what the writer is referring to." (Beverly Pearlman in *Library Journal* found the "concentric eccentricity of a poet" in *The Orgy*.) Johnston also saw the influence of film on the book. "Miss Rukeyser's technique . . . has a strong resemblance to that of the documentary cinema—a montage in which the writer piles up a catalogue of visual images, untrammeled on the whole by verbs, in the course of which, like the camera, she is able to focus the attention not on the scene as a whole but on some special element that impresses her." [6]

Benedict Kiely in the New York *Times*, praising the author's "honest and inquiring mind," called *The Orgy* "a long prose poem in the shape of a novel." Kenneth Lamott in the *Tribune*'s *Book Week* hailed the book as "less a conventional novel than a record of the experience of Puck Fair as felt through a thoroughly modern sensibility steeped in the literature of anthropology and psy-

5. Muriel Rukeyser, *The Orgy* (New York, 1965). Bernard Bergonzi, review of *The Orgy*, in *New York Review of Books*, April 22, 1965, p. 15; unsigned review of *Orgy*, in *Choice*, II (January, 1966), 774; P. Mortimer, review of *Orgy*, in *New Statesman*, March 25, 1966, p. 435; Ronald Hingley, review of *Orgy*, in *Spectator*, May 13, 1966, p. 605.
6. Denis Johnston, review of *Orgy*, in *Nation*, March 15, 1965, p. 282; Beverly Pearlman, review of *Orgy*, in *Library Journal*, XC (March 1, 1965), 282.

chology. . . . This is a poet's book in a real sense—distilled, allusive, with more suggested than is in plain sight. I read it with great
interest, with enthusiasm even, and still feel somewhat under the
brooding influence of its dark and troubling beauty." Helen Lynd
in the *American Scholar* wrote the most illuminating review. "Some
may be embarrassed by an author who gives so much of herself in
a book that is not labeled autobiography. More are bewildered by
not knowing what label to put on it. . . . The impossibility of putting this book into a customary classification is one reason for
reading it. We cope with the complexity of existence by slogans
and labels, and what we cannot classify we tend to brush aside like
an Aristotelian accident." Mrs. Lynd readily accepted the presence
of the narrator's personal life in the book. "We know that there is
no such thing as 'objectivity' apart from a perceiving person. A
'factual' account of Puck Fair would be what any particular observer calls facts. But few writers would have the courage or the
skill to make us aware of what experience she brought to this
ritual that determined what she saw in it. Miss Rukeyser's doing
this is one thing that perplexes and embarrasses the reviewers. . . .
But Miss Rukeyser's allowing us to become aware of what associations she brought to Kerry and what those three days unfolded in
her is what makes reading this book the unforgettable experience
it is." [7]

The reviewer for *Choice* did not admit the book's particular
structure, a story line involving the coming of the narrator and
others to a fair, its three-day progress, and her realizations
throughout. (Rukeyser readily offers that *The Orgy* is based on the
notebook she kept for three days when she was in Kerry for Puck
Fair.) There are flashbacks and passages of meditation which spring
unpredictably (and thus believably) from experiences the narrator
has during those three days in Kerry. These passages give the nar-

---

7. Benedict Kiely, review of *Orgy*, in *New York Times Book Review*, February 28,
1965, p. 52; Kenneth Lamott, review of *Orgy*, in *New York Herald Tribune Book Week*,
February 28, 1965, p. 20; Helen Merrell Lynd, "Three Days Off for Puck," review of *Orgy*,
in *American Scholar*, XXXIV (August, 1965), 668–72.

rative an added dimension. The second sentence in the book, after
"I came to that coast," is her utterly honest question: "But what
kind of book is this?" It will be the reader's question as the chapters unfold. The third sentence repeats the poet's concern: "That
place I did not know, the wildness turned loose in the crowd looking up to the goat on his blue tower." The "wildness," the same intense life Rukeyser traced in *One Life*, she now recognizes in the
celebrants at Killorglin: "all things roused up among the music,
the lights and the filth of cattle. I don't know what it is saying to
me." Again the insistence that "wildness," currents of life beyond
the predictable and explainable, is precious and must be attended
to. She is honest in admitting at the outset that she does not know
what this new wildness means to her. Her book is a listening and a
recording.

Helen Lynd in her review noted that a second reading of the
book is more than doubly rewarding. I agree; the cryptic statements in the introductory paragraphs mean a universe more at the
beginning of a second reading of the book. "The curious banal
thing that Nicholas finally said to me, that I could never set down
in writing. But if I tell that story, these are its pieces. They move
together, flowing and racing with that sea in the channel." One
good fact we have with which to begin a second reading of the
book is the narrator's name. It is given in one of the last chapters as
"Muriel." (The narrator of the book, however, is recognizably
Muriel Rukeyser—to anyone familiar with the rest of her work.
Muriel in *The Orgy* is a poet with a young son; she has been to
Spain and loved Otto who was killed; her themes and concerns are
those of the writer Muriel Rukeyser.) But must we read books
twice, even three times? The notion is foreign to most readers today. Yet in a survey of British literature course Rukeyser gave at
Sarah Lawrence, she required her students to read Virginia Woolf's
Orlando three times, at three points in the semester. The purpose
was to illustrate how much more one found in a book when one
came equipped with new knowledge and associations. In the first
chapter Muriel wonders aloud what kind of book she is writing,

what the Irish phenomena are saying to her. Equally important, she makes the reader wonder, for the questions she asks are meaningless to the reader at this point. Unknowing is her theme at the outset. The first chapter ends, "Alone, lit up by newness, ignorant."

The second chapter introduces two personal notes. One is familiar. The presence of Spanish boats in the harbor prompts her to think, "I have something against the Spanish. For the Spanish, too, in their bravery and defeat." Another personal note is completely unfamiliar, even to a reader of Rukeyser's other books. "But many men and almost all things reminded me of Jonah these days." We are given hardly more than that. We are kept in ignorance of the rest. We must accept Jonah as Rukeyser accepts Kerry. "The grief-stricken children with their father leaving; suffering of poverty, ragged along the roads . . . and if this, whatever it was, emerged from these bodies, this suffering known and unknown to me, a day like this reaching into this landscape. If this were goat-haunted as I had been goat-haunted the last month. I wanted to be open to it; I had ignorance; something was coming that spoke for what had spoken to me today. I did not know what that was." Readers must be as patient and open to what Muriel is divulging as she is patient and open to what Kerry is revealing to her. She makes no demands on us that she has not made on herself. She is meeting experience with her freight of current concerns and her lifetime of associations. To read *The Orgy* we must admit that this is indeed how one meets experience.

We learn at the end of the second chapter that Muriel is in Kerry to look over the last goat festival in the Western world for Paul Rotha, who would like to film it. But at the beginning of the next chapter we see her resisting the original purpose of her mission. "Let him bring his cameras, I am not going to be an American woman carrying a camera. I have a small blue notebook that will fit in my pocket, or in a pocket of my bag." She is determined to be there as poet. Her poet's personal associations and developing images come rushing in throughout the account. No camera could capture these. "There is a Spanish sailor hurt in the hospital at Valentia . . . I dreamed that night of Jonah . . . then in the dream his face changed to Otto's killed so long ago in Spain. His face as soft as rock under clear water and my face near his, under the clear wave with sun ripples on us, and an invisible brush that went over the drowned faces, brushing, brushing, until the features were obliterated" (O, 23). As we have seen throughout her work, the features of individuals, places, and concerns are brushed by time until chiefly the flowing, "the rhyming of those scenes" ("The Gates"), remains. That is the green wave, or it is her life perceived as a "long body" of linked images ("This Morning," from *Breaking Open*) or "the long strip of our many / Shapes, as we range shifting through time" ("Waterlily Fire"). The wave and the long body of linked images are here again in her perception of her experience in Kerry. "The wild red of a hedge" which her guide, Owen Cross, calls "our plant . . . the tears of Kerry" is "fuller and wilder than the reds I remembered from Carmel, that other coast of memory where there it hung in the gardens, hanging from chains, spilling over pots, red-orange beneath the sexual bells of red. . . . Here it flashed by wild, generous, run to miles of reds." The passage is emblematic of her personal progress from the sexual involvement in California (with the father of her child) to the more than sexual dimension of her experience in Kerry.

People tease Muriel several times about being American, about not being able to understand what will be going on at Puck, about Americans saying "bathroom" instead of "toilet." But she is not the American who will be unable to tolerate the filth and rowdiness of Puck nor understand its connection with death and life. For she has been to Mexico and written poems about eating and drinking in a graveyard on All Souls' Day (*Beast in View.*) Katy Evans, the innkeeper where Muriel stays, says of the fair, "I hate visitors to see it. . . . Everything in Ireland looks shabby and dirty after America." But Muriel thinks, "Everything looks very real to me." She knows she's ignorant and the theme of unknowing, of attending respectfully on the flickering experience until its meaning emerges, is a strong theme in Rukeyser's most recent work, going as far back as *One Life*, when she says in the introduction, "When I began to write this book, the people and the images moving through the story had begun to open up the present for me, and my childhood and a great deal that I knew and imagined about our bonds with the world." Rukeyser is a follower of images as they move, of meanings as they move.

As in *One Life*, children will figure in her perception of Puck Fair. Muriel asks a police officer if the third day of the fair is called "the day of the children." The officer denies it, saying he would keep his children indoors during the fair. She has a flashback to a time ten years ago when she went to Vancouver Island with her small son "on the trace of Franz Boas" and one of the Kwakiutl informants of Boas said, "It is good that you brought your child with you; you know, none of these white scientists bring any family with them. . . . no children, nothing; they just appear here, one white man, another white man, asking us silly questions and mispronouncing" (O, 33). Rukeyser is far from that "scientific" way. She has brought childbirth, children, and family into her developing perception. Although she does not have her son with her, she is keenly aware of the children of Kerry, of their place in the significance of the fair. They will appear at Puck, despite the sergeant's claims.

While in Kerry, though she misses those she loves and senses a "break of time with all I love," they are with her. Their presence colors and shapes her perceptions of Kerry. "The long night of love before I took the plane. . . . The station, with its kerosene light, green how I love you green, waving at the stations *as* I love you green, wrapping the salmon, the green branch, the green sleeves of the ragged children crying for their father. Their Daddy, their Da, gone off by train" (O, 37). The crying for father, in the rhythms of this chapter's phrasing, will recur later in the book. The need is part of the pattern of concerns in Muriel's personal life which is casting its radiance onto the Irish scene. "The great mountains turn the coast of the heart."

We meet the other main characters in Chapter 16: Nicholas

Hilliard, an English psychoanalyst practicing in Dublin, his Irish wife Liadain, and their friend Chris Dermot. Nicholas explains to Muriel that Puck Fair is popular because sex is repressed in Ireland. Chris adds, "Sex is disconnected. It's all loathing." During Puck Fair Muriel will have insights into how sex is connected with much that is known and still unknown in human life. They and Muriel go to Killorglin, the site of the fair, and they enter a bar where the first ritual drink of this increasingly ritual experience is taken:

We went in. They were three-deep at the bar, the dark, grainy smell of Guinness over them, keen and soft like a knife in a cloud. The drink would be bitter if it were thin, I thought, discovering my thirst for it in the sound of words and glasses. Its fine black thickness reassures the throat; it surely is only a bitter beginning like the kick of the donkey at the fence. It sealed in me the days and nights of preparation and the flight and the last nights before, the long sleep after them, the mixed dread and excitement, the waking today and the prologue, the taste and ringing with which things begin. (o, 46)

Shortly afterward, Muriel takes another, which she herself now recognizes as "a ritual drink." "The Irish touched my lips, cool, and then branched out in purity of fire, lips, breath, breasts, and reaching out and down, in a concentration more like cognac, in the most noble white strength. . . . All other whisky is the shadow of Power's."

She describes the goat with the perceptions of a city-dweller, a dweller among skyscrapers and bridges:

[His horns] rose thick from his forehead, branching out to left and right, soaring out and beginning to twist in a hint of wide spirals. Corrugated and pointed, without warp, without distortion. . . . The seams were along the edges, and the texture of horn seemed at first like that of wood until you saw the laminations by which they were forged, built up, the pattern welded, and the fibrous structure of these swords, harder than any one material, welded of materials of different quality. . . . and on the left groove, like a graph recorded by some even sharper sword, or acid, or steely rocks, the scar. The faces of the horns were stiff-cut, they ran to their jagged edges; smooth as they looked at first . . . they soon showed knots and nodes of formation, and something like strips, something like rings of iron. (O, 62)

This is a goat right out of "The Structure of the Plane" in "Theory of Flight." But "Mrs. Houlihan's friend," lacking Muriel's particular perception, says, "The smell is killing me."

The goat appears in a procession accompanied by a little girl, the "Green Queen." "The goat has begun to take on his new life. A curious shudder goes through the crowd, in recognition." A truck passes with a phoenix painted on it and Muriel responds: "I feel myself start, hard against Hilliard's arm, and the points of my breasts stand up: I can see the big word below the red creature. It says PHOENIX, below the painted bird. It is all there: king, queen, and resurrection." But the poet with all her mythic associations discovers that the truck is not ceremonial at all; it is delivering Phoenix Ale. In all these deep movements of her psyche, she can take herself lightly: "I laugh at myself." But the connections are made nonetheless. "The phoenix is still there, red and eternal." Indeed, coincidences like these often lead us to discover, or realize again, what is most important to us.

The little girl then crowns the king and he is lifted up to his platform on the tower. Here Muriel, hesitating momentarily at the blatant fact of goat, recognizes what he symbolizes: "The huge white balls were before my eyes, great in their power and whiteness. The life of the King was in them, making reasons for the eye's glint, the curl of lip, the hard spread of bone lifting out of his forehead. Energy bulged here, a double bulge robed in the smoothness of white fur, hidden and trumpeting, open and recondite, worlds creating worlds, something secret and understood" (O, 72). For Muriel and for the reader, the opposites of regality, great power, and the "cruder" aspects of the animal world are now wed: bluntly, rather humorously, and in all seriousness too. "His eyes glinted yellow. A long strong scent, a great pennant of smell of goat, goat of the world and the world of goat in his kingship, on his height, streamed across all of us, flowing on air. The huge cheer went up: 'King! Puck!' Up, on the air, a sound that was a tower around a tower, in the filled and male upper air of the King."

Helen Lynd said in her review of *The Orgy*, "It is not easy to confront the essential contradictions of existence," but the book confronts them continually. It begins to do so most earnestly with Muriel's confrontation of the goat, its animality, its associations and symbolism. The goat becomes the core of the growing meaning of her (and the reader's) experience in Kerry. (Here is the "direction" the reviewer for *Choice* failed to see.) That meaning develops for Muriel and for the reader as it does in certain films, according to Eisenstein's explanation; the reader must creatively imagine the connection between the various sequences, some of them smoothly linked in meaning, some of them in "collision." Muriel perceives this growth of meaning moment by moment in Kerry and she communicates her perception by focusing on individual phenomena which become emblematic of that growth. Since she has the senses of a poet, the details of Kerry are delivered with consummate skill. But always we receive more than details.

Muriel's experience begins to "deepen" in a curious way.

As I felt myself say "I'm staying," a movement of nervous certainty swung me away from that moment and everything that had gone before, whatever I had been feeling, known and unknown, and into another state, the deeper water of what I had come for. I swung into a movement that had begun when the King was crowned. . . . No, before that, when we stopped at Killorglin. . . . No, long times ago, in all the movements of the rousing of these storms of passion, rages and lightnings of wish, storms of action, all narrowed down to my life in these last few hours with these new three friends. (O, 78)

She has a profound realization, the same she expressed in the early pages of *Willard Gibbs* and in many poems, of the past blazing upon the present moment. This realization deepens her and she can't make small talk. "I felt strange, estranged from all of them, on a wave of the opposite just after a wave of strength." But she can communicate with Nicholas. "I went to Nicholas, as the others moved away again. Now it all changed, fluid and clear, Nicholas and myself and the dance knew one creature, were one creature, declaring something the music was, something the tower outside was. The goat on the black air." The book moves this way, from pole to pole, reflecting the turbulence in the narrator's life and in her memories, the alternating currents of isolation and contact, rejection and acceptance, ignorance and understanding. But as in "Theory of Flight" and the elegies she feels that the immense human wish she has been recognizing from her earliest poems will find its fulfillment.

Part II, "The Day of the Fair," is the day the cattle are driven into Killorglin, and the description Muriel gives is replete with the contradictions that the fair has begun to unfold for her. "A storm of smell came down and smote the face, the whole body, entered the clothes, the ears, the sleeves, invaded. From the bridge itself, up the hill, the whole town, streets, sidewalks, all, was covered and painted with manure of cattle. . . . A moment of quiet, as if a conversation between giants has paused. Near us, as we put our feet down slowly, not to slip please not to slip" (o, 98). The image of Muriel stepping gingerly so as not to fall into the dung is amusing—and emblematic. "The hill, the town, became so intensely what it was—a cattle market that was one root of the fair, without which there would be no fair—that the black cows and bulls, the unshipped, plastered, overspread excrement became itself: part of whatever was unfolding, part of whatever was being bargained for." The world of beauty and form and meaning is also the world of filth and haggling and greed. The thought can be paralyzing: "At this moment I knew that my knees had been shaking for some time. My feet refused the move." But one must acknowledge the "dirt" of the world. "And the excrement, the wet and dirty—you know how they work on our cities to keep them dry? to try to display life as *not* sticky, *not* wet?" We have learned to turn in disgust, to conceal: but it is all part of reality, part of us. In "Despisals" in *Breaking Open* Rukeyser will write:

> In the body's ghetto
> never to go despising the asshole
> nor the useful shit that is our clean clue
> to what we need. Never to despise
> the clitoris in her least speech.

Never to despise in myself what I have been taught
to despise. Not to despise the other.
Not to despise the *it*. To make this relation
with the it: to know that I am it.[8]

Despised as "dirt" by many, but not by Muriel, are the tinkers,
the gypsies who come to the fair. Nicholas despises them. "Para-
sites," he says. But the poet sees them "like the tribes, tribes of Indians cut off from the ways and still aware of the tribe. As these
tinkers, even when they put cars before the caravans instead of
horses, even when it's plastics and not tin. . . . They still have their
signs, their patterans, a broken branch by the road, a sign of leaves
and ashes, a way they are" (O, 113). Besides the focus on sexual
energy and its cosmic counterparts, what gives *The Orgy* its Lawrentian tone is this veneration for primitive traces in society and
their value to mechanized people.

It is characteristic of this book that Muriel not tell us exactly
what the tinkers gave her. We have to imagine the gift to her, to us.
She does tell us that she observes a tinker doing something which
impresses her and which she will, later in the narrative, apply to
her own life. "He had bent to the grass, a place blackened by the
tinker's cookfire. He leaned over the dead embers; the set of his
head was that of a man reading. There were stones among the
ashes. He walked to where we sat. 'Do they tell you something?
The stones?' I asked. 'Yes,' he said. 'It is a patteran; it gives me a
sign. Sometimes leaves, sometimes branches, sometimes stones.
One family has already moved on. This tells us where.'" Shortly afterward Muriel and Nicholas converse about Jonathan Hanaghan,
who "is making a religious bridge for Freud" (O, 123). It is just a
snippet of conversation, but Hanaghan's vision will eventually illuminate Muriel's experience in Kerry and its reverberations in her
lifetime.

The rest of that day, described in Chapter 8, plunges Muriel
into loneliness, old fears, the overwhelming sense that she will not

8. Muriel Rukeyser, *Breaking Open* (New York, 1973).

understand these vivid phenomena at all. She must remind herself
that meanings arrive in life, as in film, through "linkage, collision,"
that, as she said in "Theory of Flight," we must "open [our] flesh
. . . to opposites." So here in Kerry she asks, "All right, then. What
have we done, on the second day? Have we turned into our opposites? . . . What is it? I thought. I know nothing of this country. . . .
I can do nothing with it, nothing with my own storm of feeling, or
my speechlessness. Or my own desire that looks at him. . . . I am
the stream of chastisement, I thought." She goes for a walk. "The
road I took was toward Killorglin, and toward some kind of
death. . . . It was my death I was facing, through weakness, through
inability to act, through ignorance. I was completely inadequate to
deal with what was going through me. I could not even see these
people clearly, or hear the words they were saying to me." She is
besieged by a "great rushing" of memories and associations which
is finally halted after she receives an account of Saint Fursey, "the
vision-man. Torn in two by love of mankind, driving him to active
work, and love of solitude, driving him to his hermit's cell." She is
also watching a painting grow, staying by the side of Eileen Cos-
tello as she works on the canvas. The growth of the painting and
the story of Fursey (who encompassed intense contradictions) and
the river flowing by all contribute to an enlightenment for Muriel.
The reader doesn't know exactly how these elements combine to
relieve Muriel of her sense of inadequacy and death; but the process of enlightenment through a series of ordinary happenings is
believable. Rukeyser will express it succinctly in "A Little Stone in
the Middle of the Road, in Florida":

> My son as a child saying
> God
> is anything, even a little stone in the middle of the road,
>
> Yesterday
> Nancy, my friend, after long illness:
> You know what can lift me up, take me right out of
>   despair?

No, what?
Anything.[9]

Chapter 9 brings a striking coincidence that deepens the personal significance of the fair for Muriel. Killorglin means "Church of Lawrence." " 'It is my father's name,' I heard myself slowly say. 'And will you phone him when you phone your friend, who is going to China? And send him word from Puck?' 'He died this spring,' I told him. 'Hah!' said Nicholas. 'And the Puck reminds you, then, also of him?' 'Perhaps he does. I know that when I saw his legs were tied—my father died with his feet gone, of gangrene.' 'But King, power, giver,' Nicholas said on a deep note. 'He died—both his children disinherited. For disobedience.' " One remembers the children earlier in the narrative crying for their Da at the railroad station. Clearly the meanings must move to some reunion with the father.

Chapter 10 has Muriel in an excitingly close gathering in a pub. After the bleak account of disinheritance by the father, the movement now is toward union and acceptance. "Then we turned into one of the pubs in that street. . . . It had an earth floor, its walls were painted dark red, thick red daub. A wooden staircase went up over the smoke. An unpainted door was slightly open on the black rainy night behind the room. It was one of the best places I have ever walked into."

The evening is intense with contact and release; so that when Muriel is back in her room at the inn she feels ever so much more alone. "Jonah, really not for me. . . . I wishing only to act out my love, my wedding undone, my child two-thirds of the world away, almost as far as that China of unbelief to which Ella was flying." Muriel has a stunning perception of the unknown forces in herself, of the need to admit these unknowns as shapers of this moment. "Where is the real desire? Among the stars, the constellations, of desire, all approached in me, all unfinished, unbegun now in this

9. Rukeyser, *The Speed of Darkness*.

quiet. This moment which is the only moment, the present, with the rout of the past all there, in love, in touching, in violation, in sorting out, in arrival." At the same time she must admit all the unknown of the universe and fiercely, steadily accommodate it, especially that unknown which one might hastily interpret as failure, finality, death. In "Poetry and the Unverifiable Fact," a lecture she gave at Scripps College in 1968, Rukeyser spoke of "a constant which tends to be forgotten and neglected, often despised—which is the unknown, which is a constant in science, as it is in art and the uncertain." When one deals with experience and art in such a way as to acknowledge the unknown while linking and unifying meanings when possible, then one has the right attitude toward the world. In that lecture Rukeyser quoted Giordano Bruno: "*Est animal sanctum, sacrum, venerabile, mundus.*" She commented, "I think . . . the world is a living creature, an animal in the deep sense . . . sacred, holy, to be loved. And I think that these unifying things [linked images and meanings], and the security—the actual security that comes from dealing with them and dealing with them in change—as one goes through a poem and it changes, that this has something to do with human security, swimming in the world."[10] Rukeyser said in an interview that she cares very much about the sense of mystery, of unanswered questions, about "a suspense of images" in art. *The Orgy* is filled with that suspense. Muriel must swim, and so must her readers.

The very structure of *The Orgy* acknowledges the unknown. The prose is like her poetry, which moves in clusters, not as *abcd*, "a movement going from one point to another to another, but rather as a constellation moves, as many lives in their movement, and related always with another constant . . . the unknown." Straight journalistic prose which makes everything plain gives the impression and is structured on the assumption that one *can* eliminate the unknown, at least in the areas one is writing about. Art, Rukeyser's especially, is designed to counteract this simplistic vi-

10. Muriel Rukeyser, "Poetry and the Unverifiable Fact," *Scripps College Bulletin*, XLII, no. 4 (Claremont, Calif., 1968), 6.

sion which is tyrannical today because of the prose of newspapers, textbooks, catalogues, and other linear communications (with their line to our pocketbooks).

Part III, "Scattering Day," begins with Muriel reading Hanaghan (*Society, Evolution, and Revelation*), who is saying that we must know the opposites that we have created. "He says, 'European man declares his deceit and snobbery in his houses, their arrangement and decorations. Their fronts are often artistically decorated whilst the backs are barbaric. Take a walk down your back lanes and look at your houses from the rear and you will be looking into the European soul.' He talks about the abruptness of difference between front and back." (Rukeyser will build this realization into poems such as "The Backside of the Academy" and "Despisals" in *The Speed of Darkness* and *Breaking Open*.) She reads at random and discovers at random, as people do. "I went through Hanaghan's setting-forth of the choice before each of us: whether to go ahead with evolution itself, or whether to turn our libido to devolution, away from the life task: to bind ourself to ever widening circles of interest by the bonds of love" (O, 159). Hanaghan's vision is of a whole humankind evolving toward mutual acceptance and love. He calls—as this book does, as Rukeyser's other works do—for an imaginative "forth-flowering love and interest" which will enable us to accept the wholeness of reality (hear Willkie's "one world"). Muriel continues to read Hanaghan, with her characteristic openness, waiting for the development of meaning. "What is this saying to me?" She comes to the blinding passage about the hero: "the Myth as an imaginative creation veiling a wish of the child-self to be loved beyond human loving and honored beyond all human honoring." The child turns from what he sees as his parents' inadequate love to love of an "unseen father." But who that has been in an individual life—in Muriel's life—is not immediately perceivable. It must be someone one's parents honored; that is a law of our being. " 'But whom did your parents honor?' Reverberation of the question. A tide among the flowers, up through the hills, sonorities.' "

Nicholas arrives and they drive to Killorglin for the last day of the fair. She has Hanaghan's book along, for she wants to read it that day. The day unfolds in minor marvels. A dolphin is in a bathrub at the Nolans; the guard brought him there after finding him on a beach at Inch. "Every time they drove the 'sea-creature' away, he returned. He had made repeated efforts to leave the sea, in order to play with the children on the beach. . . . Nolan and Looby flung the blanket out over him; and, more through his willingness to stay near the children than through any skill of theirs, he had let himself be taken prisoner" (o, 166). The dolphin is an emblem of the mysteries that have swum into Muriel's consciousness in Kerry.

Muriel sees a fisherman on a bridge. "If I had the patience of that fisherman, I thought, to stand and cast again and again, like trying to write one thing all my life. It may be that, I thought. I could never tell any of this except in what I do, except in what I am, leaving something behind me like a pattern." Here Muriel connects herself with the tinkers (of the day before) who left their "patteran" in their cookfire. She also invests her experience and her work with the meaning she assigned those tinkers, saying they give to her, to society, in their ways. Rukeyser will write in the title poem of *The Speed of Darkness*:

> Time comes into it.
> Say it. Say it.
>
> The universe is made of stories,
> not of atoms.

This is an artist's sense of the worth of her art, her "patteran," to the rest of humankind; and by implication it is the sense of being despised as tinkers are despised for being "outside" society. Rukeyser has had this sense, or the sense of being undervalued, and expressed it in "In Our Time" (*The Speed of Darkness*).

> In our period, they say there is free speech.
> They say there is no penalty for poets,
> There is no penalty for writing poems.
> They say this. This is the penalty.

Nevertheless she is leaving her "patteran" for us. It is a sign.

Helen Lynd in her review said, "The book trails off, as *War and Peace*, as life, trails off: King Puck goes back to being a goat, and the narrator goes back to being a human being among other human beings in a more ordinary existence." But not before Nicholas and Muriel have a final communication which moves toward that reconcilement with the father Muriel needed.

God is your dad, he is saying in a rasping voice, God is your daddy, yes, say it in the familiar way, the way you remember when you ran across the room with your arms up. He is, he needs you as much as you need him. . . . We kiss, it is he that I am kissing and he kisses me, constellating a scene. We are on an enormous pier, the ship so tall behind him that will carry him away, lifting him, lifting him as he kisses me, in love that now belongs to him as I belong to love, carrying him far and forever away in the kiss.

It has all come through for me, in the most curious brief endless random moment, the moment and all it contains, with a man speaking to me as a wise and loving and sacred man. (O, 190)

When she and Nicholas return to the others, images come together for her:

The goat king standing there, white and archetypal in the Square. Dominant, isolated, tied by the ankles and ruling my fantasy.

The sight shifted within me. The goat alone gave way to Fursey in the air. The saint on the night sky, the gloom and press of the world at night, Ireland spread out, beneath him. He lived in that black air, moving on nothing like a world in its space. Four flames stood there, as he turned his head, in the four corners of his square of night. As he watched them, they flared up and coalesced. A voice said, "RESPICE MUNDUM." What the orgy says: "Look at the world." . . . The orgy is experience, I thought. The sacred feast.

For the artist the linking of these images in this knowledge is especially right: Look at the world. But one can't hold this knowing forever in the mind. Polar opposition returns, ineluctably. "The moment had turned. . . . I went into the little room. Alone, I thought. . . . Until I know the opposite and the other side of the moment, what we are kept in ignorance of. What I keep myself in ignorance of. And none of this is possible to say. How could I ever say it to anyone? What is it saying to me? Look at the world again." One thing Muriel is certain of is that no movie can do justice to Puck Fair. "I would rather a film crew never came to this town, or set its actors here and there, gleaming, false."

The book ends with Muriel affirming, "There had been a revelation." But she continues, "Of what?" She can't say it in any other way but the way of her narrative, of her massing of incident, scene, thought, dialogue. The revelation had something to do with "all that quickness that transforms and comes through." It had something to do with the oppositions glowing in Puck Fair. Muriel knows she must proceed from that revelation to lead a different kind of life, to "try to avoid everything I might interpose between myself and what was in me, what I was in. No myth, no mask, no legendary figure." (This statement will become "No more masks. No more mythologies" in "The Poem as Mask," *The Speed of Darkness*.) The task seems staggering. "God, how can any of it be met? . . . And how will I, anyway? What is it? Something like the fisherman doing his long endless casts over the Laune, a river that is before one, and the endless attempt at art, or life? How do I do it?"

The last two pages of the book present an "unfinished symbol" whose reverberations indicate the way one must "proceed from revelation," the way some of "it" at least can be met. Muriel's final conversation in the book is with Bill Higgins, who does not want to speak of Kerry because he is full of memories and impressions of China—"the whole other side of the world. The side that may be as far from us—but it isn't, it's only opposite. Just there. At hand." What impressed Bill Higgins most about China was "one man we saw in Peking."

"Shipwrecked, he was, in the South Atlantic; for three months he was alone on a raft, and he lived. Naked; without food or drink; without anything. No help anywhere. The flying-fish came by in the air, sometimes beside him, but sometimes they flew right over his square raft. At first he couldn't get his hand on them; but then, later, he could, they said. I saw him there, as close as I am to you. He reached up his hand right into the air; he caught them, he lived off of them. Patience. And skill. Alone on that floating square. Around the earth from here. And then plunged into the crowd in Peking. An endless crowd it was.

"Alone and naked he floated.

"It's a whole new world."

This is what we are left with at the end of a book on Ireland and on an ancient Western festival with its traditions and rituals. We are left with the East, with man alone and unpropped by old ways. The last image in the book, of that shipwrecked man from Peking, is in collision with all that has come before (though it is linked with the idea of encompassing one's opposites and with the floating square of the goat and of Fursey). We must imagine the relationship of this last image with the other images and meanings in the book and thus participate in creating the meaning of *The Orgy*. Such creative participation is what Rukeyser has been inviting, in poetry and in prose.

Helen Lynd ended her review thus: "Some books enlarge the meaning of the words with which we try to describe them. *The Orgy* has, for me, enlarged the meaning of 'luminous.'" Similarly, Hiram Haydn said, "The book is a jewel and a flame."[11] *The Orgy* does glow; what it lights up in each reader's life depends on one's willingness to stay with it for some contemplative time.

11. Hiram Haydn quoted on the dustjacket of *The Orgy*.

SEVEN

Into the Seventies

The Speed of Darkness, Breaking Open, and *The Gates*

Rukeyser's three latest volumes of poetry have come in almost as quick succession as those of her early career. To have *The Speed of Darkness* (1968), *Breaking Open* (1973), and *The Gates* (1976) before one—with the substantial *The Traces of Thomas Hariot,* prose (1971), off to one side—, to know these poems were written by a woman in her fifties and sixties who was teaching, working with the Writers' and Teachers' Collaborative in East Harlem (thus "The Ballad of Orange and Grape"), suffering a paralyzing stroke and pneumonia that required hospitalization, working in the antiwar movement, going to Hanoi, going to jail, establishing the Exploratorium, a museum of perception, in San Francisco, working as president of American Association of Poets, Playwrights, Editors, Essayists and Novelists (P.E.N.), going to Korea to plead for the life of poet Kim Chi-Ha: this is to know a continually fertile spirit. From the inscription to *The Gates* ("for Jacob & Kang & the future") to the increasingly open and exploring lyrics in the three volumes, one marvels at Rukeyser's positiveness, energy, and accomplishment. The poems become at once simpler and more reverberating. Here are the essentials of what she has been saying all along. The poems seem condensations of her vision, and that lifetime vision and achievement were recognized by the American Academy of Arts and Letters with the Copernicus Prize in the spring of 1977.

The new horror, in the first two of these recent volumes, is the war in Vietnam. It is, of course, the same old horror, another war, another failure of the imagination to recognize the unity of human beings. She says it in "Endless," addressing Otto Boch:

I look down at the one earth under me,
through to you and all the fallen
the broken and their children born and unborn
of the endless war. (SD, 67)

It is the same old despisal of one group by another, the same non-touching, non-communicating. Her hope for poetry is the same hope she expressed in the early forties. In the Scripps College lecture (1968) she repeated that the power of poetry is the power to evoke people's sense of "the resonance in the world . . . the world we breathe." This power is "more living than the dead enormous powers that keep the war going." Quoting Jonathan Hanaghan in this lecture, she compared the poem to the powerless infant whose cries are powerful enough to evoke protection, care, community. "The weakness and strength of the art of poetry . . . is taken as so small a thing with so small an audience. We know the audience is small but we know the people come to it out of some necessity, and that this necessity draws the meaning deep into their lives."[1]

Looked at in the context of the late seventies, these three volumes attest to a remarkable constancy amid radical change in poetic fashion. Reviewing the *American Poetry Anthology* (Daniel Halpern's anthology of American poets under forty) in the New York *Times* in January, 1976, Louis Simpson said,

The anthology . . . shows certain tendencies that are very much of the present time: freedom of form and disengagement from political or social involvement. . . . The disengagement is a more recent symptom—only yesterday poets were writing against the war in Vietnam or as members of an oppressed minority. But these poets, like most people nowadays, seem to have retreated into their own private lives. . . . It's not just disengagement—it's disaffection. . . . Casualness, the throw-away, is the besetting mannerism of the age. Most of the poets don't want to be thought to be taking themselves too seriously.

Simpson found only "a handful of writers who break through the fashion of keeping a 'low profile,' " commenting that "in every age, whatever the fashion may be, there are writers impelled by an in-

---

1. Rukeyser, "Poetry and the Unverifiable Fact," 11–12.

ner necessity." Quite undeniably "impelled by an inner necessity," Rukeyser is still affirming in 1976, in *The Gates*. As Linda Wagner wrote in her review of that volume in *The Nation*, "The mythic quest . . . brings neither sorrow nor stasis but a moving affirmation." Unlike most poets in the *American Poetry Anthology*, Rukeyser is still writing out of a political and social consciousness while at the same time revealing her private life more directly than ever. And as Louise Bernikow said of *Breaking Open* in *Ms.*, "It is all political; it is all personal; it is all fusion."[2]

In 1968 Laurence Lieberman said in his review of *The Speed of Darkness* that Rukeyser is "weighty and high-minded. . . . The title of her new book is indicative of the oracular soothsaying of much of her writing. . . . Her mystical vision is so dominant in the mentality of some poems, the writing becomes inscrutable, as she packs her lines with excessive symbolism or metaphorical density." Although he ends his review with a reference to "her frequent tendency to drift into cloudy abstraction," Lieberman says, "Her firmest art is in the linear and straightforward delivery of her story-telling anecdotal poems, the longer biographical poems, and letter-poems to friends expressing an open declaration of personal faith." Rukeyser can be masterfully linear. But she refuses to disallow the constellations of meaning as they arise from the unconscious. And she refuses to forswear the mystic, holy words, as in the phrase "the sacred body of thirst" ("What Do I Give You") for, as a reader of her volumes from the thirties to the present readily sees, her vision *is* mystical, though grounded in the body, on earth, like Blake's and Whitman's. Lieberman never gives an example of what he calls "oracular soothsaying" in her poetry, but one senses he was referring to poems like "The Six Canons":

> Seize structure.
> Correspond with the real.

---

2. Louis Simpson, review of *American Poetry Anthology*, ed. Daniel Halpern (New York, 1975), in *New York Times Book Review*, January 4, 1976, p. 17; Linda Wagner, review of *The Gates*, in *Nation*, March 19, 1977, p. 348; Louise Bernikow, review of *Breaking Open*, in *Ms.*, II (April, 1974), 35–36.

Fuse spirit and matter.
Know your own secrets.
Announce your soul in discovery.
Go toward the essence, the impulse of creation,
where power comes in music from the sex,
where power comes in music from the spirit,
where sex and spirit are one self
passing among
and acting on all things
and their relationships,
moving the constellations of all things.

This style in Rukeyser is to be held dear, for we have an abundance of what Lieberman praises as "a precision in the enumeration of items of dailiness," in Rukeyser and in other writers today. But we have little of the Whitmanesque, or Blake saying, "I question not my Corporeal or Vegetative Eye any more than I would Question a Window concerning a Sight. I look thro it & not with it"—affirming the vision in dailiness. In a long piece on John Ashbery in the *American Poetry Review* Lieberman in 1977 defends visionary poetry, with great enthusiasm. "In this major poem [*"Self-Portrait in a Convex Mirror"*] Ashbery [is] engaged profoundly with both the life of dreams and the public life of today. In our day, we must struggle to retrieve the institution of dreaming from our culture's rubbish heap, since our Age is more impoverished than most by neglect and outright scorn of the world of dreams." Lieberman praises Ashbery's dedication to "the task of vision . . . the service of the dream" and his "Messianic calling and mission to connect with American readers." His remarks could be applied to Rukeyser's art throughout her career.[3] But he apparently makes a severe distinction between her "task of vision" and Ashbery's.

Karl Shapiro noted in *The Poetry Wreck* (1973) that the "poetic motive" has been sacrificed to the "rational motive" in the

3. Laurence Lieberman, review of *The Speed of Darkness*, in *Poetry*, CXIV (April, 1969), 42; "A Vision of the Last Judgment," in David V. Erdman (ed.), *The Poetry and Prose of William Blake* (Garden City, N.Y., 1965), 555; Laurence Lieberman, "Whispers Out of Time, A Reading of John Ashbery's 'Self-Portrait in a Convex Mirror,'" *American Poetry Review*, VI (March/April, 1977), 4–5.

later Auden and in much twentieth-century poetry which he calls "a poetry of perfection." In Whitman's imperfections Shapiro finds a more wonderful and satisfying poetry: "The greatness of the body and the greatness of the soul; the touching of the world and the heroism of departure; the magnificent motion of death; the expanding cycle of consciousness; the essential holiness of all things. And always at the center, the self, the moment of incarnation, the Walt Whitman of one's self."[4] Rukeyser's voice and vision are like Whitman's—rare today and valuable. To quote Shapiro again, "Our anthologies are fat and blowsy, strewn with suicides, treasons, and psychic breakdowns." We desperately need the affirmations of those who have seen and felt the worst and still can sing faithfulness to the dream and the visitations of what Shelley called "intellectual beauty."

But if Rukeyser's work has remained constant in its major concerns (personal and political) and in its affirmation, decade after decade, of the spirit thrusting through dailiness, the last three volumes show a progression toward a naked, unmasked poetry. This directness could be found in certain lines of *Theory of Flight*, but the flow, the subsuming myth of process bore it along, often submerging it. Now the current reveals its atoms. Denise Levertov has referred to Rukeyser's first stroke as "that crucial illness after which her work changed so much." It is not so much a change as a purification, an intensification. She came out of her first stroke stammering; when that cleared, she spoke more directly than ever. She comments, "It rhymes with my childhood in which I lisped very badly and came out of that."[5]

Victor Howes in the *Christian Science Monitor* said of *The Speed of Darkness*, "Compared to *Waterlilly Fire* . . . the latest poems look as if they had exploded onto the page. Short lines, short phrases, stairways of lines across the page." What Peter Meinke said about *Breaking Open* and Elizabeth Stone said about *The Gates* can be applied to all three of her latest volumes. Here is Meinke:

4. Karl Shapiro, *The Poetry Wreck* (New York, 1975), quoted in Anatole Broyard's review, in New York *Times*, March 13, 1975, p. 37.
5. Denise Levertov, in a letter to the author, July, 1977.

Breaking Open overflows with "naked" poetry about her family, her friends, her country, her religion, herself. The poems seek to break through to "touch". . . . She has absorbed both the rolling rhythms of Whitman and the tighter cadences of Yeats. Her imagery is not wild but natural: water and earth, flowers, moon, shoreline. Life is a flowing, an outpouring, the makers and touchers lining up against the destroyers, the "anti-touch people". . . . In the face of a society that seems bent on self-deception and self-destruction, *Breaking Open* stands as a testament of human toughness and compassion, even against overwhelming odds.

Here is Stone on *The Gates*:

Rukeyser continues to explore the themes which have haunted and moved her through 13 earlier volumes: She writes of the political and the political-cum-metaphysical; of herself—as someone's mother, someone's child. She continues her celebration, often mystical in overtone, of creativity, the poetic process, sexuality. And, as always, in the midst of the symphonic and transcendent are the earthly grace notes—about a roach, say, or a new false tooth. . . . It is frequently young poets and suicidal poets who write of death, often with an aura of eroticism or urgency. Muriel Rukeyser does neither, and it is worth underscoring that her perspective is one that probes what of herself can survive.

She uses both affliction and mortality in order to affirm the value of life. . . . Rukeyser is neither innocent-and-optimistic nor knowing-and-in-despair, but in some third place which Blake called Second Innocence.[6]

Except for Lieberman on *The Speed of Darkness* and Thomas Stumpf and a reviewer in the *Times Literary Supplement* on *Breaking Open* Rukeyser's last three volumes drew praise. But Victor Howes had these reservations: "With this poet there is always the danger of emotion running away with the poem, or of a private connection serving for a public one." And Jerome McGann, reviewing *Breaking Open* in *Poetry*, found it uneven and sensed a "rhetorical pose" in the poems that express her need to touch and to speak. Yet, though the reviews were generally favorable, they were not numerous. The New York *Times* carried Eberhart's magnificent review of *The Speed of Darkness* (see pp. 240

6. Victor Howes, review of SD, in *Christian Science Monitor*, July 23, 1968, p. 9; Peter Meinke, review of BO, in *New Republic*, November 24, 1973, p. 25; Elizabeth Stone, review of *Gates*, in *Village Voice*, November 22, 1976, p. 93.

and 318 herein), but no reviews of *Breaking Open*. The *Times'* brief review of *The Gates* appeared nearly a year after its publication. William Meredith begins by acknowledging the familiar hesitations: "If you are not used to thinking of poetry the way Muriel Rukeyser does, her work can be hard to read. The reader must acquiesce, perhaps more openly than with more conventional poems. Many people seem to have trouble with this beautifully voiced verse." Though Meredith says "I would like to make this a review that will move the unconverted," he was obviously given few column inches in which to argue. Rather he quotes two poems from the volume in their entirety, asserting (to all those who have said otherwise throughout the years) that there is no rhetoric in Rukeyser. "The concerns of her poetry and her life remain inextricable, as with a person who can only tell the truth and take the consequences. The poetry in this fine book moves toward form, using all her fears—it is crafted in that hard way."[7]

After Bogan's death, the *New Yorker* published no more reviews of Rukeyser's poetry. We know that publications like the *Times* are not paying much attention to poetry these years; the *American Poetry Review* was launched because many publications which once published poetry and reviews of poetry no longer do so with regularity or thoroughness. In the pages of this vital new journal Rukeyser's work has been featured: first came Virginia Terris' long retrospective analysis and the publication of several new poems and of "Ives" from the "Lives" sequence. Then *APR* published "The Gates" in a special section. It is gratifying to find Rukeyser's work and criticism of her work in this lively periodical, but it is not surprising. Geof Hewitt, writing in Rosalie Murphy's *Contemporary Poets of the English Language* (1970), said, "Some of Rukeyser's long poems, in particular 'The Speed of Darkness' . . . are among the finest we'll have to carry with us into the next century. Her vocabulary is truly of our generation, but she's writing poems of a longer endurance." Hewitt praises Rukeyser's

---

7. William Meredith, "A Life of Poetry," review of *Gates*, in *New York Times Book Review*, September 25, 1977, p. 26.

toughness and optimism, saying she "never assumes the false authority that is so often mistaken for wisdom. She investigates nearly every aspect of life."[8]

But never a decade has gone by for Rukeyser without at least one scathing review based on the reviewer's superficial reading. Here is Thomas Stumpf in the *Carolina Quarterly*:

Muriel Rukeyser's collection of poems, *Breaking Open*, is the dry product of a careful cultivation of the poetic reflex and many years spent thinking the right thoughts and lingering over the right feelings. It has all the liberal virtues: high seriousness, indefatigable optimism, hand-clasping brotherhood, and love for all ethnic groups. . . . Rukeyser is nothing if not sympathetic, loudly proclaiming her identity with the blacks ("my black voice bleeding") and, of course, the Vietnamese. . . . This is verse that, like rolled oats, is unappetizing but good for you. It is nice to be against death and oppression, to feel that there is a new dawn breaking and that the good people will soon be at the head of the parade. . . . These healthful sentiments feed a poetry that is without muscle, without alertness . . . poetry that is fatally in love with exhortations and public promises, with first person posturings. . . . What she would like to do is to convert her daily bread—the streets of New York, the hospital rooms, the soft drink vendors—into food for the soul, to see the sublime in the particular, the infinite in a grain of sand. What she succeeds in doing is merely juxtaposing the mean with the magniloquent, Muriel the hot-dog muncher with Muriel the martyr. That, however compassionate the motive, is the stuff of bathos. . . . Too much compassion, as Rukeyser proves, can be the death of poetry.

Stumpf, like many critics and reviewers before him, seems simply to reject the spirit of the poems as inadmissible, incredible, fake enough to merit belittling treatment. Something in Rukeyser's work is an irritant to reviewers. As one recalls the objections to her work over the years one finds a common denominator: the reviewers sense that she doesn't *really* feel these things. She is "posturing." She is kidding herself (Rosenthal's "unearned conclusions.") Such antagonism blinds reviewers to aspects of her work that they can and do appreciate in other poets. For example, Stumpf could write

8. Geof Hewitt in Murphy (ed.), *Contemporary Poets of the English Language*, 946–49.

in the same omnibus review quoted above that Daniel Berrigan, like Rukeyser, writes "public poems . . . but they are poems that take private moods, private quirks into account. Berrigan remains an individual with an individual past. . . . *[His]* poems display that gift which is the greatest enemy of the false sublime, the ability to distinguish between one detail and the next, between Tom and Dick, between today's mood and yesterday's."[9] But to claim, as Stumpf does, that Rukeyser's poetry lacks such individuality is nonsense. One needn't read more than *Breaking Open* to encounter a persona who acknowledges a very individualistic development and response. (See poems such as "H.F.D." on her dying friend, Hallie Flanagan, and "Gradus ad Parnassum," a wry satiric poem on the choices that kept her from the "security" of a matron's life in New Rochelle.) Much of Rukeyser's private past and present informs her "public" poetry.

The three latest books contain, like *U.S.1.*, reports from crucial zones, frontiers. In the thirties Rukeyser went to Alabama, West Virginia, and Spain. In the sixties and seventies she returned to the Catalan border. She also traveled to the Outer Banks of North Carolina (and from there in spirit to Selma, Alabama), to Hanoi, to prison for protesting the war, to Korea to intercede for Kim Chi-Ha. In *The Speed of Darkness* she writes of the Outer Banks of North Carolina as

> the edge of experience, *grenzen der seele*
> where those on the verge of human understanding
> the borderline people stand on the shifting islands
> among the drowned stars and the tempest.
> "Everyman's mind, like the dumbest,
> claws at his own furthest limits of knowing the world,"
> a man in a locked room said. ("The Outer Banks")

She is standing on the beach thinking of the events in the South in the mid-sixties. The poem tells of her own coming to the sense of the edge of experience, the precipice over the unknown. It is the

9. Thomas Stumpf, review of BO, in *Carolina Quarterly*, XXVI (Spring, 1974), 101.

sense of death and of possible rebirth as well. The poem is filled with her images of the life-bringing turning wind, the spiral. The life-giving change that is to come now involves racial justice.

> Dragon of the winds forms over me.
> Your dance, goddesses in your circle
> sea-wreath, whirling of the event
> behind me on land as deep in our own lives
> we begin to know the movement to come.

"A man who is white and who has been fishing" and is pulling a boat approaches her; he changes into

> A black man in the sun.
> He now is a black man speaking to my heart
> crisis of darkness in this century
> of moments of this speech.
>
> . . . .
>
> The zigzag power coming straight, in stones,
>   in arcs, metal, crystal, the spiral
> in sacred wet
>   schematic elements of
> cities, music, arrangement.

(Here again is the "sacred wet" of the essential ways of Killorglin.) Her "looking into the sun and the blaze inner water" affects her perception of the figure coming toward her; now he becomes "A man who is bones . . . drawing a boat of bones" and "A man whose body flames and tapers in flame." She gets in his boat, for the flames of his body are "twisted tines of remembrance that dissolve." She is compelled to go with him because he reminds her of someone, some force in her life: the force which compels her to trust in change. The boat is "the boat of death"; but it can be seen as the death of old ways. Again her theme, as in, for example, "Nine Poems for the Unborn Child": we can choose. She begins the poem with reference to "the guardians of this landscape," explaining in a note that these are "the truncated wing . . . a monument to the Wright Brothers" and "the spiral lighthouse" of Hatteras light. But as the poem comes to a close

no longer wing and lighthouse
no longer the guardians.
They are in me, in my speechless
life of barrier beach
As it lies open
to the night, out there.

. . . .

Out there? Father of rhythms,
deep wave, mother.
There is no *out there*.
All is open.
Open water. Open I.

Again, as in the thirties, she affirms that security is in risk, in moving through uncertainty, in being open to the night. The "rhythms"
referred to above are "the deep rhythms of your experience" ("The
Overthrow of One O'Clock at Night.") The open, the opening, is
a flash-forward to the wish of her next volume, *Breaking Open*.

The last stanza, in Whitman's rolling rhythms, brings together
images of "whatever has dissolved in our waves," hard, precise images of what the "wave of the sea" (that single phrase constitutes
stanza three) of time has carried along: "the blood-clam's ark, the
tern's acute eye, all buried mathematical instruments, castaways."
At the center of the open sea, the crucial moment of our people
now, she is "a lost voice" and she identifies with the voices of the
Freedom Riders, "the dark young living people."

Rukeyser's trip to Hanoi in 1972 is foreshadowed in the poems
of *The Speed of Darkness*; in these she says the war comes into her
room. "The Overthrow of One O'Clock at Night" is a "linear"
poem giving the harrowing thoughts of an American during the
war in Vietnam:

little children
half world over tonight rained on by fire—that's us—
calling on somebody—that's us—to come
and help them.

Another such poem is "The War Comes into My Room" with its

urgent consciousness (the same she nurtured in the thirties) that poets must sing their complete response to the moment which is constantly changing:

> nothing
>   has been spoken
>   not now
>   not in this night time
> the broken singing
>   as we move.

The singing will be "broken," inevitably. It will not be a closed, wholly linear poetry, not if it is to capture the movement, the groping, agonized reach for meaning during the "endless war." Richard Eberhart said her poetry in *The Speed of Darkness* was open-ended, not systematic "except in the inchoate system and thrust of the passions throwing off poems in a continuum of poetic realization."[10] "Delta Poems" is linear, but the nightmare of two young Vietnamese dying flashes and flashes; the linearity of the poem breaks into a nightmare of returns. Otto returns.

> I remember you. We walked near the harbor.
> You a young man believing in the future of summer
>
> . . . .
>
> They are walking again at the edge of waters.
> They are killed again near the lives, near the waves.

Rukeyser writes these poems aware of her place in history. She has been aware of that place since *Theory of Flight* where she wrote "Prinzip's year bore us." She writes in "Delta Poems,"

> I am a woman
> in a New York room
> late in the twentieth century.
> I am crying. I will write no more.

In "Poem" she writes, "I lived in the first century of world wars." She is intensely conscious of her art arising from a matrix of horror. But it does rise. Though she says "Most mornings I would be

10. Richard Eberhart, review of SD.

more or less insane" because of the newspaper headlines about these wars, she shows us in this poem her program of sanity, survival, and hope. The *"grenzen der seele"* is referred to again—the sense of a crucial limit to be pierced in order to grow. This "waking" is the state Blake and MacDiarmid tried to describe: a sense of the possibility of human life. It can't be noted enough that Rukeyser, who lived through the crushing of the visions of the thirties, still finds value in "considering a nameless way of living, of unimagined values." In poems like "Not Yet" Rukeyser tries to imagine how a time of "rigor, hatred and doom" can be overthrown. She imagines the bursting will come from the children: "The children are marvelous singing among the wars." In the wish of children for understanding, words take on new meanings, and revolutions are born.

The war poems in *The Speed of Darkness* cannot be completely "linear and straightforward," for Rukeyser considers the war in Vietnam as part of the continuing war of our century. She renders the nightmare recurrence in dreamlike imagery, and she finds her vision of possibility in dreamlike recurrence. In "Endless" she addresses Otto:

> your body with its touch its weight   smelling of new
>   wood
> as on the day the news of battle reached us
> falls beside the endless river.

The countermovement of possibility arises:

> Your body of new wood your eyes alive barkbrown of tree-
>   trunks
> the leaves and flowers of trees   stars all caught in crowns
>   of trees.

Otto's body becomes "endless earth." Here, as in "The Speed of Darkness," she plunges into the dark body connection of generations where she hopes to find a redeeming vision—again, a "body of waking." She imagines the dark, the unconscious forces of energy and renewal and associates them with the body in a most Lawrentian way. Through her body, her body rhythms, sex, dream, she is connected with the life-renewing forces. The poetry which renders this mystic vision rings true to those who have not ruled out such vision as, in Lieberman's words of 1968, "inscrutable . . . cloudy abstraction" or "oracular soothsaying."

> No longer speaking
> Listening with the whole body
> And with every drop of blood
> Overtaken by silence
>
> But this same silence is become speech
> With the speed of darkness.

Awareness of the body speaking for the cosmos leads to an awareness of the destruction wreaked upon the body, at this moment by the war in Vietnam. Nevertheless the vision continually arises from the body; the body is emblem of the struggle of the world to be whole.

> Lying
> blazing beside me
> you rear beautifully and up—
> your thinking face—
> erotic body reaching
>
> . . . .
>
> colors   lights   the world thinking and reaching.

Here a human body is identified with the body of the world, which she will elsewhere picture as "breathing" ("This Morning," in *Breaking Open*.) In the Scripps College lecture she quoted Giordano Bruno's poem *"De Immenso"*: *"Est animal sanctum, sacrum, venerabile, mundus."* She commented: "I think it means that the world is a living creature, an animal in the deep sense . . . sacred, holy, to be loved."

At the end of "The Speed of Darkness" poetry is imaged as body-based, connected to the unconscious, to vital, undeniable primal forces:

> A bird with a curved beak.
> It could slit anything, the throat-bird.
>
> Drawn up slowly.   The curved blades, not large,

Bird emerges   wet   being born
Begins to sing.

In "Endless" Otto's body is broken but the body still makes the sacred, powerful connections: the war is endless but so is the unkillable consciousness that we must stop the killing. As she says in
"Segre Song,"

Your song where you lie long dead on the shore of a Spanish
river—
your song moves under the earth and through time,
through air—
your song I sing to the sun as we move. . . .

The deep song, poetry, the throat bird, "could slit anything," she
has said, even the silence of the "recurrent dream of a locked
room" ("Not Yet"), which is an image of the spirit in all generations unable to speak its human wish. In "Word of Mouth" the
poet affirms that the silence is being shattered today.

Something is flying out of the sky behind me.
Turning, stirring of dream, something is speeding,
something is overtaking.

Stirrings in prisons, on beds, the mouths of the young,
resist, dance, love. It drives through the back of my
head,
through my eyes and breasts and mouth.

. . . .
Something out of Spain, into the general light!

In these war poems from *The Speed of Darkness* Rukeyser
asserts again that the promise of Spain in the thirties will not be
denied, is flowering in the rest of the century. The promise has
something to do with speech, touch, look: a freeing, an openness,
a confronting—just as the horror which also began in Spain in our
time involves the opposites of all these. The promise of openness
and the forces which seek to stifle it are Rukeyser's concerns in her
personal life. It is no wonder "it is all personal; it is all political"
(Bernikow). As the poems become more unmasked, so do the sin-
ews which bind all her work.

"Käthe Kollwitz," one of the "Lives," is also a war poem. It begins,

> Held between wars
> my lifetime
> among wars, the big hands of the world of death
> my lifetime
> listens to yours.

Lieberman referred to the "absorptively sympathetic portrait" Rukeyser draws of Kollwitz. One recognizes in this portrait Rukeyser's own personal and artistic ideals:

> a look as of music
> the revolutionary look
> that says   I am in the world
> to change the world
> my lifetime
> is to love to endure to suffer the music
> to set its portrait
> up as a sheet of the world
> the most moving the most alive
> Easter and bone
>
> . . . .
>
> the hands of enduring life
> that suffers the gifts and madness of full life. . . .

In this volume, in "Gift," she writes of "the dreams of madness and of an impossible complete time." And in "Song: Love in Whose Rich Honor" she says she is receiving

> the gift longed for so long
> The power
> to write
> out of the desperate ecstasy at last
> death and madness.

Rukeyser calls Kollwitz "Woman as gates," thus flashing forward to her volume of 1976, *The Gates*. In "Käthe Kollwitz" the German artist is speaking what we know Rukeyser believes about her own work, something I hope this study has been tracing:

Woman as gates, saying:
"The process is after all like music,
 like the development of a piece of music.
 The fugues come back and
                         again and again
    interweave.
 A theme may seem to have been put aside,
 but it keeps returning—
 the same thing modulated,
 somewhat changed in form.
 Usually richer.
 And it is very good that this is so."

Kollwitz's life was filled with personal tragedy as a result of wars: a son killed in a first war, a grandson killed in a later war. She reminds one of the women in "Letter to the Front" (*Beast in View*) who must watch and weep at the violence of war. Again the poet asserts that women and artists see the truth that others, for various reasons, do not.

What would happen if one woman told the truth about her
    life?
The world would split open

This now classic couplet with its shocking image associated with sex and birth is thus, too, grounded in the body, on the poet's own experience of birthing. In "The Poem as Mask" she shows how that experience is associated with the birth of a stronger self, a stronger art:

when I wrote of the god,
fragmented, exiled from himself, his life, the love gone
    down with song,
it was myself, split open, unable to speak, in exile from
    myself.

There is no mountain, there is no god, there is memory
of my torn life, myself split open in sleep, the rescued child
beside me among the doctors, and a word
of rescue from the great eyes.

No more masks! No more mythologies!

In "Käthe Kollwitz" Rukeyser asserts that an unmasked art can bring about this splitting-open throughout the world. (Her next volume will be entitled *Breaking Open*.)

The first section of "Akiba," another of the "Lives," appeared in *Waterlily Fire*. Rukeyser says in a note, "The story in my mother's family is that we are descended from Akiba—unverifiable, but a great gift to a child." The gift is the marvelously inspiring image of Akiba "identified with the Song of Songs and with the insurrection against Hadrian's Rome, led in A.D. 132 by Bar Cochba (Son of the Star)." Akiba is thus identified with sacred eroticism and revolution; one can see how he would appeal to this poet. Her poem about him explores his emblematic life. As we have seen, the first section, "The Way Out," is music of possibility, the images and rhythms and assertions moving to affirm.

The second section, "For *The Song of Songs*," is a hymn to "Holy desire," that "wish" the poet has been singing since "Theory of Flight" and the elegies. It is "the sacred body of thirst" ("What Do I Give You?"), the energy of wanting in a human being that makes the journey possible. It is the cosmic desire expressed in "The Gyroscope," desire as the begetter of all things.

> This song
> Is the creation
> The day of this song
> The day of the birth of the world.
>
> . . . .
> The desire will make
> A way through the wilderness

These imaged metaphysical assertions flow from the heart of the poet's vision, which essentially equates the desires of the body and spirit with the creativity of God.

> In these delights
> Is eternity of seed,
> The verge of life,
> Body of dreaming.

Our desires will lead us to truth. Thus she wrote in "A Song of Another Tribe" (*Waterlily Fire*) that she feels guilt not when she has certain desires but when her desires find no way. One recalls Blake saying in "A Vision of the Last Judgment" that the kingdom of heaven is not for those who have curbed their passions or who have no passions but for those who have cultivated their understandings. To Blake the worst thing a person can do to another is what the "priests in black gowns" did in "The Garden of Love": "binding with briars my joys and desires."[11]

In "The Bonds" Akiba is considered in his desire, his "immense need" to speak, "to find the burning Word." He learns to speak; he develops bonds with the world. The world becomes a sacred exchange, a continual bonding. The poet has explored this theme before in her search for a sense of union with the world. (In "This Place in the Ways" in *The Green Wave* she said, "I offered and all was well.") The vision is of a creative life of personal growth, which at the same time nurtures others. For the poet the nurturing is through speech: "Go answering, answering," she said in "Theory of Flight."

> In giving, praising, we move beneath clouds of honor,
> In giving, in praise, we take gifts that are given,
> The spark from one to the other leaping, a bond
> Of light
>
> . . . .
>
> The need to give having found the need to become

The section on the martyrdom of Akiba is a paean to a hero of the race whose heroism is germane to our times. Here Rukeyser succeeds in creating a living myth.

> This was an old man under iron rakes
> Tearing through to the bone. He made no cry.
>
> . . . .
>
> He accepts his harvest, failures. He accepts faithlessness,
> Madness of friends, a failed life
>
> . . . .
>
> Does he preach passion and non-violence?

11. "The Garden of Love," in Erdman (ed.), *Poetry and Prose of William Blake*, 26.

> Yes, and trees, crops, children honestly taught.
>
> . . . .
>
> My hope, my life, my burst of consciousness:
> To confirm my life in the time of confrontation.

In the lyric first person of the last lines the poet speaks of her own life through the images of Akiba. She will write more directly of her personal political confrontation with the enslaving powers in *Breaking Open* and *The Gates*, where she, like Akiba, will preach "passion and non-violence."

The last section of "Akiba" is entitled "The Witness": it is a term she has used for the responsive reader of poetry. In this section, repeating lines and phrases from the rest of the poem, she asks her reader to take her work into her/his transforming life, as she (as witness) has taken the legend of Akiba into her own life.

> You who come after me far from tonight finding
> These lives that ask you always Who is the witness—
> Take from us acts of encounter we at night
> Wake to attempt, as signs, seeds of beginning
>
> . . . .
>
> Time tells us men and women, tells us You
> The witness, your moment covered with signs, your self.

In "This Morning" in *Breaking Open* she gives her resolve, born of her witness to Akiba's life:

> I say across the waves of the air to you:
> today once more
> I will try to be non-violent
> one more day
> this morning, waking the world away
> in the violent day.

After "Akiba," the witnessing, the confronting, will consist of political speech. Rukeyser has been witnessing through speech all along; but in these latest three volumes the political witnessing becomes increasingly direct, just as references to her personal life become unmasked. In "Facing Sentencing":

> the world

Is almost silent, and suppose we did not know
This power to fall into each other's eyes
And say We love; and say We know each other
And say among silence We will help stop this war.

The long poem "Searching/Not Searching" explores the themes of bearing witness to truth in times of political crisis. The inscription (credited as "after Robert Duncan") is "Responsibility is to / use the power to respond." The poem begins, "What kind of woman goes searching and searching?" A woman like this poet, like Miriam:

> I alone stand here
> ankle-deep
> and I sing, I sing,
> until the lands
> sing to each other.

Each section of the poem is another witness to wholeness and unity, despite the discouragement of silence and unresponsiveness. The direct vision and speech of children will help the poet in her search to speak the truth. In the next section searching becomes building in speech:

> They are setting the forms,
> pouring the new buildings.
> Our days pour down.
> I am pouring my poems.

The poem moves through several subjects on the theme of bearing witness despite enormous difficulties. In images as diverse as Galileo constructing a spinning toy earth to teach his student "on the shore of a new era," to the heroine of the epic of Vietnam, the *Kieu*, "in which being handed to soldiers is the journey," to a description of the floor of the Sistine Chapel as a sea of arms "pointing straight up closing the gap between / continual creation and the daily touch," the poem affirms the possibility of continual new wholeness and spiritual discovery even in a society corrupted by war. Addressing her dying friend Hallie Flanagan (director of the w.p.a. Theatre Project), "lying all gone to bone," she says,

> I knew Hallie then I could move without answer,
> like the veterans for peace, hurling back their medals
> and not expecting an answer from the grass.
> You taught me this in your dying, for poems and theatre
> and love and peace-making that living and my love
> are where response and no-response
> meet at last, Hallie, in infinity.

The speech of the witness, the poet, the discoverer is contrasted with the speech of the politician in "The President and the Laser Bomb," section ten of "Searching/Not Searching." In our time when the lie is widely broadcast by technology, the awful deeds masked by the speech of politicians must be spoken by the poet, in her own voice. Real speech, real communication is the hope of the world, in *Breaking Open* as in *The Life of Poetry*. Real speech is the deep mutual recognition that made possible the event described in "Don Baty, the Draft Resister." Several people, including the poet, gather in a church and in a religious ceremony they all say, "I am Don Baty," so that when the police come to arrest him, all his friends say they are he. It is speech nonviolently affirming union and confronting violence and the lie. Though the poet now sings all the brave acts of those who resist, as in "Bringing," she recognizes that her own political acts characteristically involve speech. From "Flying There: Hanoi":

> I thought I was going to the inventors of peace,
> but I am going to the poets.
> My life is flying to your life.

In the title poem, "Breaking Open," the poet struggles to regain "a language just forgotten":

> it means
> Something in our experience you do not know
> When will it open open opening.

Like Akiba she struggles to speak the burning words needed in this time when "we are Asia and New York/Bombs, roaches, mutilation." The world is speaking; she has always known this. She must ever struggle to hear and transmit the whole meaning. She does not want to stop at disgust and negation, even in this time when a deteriorating New York City parallels the crumbling of our national ideals in the Vietnam War.

> The whole thing—waterfront, war, city,
>   sons, daughters, me—
> Must be re-imagined.

The facts of war and wrecked city are overwhelming. At first she protests with her voice, but not in the ordered achievement of speech (though she will make a powerful poem out of that first agonized frustration).

> Walking into the elevator at Westbeth
> Yelling in the empty stainless-steel
> Room like the room of this tormented year.
> Like the year
> The metal nor absorbs nor reflects
> My yelling.
> My pulled face looks at me
> From the steel walls.

The stainless-steel walls of those huge elevators at Westbeth (former telephone company offices, now improbably artists' and writers' housing) effectively symbolize her unresponsive countrymen and women during the height of the Vietnam War. The progress of her agony is into physical demonstration:

> and some of us lie gravely down
> on that cool mosaic floor,
> the Senate.
> Washington! Your bombs rain down!
> I mourn, I lie down, I grieve.

During a flight to Hanoi (for the Committee for Solidarity, to demonstrate many Americans' desire for peace) she senses acutely the connection between the political and the personal. "In facing history, we look at each other, and in facing our entire personal life, we look at each other. I want to break open." She must be fully personal and honest if she is to have that "inner greet" (BO, 31) which is to save the world, make it one world. Political relations must grown out of open personal relations or they will not grow. An ideal openness is possible among the few—for now. The new world is not yet. The openness begins, as it has always begun for Rukeyser, in the solitude of her room where she writes poetry.

> To the high cold mountains, to the source of the river,
> I too go,
> Deeper into this room.

She can say to the witness, "Answer me. Dance my dance." But the time (at the height of the war) is unutterably discouraging.

> Sobbing, lost, alone. The river darkens.
> Black flow, bronze lights, white lights.
> Something must answer that light, that dark.

> Love,
> The door opens, you walk in.

Relief is found only in the "inner greet" of the few friends and lovers. For a time, political acts must substitute for speech.

> I try to turn my acts inward and deeper.
> Almost a poem. If it splash outside,
> All right.
>
> . . . .
>
> Going to prison. The clang of the steel door.
> It is my choice. But the steel door does clang.
> The introversion of this act
> Past its seeming, past all thought of effect,
> Until it is something like
> writing a poem in my silent room.

In prison, everyone and everything is locked up, including speech. How can it be otherwise? Prisoners are "objects." To those whom society has treated like objects, the sacred words are meaningless.

> In prison, the prisoners.
> One black girl, 19 years.
> She has killed her child
> and she grieves, she grieves.
> She crosses to my bed.
> "What do *Free* mean?"

I look at her.
"You don't understand English."
"Yes, I understand English."
"What do *Free* mean?"

("The Backside of the Academy" in *The Speed of Darkness* also effectively contrasts our society's "sacred" words with the sordid realities of those who live on the streets of New York. The academy is the American Academy of Arts and Letters on 156th Street.)

the shut wall with the words carved across its head
ART REMAINS THE ONE WAY POSSIBLE OF SPEAKING
TRUTH.—

. . . .

and further along Viva Fidel now altered to Muera Fidel.

. . . .

and also Margaret is a shit and also fuck and shit;
far up, invisible at the side of the building:
WITHOUT VISION THE PEO

The prison sequence in "Breaking Open" ends with the poet on her way back to Westbeth. She is finding a way to reimagine the whole thing: "Nothing buried in her but is lit and transformed." On one of the final pages of *Breaking Open* one finds a horrifying vision of what "Rational man has done." But after facing these horrors the poet can turn once again to affirmation and making.

I do and I do.
Life and this under war.
Deep under protest, make.
For we are makers more.

but touching teaching going
the young and the old
they reach they break they are moving
to make the world

The section of *Breaking Open* called "The Hostages" introduces those to whom sacred words are live and meaningful: workers for peace in Vietnam. They give the poet new faith in speech.

When I stand with these three
My new brothers my new sister

> . . . .
> I can speak,
> And I speak openly on the church steps,
> At the peace center saying: We affirm
> Our closeness forever with the eyes in Asia,
> Those who resist the forces we resist.

This feeling of community and love with those who are open to history and to themselves makes her say, "It is something like the breaking open of my youth." She feels now that "a way is open: transformation." Again she has a spiritual sense of "the edge of experience."

> Then came I entire to this moment
> process and light
>   to discover the country of our waking
> breaking open.

The final phrase suggests hope not only for personal growth but for a nation's growth in consciousness—that nation in which she has been protesting and also "feeding and seeding" ("Wherever"). In retrospect we can say of the time of the war in Vietnam that many Americans did indeed wake to a new realization of American ideals. In a sense there was indeed a breaking open in the United States in the sixties.

Breaking Open contains several poems that explore the paralysis of speech, the great "effort at speech." I have discussed that effort in its political context. In some of the poems her struggles in personal relationships are tightly interwoven with her political struggles. Such a poem is "Desdichada," where the poet asserts that her speech and her affirmation grow out of others' personal denial of her.

> Disinherited, annulled, finally disacknowledged
> and all of my own asking. I keep that wild dimension
> of life and making and the spasm
> upon my mouth as I say this word of acknowledge
> to you forever. *Ewig.*

Rukeyser has felt the suffering of personal repudiation. Her father

disinherited her. She had her marriage annulled. The father of her
son did not acknowledge the family. Yet she acknowledges:

> Then I do take you,
> but far under consciousness, knowing
> that under under flows a river wanting
> the other: to go open-handed in Asia,
> to cleanse the tributaries and the air, to make for making,
> to stop selling death and its trash, pour plastic down
> men's throats.

She acknowledges her life-task and its potential in a new generation: "my broken mouth / and the whole beautiful mouth of the
child."

Rukeyser reveals in several poems that her need for speech and
her achievement of genuine speech come, paradoxically, from not
having been spoken to in crucial moments of childhood.

> I ask the first grown sexual
> question.   She cannot reply.
> And from then on even past her death, I cannot fully
> have language with my mother
>
> .   .   .   .
>
>   although it has taken me all these years
> and sunsets to come to you, past the dying, I know,
> I come with my word alive.

Again, in "More Clues,"

> Mother because you never spoke to me
> I go my life, do I, searching in women's faces
> the lost word, a word in the shape of a breast?

Breaking Open contains a section of Eskimo songs translated
by Rukeyser and Paul Radin. In his review Thomas Stumpf referred to these primitive songs derogatorily as exhibiting Rukeyser's "hand-clasping brotherhood, and love for all ethnic groups. . . .
Even for a poet who is all heart, it must be difficult to identify with
long distance caribou hunting, hunkering down over an ice hole,
or making love in an igloo: but Rukeyser is nothing if not sympathetic." Stumpf missed the relevance of the poems entirely. Rukey-

ser was not writing of Eskimos as she has written of blacks, sympathetically identifying with their oppression, struggle, and pain. Rather she was obviously captivated by the haunting sense of loss and yearning of some of the poems, the doggedness of others about the pursuit of song or of fish, and the simplicity of the "stroking songs" which are related to her "touch poems" ("This Morning") and to the theme and phrasing of "A Simple Experiment." From that poem:

> stroke it
> stroke it,
> the molecules
> can be given
> their tending grace
>
> by a strong magnet
> stroking stroking.

Some Eskimo songs are obviously thematically connected to her poems about the effort at speech.

> Song-calling.
> Breathing deep, my heart laboring,
> Calling the song. (BO, 87)
>
> I cannot even make my difficult song,
> For easy birdsong is not given to me. (BO, 96)
>
> How lovely it is to
> Put a little song together.
> Many of mine fail, yes they do. (BO, 97)
>
> I know what I want in my words
> But it will not turn into song. (BO, 98)

Speech is the central concern of *The Gates*. The long title poem presents the poet on a mission to Korea to plead for the life of the "stinging" poet Kim Chi. He has written work "like that of Burns or Brecht—and it has got under the skin of the highest officials." The first section shows how the words of the imprisoned poet live:

> Waiting to leave all day I hear the words;
> that poet in prison, that poet newly-died
> whose words we wear, reading, all of us. I and my son.

She goes "to find the poet of these cries." But when she arrives in his country she finds "the marvelous / hard-gripped people silent among their rulers, looking / at me." In the third section she learns the caution she must now observe in speaking:

> A missionary comes to visit me.
> Looks into my eyes. Says,
> "Turn on the music so we can talk."

Later she and the Cabinet minister talk of "Liberation." That theme in Kim's work, she says, "bind[s] his people and mine in these new ways / for the first time past strangeness and despisal." But he is imprisoned, for officials have broken into his house and stolen his diaries with their revolutionary words. She goes to the poet's house, "books making every wall / a wall of speech." She goes to the church of Galilee and learns that the police listen to everything, "standing before all doors, / hearing over all wires." "Let them listen to the dispossessed," she exclaims. She connects her mission to Korea with Akiba.

> That night, a flute
> across the dark, the sound
> opening times to me, a time
> when I stood on the green hillside
> before the great white stone.
> Grave of my ancestor
> Akiba at rest over Kinneret.
> The holy poem, he said to me,
> the Song of Songs always;
> and know what I know, to love
> your belief with all your life.

Section eight builds a striking image of Kim Chi's mother standing in the prison Yard:

> Woman as fine tines blazing against sunset,
>
> . . . .
>
> as the tines of a pitchfork
> that stands to us as her son's voice does stand
> across the world speaking.

The American poet speaks with others to free the Korean poet:

> in long despair we work   write   speak   pray   call to others
> Free our night   free our lives   free our poet.

The worst thing Rukeyser imagines in the imprisonment of Kim Chi is his loss of words. Section ten begins with images of silence and paralysis:

> The fear of the child among the tyrannical
> unanswerable men and women, they dominate day and night.
> . . . .
> Giant fears: massacres, the butchered that across the fields
>   of the world
> lie screaming, and their screams are heard as silence.

Finally, she imagines the horror for Kim Chi:

> without books, without pen and paper.
> Does he draw a pencil out of his throat,
> out of his veins, out of his sex?
> There are cells all around him, emptied.
> He can signal on these walls till he runs mad.

At this point in this political poem, the poet breaks open her personal life. After imagining a dreadful silence in the larger world, the world of political prisoners, she flashes to the silence she has maintained in her own life. Seeing Kim Chi's son causes her to speak more freely than ever before about her own son and the feelings she had as a new mother.

> Long ago, soon after my son's birth
> —this scene comes in arousal with the sight of a strong
>   child
> just beginning to run—
> when all life seemed prisoned off, because the father's
>   other son
> born three weeks before my child
> had opened the world
> that other son and his father closed the world—
> in my fierce loneliness and fine well-being
> torn apart but with my amazing child
> I celebrated and grieved.

In Section twelve, after connecting the silence of her life with that of Kim Chi, through the inability of their children to speak with their fathers, she cries out for speech, for naming. But even now speech still cannot come.

> For that I cannot name the names,
> my child's own father, the flashing, the horseman,
> the son of the poet—
>
> . . . .
> Again I am struck nameless, unable to name
>
> . . . .
> silent in this terrifying moment under all moonlight,
> all sunlight turning in all our unfree lands.
> Name them, name them all, light of our own time.

In the past her own child, like the son of Kim Chi, was "crucified . . . kept away from his father." Both fathers are jailed, one in an actual prison, the other, in the past, "by his own fantasies."

Rukeyser sees this tragic series of events in her personal life as the cause of her particular development as a poet: she has become a poet who focuses on recurrences, a poet who fiercely accepts life ("among us who carry our own time") as she accepted the responsibility of rearing her child alone despite all the advice to the contrary (see "All the Little Animals" in *Breaking Open*), a poet who waits for the gifts of life with determined good humor even in her agonies:

> And before that baby
> had ever started to begin to run
> then Mary said,
> smiling and looking out of her Irish eyes,
> "Never mind, Muriel.
> Life will come will come again
> knocking and coughing and farting at your door."
>
> So I became very dark very large
> a silent woman this time given to speech
> a woman of the river of that song
> and on the beach of the world in storm given
> in long lightning seeing the rhyming of those scenes
> that make our lives.

She asks urgent, reverberating questions at the end of the poem and the volume.

> How shall we free him?
> How shall we speak to the infant beginning to run?
> All those beginning to run?

In our time, as in all times, parents and others have asked themselves how to prepare the young for a world where beauty, energy, and idealism are prey to the perpetual currents of evil, denial, and destruction. Rukeyser writes of our concerns with a simplicity and forcefulness that dignify our wish and give us courage. The sociologist Robert Coles, in a deeply sympathetic review of *The Gates* in *American Poetry Review*, writes of feeling "silent, sad, instructed, grateful" after reading the latest volume of "a gifted observer of this world; a person who can sing to us and make our duller, less responsive minds come more alive."[12]

It is evident in these last three volumes that Rukeyser has been engaged in an "unmasking," a demythologizing. She announced it in "The Poem as Mask" (SD, 3): "No more masks! No more mythologies." Several poems in these three volumes announce her desire to be more direct in her art; several striking images convey her resolve. From "The Transgress" (SD, 5):

> bed of forbidden things finally known—
> art from the symbol struck, living and made.

From "What Do I Give You?" (SD, 4):

> Seeds of all memory
> Given me give I you
> My own self. Voice of my days.

Other "unmasked" poems in *The Speed of Darkness* reveal her more personally than ever. Such are "What I See," with its description of the poet sweating and dreaming of a lover "perfectly at climax" on another bed and "Song: Love in Whose Rich Honor" with its frank avowal of the impulse behind much of her recent poetry.

12. Robert Coles, review of *Gates*, in *American Poetry Review*, VII (May/June, 1978), 15.

> Love
> deep and so far forbidden
> is bringing me
> a gift
> to claw at my skin
> to break open my eyes
> the gift longed for so long
> The power
> to write
> out of the desperate esctasy at last
> death and madness.

"Anemone" is another such imaging of that impulse:

> My sex is closing, my sex is opening.
> You are singing and offering: the way in.

"For My Son" is a catalog of the ancestry of her "fatherless" son, an unmasking and demythologizing of traditional notions of ancestry:

> You come from poets, kings, bankrupts, preachers,
>   attempted bankrupts, builders of cities, salesmen,
> the great rabbis, the kings of Ireland, failed drygoods
>   storekeepers, beautiful women of the songs,
> great horsemen, tyrannical fathers at the shore of ocean.

By the end of the poem one realizes that the poet has made myth out of our ordinary human condition in which every one of us, not just the pedigreed and "legitimate," is related to the great ones of the universe:

> in your self made whole, whole with yourself and
>   whole with others
> the stars your ancestors.

Though the unmasking in these three latest volumes involves, as it did in the poems from the thirties such as "Effort at Speech," a revelation in words, now *look* and *touch* are equally emphasized. The goal, as set forth in *The Life of Poetry*, is communication, communion. In *The Speed of Darkness* the communication is first with her deepest self, her unconscious, which she must touch and make her own in waking life.

Clues
How will you catch these clues at the moment of waking
take them, make them yours?

. . . .

   write what streamed
from you in darkness
into you by dark?

Indian Baptiste saying, We painted our dreams
We painted our dreams on our faces and bodies.
We took them into us by painting them on ourselves.

"Forerunners" also describes the poet's coming into contact with
her unconscious; here her conscious perceptions of scenes in the
world ("forerunners of images") are seen about to deepen, to dip
into the unconscious where they will generate the compelling images of art.

In morning, on the river-mouth,
I came to my waking
seeing carried in air
seaward, a ship.

. . . .

Day conscious and unconscious.
Words on the air.
Before the great
images arrive, riderless horses.

In "Woman as Market" the poet senses that the world may call
up meaning from the unconscious:

the reds, the yellows, all the calling boxes.
What did those forms say? What words have I forgotten?
what spoke to me from the day?

Once the darkness has sped to consciousness, once the dream of
love and wholeness has been dreamt, the need to touch, to look, to
speak with others is strong. It is unbearable in a country of non-
communicators. From "Among Grass":

amazed among silences   you touch me never

. . . .

no touch no touch   a tactless land

denies my death my fallen hand
silence runs down the riverbeds.

But for Rukeyser the unconscious is in touch with the inform-
ing power of the cosmos; when the artist works from the unconscious, its universal images and rhythms, communion may be
achieved.

> Spirals and fugues, the power most like music
> Turneth all worlds to meaning
> And meaning to matter, all continually,
> And sweeps in the sacred motion,
> Spirals and fugues its lifetime
> To move my life to yours,
>   and all women and men and the children in their light,
> The little stone in the middle of the road, its veins and
>   patience,
> Moving the constellations of all things.

In "Poem," describing her life "in the first century of world wars,"
she tells why she still writes poetry: to bring the unconscious powers of wholeness into consciousness, "to reconcile / Waking with
sleeping, ourselves with each other, / Ourselves with ourselves."
She wants to touch deep with deep. This is poetry as "the type of
the creation in which we may live and which will save us" (LP,
228). In the beautiful "The Seeming," dedicated to Helen Lynd,
the progressive verbs and nouns ending in "ing" define a coming to
consciousness from the unconscious:

> We do not know the springs of these colored and loving
>   acts   or what triggers birth   what sleep is.

There are those who show us how to bring our deepest unitive
powers to our conscious life and work:

> we do not even   not even know why we wake
> but some of us showing the others
> a kind of welcoming
> bringing a form to morning
> we see in a man a theme
> a dream taking over
> or in this woman going today who has shown us

. . . .
> morning and every time the way to naming.

In the short poem "Air" the poet affirms that universal spirit which informs all matter and gives it meaning and which allows people to communicate.

Several poems in *The Gates* describe the artist's relationship with creative forces. In "Work for the Day is Coming" they are imperious:

> For that I move through states of being
>
> . . . .
>   and all night long
> am invited led whipped dragged through states of being
> toward the
>   inviting you through states of being
>   poem.

In "The Sun-Artist" the power of the cosmos is symbolized by the sun. The poem describes how Bob Miller at the Exploratorium in San Francisco constructed a motor that follows the sun by counteracting the motion of the earth. The sun's rays refracted through prisms are a skein of moving colors on a screen. The viewer may block one color with an arm or another part of the body and become "part of the color . . . part of the sun." Thus the sun symbolizes that creative power which comes from the world, through the unconscious (and the body) and gives rise to art. Allow the forces, move with the forces, she has said. Now she sees the sun-artist saying it in his most essential medium. It delights her that she is invited to participate in the creation of this art, to dance her own dance in the sun's beams.

Paradoxically, the forces are fragile. And ironically those who work with them most closely may be denied the name of artist.

> Frail it is and can be intercepted.
> Fragile, like ourselves. Mirrors and prisms, they
>   can be broken.
> Children shattered by anything.
> Strong, pouring strong, wild as the power of the great sun.
> Not art, but light. In distance, in smiting winter,

the artist speaks : No art.
This is not art.
What is *an artist*? I bear the song of the sun.

The last line affirms both that the sun-artist's work communicated the forces to the perceiving poet and that she herself has been singing the sun, the universal creative spirit. The artist who smites the sun-artist from a cold distance, denying the value of his work, denies what Rukeyser described in *Willard Gibbs*: "the worker in pure imagination: scientist, poet, abstract artist, pioneer of system— those few working closest to the spirit in any field."

Besides the poems focusing on speech and exploring contact with the creative forces, the latest volumes also celebrate an unmasked "looking" and "touching." In *Breaking Open*, "Despisals" wishes

> never to despise
> the homosexual who goes building another
>
> with touch   with touch   (not to despise any touch).

In certain poems such as "In Her Burning," Rukeyser in aging has come around to Yeats's "rag and bone shop of the heart."

> The randy old
> woman said
> Tickle me up
> I'll be dead very soon—
> Nothing will
> touch me then.

But in only one poem does she share Yeats's "cold eye" at this stage:

> Rondel
> What happens to song and sex
> Now that I am fifty-six?
> They dance, but differently,
> Death and distance in the mix;
> Now that I'm fifty-six.

There is usually no "distance" in this poet's "dance," her call to touch and look and speech. In "Welcome from War" she says, "I kiss your hands, I kiss your eyes, / I kiss your sex," and in "Facing Sentencing": "fear is not to be so feared. / Numbness is." In "Looking" she alludes to a painfully personal connection in her larger commitment—her son was in Canada during the war.

> Battles whose names I do not know
> Weapons whose wish they dare not teach
> Wars whose need they will not show
> Tear us tear us each from each,
> O my dear
> Great sun and daily touch.
>
> . . . .
> I saw you stare out over Canada
> As I stare over the Hudson River.

What strikes a reader who has progressed through these three volumes is a new emphasis on illness, aging, and death in *The Gates*. The focus is not completely new, for several poems in *Breaking Open* deal with the poet's aging and with her meditations on death. And by no means do we find the fascination with death of Plath or Sexton. A short poem asserts, "I'd rather be Muriel than be dead and be Ariel" (BO, 63). But there is in *The Gates* a new consciousness of the imminence of death. Several poems describe recovering from serious illness. Rukeyser had a stroke in 1965, described in "Resurrection of the Right Side," which left her partially paralyzed and for a while impeded in her speech. It took eleven years for the poem to "come through," as she says. But it is here now, and one sees how terrible is this particular illness to one who bases her perceptions and her song on the rhythms of the body. In this volume she describes her writing:

> Poem   white page   white page   poem
> something is streaming out of a body in waves
> something is beginning from the fingertips.

She also proclaims in "Dream Drumming," "I turned into the infinity figure, reaching down into / the earth of music with my legs at last . . . turned into music." Here is the loss of that body-based art:

When the half-body dies its frightful death
forked pain, infection of snakes, lightning, pull down
   the voice. Waking
and I begin to climb the mountain on my mouth,
word by stammer, walk stammered, the lurching deck of
   earth.
Left-right with none of my own rhythms
the long-established sex and poetry.
                     I go running in sleep,
but waking stumble down corridors of self, all rhythms
   gone.

Yet despite, or perhaps because of, this actual experience of half-death, more frightful than her dangerous Caesarean delivery because completely unexpected, her determination to recover and to make crisis yield new force is stronger than ever. This determination is found not only in poems about her own illnesses but also in poems about the illness and death of others, of society at large. In "Slow Death of the Dragon," about Spain's Franco, she describes the first illness of that country:

The sickness poured through the roads,
The vineyards shook.
A clot formed on the wild river.
The streets and squares were full of crevices.
Poison ran on the church-towers.

It is an illness of over thirty years. But she can also describe recovery:

They have been speaking all along.
We can tell by their eyes,
Although their mouths are broken.
Now they are healing their mouths.

In "Neruda, the Wine," she declares that

We are the seas through whom the great fish passed
And passes. He died in a moment of general dying.
Something was reborn.

· · · · · · · · · · · · · · · ·
                 Spain, that core of all our lives,
The long defeat that brings us what we know.

Since "Theory of Flight" she has been singing new beginnings, birth out of death. Now the singing has a new edge, even a frenzy, for she too has felt death.

> Father with your feet cut off
> mother cut down to death
> cut down my sister in the selfsame way
>
> . . . .
>
> The song flies out of all of you the song
> starts in my body, the song
> it is in my mouth, the song
> it is on my teeth, the song
> it is pouring the song
> wine and lightning
> the rivers coming to confluence
> in me entire.

Science tells us that as we age we see through dead cells in our eyes. The poet seizes this scientific fact (as she has many others) and draws out its spiritual meanings. The spiritual mastery she enjoys over the process of aging is symbolized by the bodily eye's own accomplishments. Like Blake she proclaims a spiritual sight and independence from what he called the "vegetative eye"; but first she notes what the eye does in the grip of dying.

> . . . I pass, my eyes seeing through corpses of dead cells
> Glassy, a world hardening with my hardening eyes
> My look is through the corpses of all the living
> Men and women who stood with me and died before
> But my young look still blazes from my changing
> Eyes. . . .

In a poem that recalls the androgynous vision of "Letter to the Front" Rukeyser refers in "Double Ode" to her "female powers" and says,

> I am the poet of the night of women
> and my two parents are the sun and the moon,
>
> . . . .
>
> their silvery line of music gave me girlhood
> and fierce male prowess and a woman's grave
> eternal double music male and female.

("Night," of course, has no evil connotation here, not for the poet of *The Speed of Darkness*, celebrator of the dark creative force.) Associating "the sun and the moon" with her mother and father she says, "I knew that the sun and the moon / Stood in me with one light." Indeed, in her three latest volumes Rukeyser has been especially "woman-conscious," exploring feminist themes. In "Waiting for Icarus" and "Myth" (a retelling of the Oedipus story in *Breaking Open*), she humorously protests that the male role and society's attitudes toward women assign them an unsatisfactory position. In *The Gates* "Ms. Lot" is another rewriting of a myth with an emphasis on the inadequate consideration given women in the great story. But in "Painters" there is more than wry protest. Here Rukeyser sings of her ancestor in prehistory:

> In the cave with a long-ago flare
>
> . . . .
>
> one or two men, painting
> and a woman among them.
> Great living animals grow on the stone walls,
> their pelts, their eyes, their sex, their hearts,
> and the cave-painters touch them with life, red, brown,
>   black,
> a woman among them, painting.

In "Fable" she joins two themes for a most effective insight into the nature of human growth as she has explored it in several poems and in her prose. The poem begins like her other poems retelling myths from a feminist point of view:

> Yes it was the prince's kiss.
> But the way was prepared for the prince.
> It had to be.

But the poem continues to develop a theme she has traced elsewhere.

> When the attendants carrying the woman
> —dead they thought her lying on the litter—
> stumbled over the root of a tree
> the bit of deathly apple in her throat
> jolted free.
>
> . . . .

. . . .
A miracle has even deeper roots,
Something like error, some profound defeat.
Stumbled-over, the startle, the arousal,
Something never perceived till now, the taproot.

In "Chapman," one of her first *Lives* (TW, 1939), she described a hero who was "many-born" through a series of defeats which opened new ways of being for him. She depicted Willkie in *One Life* as a man who leaped to new growth each time he met defeat. Each failure was, for Willkie, that "jolt" which pushed him over a new threshold. Of Thomas Hariot she said, "He is a rebel who appears to fail at every climax of his life. He can be seen to go deeper at these times." And again, "Beaten down he was, step by step, and at each step he opened his life beyond the beating."[13]

Defeat may catapult the spirit over a threshold. Rukeyser has been fascinated by such paradoxes since "Theory of Flight" with its visions of new life wrenched from the teeth of death. Flight was, in that poem, "intolerable contradiction." She urged, "Open your flesh . . . to opposites." Thus from her very first published works she has given us images of possibility flowing from the dialectical process which is, to her, the music of growth and life, the hands of enduring life, the gates.

The Traces of Thomas Hariot

The Traces of Thomas Hariot (1971) which is, like *Willard Gibbs*, the biography of a scientist, tells the reader, especially the reader of the poems, as much about the poet as it does about Hariot. John Hollander, praising the book highly in *Harper's*, said it "is a very special kind of poetic work. . . . Ultimately . . . the author's concern focuses on her own imaginative act, and the historical research behind her essay becomes part of it—not coded in the notes

13. Muriel Rukeyser, *The Traces of Thomas Hariot* (New York, 1971), 4, 12.

and apparatus of a technical historian . . . but internalized as part of a continuing imaginative quest."[14] The quest is for another living ancestor, a "risen image" like those of the "Lives": Ryder, Chapman, Gibbs, Akiba, emblems of the brave, full life which denies or simplifies no part of the human journey and which, beaten down or blocked, transforms itself into new modes. Rukeyser's view of history is the same in *Hariot* as it is in *Willard Gibbs*, as it is in the poems. The first sentence of *Gibbs*—"Whatever has happened, whatever is going to happen in the world, it is the living moment that contains the sum of the excitement, this moment in which we touch life and all the energy of the past and future"—is reiterated in *Hariot*: "The facts of history are the facts of the present, with the past acknowledged and alive." Quoting R. G. Collingwood, she continues, " 'The historical past is the world of ideas which the present evidence creates in the present. In historical inference we do not move from our present world to a past world; the movement in experience is always a movement within a present world of ideas.' " (TTH, 62) Her book shows us her imagination vividly discovering the "present world of ideas," images, speculations, hopes, linkages which are the traces of Hariot. We are given the traces as strokes, gestures of the imagination seizing; most often we are encouraged to make our own connections between the strokes, using our own imaginations.

Reading *Hariot* is exhilarating but also tiring and often annoying. One wonders why there are so many typographical errors in such a beautifully produced book. Why do footnotes not always satisfactorily indicate the source of material used? What is the logic of an index which omits the titles of important books mentioned in the text while listing other books? There are blocks of untranslated Latin. There are very difficult sentences, some of which, though tantalizing, make little sense until several chapters later. Rukeyser explains that Random House was very careless with the book because they didn't like it. They remaindered it soon

14. John Hollander, review of *The Traces of Thomas Hariot*, in *Harper's*, CCXLII (February, 1971), 109.

after publication. Paul Johnson, reviewing the book in the *New Statesman*, said: "Though she has examined many unpublished manuscripts, her gleanings are obscured by an inflated style which defies description and baffles the reader." John Hollander wrote with understanding of the "quotations whose immediate significance will owe more to the methods of modern long poems than to those of historical demonstration," but he also said, "This book is in many ways very unruly." Geoffrey Wolff in his sympathetic and admiring *Newsweek* review noted that Rukeyser seems "to be striking out for a voice in prose that will catch the spirit of Elizabethan and Jacobean diction." He said her sentences "surprise the reader with an odd usage, to please him by making him work to solve the sentence as well as the story." He concluded by saying that the book was occasionally exhausting, but he called it "a book of great learning and of loving patience." Readers must bring an appreciation of learning and their own patience to the book. If one does not close the book prematurely one may reach and "touch life and all the energy of the past and future." One is invited to respond, to create the image, again, as in the other prose books, as in many of the poems. Clive Bush noted in "Muriel Rukeyser: The Poet as Scientific Biographer," that "Muriel Rukeyser's own method . . . encourages the reader to bring his own experience to the most obdurate of traces so that the meanings gradually discover themselves."[15]

We are given great clusters of vibrant detail. Of the accounts of the fiery Elizabethan men and women whose lives and deaths impinged on Hariot Rukeyser explains, "With all the other pieces of evidence in this story, these pieces shine, quiver, move. They are ambiguous only in this: that the pieces are very often not identifiable. They are live, but cannot be measured. They are traces" (TTH, 90). Often the manner of impingement is not exactly known; the poet fashions the pieces and lets them speak for themselves, in con-

15. Paul Johnson, review of *Hariot*, in *New Statesman*, March 3, 1972, p. 277; Geoffrey Wolff, review of *Hariot*, in *Newsweek*, March 29, 1971, p. 101; Bush, "Muriel Rukeyser: The Poet as Scientific Biographer," p. 30.

junction with other pieces. This is her justification for this method:

The evidence that I offer here has never been offered, and is only a stroke, and so much of this story consists of a silvery stroke in a place, and a great gap then of ignorance and destruction, another stroke, and a greater gap. But soon, with all the gaps, a large structure begins to be evident, a structure before which surmise strikes deep into one's life. (TTH, 89)

The question of the portrait [of Hariot] is like many others in this history, mysterious, equivocal, capable of at least two interpretations, and of extreme interest taken together with the other live and mysteriously moving pieces of this evidence. It is possible to swim among many unknowns. (TTH, 168)

It is obvious to the reader that Rukeyser finds the swim exhilarating, compelling, vastly satisfying. She has been swimming this way in her prose: in dealing with the difficult, disparate material for the Gibbs book, in portraying Willkie's "wild" changes of phase, in tracing her experience in Kerry. Writing is to Rukeyser a risk, a flight, a swim. She is almost always able to communicate the exhilaration of this risk to the receptive reader. Wolff said, "She explores Hariot as he must have explored the New World: now gingerly feeling the sand yield beneath his step . . . now plunging recklessly into the forest; now mapping his progress."

But Wilbur Applebaum, writing in *Isis*, explained the reservations of those who are not inclined to swim with Rukeyser among unknowns:

Miss Rukeyser uses some of the techniques of modern film-making in which the plot is immaterial and the images, which multiply, shift, and blend in rapid, vivid and startling juxtapositions, are themselves all-important. Instead of building to a single vision, however, they tend to confuse rather than illuminate and to exhibit lack of control, discipline, and firmness, so that the eye of imagination veers widely from point to point. The whole is an impressionistic panorama which in the end leaves us dissatisfied, confused, and defeated in trying to reach Harriot the man and his age, or to measure his impact on our time.[16]

16. Wilbur Applebaum, review of *Hariot*, in *Isis*, LXIII (June, 1972), 278–80.

Measure is the key word. As Rukeyser has said, often the traces she presents "cannot be measured." Besides, she is not interested in measuring the particular contributions of Hariot, though she vividly details (with excerpts from his papers) Hariot's pioneering account of Virginia and its inhabitants, his work in optics, algebra, astronomy, and atomic theory. Rather, as Applebaum noted, "Hariot's 'achievements' as a scientist matter less to Rukeyser than the wholeness of his life and its lessons for us." That wholeness she must reach by "surmise," and it "strikes deep into one's life." The wholeness of Hariot is the wholeness of the Renaissance man who is "the pilgrim of the joined life" of action and contemplation (TTH, 268). He was scientist, philosopher, and explorer of a new continent. His spiritual ancestors, Nicholas of Cusa, Giordano Bruno, and Roger Bacon, among others, inspire in him the concerns Rukeyser will make her own in the twentieth century. Seeking Hariot's ancestry and philosophical links, she seeks and finds her own. She also finds justification for her own method of proceeding in this unorthodox biography. Rukeyser discovers and conveys these links in the "climate of revelation" she wrote of in *The Life of Poetry*, for they are her lineage. The reader of her poems will recognize phrases and images from the poems and prose in descriptions of Hariot and in what Hollander called "the constellations of figures which surround Hariot." Examples are innumerable, but take the paragraph on Hariot's boyhood, which reminds the reader of *The Orgy* of those tinkers at Puck Fair and Rukeyser's fascination with them:

But very much may be deduced, projected backwards from the loose papers that have come down to us, part of the traces in his own hand, in many hands, in notes and fragments, signals for which the best term perhaps is that word used by the travelling people for the signs which tell where they have been and in what direction they are moving—"patterans." By these inscriptions and objects, the diagrams covering this folio, the writing this-side-up on half the sheet, that-side-up on the other, that lets us know that here the master sat and there the students, by deaths and forgettings, tortures and instruments, the little pit where the foot of a compass was planted long ago, silk-grass waving near Hatteras—by these we guess, and ourselves move leaving our patterans. (TTH, 54)

Of Roger Bacon she says, he "thrives on what other people call intuition, but which is apparent as a most subtle and representative
human power—attention, or noticing, or trust in experience" (TTH,
55). Is this not the human power she has been calling upon in
poems like "The Overthrow of One O'Clock at Night"? ("Trust in
experience . . . / The deep rhythms of your experience.") She writes
of Nicholas of Cusa that he "is loved by Hariot," that "he is related to The Cloud of Unknowing, and to many other darknesses."
She quotes from Nicholas of Cusa:

"In all faces is shown the Face of faces, veiled and in a riddle. Howbeit,
unveiled it is not seen, until above all faces a man enter into a certain secret and mystic silence, where there is no knowing or concept of a face.
This mist, cloud, darkness or ignorance, into which he that seeketh thy
Face entereth, when he goes beyond all knowledge or concept, is the state
below which thy Face cannot be found, except veiled; but that very darkness revealeth the Face to be there beyond all veils. Hence I observe how
needful it is for me to enter into the darkness and to admit the coincidence to opposites, beyond all the grasp of reason, and there to seek the
truth, where impossibility meeteth us." (TTH, 68)

To the reader of *The Speed of Darkness*, this passage seems a
source. Rukeyser has written many poems besides those in that
volume celebrating the nonrational consciousness, the presence of
oppositions that cause us to make the leap into new states of understanding and being.

Bruno as she describes him is the spirit that informs many of
her poems. We have already seen how his *De Immenso*—on the
world as sacred animal, to be loved—is reflected in many poems.
She says, "His vigor would not let anything be driven apart from
the rest of life" (TTH, 73). (Hear her calls for unity in consciousness
and learning in *The Life of Poetry* and *Willard Gibbs* and her
words in the 1974 *Esquire* piece recalling the antifascist Olympics:
"Not to let our lives be shredded, sports away from politics, poetry
away from anything. Anything away from anything.") She also
says of Bruno, "He adored the contraries. He acknowledged them
fully, he was the contraries." (Hear her praise for Whitman, for the
same reasons; hear her in "Despisals," "Not to despise the *it*. To
make this relation / with the it: to know that I am it.") Rukeyser

admires Bruno's courage in maintaining his unorthodox ideas, and she associates him with all those in the forefront of knowledge to whom the world's prejudice has been directed through the years. He is an ancestor of Willkie: "the prior of the monastery had said that Bruno was 'a universal man' who 'could, if he wished, make the whole world of one religion'" (TTH, 109). "He said of himself that he was a 'citizen and servant of the world, child of the sun and mother earth'" (TTH, 112). One of Bruno's beliefs underlies Rukeyser's in many poems, beginning with "Theory of Flight": that energy is inexhaustible, that human desire is part of the eternal creative force. "Yes, he had praised the infinity of worlds, believing that infinite divine power could bring into being an infinity of worlds" (TTH, 158). "He rejoices: the universe is eternal, its worlds decay, we die, the parts of all things enter into new arrangements" (TTH, 113).

Other intellectual kin of Hariot are attractive to the poet. George Chapman "is close to Hariot, or to any man who binds science, poetry, exploration." Rukeyser quotes Phyllis Brooks Bartlett:

> "Chapman was one of a group of men, including Ralegh and Marlowe, who were interested in pushing science and philosophy beyond the bounds of contemporary beliefs and decorum, a group bound together by a common curiosity, suspected of being atheists and hence condemned by most of their fellows, but mocked by Shakespeare in his *Love's Labour's Lost* as 'the school of night.'" (TTH, 147–48)

To the poet of *The Speed of Darkness* and "the night of women," Shakespeare's designation of these wild exploring spirits as a school of "night" is encouraging.

The most striking passage in *Hariot* to the reader of the poems is that which describes George Ripley's *The Twelve Gates of Alchemy* (1471). The book is mentioned first as *The Twelve Gates*, a "treatise in verse." Although the terms are not completely clear (they are poetic, suggestive, a tantalizing abridgement of research and therefore not orthodox scholarly exposition and analysis), they illuminate the poet's fascination with the phrase "the gates." In "Käthe Kollwitz" Rukeyser referred to the German artist as "woman as gates." The title of her latest collection is *The Gates*. She called them "the gates of perception" in a note to the title poem. But "the gates" is a phrase with wider reverberations. One must remember that alchemy was the sought process of transforming the gross metals into gold, common things into more precious substances: a process of transformation. Rukeyser writes later in *Hariot* of "the statement at the core of this art [alchemy]: there is transformation of all things, our dreams are the language of transformation" (TTH, 209). Here are some of the reverberations of "the gates" in *Hariot*:

The gates are the process: Of Calcination, Of Solution, Of Separation, Of Conjunction, of Putrefaction, Of Congelation, Of Cibation, Of Sublimation:

> The fyrst cause ys to make the body spirituall
> The second that the spryt may corporall be,
> And become fyx wyth hyt and substantyall;

Of Fermentation, of Exaltation, Of Multiplication, Of Projection. (TTH, 116)

These must be Ripley's words, but they are not in quotation marks. The method is not that of orthodox scholarship. Nevertheless it is very effective: one can see the author absorbing her source in this text as she will in another transmutation, the poems. (Another way Rukeyser enlivens her presentation is to shift the person of narration. At the beginning of the book as Hariot sails from England the narrative is in the conventional third person. Then, without preparation or quotation marks, the narrative shifts to the first person of Hariot's *A Brief and True Report*.)

After presenting Ripley's theory, Rukeyser gives us an excerpt from Hariot's papers.

This is what Hariot was doing: "Let not thy heat be over strong, and yet strong enough, and between Scylla and Charybdis sail like unto a skillfull pilot, so shalt thou attain the wealth of either India; sometimes thou shalt see as it were little Island floating, and shooting out as it were little sprigs and buds, which will be changeable in colors, which soon will be melted and others arrive; for the earth as inclining to a vegetation, is always sending forth some new thing or other;—sometimes thy fance will be that thou seest in thy glass birds or beasts, or creeping things, and thou shalt each day behold colors most beautiful to sight . . . "

This is what Hariot was doing : Attend then to my doctrine: take the body which I have shewed you, and put it into the water of our sea, and decoct it continually with a due heat of fire, that both dews and clouds may ascend, and day, without intermission. . . .

"And the drops which are continually running down to perforate the mass marvelously, and by continual circulation the water is made more subtle, and doth sweetly extract the soul of the Sun; so by the mediation of the soul the spirit is reconciled with the body." (TTH, 116–17)

The reader has to use imagination here and be very attentive for clues. What the devil *is* Hariot doing? He is doing something with a "glass"—is it a test tube or beaker? And the wealth of Indies—is he following Ripley's instructions and performing an alchemical experiment? The application to human life is most interesting. One must swim among many unknowns in this passage and grasp what one can.

One could draw many more parallels between the scores of figures and theories in *Hariot* and Rukeyser's own philosophy. She found surrounding Hariot a most congenial confluence of world views, for the late 1500s were "a threshold of all things, for in England the old style of religion, calendar, the sea, and essential being, England itself, have all broken open into another life" (TTH, 4). To the twentieth-century poet, Thomas Hariot himself is the most attractive figure in this scene. That he exists in allusions but that not much is directly known of him today fascinates the poet who has encountered the wasteful ways of history before, in her research for *Willard Gibbs*. He was, as we have seen, a "whole" man, exercising his powers widely and fully. He is, like Gibbs, a source of strength to us today: "In a very real way, he is the first explorer on this land of a way of thinking, a real and possible strength to our time." That way is the way of nonspecialization, of daring imagination and intellect. "His work is part of the long work in history and the present to expand the limits, to risk, to break bounds and establish further imagining, that is, to change the world and the body of man in its possibilities" (TTH, 15). As Gibbs pursued his highly individualistic researches which were not the popular work of science in his age of invention and practicality, Hariot worked steadily in a climate of rapacity and violence. He lived the final decades of his life in the midst of horrors and fears, blamed for treasons and blasphemies, both his patrons in the Tower of London. Rukeyser's presentation effectively displays his steady life of experiment and thought, for she gives us excerpts from the papers interspersed among accounts of intrigue, torture, and execution.

Hariot had to "trust in experience" at most crucial points in his life. After making careful notes of the voyage to the New World he saw them dumped overboard when a pinnace struck a sandbar. Hariot coming back to England had "only himself, his experience, what he carried in his body and head, that is, in his body, in himself" (TTH, 61). He overcame his loss. The account of the solar eclipse he witnessed on the way to America foreshadows Hariot's rebirth into a new phase. "The Indians of America saw the total and full eclipse. They met it dancing; they danced and stamped all night in one long sustaining rhythm, carrying themselves through, carrying the sun through till it rose in the morning as they danced and shouted, reborn. Born again whole" (TTH, 21). The De Bry edition of Hariot's voyage, called *America*, which Hariot worked on after his *Brief and True Report*, "extends the *Report* not only in material, but in language. The writing here is not a description for the purpose of getting support. The further disappointments have been lived through; Hariot is writing in a mood of the next phase of his life. He has gone deeper. . . . The terms are . . . those of reality and delight" (TTH, 110–11). When his patrons, Ralegh and Northumberland, are in the Tower, he voluntarily works and lives there. "The world is here. The New World is asleep. Hariot makes the leap in this prison from the New World to the moon. He makes his great picture of the moon. He observes and maps and makes his leap" (TTH, 207). Hariot is for the rest of his life a "magus," a man of science with an overtone of magician, for such were the marvels he dealt with. It delights the poet that Hariot was called "Matheseos" by his friend Lawrence Keymis. "The word signifies," according to Frances Yates, quoted in *Hariot*, "one of the four 'guides in religion' of which the others are Love, Art, and Magic." Rukeyser continues, "The word swims among its meanings of learning in general and (accented differently) magic" (TTH, 141). That such an inclusive faculty should have been considered magical during the Renaissance is encouraging to the poet who has celebrated the faculty and manifested it in her own work. She quotes an anonymous contemporary of Gabriel Harvey who praises Hariot: "It is not sufficient for poets to be superficial humanists : but they must be exquisite artists, & curious universal scholars" (TTH, 198).

Hariot "kept with him" the drawing of the constellation Serpentarius, the Serpent-Bearer (now called Ophiucus), and Rukeyser probes the meanings of that figure for Hariot and for herself. The drawing "of a strong, broad man . . . gripping in his hands the coils of a snake spread across the sky" is superimposed on the stars, clusters, and nebulae of the constellation. Four novae were seen in Serpentarius in Hariot's time—"these bursting energies that seem to mean continual creation and defiance of entropy": here the poet links Hariot's beliefs with Bruno's and her own. The interpretation that many cultures gave to the constellation is also of personal interest to the poet. It "has . . . been seen as a man carrying the serpent of wisdom." Rukeyser concludes, "It is Hariot's constellation, of the man undergoing the struggle with wisdom, of the region of clusters and nebulae." This is her own view of human struggle, of swimming in the fertile, rarefied unknown. This image of the pursuit of a nebular wisdom is linked with a striking description of natural landscape at the very beginning of the book to reinforce a theme. Hariot's landscape is the Outer Banks of North Carolina, where he came on his first voyage of discovery and where all his notes, books, and instruments were drowned.

Sand at the sea-bottom shifts, the water moves, the sandbars are shifting slowly. It is the landscape of imagination. You are looking straight across from the site of the City of Ralegh to the short truncated wing of stainless steel and granite at Kitty Hawk which marks the first flight of the Wright Brothers. Actually, since the dunes shift, it does not mark the place; a big boulder pins down the spot. The wing is a monument to that kind of imagination.

Beyond it is the sea. (TTH, 16)

"All things shift" in this landscape—and in the landscape of what we call "knowledge" or "truth" or "fact"—and the imagination must fly (or swim) as Hariot's did, as the followers of his traces must, to pursue the developing image of the real. The Outer Banks and Serpentarius: two images of Hariot and of the task of imagination as Rukeyser understands it and carries it forward in her book.

There is a passage in *Hariot* which is central to the imaginative working behind a book like this, behind *One Life*, *Gibbs*, and the poetry as well. A familiar phrase flags to *One Life* and "Akiba": "the bonds." Rukeyser gives her thoughts as she is examining (as she has many times) the drawing, which is also a map, that Hariot made of the moon and a "map with which Hariot is identified, the map of Virginia. . . . On the table, side by side, the two maps seem to have very little in common." Here Rukeyser shows us her approach to reality.

Suddenly something jumps out of the maps, with that startling abrupt movement by which I recognize the authentic, a movement that is no movement at all, like the famous moment in Zen doctrine when the snow is let fall from the branches of trees. An identity seemed to leap out before me from the maps. From one, the circles which we know as the craters of the moon, and named for astronomers. From the other, the circles which are the palisaded villages of the Virginia Indians. Both with their vertical lines—one to show steep darkness, the other the stockade of poles. Both circles very human, part of the bonds that link Virginia and the moon through human perception. Through Hariot. Through ourselves. (TTH, 224)

Rukeyser's patient attention and openness allow her imagination to discover how art (someone else's imagination) has (perhaps unconsciously) linked Virginia and the moon. The poet is touched by this insight into a human process which reveals a human need for bonding. In perceiving the bond she enters into the union originating in the past, now carried through into this moment of her writing, this moment of our reading. From "Käthe Kollwitz":

> and through my life, through my eyes, through my arms
> and hands
> may give the face of this music in portrait waiting for
> the unknown person
> held in the two hands, you. (SD, 100)

"The bonds that link" us to the wholeness of reality—past, present, future—are the bonds of free perception, what she has called in the foreword to *One Life* "our bonds with the world."

Rukeyser's quest in prose and poetry is for the wholeness of experience; therefore she does not superimpose unifying structures or forms on experience (the poems, *The Orgy*) or on the data of research (the biographies). Rather she allows the material to generate its own form, and she is informed in the process. This process is what critics are now calling one of the hallmarks of the "post-modern" sensibility. In the words of poet Robert Duncan, who is quoted in Charles Altieri's "From Symbolist Thought to Immanence: The Ground of Postmodern American Poetics," "Central to and defining the poetics I am trying to suggest here is the conviction that the order man may contrive or impose upon the things about him or upon his own language is trivial beside the divine order or natural order he may discover in them." Similarly, Robert Bly said poetry is a way of uncovering "secrets objects share." David Antin in "Modernism and Postmodernism: Approaching the Present in American Poetry" wrote that the Beats, the Black Mountain poets, and the New York poets in the fifties and sixties "offered a great claim for the meaning of poetry: that phenomenological reality is 'discovered' and 'constructed' by poets. . . . It is part of a great Romantic metaphysic and epistemology that has

sustained European poetry since Ossian and Blake and Words-
worth and is still sustaining it now."[17]

Critics cite Olson and his group as the first postmoderns. Their
view of history is Rukeyser's. Altieri explains that postmoderns believe that history "need not be primarily analytic and interpretive. . . .
Both [Olson and Snyder] see history as the presence of the past,
and both look for concrete instances of that presence" (Rukeyser's
"traces"). Antin called Olson and Duncan pioneers of the shift of
emphasis from Pound's idea of establishing a "cultural heritage" to
"an attempt to recover the cultural heritage of *humanity*, 'The Human Universe.' " Duncan "sets out to recover his version of the human universe and starts out to look for it in the exiled, abandoned
and discarded knowledges, hopes, and fears, magic, alchemy, the
Gnosis, Spiritualism, etc."[18] Rukeyser has been engaged in such an
attempt from the time she wrote of Bruno in "Theory of Flight,"
through her exploration of the "discarded" lives of miners in
U.S.1, through history's loss of Gibbs, the apparent failures of
Whitman and Melville, Ives and Willkie, and Hariot's life "gone
down, almost forgotten among great waves of crushing powers"
(TTH, 3). Though she may have been castigated for "free handed
forays into historiography," Rukeyser was a postmodern before
the coining of the term.

The central and most tantalizing analogy in the book is that
which connects Hariot with Ariel. Rukeyser chose the spelling
Hariot because it sounds most like the name of Shakespeare's
spirit who "sings transformation" (TTH, 246). How can Hariot be
Ariel? Rukeyser makes no authoritative claims. "The play is itself;
its people cannot be chained to other figures, its meanings cannot
be chained to prose or philosophical meanings. These meanings

17. Charles Altieri, "From Symbolist Thought to Immanence: The Ground of Postmodern American Poetics," *Boundary 2* (Spring, 1973), 610; David Antin, "Modernism
and Postmodernism: Approaching the Present in American Poetry," *Boundary 2* (Fall,
1972), 132–33.
18. Altieri, "From Symbolist Thought to Immanence," 631; Antin, "Modernism and
Postmodernism," 125.

are in their music, and move there. Only certain questions can be reached" (TTH, 245). Rukeyser asks her questions imaginatively, patiently, wondering what secrets certain things share:

What is this island? What, in England, is an island, cut off by magic and water from the rest, where amazing events, further imprisonments, take place; from which release may also by magic come? Is not the Tower of London such an island?

What sonorities are here? What does the name Prospero have in it, along with the overtones of fortune and hope, and perhaps even the prospective glass, through which magically the future could be seen? Are there sounds here like Hotspur, and like Percy?

And of the magi, the spirits around the great prince Percy, is there one that has a name like Ariel? It is nonsense to look at Hariot for these qualities and this name.

But where is the instigating event behind

I'll break my staff . . .

I'll drown my book.

What staff was broken? What book drowned? The loss that overtook Hariot in the last moments in the shallow waters, after the four-day tempest; a loss beyond which he imagined and went forward. (TTH, 248–49)

It was with Hariot's assistance that Ralegh wrote his *History of the World*, while in the Tower of London. Rukeyser quotes Henry Stevens, "He had at command a Hariot, a sort of winged Mercury" (TTH, 254). When Hariot died he was buried in the Church of St. Christopher, which was taken down in an expansion of the Bank of England in 1781. "A garden with a fountain marked the site of the burial-ground attached to St. Christopher le Stocks. As the bank grew and was rebuilt, the garden became completely surrounded. . . . It is today a place of intense stillness and greenness, completely surrounded by money" (TTH, 297). Rukeyser has gone to stand on this spot where, she writes in *Hariot*, "I felt many forces." She describes her mind proceeding to certain linkings: "Outside the garden, just within the wall, there is something very curious. There is nothing to declare here; it is again a matter of raising a question. You see the flash of this image from outside the wall of the Bank of England, at the busy corner of Princes and Threadneedle Streets. It is a gold flying figure poised on one foot, high over the wall, based on a small dome. *London for Everyman* says, 'Above is a charming figure of Ariel.' " "A bobby at the corner" told Rukeyser, "It's just a figger, 's far's we're concerned." But a Bank of England guard said, "It's Mercury." It turns out that "Ariel has been a traditional figure" to the Bank of England (one of whose governours regarded him as "a variant of Mercury") and that it is indeed Ariel "that now stands, gold, fleet, on the dome of a modified temple," the Bank of England, which occupies the place where once Hariot was buried (TTH, 298–99). Thus Rukeyser has, sometimes whimsically, often with moving insights, discovered "the secrets objects share" and the strange linkings of the traces of Hariot.

A. L. Rowse, distinguished biographer of several Elizabethans, said in his review in the *New York Times Book Review*: "The author is a poetic lady, not a scientist . . . and there are occasional flashes of poetic insight . . . though she . . . did not really qualify to write about the subject." Rowse found that Rukeyser's conjectures create "superfluous confusion." But Cyril Stanley Smith, Professor at MIT, historian of science, and expert in the history of metallurgy, has defended Rukeyser's poetic approach to Hariot. "Kepler may have heard of Harriot's piled balls, but there is no hard evidence that they led to any of the later thought on crystals. In any case jewelers had made similar geometric designs with their granulation techniques several centuries before. Muriel Rukeyser's story of crystallography is not well-documented history, but the picture she gives with all of the threads stretching tangled and interwoven from Harriot is wonderful: moving and humanly right even if the connections were vaguely in the environment rather than demonstrably connected from one man to another through subsequent history. This is part of what poetry is about." The bibliography of *Thomas Harriot, Renaissance Scientist* by Oxford's Harriot Seminar scholar John Shirley says that Rukeyser's book is "a poetic and literary account, but sensitive and effective in developing a sympathetic understanding of Harriot."[19]

19. A. L. Rowse, review of *Hariot*, in *New York Times Book Review*, April 18, 1971, p. 28; from the letter of Cyril Stanley Smith to the author; John W. Shirley (ed.), *Thomas Harriot, Renaissance Scientist* (Oxford, 1974), 171–72.

EIGHT

Muriel Rukeyser — Before and Beyond Postmodernism

"POSTMODERNISM" was first noted among the poets of the San Francisco Renaissance of the late fifties (Ginsberg, Corso, Duncan, Ferlinghetti, and others.) Critics identified postmodern sensibilities as those which departed from the ironic aloofness of the alienated poets of the forties and fifties who followed Eliot. In the San Francisco Renaissance the poet, aware of and often detailing the insanities of a superabundant yet repressive society, became again the person with a special vision into the wholeness, joy, and potential of life. Ginsberg's *Howl* (1956) became the manifesto of the new poetry now called postmodernist.[1] But as Rukeyser offered in an interview in 1977, "It isn't post anything. It's the moment. It's believing in the reality of the moment." For Rukeyser, to give the "full reality, the full texture of reality, one must give the potential of the moment." To do less is to respond less than fully to reality. Among her working papers of the forties Rukeyser wrote, "To see the thing—not only in itself, but in its direction . . . to balance perception with hope." Without such balance we have, as she wrote in *The Life of Poetry*, "the poetry of the sense of annihilation, of the smallness of things, of aversion, guilt" (LP, 189).

"Wish" and "desire" for potential and fullness recur in her poetry again and again until she says most effectively in "Song of Another Tribe" (WF), "I feel guilt when my desire finds no way." Wish in Rukeyser and in poets associated with postmodernism is often

1. For a good survey of the numerous articles and books on postmodernism, see the bibliographies in the *Journal of Modern Literature*, III (July, 1974), an entire issue devoted to Modernism and Postmodernism.

Among the characteristics critics always note as postmodern, of course, are the raw directness and personalism Rukeyser was castigated for in the Forties and Fifties.

expressed in incantatory style. But Rukeyser believes that before focusing on stylistic terms such as "incantatory" one should recognize that her own poetry involves the age-old question of "the amount of faith and validity you allow for the potential in life." She says, "I hope always to deal with the potential as as real as any other part of life." In this study I have connected her attitude, as did Rosenthal, with American "meliorism." Rukeyser herself says, "I think of it as going as far back as we go. People have been comparing me to Whitman, and although I love and adore and am a child of Whitman, both of us come from the Bible and from the religious writings where the parallelism enables contradictions to be contained and synthesis to be achieved. We are talking about the endless quarrel between the establishment and the prophets, and I hope to be forever on the side of the prophets." To be a prophet in poetry and utter "unverifiable facts" running counter to prevailing dark moods was to be sneered at in the forties and fifties. "It seems to be a question of the times, more than anything," says Rukeyser.

"Body of Waking" appeared within two years of *Howl* (in 1958) and contains the same agonizing protest at the insanity of our culture as well as great, prophetic hope for

> Bodies exchanging life.
> Where the belief flows somewhere
> Uncorrupt, hidden, under violence,
> Making its own and dawn-announcing act,
> River of daybreak, where the waking is,
> Still to be sung among the deaths and days.
>
> These meanings become the light we breathe,
> The breathing of a theme; in our own time.

Of course Ginsberg's language is wildly different from Rukeyser's. But both poets defy, in Ginsberg's words in *Howl*,

> Moloch the loveless! Mental Moloch!
> . . . .
> Moloch whose blood is
> running money! Moloch whose fingers are ten armies!
> . . . .
> Moloch in whom I am a consciousness without a body! Moloch

who frightened me out of my natural ecstasy! Moloch whom I
abandon.

The poets of San Francisco discovered the spirit Rukeyser has
been identified with since the thirties and which she has clarified in
her increasingly open and direct poetry. Rexroth explains that
these poets "write much like the Proletarians of the Thirties. . . .
Practically all revolutions in poetry since time began have been
nothing but reassertions, after a period of academic sterility, of the
abiding principles of all poetry everywhere." This particular revolution came to flower in a community that had been vigorously independent of the Eastern literary establishment in the forties and
fifties. Postwar San Francisco had "its own magazines, its own
presses, its own literary reputation, but the rest of the country was
unaware of this faraway ferment." Poetry readings, which became
popular in the coffeehouses of New York in the late fifties,
abounded in San Francisco even before the war.[2] Rukeyser began
Body of Waking toward the end of her stay in San Francisco where
she bore a child, "was writing my head off," and participated as
much as a new, single mother could in the artistic and intellectual
life of the community. (*Body of Waking* attracted little attention
compared to *Howl*. One reason is surely Ginsberg's shocking new
idiom. But Rukeyser says Harper's brought her book out "almost
secretly," perhaps because of the poor reception *One Life* had received in 1957.)

Rukeyser first went to San Francisco in 1937 for the opening of
the Golden Gate Bridge, an event which excited her as did the rise
of skyscrapers in New York when she was a child. (In an interview
in the *Chronicle* a few years later she said she found San Francisco
still had the stimulating climate of growth and expansion that
New York was losing.) In December, 1943, when she heard of
Otto's death, she contemplated going to San Francisco again.
From "Diary of a Change," among her unpublished papers: "If I
go to San Francisco I want my life as a woman. That is also my life

2. Kenneth Rexroth, *Assays* (Norfolk, Conn., 1961), pp. 185–87.

as a poet. It can only be lived by my giving enough life for me to reach the stillness out of which the poems come." The last words are amended to read, "to reach the central motion out of which the poems come—in that motion which seems to us as stillness, since it is our own right motion, the place where we speak to each other." She identified this place in *The Life of Poetry*: "If we go deep enough, we reach the common life, the shared experience of man, the world of possibility" (LP, 201). San Francisco seemed to offer the opportunity for growth. She did not go there right away, however, but took the job with the Office of War Information poster division, "charmed by the presence of artists I would be working with": Perlin, Dali, Benton, Shahn. She resigned after six months ("not soon enough"), as did many other artists and writers, because the posters she was designing were rejected for displaying the underlying meanings of the war. As Pulitzer-prizewinner Henry F. Pringle charged when he led the exodus from OWI, the agency was "being turned into an 'office of war ballyhoo' by high-pressure promoters who prefer slick salesmanship to honest information."[3]

According to Rexroth, after the war most poets went from "the propaganda gravy train" and "swivel chairs in Washington" to chairs of poetry or creative writing in colleges and universities.[4] It is indeed a fact that most American poets are now associated with academe and that this association dates from immediately after World War II. But Rukeyser's associations have been different. The Berkeley biologist Herbert Evans, who isolated vitamin E, was a great admirer of the Gibbs book. He came to see Rukeyser in New York and subsequently helped her find her first apartment on the Berkeley border. Since she was having difficulty earning a living, she tried to get a teaching fellowship in California, and she asked poet Josephine Miles to write a recommendation for her. Miles refused, saying, "It is like a sailor wanting to have a farm." Rukeyser heeded the advice. From then on, she says, "I began to

3. New York *Herald Tribune*, "Miss Rukeyser Quitting O.W.I. Over 'Policies,'" May 12, 1945.
4. Rexroth, *American Poetry*, p. 130.

teach in the alternate places." In 1945 she taught a workshop in poetry at the California Labor School. Communists there at first argued against hiring her because she had been attacked by New York Communists for defending Horace Gregory and for being what they called a nationalist. She was finally hired when someone effectively defended her by saying, "New York can make mistakes." Among her friends and acquaintances in San Francisco were the writer Ella Winter (widow of Lincoln Steffens), poet Robert Duncan, poet Marie de L. Welch, geneticist and radical Alfred Marshak, renal scientist, radical, and great admirer of *Willard Gibbs* Thomas Addis, Eric Berne, Octavio Paz, Robert Payne, Paul Radin, painter Glyn Collins (whom she married), Donnan Jeffers (one of the twin sons of Robinson Jeffers), Charles Olson, and Kenneth Rexroth. She participated in poetry readings such as those sponsored by Pierre Salinger's mother. Often the audiences were small in those years, but Rukeyser rightly believes that these readings laid the foundation for the San Francisco Renaissance and the national revival of interest in poetry readings. She says she especially enjoyed the people she met at Kenneth Rexroth's house. "We knew each other rather well although we didn't see each other often," she says of Rexroth. She introduced him to painter Morris Graves, a relationship she points to as fruitful since it stimulated Rexroth's interest in Japan. She began what was to become a lifelong friendship with Robert Duncan, whom Rexroth calls the most influential older poet of the Renaissance; her unpublished correspondence includes Duncan's letters of admiration for her poetry as well as manuscripts and typescripts of his own poems. In fact many letters (now in the Berg Collection of the New York Public Library) show that her friends and acquaintances in San Francisco admiringly encouraged her to continue in her own vein of poetry and prose, while what she calls "wit writing" flourished on Eastern campuses. Ella Winter wrote, "You do the greatest service to other people man can do—or poetry can do—you make one live life more fully and with greater insight. You are a very great person, Muriel."

Rukeyser spent a great deal of time at Marie de L. Welch's

home at Los Gatos; they met shortly after Welch's husband died, and they became very close. Welch dedicated a poem to Rukeyser which shows how highly her vision was prized by a friend and fellow poet.

Verde Verde
For M.R.

The green hill rises under the bloody
Bodies and ditches of your death
And all the wounds in your world of agony
Move with the healing earth.

> So many springtimes and love
> In each one murdered.
> So much good fire and birth
> Everywhere frozen.

> If it were death at last
> I might accept it
> For one more memory, surely
> One, in my own island.

> But all around there
> Wind and surf ring,
> Ring and bring in the seeds,
> Letting no life end.

The green hill rises in the thunder-shadowed
Images and arguments of your myth
And all the wills in your broken world
Move wholly against death.[5]

Rukeyser says, "I'm grateful to her for that poem because it seems to me she uses me as part of the fight against death in one's own life." Indeed the poem celebrates Rukeyser's strength in images that echo those in *The Green Wave* (composed in California), notably the "powerful green hill" of "Then I Saw What the Calling Was." That hill is at Los Gatos. Rukeyser dedicated *The Green Wave* and *The Orgy* to Marie de L. Welch.

Thus in San Francisco she continued to write the kind of poetry John Brinnin referred to in his letter to her when she was still

---

5. Marie de L. Welch, *The Otherwise* (San Francisco, 1976), p. 77. Rukeyser's deep appreciation of this singular poet, who is yet to be discovered by readers of contemporary poetry, is evident in the introduction to this posthumous volume.

in New York. "Last summer I think we made some attempt toward definition of the 'continuity' you mentioned. Its expression in poetry is our only value ultimately." That continuity, she has explained, is the awareness shared by what Gary Snyder (of the second generation of San Francisco poets) calls The Tribe or The Great Subculture. From his *Earth House Hold*:

Peasant witchcraft in Europe, Tantrism in Bengal, Quakers in England, Tachikawa-ryū in Japan, Ch'an in China. These are all outcroppings of the Great Subculture which runs underground all through history. This is the tradition that runs without break from Paleo-Siberian Shamanism and Magdalenian cave-painting; through megaliths and Mysteries, astonomers, ritualists, alchemists and Albigensians; gnostics and vagantes, right down to Golden Gate Park.

The Great Subculture has been attached in part to the official religions but is different in that it transmits a community style of life, with an ecstatically positive vision of spiritual and physical love; and is opposed for very fundamental reasons to the Civilization Establishment.

It has taught that man's natural being is to be trusted and followed; that we need not look to a model or rule imposed from outside in searching for the center; and that in following the grain, one is being truly "moral."

Significantly, Snyder explains that in the thirties and early forties "all the anarchists and left-deviationists . . . were tribesmen at heart."[6] Much of what is called postmodernism is a new flowering of the spirit of this Great Subculture and of the prophets—versus the establishment.

Rukeyser wrote a great deal in California, putting together the original lectures to form *The Life of Poetry* and composing *Orpheus, The Green Wave*, and parts of *Body of Waking*. Yet she is not associated with the San Francisco Renaissance because, she says, she has never been a group person and because she was "pushing a baby carriage" much of the time. She explains that when she gave up teaching at the Labor School after the birth of her child in 1947, she was "saved by a benefactor in a curious and wonderful way." An anonymous patron left her a yearly sum of

6. From a letter from John Malcolm Brinnin to Rukeyser, January 5, 1941, in the Berg Collection of the New York Public Library; Gary Snyder, *Earth House Hold* (N.Y., 1969), pp. 113–15.

money on condition that she not ask her name (it was believed Rukeyser would not accept the money if she knew the source—which she found out later was Henriette Durham, of the well-known California family). This sum carried her through until her return to New York when she began to teach part-time at Sarah Lawrence in 1954. She then stopped that gift because she felt she no longer needed it. (At her benefactor's death Rukeyser received a lifelong trust, which will pass to her son at her death.) She became no ordinary college professor on tenure track, however. She never wanted more than part-time teaching because she felt her students' response obviated the need to go home and write a poem. But she found that she had to take other part-time jobs "to support the teaching." When I spoke of what Richard Eberhart's biographer calls that poet's "enviable position" as a tenured professor at Dartmouth, she said wryly, "Mine is not enviable. Mine is also stupid. The next most unpractical thing—next to writing poetry—is part-time teaching." Nevertheless when Sarah Lawrence wanted to give her tenure she said, "Give me tenure and I'll leave." "Nonsense," they said, "it's for your own protection." So they gave her tenure and she left in 1967. Her explanation: "I couldn't be a tenured professor at any college; it would make me very nervous." She has never solved it practically, she says, though with the contracts, the part-time teaching, the poetry readings, and help from friends, she has managed. She still occasionally teaches between semesters at Sarah Lawrence; she calls it reading poems with people—all kinds of people associated with the college: students, the manager of the bookstore, grounds workers. It has been an unusual career for a poet in a period when academe has proved the mainstay for so many poets.

Rukeyser's students found her a charismatic teacher, and their recollections of her are vivid even after many years. Miriam Reik, author of *The Golden Lands of Thomas Hobbes*, was at Sarah Lawrence from 1956 to 1960. She wrote:

Muriel would find ways, often wonderfully simple and direct, of opening a door to the meanings of literature by getting a student to focus on how she or he was relating to a text. . . . We were assigned some poetry by Blake for one class. When we came to class, presumably having read it, Muriel asked us to write a description of Newton on the spot. Surprised by the instructions, most of the students set about the task armed with a set of predictable ideas: Newton meant reason as opposed to imagination, science as opposed to poetry; Blake was a mystic and disliked Newton and said so. . . . When we finished, Muriel managed to jiggle all of those simplicities out of our heads, merely by passing around Blake's painting of Newton, in which he looks rather like a Greek God, preoccupied with the wonderful symmetries of geometry. This strategy did not solve the question of the relations between science and poetry, and it did not offer a specific interpretation of Blake, but for anyone with half a brain, it set you down a track, gave you new access to the poems, and broke down what Muriel has called "the resistances" to the work of the imagination. . . . Muriel's language, so much her own, was obviously also part of her teaching, but I would fail in any attempt to describe it. Suffice it to say that some students found it difficult, because "original," but I always found it clear and designed to capture meanings without destroying them.[7]

Poet and painter Mary Baldwin North was in Rukeyser's poetry course at Sarah Lawrence in 1966, "in the small stone house in the middle of campus on a hill." North wrote from Virginia:

Her desk was near the fireplace; we were stretched on either side of the room on benches under the rows of windows. I remember staring at legs; it was an atmosphere of fierce attack, dead silence, the calm before the storm. . . . I felt numb. Dumb. My anxiety before this presence which grew to granite statue proportions of the gods was immense; and yet, she was smiling at me, urging a voice from the very depths of an infinite presence of ME. . . . There was no shield or block or defense against the utter determination of the assault. And those students who had more sophisticated fronts came running from the house in tears, in fright, in anger. . . . How can I say here in the isolated hollow of the Blue Ridge that she is still with me, as clearly as the face of my two-year old son?. . . . She gave the deepest reassurance of self-presence in what is more of an Eastern student/master relationship. . . . If a woman can fill her child with the power that the child alone has, if as mother she can stand separate to allow for the child's presence, then it is the same most powerful balance

---

7. From a letter to the author from Miriam Reik, August 23, 1978.

that is nurtured in the student-teacher relationship. That is what I felt with Muriel. But, oh, this is rare—she is an extraordinary being.[8]

Rukeyser's unorthodox career, with its constant involvement in the work of many libertarian organizations befits a poet of "the alternative society" as described by Rexroth.

Already a new set of artistic and literary values or criteria are emerging. They reflect the interpersonal relationships and their attendant values of a quite different kind of society—anti-predatory, anti-exploitative, personally, morally engaged. This results in a quite different formal esthetic—and through all the apparent chaos, a new concept of form can be seen emerging. . . . The Seceders have attacked precisely alienation and I suppose that is the fundamental criterion: does this poem . . . overcome the gulf between man and man and between man and himself—even a very little?[9]

Rexroth said that the new poetry presented "an alternative kind of human being," one who was "preternaturally unassimilable" by establishments (as opposed to genuine communities.) He cites Gary Snyder, who has held jobs from lumberjack to merchant seaman, Philip Whalen, and Allen Ginsberg as "the most influential spokesmen, or even ideologists, of a new and revolutionary system of values, based on a constant, prayerful sense of the interlocking responsibilities of the community of all life on earth."

Rexroth notes the amazing variety of the new poetry which grew out of the San Francisco Renaissance. But he finds a common denominator: the new poets all believe in poetry as communication, as opposed to the "I. A. Richards-Valéry thesis that a poem is an end in itself, an anonymous machine for providing esthetic experience." Rukeyser wrote in the early forties, "This is one skill we have not used, reaching that makes a meeting-place. Facing and communicating, that will be our life, in the world and in poetry" (LP, 40). What will we communicate, it will be asked? Poets like Snyder, Ginsberg, Levertov are writing of the need to communicate a sense of reverence for life, of caring for the world and all

8. From a letter to the author from Mary Baldwin North, September 12, 1978.
9. Kenneth Rexroth, *The Alternative Society* (N.Y., 1970), pp. 113, 165, 14.

within it, a sense that we must grow in consciousness, that the work to be done, now that material abundance is within the reach of so many, is inner work as prelude to community. Rukeyser has urged inner growth since "Theory of Flight." She has always maintained the power of poetry to "make things happen" in consciousness. "But to go on, to recognize the energies that are transferred between people when a poem is given and taken, to know the relationships in modern life that can make the next step . . . that is for the new poets. . . . Exchange is creation; and the human energy involved is consciousness, the capacity to produce change from the existing conditions" (LP, 183).

Rukeyser's themes and concerns recur in the much younger Gary Snyder, in his characteristic Zen and Western American idiom. In *Earth House Hold* (1969)—with the magnified spiral of a conch shell on its cover—there is the insistence on the community of all life and the responsibility to go into the mind to achieve clarity of vision and to bring it

back out in the way you live, through personal example and responsible action, ultimately toward the true community (sangha) of "all beings." This last aspect means for me, supporting any cultural and economic revolution that moves clearly toward a free, international, classless world. It means using such means as civil disobedience, outspoken criticism, protest, pacifism, voluntary poverty . . . affirming the widest possible spectrum of non-harmful individual behavior—defending the right of individuals to smoke hemp, eat peyote, be polygynous, polyandrous or homosexual.[10]

The citation that accompanied the Copernicus Award given to Rukeyser in May, 1977, read:

From her first book . . . through her recent collection *The Gates* (the title poem finds her characteristically outside the prison of the South Korean poet Kim Chi Ha), the work of Muriel Rukeyser has been committed to ideas of freedom. Throughout her life she has been sensitive to encroachments on the freedom of individuals or peoples. She has responded in actions of which poetry was only the highest form.

10. *Earth House Hold*, p. 92.

Rukeyser says that the causes she has worked for have involved "the bonds between people and the freedom of those bonds such as free speech and freedom from the very heavy tyrannical hand that is on us and wants only a partial response." She has worked with and supported many organizations besides P.E.N., including committees against war and fascism, the League for Industrial Democracy, the National Student League, Medical Services for the Spanish Republic, the American League for Peace and Democracy, the American Student Union, American Friends of the Chinese People, the American Writers' Union, and Amnesty International. In 1978 she was trying to put together a group to be called "ARNO" which would work to remove the stigma of illegitimacy from people's lives.

Thus Rukeyser, and other contemporary poets embody what Richard Wasson (in "From Priest to Prometheus: Culture and Criticism in the Post-Modernist Period") calls "metaphors of culture which we might categorize as incarnational: culture leaves its sacred cloister and goes into the world to participate in the joys and sorrows of the human community and to work for its redemption. . . . The old image of culture expressed itself in terms of the defense of an embattled fortress; the new images express what [Northrop] Frye calls a myth of concern, a concern that mankind will choose life, freedom, and happiness rather than their opposites."[11] On one of the most touching pages of her working papers Rukeyser wishes for "an age when poetry shall roll in breakers on their hearts."

Many postmoderns share Rukeyser's interest in primitive beliefs which reinforce the vision of unity of the sacred world. Rukeyser discussed the cultural resources of American Indians in *The Life of Poetry*, urging poetry as a means for civilized people to achieve the primitives' integration of body and mind. With Paul Radin she translated songs of the Marquesans and of the Eskimo. She loved the Indians of Vancouver Island, whom she visited with

11. Richard Wasson, "From Priest to Prometheus: Culture and Criticism in the Post-Modernist Period," *Journal of Modern Literature*, III (July, 1974), 1201–02.

her small son when she began her study of Franz Boas (another subject for the "Lives" series.) She has found the unifying primitive vision helpful in her own imagining of the world. As a poet her interest in anthropology stems from her discovery as a young woman that "the fantasies that I was afraid to tell people and that I was afraid of in myself were not at all unique but were things that were common in many tribes. It was a happiness to me to find that I was like others."

In his introductory note to *Turtle Island* Gary Snyder says his poems

speak of place, and the energy-pathways that sustain life. Each living being is a swirl in the flow, a formal turbulence, a "song." The land, the planet itself, is also a living being—at another pace. Anglos, Black people, Chicanos, and others beached up on these shores all share such views at the deepest levels of their old cultural traditions—African, Asian, or European. Hark again to those roots, to see our ancient solidarity, and then to the work of being together on Turtle Island.[12]

When *The Life of Poetry* was reissued in 1974, Grace Schulman reviewed it in *The Hudson Review* along with *The Lives of a Cell* by Lewis Thomas. In this insightful piece Schulman explained the "unexpected resemblance" she found "between two . . . books that would seem to be worlds apart." She noted that "Dr. Thomas returns over and again to the theme of unity, finding connectedness to be the principle of living things: 'The new phenomenon of cell fusion . . . is the most unbiologic of all phenomena, violating the most fundamental myth of the last century for it denies the importance of specificity, integrity, and separateness in living things. Any cell—man, animal, fish, fowl, or insect—given the chance and under the right conditions, brought into contact with any other cell, however foreign, will fuse with it.'" Schulman recognized that Rukeyser's vision as a poet and critic was borne out by the scientist's findings. "According to Rukeyser, the human quest is not for truth as isolated phenomena but for the reality of relationships, a method

12. Gary Snyder, *Turtle Island* (N.Y., 1974).

she has learned from biology. The poet's perception of truth is comparable, she believes, to the scientist's apprehension of facts not as isolated things but as phenomena that interact, feeding or destroying one another. . . . What emerged from my reading of both works was the staggering truth of unity, the conviction that all life is part of the same fabric. Together, the writers have a mysterious, insisting, latent voice murmuring, 'ONE WORLD, ONE WORLD.'" [13] This voice is heard in much postmodern poetry.

Postmodernist critics have found the mainspring of the new poetic sensibility to be eros, the pleasure principle: the focus on inhabiting or the great wish to inhabit the world in delight, as opposed to the focus on various codes and systems that propose to hold eros in check in the name of "higher" values. Richard Wasson noted that in the sixties Norman O. Brown and Herbert Marcuse were "the chief spokesmen for Eros." This "wish for fulfillment in love and unity, in work" informs the poetry of Rukeyser, Levertov, Snyder, Rexroth, and other contemporary poets. It is the liberating force that abjures specialization, domination, despisal. Wasson explains that Brown and Marcuse clarify Freud's inadequacy to our times by arguing effectively that the reality principle is not as rigid as Freud and capitalism would have us believe. We do not have to relinquish the sense of union we enjoyed at our mothers' breasts and turn to various forms of often destructive gratification.

Freud, they say, made the mistake of assuming that the reality principle of his time was right and rational, when in fact it was destructive and irrational in its severe limits and restrictions on the pleasure principle. A capitalist industrial society not only reduces to a minimum the possible satisfactions of the wishes of the pleasure principle, but releases dangerous forces of aggression and finally death. An individualist industrialism encourages the child to channel his wishes for pleasure not only into productive work, but into a struggle for dominance over the world and other men. The world becomes not something one takes pleasure in, but something one dominates and controls. . . . Other men are not beings with

13. Grace Schulman, "Song of Our Cells," in *Hudson Review*, XXIX (Spring, 1976), 132.

whom one establishes a community, but creatures against whom one struggles and over whom one exercises control. . . . What is called health then is disease; what is called sanity is a justification for an insane system.[14]

Eros, denying this false reality principle, is the energy of postmodernist literature, and Rukeyser everywhere celebrates it:

> Power never dominion.
> Some other power.
> Some force flaking in light, avalanches of lilies,
> Days and the sun renewed in semen, pure
> Among the uncorrupted fires. (BW, 98)
>
> Wish at the center of growth
> We feel as peace. (BW, 108)

The imagination, especially through art, can allow eros back into the world and encourage a liberation of which society is much in need. "In its refusal to accept as final the limitations imposed upon freedom and happiness by the reality principle," says Marcuse, "in its refusal to forget what *can be*, lies the critical function of phantasy."[15] Since the thirties Rukeyser has written in defense of a wider, more intense imaginative and emotional life, for eros and its embodiment in poetry and in human relations.

For if we lived in full response to the earth, to each other, and to ourselves, we would not breathe a supernatural climate; we would be more human. The tendency of art and religion, and the tendency of poetic meaning, is toward the most human. It is a further humanity we are trying to achieve, at our most conscious, and to communicate. The thinning-out of our response is the weakness turning us inward to devour our own humanity, and outward only to sell and kill nature and each other. . . . The outward and predatory are glorified by business society, and the young are brought up in conduct leading toward aggression surrounded by strict tabus. (LP, 41–42)

From her first published poems, Rukeyser has been imagining the power of desire or wish for what *can be* in human relations. An early symbol of desire was the gyroscope. Another was the miracle

---

14. Wasson, "From Priest to Prometheus," 1199.
15. Herbert Marcuse, *Eros and Civilization* (Boston, 1966), p. 149.

of the plane in flight, which mirrored the human personality's full, joyful exercise of unrepressed powers. In "Theory of Flight" the energy of desire leads to a sense of fruitful communion with others and a resolve to work for human progress. In the shorter poems of that volume the young poet is seen achieving communion with those who share her vision. In "Diary of a Change," among her unpublished papers, she writes on Christmas Eve, 1943, after learning of Otto's death, "I believe in faith and resistance. Not: faith, meaning belief in that which is *against* rational processes, but an extension, the conclusion to which the *images* lead me." She has placed utter faith in her imagination's power to envision a more satisfying human condition. As the poems become more direct and personal it is apparent that her creative energy as poet springs from her "untamable need" ("First Elegy"), from her sense of a full sensual and sexual self ("Ajanta") which offers itself to others in quest of communion; after the crushing disappointment of war and loss, "World, not yet one, / Enters the heart again." Rukeyser even retells the Freudian story with a happy ending for eros. From *Body of Waking*:

> He is born; and asleep, awake, and soon the warm
> Taste of the second world calls him to understand
> Power drawn on the tides of sweetness in.
>
> . . . .
>
> Not now, but much later, does the world fall away.
> This is myself, says the child. My self, we all did say.
> There is my mother, whose pleasure, whose deep need
> It was to feed me singing, or recoil.
> And then the fable, the terrible forgetting.
> A cold distortion twisting past the leaves.
> Was there a Garden? Was there a Tree of Sin?
> What was my exile but from memory?
> Refusal, flowering, was the only tree.
>
> . . . .
>
> Dream and the sea open.
> All things find their change.
>
> The child remembers: the child is the tree;
> The tides, the leaves, the city, the true relation.

The world was the mother, the world; it was always the world
Pure, fierce, all moving and all reconciled. (BW, 89)

Thus for Rukeyser original sin is the refusal to dream, to remember, to imagine. Marcuse, analyzing a passage of Valéry's *Narcisse Parle* in explaining the hero of eros, says: "The climate of this language is that of the *'diminution des traces du péché originel,'*—the revolt against culture based on toil, domination, and renunciation. The images . . . [evoke] pleasure, the halt of time, the absorption of death; silence, sleep, night, paradise—the Nirvana principle not as death but as life."[16]

In "In the Underworld" (*Breaking Open*) Istar, goddess of love, acknowledges the power of eros as savior, particularly in the love of a woman:

> Now I remember love
> who has set my being on me,
> who permits me move
> into all being,
> who puts on me perceiving
> and my bones
> in a live chain
> and my flesh that perceives
> and acts
> and my acknowledging skin
> my underdress, my dress
> and my robe
> the jewels of the world
> I touch and find.
> —I know him and I know
> the breast speaking
> out of a gone woman
> across distances.

After reading *Orpheus* (a supreme hero of eros, according to Marcuse), Hallie Flanagan wrote to Rukeyser, "No poetry of our own age moves me as yours does. I never understood it with my mind—but with my blood, my pain, and my love. . . . To me there is in

16. Marcuse, *Eros and Civilization*, 164.

everything you have written, the strongest possible erotic power, as if your womanhood had taken pain, rapture, beauty—and through physical experience 'dissolved into the body of song.' " In her contemplation of Willkie's journey Rukeyser recognizes that the force that moves all creation through time, process, and change in the vast sea of possibility is love: eros is the divine creative energy. It can explode the most frozen rigidities—even in Spain. "Has the dragon died? / . . . O love. Make the song start" (*The Gates*, 76). Love is our core: "ripples of change out from the center / of me, of you, of love the inventor" (*The Gates*, 60).

Rukeyser is a poet of liberating eros, of the unembarrassed, vulnerable admission of need. She admits that there is a needing child in her who cannot be repressed: "And the child I among my veins / Sings and says with every breath" (BW, 31). In a startlingly personal idiom for a book which is categorized as "literary criticism," she writes in *The Life of Poetry*, "My one reader, you reading this book, who are you? What is your face like, your hands holding the pages, the child forsaken in you, who now looks through your eyes at mine?" She recognizes eros in its wish, born in infancy and yearning ever to find its object, what Northrop Frye calls "the more abundant life that the social structure fears and resists."[17] Thus she has always urged communication, "more freedom, more imagination, more poetry with all its meanings" (LP, 28).

The divine energy of desire in human beings is celebrated by poets such as Rexroth, Snyder, and Levertov in the same spirit that has impelled Rukeyser, as in the conclusion to Rexroth's long poem, *The Dragon and the Unicorn* (1952):

> Deep in myself arise the rays
> Called Artemis and Apollo
> Helios, Luna, Sun and Moon,
> Flowing forever out into
> The void, towards the unknown others.
> The heavens and hells of man,
> The gods and demons

17. Northrop Frye, quoted in Wasson, 1198.

. . . .
are more or less successful
Mythological descriptions
Of knowing, acting, loving—
You are Shiva, but you dream.

In that poem Rexroth also wrote, "insanity is the crippling / Of
the organ of reciprocity," for when eros is not allowed freedom,
there is aggression (including economic aggression), brutality, the
insanity of Rukeyser's "Rational Man." As in "Body of Waking,"
Rexroth in "Thou Shalt Not Kill" (1956) details the insanity of an
"Age of Abundance," greed, and repression which has murdered
the young men and women of eros: Dylan Thomas, Lola Ridge, all
poets and revolutionaries.[18]

Gary Snyder has written of his "life with his family and com-
rades in the foothills of the California Sierras," a life lived in what
Marcuse calls the "Great Refusal" of the insanities of the age, a life
in which, the poems show, eros reigns. In images that recall Rukeyser's (gates, spiral, music, seed, body) he celebrates the unity of life:

the space between the thighs I reach through,
. . . .
The gates of Awe
That open back a turning double-mirror world of
wombs in wombs, in rings,
that start in music,
is this our body?
The hidden place of seed
. . . .
Kai's little scrotum up close to his groin,
the seed still tucked away, that moved from us to him
. . . .
this is our body ("The Bath," *Turtle Island*)

Denise Levertov, close personal friend and great admirer of
Rukeyser ("One of the things I most admire her for is her continu-

18. Kenneth Rexroth, *The Dragon and the Unicorn* (Norfolk, Conn., 1952), pp. 170–
71; 110; Rexroth, *The Collected Shorter Poems of Kenneth Rexroth* (N. Y., 1966), pp.
267–75.

ing growth"), writes often of the force of eros. Reading through Levertov's volumes chronologically, one finds an increasing use of the term *waking*. This is what Rukeyser celebrates in *Body of Waking*, our physically grounded great wish for and awareness of love and unity. Waking or the wish to awaken and praise gives these contemporary poets the optimism that repudiates the alienated stance. Waking, they are aware of the possibility of transformation, of a vision of the world other than the repressive and hopeless one we are familiar with in our opaque moments. (It will be recalled that Rukeyser sought "a language of transformation" as far back as the thirties when she turned to the study of Gibbs.) Levertov writes often of eros released into a new phase.

> Speak to me, little horse, beloved,
> tell me
> how to follow the iron ball,
> how to follow through to the country
> beneath the waves
> to the place where I must kill you and you step out
> of your bones and flystrewn meat
> tall, smiling, renewed,
> formed in your own likeness
> Marvelous Truth, confront us
> at every turn,
> in every guise
> . . . .
> Thrust close your smile
> that we know you, terrible joy. (*The Jacob's Ladder*, 59–60)

One poem especially recalls Rukeyser's focus on blocked lives changing phase and growing again. From "The Novel":

> Yet they do have—
> don't they—like us—
> their days of grace, they
>
> halt, stretch, a vision
> breaks in on the cramped grimace,
> inscape of transformation.
> Something sundered begins to knit.
> By scene, by sentence, something is rendered
> back into life, back to the gods. (*O Taste and See*, 65)

Levertov's central poem on this theme, "The Unknown," is dedicated, not surprisingly, to Muriel Rukeyser. The poem explores the
difficulty of attaining "enlightenment," where one's anxiety or
"fury" passes into "quiet praise." Before one can attain the miracle
of that state one must accept a "decent" routine of daily work—in
her case, housework and writing. The awakening is then, unex-
pectedly, "to transformation, word after word" (*The Sorrow
Dance*, 27–28). Waking is not easy, according to Levertov, and a
vision of our possibilities is not easily held by the imagination.

> How I woke to the color-tone
> as of peach-juice
>
> . . . .
> How I seemed a woman tall and
> full-rounded
>
> . . . .
> but continued to awake
> further, and found myself
> myself, smaller,
> not thin but thinner, nervous,
> who hurries without animal calm
>
> . . . .
> and it was not morning. (*The Sorrow Dance*, 71)
> could there be
> a reversal I cannot
> hoist myself high enough
> to see,
> plunge myself deep enough
> to know? (*Footprints*, 36) [19]

Rukeyser's poems show the desired "reversal" or changed phase
more often than those in the later volumes of Levertov. Nevertheless she (like the postmoderns as a group) repudiates what William
Hamilton quoting Saul Bellow calls "the cheap mental stimulants
of Alienation . . . Forlornness," despair. In "City Psalm," detailing
the "pain and misfortune" of a contemporary city, "walking the
thronged / pavements among crippled lives, jackhammers / raging,"

19. Denise Levertov, *The Jacob's Ladder* (N.Y. 1961); Levertov, *O Taste and See* (N.Y., 1964); Levertov, *The Sorrow Dance* (N.Y., 1966); Levertov, *Footprints* (N.Y., 1972).

Levertov has a vision of transformation, engendered by the same deep wish of the elegies:

> Nothing was changed, all was revealed otherwise;
> not that horror was not, not that the killings did not continue,
> not that I thought there was to be no more despair,
> but that as if transparent all disclosed
> an otherness that was blesséd, that was bliss.
> *I saw Paradise in the dust of the street.* (*Sorrow Dance*, 72)

Here is precisely the sort of "unearned conclusion" Rukeyser was castigated for in the forties and fifties. What postmodernist critics see in such conclusions, in Moses Herzog who refuses to go mad, in Denise Levertov who says in "The Freeing of the Dust," "I am tired of 'the fine art of unhappiness,'" is what William Hamilton calls "the new optimism." It is in fact the triumph of eros, the life instinct, the free imagination. Postmodernist writers reaffirm again Keats's "holiness of the heart's affections," what Northrop Frye calls "the total dream of man."[20] From *Body of Waking*:

> Then from the mountains of the lost,
> All the fantasies shall wake,
> Strong and real and speaking turn
> Wherever flickers your unreal.
> And my strong ghosts shall fade and pass
> My love start fiery as grass
> Wherever burn my fantasies,
> Wherever burn my fantasies. (BW, 25)

Thus acknowledging and following eros leads to an optimistic, liberating body of poetry which yields continual visions of possibility. In "Waterlily Fire," "But it is hell" becomes "Or it could be a foundation." In "Breaking Open" Rukeyser writes of people beginning to change, open, and grow:

> But this music is
> itself
> needing only other selving

20. Thomas J. J. Altizer and William Hamilton, *Radical Theology and the Death of God* (Indianapolis, 1966), p. 159; Levertov, *The Freeing of the Dust* (N.Y., 1975); Northrop Frye, *Anatomy of Criticism* (Princeton, 1957), p. 119.

It is defeated but a way is open:
transformation

Levertov in "The Freeing of the Dust" presents a striking vision of
unity by jettisoning notions of polarity, despisal, and rejection:

Unwrap the dust from its mummycloths.
Let Ariel learn
a blessing for Caliban
and Caliban drink dew from the lotus

Poets of postmodernism have shown their optimism in "documentary" poems like those in Rukeyser's volumes. Snyder, Rexroth,
and Levertov have all written powerful poems protesting war and
injustice. But always their vision is, like Rexroth's in "The American Century," of the possibility of peace, of the hope and beauty of
children or of resisters "in the century of horror." [21] While describing
bombed villages and crumbling neighborhoods, they sing their
celebration of life, their homage to eros. They insist that our wish
will find a way.

The new poets of eros who admit and explore their need for
"fulfillment in love and unity, in work" believe concomitantly
that form in art and life is organic, evolving, not superimposed but
discovered. Almost all the poets influenced by the San Francisco
Renaissance have made statements about discovering form in the
writing of poetry. Gary Snyder's statements carry this attitude into
life: "Discipline of self-restraint is an easy one; being clear-cut,
negative, and usually based on some accepted cultural values. Discipline of following desires, *always* doing what you want to do, is
hardest. It presupposes self-knowledge of motives, a careful balance of free action and sense of where the cultural taboos lay—
knowing whether a particular 'desire' is instinctive, cultural, personal, a product of thought, contemplation, or the unconscious."
(Compare Rukeyser's "I feel guilt when my desire finds no way.")
Form will arise through the following of deep wish and the admission of all meanings. "Do I move toward form, do I use all my

21. Rexroth, *Collected Shorter Poems*, p. 275.

fears?" (*The Gates*, 10) Robert Duncan, whose poems Rukeyser
says she feels very close to, wrote, "In one way or another to live
in the swarm of human speech. This is not to seek perfection but to
draw honey or poetry out of all things. After Freud, we are aware
that unwittingly we achieve our form. It is, whatever our mastery,
the inevitable use we make of the speech that betrays to ourselves
and to our hunters (our readers) the spore of what we are becoming."[22] Recalling Duncan's images are those in Levertov's "Second
Didactic Poem":

> In our gathering, in our containing, in our
> working, active within ourselves,
> slowly the pale
> dew-beads of light
> lapped up from flowers
> can thicken,
> darken to gold:
> honey of the human. (*The Sorrow Dance*, 83)

Snyder, Rukeyser, Levertov all write of the responsibility of the
poet to the tribe. Snyder calls the poet a shaman who "is simply
the man whose mind reaches easily out into all manners of shapes
and other lives, and gives song to dreams." (Rukeyser's "Dream
Drumming" from *The Gates* is a perfect title.) The shaman heals
with the power of dreams. So do these poets who offer us again a
vision of life's possibilities. Rukeyser writes several times of the
priestly, tribal function of poetry, saying she makes her work for
the "unborn." Levertov has said, "The poet—when he is writing—
is a priest."[23] In "February Evening in Boston, 1971," she looks to
future generations as Rukeyser does in "Poem" ("I lived in the first
century of world wars. . . .") from *The Speed of Darkness*. Levertov writes:

> It was the custom of my tribe
> to speak and sing;

22. *Earth House Hold*, p. 16; Duncan, *The New American Poetry*, p. 400.
23. *Earth House Hold*, p. 122; Denise Levertov, *The Poet in the World* (New York, 1973), 47.

not only to share the present, breath and sight,
but to the unborn.
Still, even now, we reach out
toward survivors. It is a covenant
of desire. (*Footprints*, 34)

Rukeyser's work will continue to encourage many to keep this covenant. Jane Cooper, poet and teacher with Rukeyser at Sarah Lawrence, wrote:

Muriel's writing has always meant an enormous amount to me. She was the first contemporary woman poet I read, when I was 13 or 14. . . . For me, who had been brought up writing in the tight, accepted forms of the Forties, she meant always an openness, a breadth—and not just because of the poems, but because of her love of science, the writing of the biographies, her political commitments . . . the links to film or theater, Jungian psychology. That kind of generosity of the total being seemed the best kind of antidote to the New Critics, whom otherwise I respected.

In a letter of 1976 essayist Vivian Gornick wrote to Rukeyser, "Yours is the true power of the poet: any three sentences you speak, like a stone penetrating a glassy liquid surface, create ripples in the mind and spirit that go on so long and reach so far that finally they seem to touch the furthest shores of thought and feeling." In Rukeyser's unpublished correspondence there are moving letters from Anne Sexton, who is not a survivor, but who felt the power of a magnificent lifework that reaches out to nurture our life wish.

Dear Wonderful Muriel,
I still keep "The Speed of Darkness" on my desk. It glistens here like the first washed flowers in spring when you sent it to me. Section one goes whammy! Then flows out like an infusion of blood into the body. I just want to tell you again, beautiful Muriel, mother of everyone, how I cherish your words. . . . Your new poem is splendid and you the high queen and you the tower and you the goddess are strange and beautiful. Your poems move like dreams and sink into my unconscious to reappear at night. They frighten. They become a memory.[24]

---

24. From a letter to the author, July 10, 1978; from a letter from Vivian Gornick to Rukeyser, March 17, 1976; from a letter and a postcard from Anne Sexton to Rukeyser, November 1 and December 19, 1967, in the Berg Collection of the New York Public Library.

A Chronology of Important Events

December 15, 1913: birth in New York City to Lawrence and Myra Lyons Rukeyser.

1921–1930: Ethical Culture School and Fieldston School.

1930–1932: Vassar College. On staff of *Student Review.*

1931 and 1932 (summers): Columbia University. Studied anthropology, short story, psychology.

1933: to Alabama for Scottsboro trials. Arrested. Typhoid fever.

1933–1934: Roosevelt School of Aviation, New York City.

1935: publication of *Theory of Flight* in Yale Series of Younger Poets. Associate Editor, *New Theatre*. Work for Theatre Union and Garrison Films (titles and commentaries for foreign films). Learned film editing with Helen Van Dongen. Work for *Coronet* and *Life* (experiments with photographs and running verse commentaries).

1936: to Gauley Bridge, West Virginia; England, Spain.

1938: publication of *U.S.1*. Published translation of Erica Mann's *School for Barbarians* (on the education of youth in Germany).

1939: *A Turning Wind*. Six months' stay in Mexico.

1940: Oscar Blumenthal Prize. *The Soul and Body of John Brown*, with etchings by Rudolph von Ripper. "Poetry and Communication" lectures at Vassar.

1941: Harriet Monroe Poetry Award (the first one given). Associate Editor, *Decision*. Translated Jean Renoir, *People of France* (film). Filmscript-documentary, *A Place to Live*.

1942: *Wake Island. Willard Gibbs*. Thousand-dollar grant from American Academy of Arts and Letters and National Institute of Arts and Letters.

1943: work at graphics division of Office of War Information, six months. (Most of her poster ideas rejected.) Guggenheim Fellowship.

1944: member, Writers' War Board. *Beast in View*.

1945: *The Middle of the Air* (a play) produced by Hallie Flanagan, Iowa City. Move to California. Lecturer at California Labor School. Marriage to Glynn Collins, painter; annulment.

1947: birth of son, (William) Laurie Rukeyser, Berkeley, California. Levinson Prize. Reading at San Francisco "Festival of Modern Poetry" with Josephine Miles, Janet Lewis, Madeleine Gleason, Kenneth Rexroth, and others.

1948: *The Green Wave*.

1949: *Elegies. The Life of Poetry. Orpheus*, with a drawing by Picasso. Trip to Vancouver Island for work on Franz Boas biography.

1951: *Selected Poems.*

1953: work with Helen Parkhurst on unpublished biography. Work with Frances Wickes on unpublished autobiographical novel. Teaching, Vassar Family Institute ("sessions with parents, teachers, children, including two-year-olds and six-year-olds, in poetry"). Writing report for White House Conference for New York State.

1954: began teaching at Sarah Lawrence.

1957: *One Life.*

1958: filmscript-documentary *All the Way Home. Body of Waking.*

1961: *The Colors of the Day,* a play for the Vassar Centennial. Honorary Doctor of Literature, Rutgers.

1962: *Waterlily Fire: Poems 1935–1962.* Eunice Tietjens Memorial Prize.

1963: publication of translation of Octavio Paz, *Selected Poems* and *Sun Stone.*

1964: stroke.

1966: *The Orgy.*

1967: elected member, National Institute of Arts and Letters. Translated with Leif Sjöberg, Gunnar Ekelöf, *Selected Poems.*

1968: "Poetry and the Unverifiable Fact." *The Speed of Darkness.*

1971: *The Traces of Thomas Hariot.*

1972: *29 Poems.* Trip to Hanoi with Denise Levertov and Jane Hart. Jail, Washington.

1973: *Breaking Open.* Published, with others, Octavio Paz, *Early Poems, 1935–1955. Houdini* produced in Massachusetts. Pneumonia, London.

1975: elected President, P.E.N. American Center. Trip to Korea for poet Kim Chi-Ha (for Friends of Kim Chi-Ha and P.E.N.).

1976: *The Gates.*

1977: stroke. Copernicus Prize, Shelley Prize.

1979: *The Collected Poems of Muriel Rukeyser.*

Bibliography

Works by Muriel Rukeyser

I. BOOKS

Beast in View. Garden City, N.Y.: Doubleday, Doran, 1944.
Body of Waking. New York: Harper, 1958.
Breaking Open. New York: Random House, 1973.
Bubbles (for children). New York: Harcourt, Brace, 1967.
The Collected Poems of Muriel Rukeyser. New York: McGraw-Hill, 1979.
The Colors of the Day: A Celebration of the Vassar Centennial (play). Poughkeep-sie, N.Y.: Vassar College, 1961.
Come Back, Paul (for children). New York: Harper, 1955.
Elegies. Norfolk, Conn.: New Directions, 1949.
The Gates. New York: McGraw-Hill, 1976.
The Green Wave. Garden City, N.Y.: Doubleday, 1948.
I Go Out (for children). New York: Harper, 1961.
The Life of Poetry. New York: Current Books, 1949.
Mazes (for children). New York: Simon and Schuster, 1970.
One Life. New York: Simon and Schuster, 1957.
The Orgy. New York: Coward McCann, 1965. London: Deutsch, 1966.
Selected Poems. New York: New Directions, 1951.
The Speed of Darkness. New York: Random House, 1968.
Theory of Flight. New Haven: Yale University Press, 1935.
The Traces of Thomas Hariot. New York: Random House, 1971. London: Gol-lancz, 1972.
A Turning Wind. New York: Viking, 1939.
29 Poems. London: Rapp and Whiting. Deutsch, 1972.
U.S.1. New York: Covici, Friede, 1938.
Wake Island. Garden City, N.Y.: Doubleday, Doran, 1942.
Waterlily Fire: Poems, 1935–1962. New York: Macmillan, 1962.
Willard Gibbs. Garden City, N.Y.: Doubleday, Doran, 1942.

II. TRANSLATIONS, SCRIPTS, INTRODUCTIONS, SEPARATE PUBLICATION OF INDIVIDUAL POEMS, ETC.

Abbott, Berenice. *Berenice Abbott Photographs*. Foreword by Muriel Rukeyser. New York: Horizon, 1970.
All the Way Home. Documentary Filmscript. Directed by Lee Bobker, 1958.

Brecht, Bertolt. *Uncle Eddie's Moustache*. Translated by Muriel Rukeyser. New York: Pantheon Books, 1974.

Ekelöf, Gunnar. *Selected Poems*. Introduction by Lief Sjöberg. Translated by Muriel Rukeyser and Lief Sjöberg. New York: Twayne, 1967.

———. *Three Poems*. Translated by Muriel Rukeyser and Lief Sjöberg. Lawrence, Kansas: T. Williams, 1967.

Houdini. (Play) Produced by Lenox Arts Center, 1973.

Mann, Erica. *School for Barbarians*. Translated by Muriel Rukeyser. New York: Modern Age Books, 1938.

Mediterranean. New York: Writers and Artists Committee, Medical Bureau to Aid Spanish Democracy, n.d.

The Middle of the Air. (Play) Produced by Hallie Flanagan. Iowa City, 1945.

Orpheus. With a Drawing by Picasso. San Francisco: Centaur Press, 1949.

The Outer Banks. Santa Barbara, Calif.: Unicorn Press, 1967.

Paz, Octavio. *Early Poems, 1935–1955*. Translated by Muriel Rukeyser and others. New York: New Directions, 1973.

———. *Selected Poems*. Translated by Muriel Rukeyser. Bloomington: Indiana University Press, 1963.

———. *Sun Stone*. Translated by Muriel Rukeyser. New York: New Directions, 1963.

A Place To Live. Documentary Filmscript. Philadelphia Housing Films, 1941.

Poetry and the Unverifiable Fact. Scripps College Bulletin, XLII, 4. Claremont, California: Scripps College, 1968.

The Soul and Body of John Brown. With etchings by Rudolf C. von Ripper. New York: Lee Ault and R. C. von Ripper, 1940.

Welch, Marie de L. *The Otherwise*. Introduction by Muriel Rukeyser. San Francisco: Adrian Wilson, 1976.

The World Split Open: Four Centuries of Women Poets in England and America, 1552–1950. Edited by Louis Bernikow. Preface by Muriel Rukeyser. New York: Random House, 1974.

III. ARTICLES AND REVIEWS

"Allusions in the Last Part of Gunnar Ekelöf's *En Mölna-elegi*." Translated by Muriel Rukeyser and Leif Sjöberg. *Germanic Review*, XL (March, 1965), 132–63.

"Amistad Mutiny." Bucklin Moon, ed. *A Primer for White Folks*. Garden City, N.Y.: Doubleday, Doran, 1945.

"The Amistad Mutiny." *Twice-a-Year*, VIII–IX (1942), 195–228.

"Barcelona, 1936." *Life and Letters Today*, XV (Autumn, 1936), 28–33.

"The Club" (story). Howard Moss, ed. *The Poet's Story*. New York: Macmillan, 1973.

"Craft Interview with Muriel Rukeyser." William Packard, ed. *The Craft of Poetry*. Garden City, N.Y.: Doubleday, 1974.

"A Crystal for the Metaphysical." Review of Marianne Moore's *Tell Me, Tell Me: Granite, Steel, and Other Topics. Saturday Review*, October 1, 1966, pp. 52–53.

"Death in Spain: Barcelona on the Barricades." *New Masses*, XX (September 1, 1936), 9–11.

"The Dividends of War." Review of Guiles Davenport's *Zaharoff—High Priest of War*. *New Masses*, XIII (December, 1934), 25–26.

Review of Faulkner's *Dr. Martino and Other Stories*. *New Masses*, XI (May 22, 1934), 25.

"The Fear." New York *Times*, June 19, 1978, p. 19.

"The Fear of Poetry." *Twice-a-Year*, VII (Fall–Winter, 1941), 15–31.

"From Scottsboro to Decatur." *Student Review*, II (April, 1933), 12–15.

"Genesis of 'Orpheus.'" John Ciardi, ed. *Mid-century American Poets*. New York: Twayne, 1950.

"Glitter and Wounds, Several Wildnesses." Review of Anne Sexton's *The Book of Folly*. *Parnassus*, II (Fall/Winter, 1973), 215–21.

Review of Knut Hamsun's *The Road Leads On*. *New Masses*, XI (July 24, 1934), 27–28.

"In a Speaking Voice." Review of Robert Frost's *Collected Poems, 1939*. *Poetry*, LIV (July, 1939), 218–24.

"Indian Fiesta Huge Success." *Nation*, May 29, 1937, pp. 616–18.

"Josiah Willard Gibbs." *Physics Today*, II (1949), 6–13, 27.

"Language of Our Theatre." *Theatre Arts*, XXXIV (January, 1950), 52–53.

"The Life to Which I Belong." Review of Franz Kafka's *Letters to Felice. American Poetry Review*, III (May/June, 1974), 8–9.

"Little." *Ladies Home Journal*, LXXXII (February, 1965), 82–85.

"Lorca in English." Review of translations of Garcia Lorca's *Blood Wedding, Poems, The Poet in New York*. *Kenyon Review*, III (1941), 123–27.

"Lyrical 'Rage.'" Review of Kenneth Rexroth's *In Defense of the Earth*. *Saturday Review*, November 9, 1957, p. 15.

Review of Archibald MacLeish's *Land of the Free*. *New Masses*, XXVII (April 26, 1938), 26–28.

"Myth and Torment." Review of Robert Duncan's *Heavenly City, Earthly City*. *Poetry*, LXXII (April, 1948), 48–51.

"Nearer to the Well-Spring." Review of R. M. Rilke's *Sonnets to Orpheus*. *Kenyon Review*, V (Summer, 1943), 451–58.

"On John Crowe Ransom's 'Master's in the Garden Again.'" A. J. Ostroff, ed. *The Contemporary Poet as Artist and Critic*. Boston: Little Brown, 1964.

"The Rhythm Is the Person." Review of Marianne Moore's *O To Be a Dragon*. *Saturday Review*, September 19, 1959, pp. 17–18.

"She Came to Us." *New Statesman*, November 8, 1958, p. 624.

"Sherwood Anderson." *Decision*, I (April, 1941), 12–13.

"A Simple Theme." Review of Charlotte Marletto's *Jewel of Our Longing*. *Poetry*, LXXIV (July, 1949), 236–39.

Review of Edith Sitwell's *The Pleasures of Poetry*. *New Masses*, XIV (February 12, 1935), 26.

"Thoreau and Poetry." W. R. Harding *et al.*, eds. *Henry David Thoreau: Studies and Commentaries*. Rutherford, N.J.: Fairleigh Dickinson University Press, 1972, pp. 103–16.

"Under Forty." *Contemporary Jewish Record*, VII (February, 1944), 4–9.
"The Usable Truth." *Poetry*, LVIII (July, 1941), 206–209.
"War and Poetry." Oscar Williams, ed. *The War Poets*. New York: John Day, 1945.
"We Came for Games." *Esquire*, LXXXII (October, 1974), 192–94.
"With Leftward Glances." Review of John Wheelwright's *Rock and Shell. New Masses*, XII (July 10, 1934), 28.
"Words and Images." *New Republic*, August 2, 1943, pp. 140–42.
Review of Marya Zaturenska's *The Listening Landscape. Decision*, I (June, 1941), 81–83.

Works about Muriel Rukeyser and Her Time

I. ARTICLES AND BOOKS DISCUSSING MURIEL RUKEYSER

Alsterlund, B. "Biographical Sketch." *Wilson Library Bulletin*, XV (October, 1940), 110.
Brinnin, John M. "Muriel Rukeyser: The Social Poet and the Problem of Communication." *Poetry*, LXI (January, 1943), 554–75.
Beach, Joseph Warren. *Obsessive Images: Symbolism in Poetry of the 1930's and 1940's*. Edited by W. V. O'Connor. Minneapolis: University of Minnesota Press, 1960.
Bush, Clive. "Muriel Rukeyser: The Poet as Scientific Biographer." *Spanner 11*, II (July, 1977).
Cooper, Jane. *Maps & Windows*. New York: Macmillan, 1974.
Current Biography, 1943.
Gilbert, Jack. "Between Verses: Report on a West Coast Poetry Festival." *New York Times Book Review*, September 9, 1962, p. 4.
"Grandeur and Misery of a Poster Girl." *Partisan Review*, X (September–October, 1943), 471–73.
Gregory, Horace. "American Poetry 1930–1940." *Decision*, I (January, 1941), 24–29.
Gregory, Horace, and Marya Zaturenska. *A History of American Poetry 1900–1940*. New York: Harcourt, Brace, 1946.
Jarrell, Randall, *Poetry and the Age*. New York: Knopf, 1953.
Kunitz, Stanley, and Howard Haycraft. *Twentieth Century American Authors*. New York: Wilson, 1942.
Levertov, Denise. *The Poet in the World*. New York: New Directions, 1973.
Madden, David, ed. *Proletarian Writers of the Thirties*. Carbondale, Ill.: Southern Illinois University Press, 1968.
"Miss Rukeyser Quitting O.W. I. over 'Policies.'" New York *Herald Tribune*, May 12, 1945.
Murphy, Rosalie. *Contemporary Poets of the English Language*. New York: St. Martin's Press, 1970.
Novak, Estelle G. "The Dynamo School of Poets." *Contemporary Literature*, II (1970), 526–39.
Parkinson, T. "Some Recent Pacific Coast Poetry." *Pacific Spectator*, IV (1950), 300–302.

Rexroth, Kenneth. *American Poetry in the Twentieth Century*. New York: Herder and Herder, 1971.

Rosenthal, M. L. "Chief Poets of the American Depression: Contributions of Kenneth Fearing, Horace Gregory, and Muriel Rukeyser to Contemporary American Poetry." Ph.D. Dissertation, New York University, 1949.

———. "On the 'Dissidents' of the Thirties." *University of Kansas City Review* (Summer, 1951), 294–300.

———. "Muriel Rukeyser: The Longer Poems." James Laughlin, ed. *New Directions in Prose and Poetry*, XIV (1953), 202–29.

———. *The New Poets: American and British Poetry Since World War II*. New York: Oxford University Press, 1967.

"The Rukeyser Imbroglio." *Partisan Review*, XI (Winter, 1944), 125–29.

"The Rukeyser Imbroglio (cont'd)." *Partisan Review*, XI (Spring, 1944), 217–18.

"Sarah Lawrence Again Under Fire." New York *Times*, November 14, 1958, p. 11.

Tate, Allen. *Recent American Poetry, a Selected List of References*. Washington: Library of Congress, 1943.

———. *Sixty American Poets, 1896–1944, Selected, with a Preface and Critical Notes*. Washington: Library of Congress, 1945.

Terris, Virginia R. "Muriel Rukeyser: A Retrospective." *American Poetry Review*, III (May/June, 1974), 10–15.

Untermeyer, Louis. "The Language of Muriel Rukeyser." *Saturday Review*, August 10, 1940, pp. 11–13.

———. *Modern American Poetry, Modern British Poetry*. New York: Harcourt, Brace, 1950.

II. REVIEWS OF RUKEYSER'S BOOKS

Theory of Flight, 1935

Benét, William Rose. *Saturday Review*, December 7, 1935, p. 47.

Booklist, XXXII (February, 1936), 166.

Boston *Transcript*, January 15, 1936, p. 3.

Burke, Kenneth. "Return after Flight." *New Masses*, XVIII (February 4, 1936), 26.

Clark, Eunice. *Common Sense*, V (January, 1936), 28.

Gregory, Horace. "A Hope for Poetry." *New Republic*, February 5, 1936, p. 374.

Jack, Peter Munro. *New York Times Book Review*, January 12, 1936, p. 15.

Lechlitner, Ruth. *Partisan Review and Anvil*, III (March, 1936), 29–30.

Maas, Willard. *New York Herald Tribune Books*, January 19, 1936, p. 7.

Matthiessen, F. O. *Yale Review*, n.s., XXV (Spring, 1936), 604.

Ransom, John Crowe. *Southern Review*, I (Winter, 1936), 615–16.

Rice, P. B. "New Poet." *Nation*, January 29, 1936, p. 134.

Roberts, Michael. *Spectator*, May 1, 1936, p. 804.

Rosenberg, H. "Youth in Protest." *Poetry*, XLVIII (May, 1936), 107–10.

Stone, Geoffrey. *American Review*, VII (April, 1936), 101.

Time, December 16, 1935, p. 81.

U.S.1., 1938

Benét, William Rose. *Saturday Review*, April 30, 1938, p. 16.

Booklist, XXXIV (March 15, 1938), 263.

Holmes, John. *Boston Transcript*, March 19, 1938, p. 2.
Maas, Willard. "Lost Between Wars." *Poetry*, LII (May, 1938), 101–104.
Quinn, Kerker. *New York Herald Tribune Books*, Feb. 20, 1938, p. 12.
Rice, P. B. *Nation*, March 19, 1938, p. 335.
Rodman, Selden. *Common Sense*, VII (March, 1938), 26.
Time. March 28, 1938, p. 63.
Untermeyer, Louis. *Yale Review*, n.s., XXVI (Spring, 1938), 608.
Walton, Edna Lou. *New York Times Book Review*, March 27, 1938, p. 19.
Wheelwright, John. *Partisan Review*, IV (March, 1938), 54–56.
Williams, William Carlos. *New Republic*, March 9, 1938, pp. 141–42.
Wolff, David. "Document and Poetry." *New Masses*, XXVI (February 22, 1938),
    23–24.
Zabel, Morton Dauwen. "Two Years of Poetry: 1937–39." *Southern Review*, V
    (1939–1940), 568–608.

A *Turning Wind*, 1939
Bishop, John P. *Collected Essays*. New York: Scribner's, 1948, pp. 313–16.
Bogan, Louise. *New Yorker*. December 16, 1939, p. 120.
———. *Selected Criticism: Prose, Poetry*. New York: Noonday, 1955, pp. 171–74.

Clark, Axton. *New York Times Book Review*, April 7, 1940, p. 2.
Friend, Robert. *Common Sense*, IX (January, 1940), 26.
Horton, Philip. "Symbols of Decay." *New Republic*, January 22, 1940, p. 123.
Lechlitner, Ruth. *New York Herald Tribune Books*, January 7, 1940, p. 10.
Millspaugh, C. A. *Kenyon Review*, II (1940), 359–63.
Rodman, Selden. "Poets of the World, Relax." *Saturday Review*, December 9, 1939,
    p. 7.
Wilson, T. C. *Poetry*, LV (January, 1940), 214–16.

Wake Island, 1942
Benét, William Rose. *Saturday Review*, August 29, 1942, p. 14.
Bogan, Louise. *New Yorker*, October 31, 1942, p. 68.
Kees, Weldon. "Miss Rukeyser's Marine Poem." *Partisan Review*, IX (November–
    December, 1942), 540.
Lechlitner, Ruth. *New York Herald Tribune Books*, September 27, 1942, p. 16.

Willard Gibbs, 1942
Atlantic, CLXXI (March, 1943), 150.
Chamberlain, John. New York *Times*, November 24, 1942, p. 23.
Clark, Eunice. *Common Sense*, XII (January, 1943), 461.
Commonweal, January 8, 1943, p. 304.
Fadiman, Clifton. *New Yorker*, November 7, 1942, p. 67.
Färber, Eduard. *Isis*, XXXIV (Summer, 1943), 414–15.
Gabriel, Ralph. *American Historical Review*, XLVIII (July, 1943), 750.
Jaffe, Bernard. *New York Herald Tribune Books*, November 22, 1942, p. 4.
Johnston, John. *Chemical and Engineering News*, XXI (March 10, 1943), 342.
Kaempffert, Waldemar. *New York Times Book Review*, December 13, 1942, p. 3.
Kazin, Alfred. "Another Ancestor." *New Republic*, December 7, 1942, p. 752.
Kirkwood, John G. *Yale Review*, n.s. XXXII (Spring, 1943), 579.

Kraus, Charles A. *Journal of the American Chemical Society*, LXV (December, 1943), 2475–76.
Krutch, Joseph Wood. "Deep Waters." *Nation*, January 16, 1943, p. 97.
Library Journal. LXVII (October 15, 1942), 908.
Masters, D. *Chicago Sun Book Week*, October 3, 1965, p. 18.
Northrop, F. S. C. "A Poet Discovers the Mathematical Physicist." *Saturday Review*, December 5, 1942, p. 10.
Rice, Philip Blair. *Kenyon Review*, V (1943), 310–12.
Smith, Henry Nash. *New England Quarterly*, XVI (September, 1943), 525.
Springfield *Republican*, November 29, 1942, p. 7e.
Time. January 4, 1943, p. 90.
Weaver, Elbert C. *Journal of Chemical Education*, XX (1943), 259–60.

Beast in View, 1944

Blackmur, R. P. *Kenyon Review*, VII (1945), 339.
Bogan, Louise. *New Yorker*, October 21, 1944, p. 91.
Chicago Sun Book Week. August 13, 1944, p. 9.
Dupee, F. W. *Nation*, November 25, 1944, p. 662.
Flint, F. C. *New York Times Book Review*, September 3, 1944, p. 4.
Lechlitner, Ruth. *New York Herald Tribune Book Review*, December 31, 1944, p. 4.
Miles, Josephine. *Accent*, V (Autumn, 1944), 60–61.
Sauer, C. M. Springfield *Republican*, August 6, 1944, p. 4d.
Williams, Oscar. *New Republic*, October 23, 1944, p. 534.

The Green Wave, 1948

Caldwell, J. R. "Margins of Terror." *Saturday Review*, March 20, 1948, p. 16.
Eberhart, Richard. "Art and *Zeitgeist*." *Poetry*, LXXIII (December, 1948), 173–76.
Freemantle, Anne. *Commonweal*, August 13, 1948, p. 430.
Jarrell, Randall. *Nation*, May 8, 1948, pp. 512–13.
———. *Poetry and the Age*. New York: Vintage, 1953.
Kay, Alfred. *San Francisco Chronicle*, February 8, 1948, p. 19.
McCarthy, F. B. *New York Times Book Review*, March 14, 1948, p. 6.
New Yorker. May 8, 1948, p. 115.
Rosenthal, M. L. *New York Herald Tribune Book Review*, June 27, 1948, p. 4.

Elegies, 1949

Bogan, Louise. *New Yorker*, May 20, 1950, p. 105.
Caldwell, J. R. "Invigoration and a Brilliant Hope." *Saturday Review*, March 11, 1950, p. 26.
Daiches, David. *New York Herald Tribune Book Review*, June 25, 1950, p. 8.
Humphries, Rolfe. *Nation*, January 28, 1950, p. 94.
Rosenthal, M. L. *New Republic*, February 6, 1950, p. 21.
Wolfert, Helen. *New York Times Book Review*, April 23, 1950, p. 28.

The Life of Poetry, 1949

Brinnin, John Malcolm. *New York Times Book Review*, March 2, 1975, p. 5.
Caldwell, J. R. "Invigoration and a Brilliant Hope." See *Elegies*.

Chicago *Sun*, May 1, 1950, p. 5.
Daiches, David. *New York Herald Tribune Book Review*, June 25, 1950, p. 8.
Rolo, Charles J. *Atlantic*, CLXXXV (March, 1950), p. 81.
San Francisco *Chronicle*, April 30, 1950, p. 22.
Schulman, Grace. "Song of Our Cells." *Hudson Review*, V (Spring, 1976), 130–38.
Wolfert, Helen. See *Elegies*.

Orpheus, 1949

Bogan, Louise. *New Yorker*, May 20, 1950, p. 114.
Caldwell, J. R. See *Elegies*.
Crane, Milton. *New York Times Book Review*, December 18, 1949, p. 14.
Daiches, David. *New York Herald Tribune Book Review*, June 25, 1950, p. 8.
Humphries, Rolfe. *Nation*, January 28, 1950, p. 94.
San Francisco *Chronicle*, January 8, 1950, p. 25.

Selected Poems, 1951

Bogan, Louise. *New Yorker*, November 3, 1951, pp. 150–51.
Eberhart, Richard. *New York Times Book Review*, September 23, 1951, p. 30.
Ferlinghetti, Lawrence. San Francisco *Chronicle*, November 18, 1951, p. 19.
New Mexico Quarterly, XX, 2, p. 225.
Salomon, I. L. "From Union Square to Parnassus." *Poetry*, LXXX (April, 1952), 52–57.

One Life, 1957

Booth, Philip. *Saturday Review*, August 3, 1957, p. 12.
Eberhart, Richard. *New York Herald Tribune Book Review*, April 28, 1957, p. 4.
Engle, Paul. *New York Times Book Review*, April 14, 1957, p. 16.
Dorn, N. K. San Francisco *Chronicle*, May 5, 1957, p. 38.
Kempton, Murray. New York *Post*, April 14, 1957.
Rolo, Charles J. *Atlantic*, CXCIX (May, 1957), 82.

Body of Waking, 1958

Gunn, Thom. *Yale Review*, n.s. XLVIII (December, 1958), 299.
Rexroth, Kenneth. *New York Times Book Review*, October 19, 1958, p. 4.
Rosenthal, M. L. "Closing in on the Self." *Nation*, March 21, 1959, pp. 259–60.
Scott, Winfield Townley. *Saturday Review*, January 3, 1959, p. 14.

Waterlily Fire, 1962

Adkins, Joan F. "The Esthetics of Science: Muriel Rukeyser's 'Waterlily Fire.'" *Contemporary Poetry*, I (1973), 23–27.
Campbell, Colin. *Christian Science Monitor*, October 25, 1962, p. 6.
Carruth, Hayden. "The Closest Permissible Approximation." *Poetry*, CI (February, 1963), 358–60.
Eberhart, Richard. *New York Times Book Review*, September 9, 1962, p. 3.
Schevill, [?]. San Francisco *Chronicle*, *This World Weekly*, December 23, 1962, p. 21.
Simpson, Louis. *Hudson Review*, XVI (Spring, 1963), 130.
Smith, W. J. *Harper's*, CCVII (September, 1963), 115.

Stauffer, R. E. *Voices*, CLXXXI (May–August, 1963), 34–36.
Stepanchev, Stephen. *Shenandoah*, XIV (Spring, 1963), 58–65.
Swenson, May. "Poetry of Three Women." *Nation*, February 23, 1963, pp. 164–66.

The Orgy, 1966

Bergonzi, Bernard. *New York Review of Books*, April 22, 1965, p. 15.
Choice, II (January, 1966), 774.
Collery, S. *Saturday Review*, March 27, 1965, p. 30.
Hingley, R. *Spectator*, May 13, 1966, p. 605.
Holland, M. *Observer*, March 27, 1966, p. 27.
Johnston, D. *Nation*, March 15, 1965, p. 282.
Kiely, B. *New York Times Book Review*, February 28, 1965, p. 52.
Lamott, K. *New York Herald Tribune Book Week*, February 28, 1965, p. 20.
Lynd, Helen M. "Three Days Off for Puck." *American Scholar*, XXXIV (Autumn, 1965), 668–72.
Mortimer, P. *New Statesman*, March 25, 1966, p. 435.
Pearlman, B. G. *Library Journal*, XC (March 1, 1965), 1112.
Time, March 12, 1965, p. 103.
Times Literary Supplement, August 11, 1966, p. 728.

The Speed of Darkness, 1968

Eberhart, Richard. *New York Times Book Review*, June 23, 1968, p. 24.
Howes, V. *Christian Science Monitor*, July 23, 1968, p. 9.
Lieberman, Laurence. "Critic of the Month." *Poetry*, CXIV (April, 1969), 42.

The Traces of Thomas Hariot, 1971

Applebaum, Wilbur. *Isis*, LXIII (June, 1972), 278–80.
Dee, John. *Times Literary Supplement*, May 19, 1972, p. 579.
Hollander, John. *Harper's*, CCXLII (February, 1971), 109.
Johnson, Paul. *New Statesman*, March 3, 1972, p. 277.
New Yorker, April 17, 1971, p. 147.
Observer, January 9, 1972, p. 32.
Rowse, A. L. *New York Times Book Review*, April 18, 1971, p. 28.
Wolff, Geoffrey. *Newsweek*, March 29, 1971, p. 101.

Breaking Open, 1973

Bernikow, Louise. *Ms.*, II (April, 1974), 35–36.
McGann, Jerome. *Poetry*, CXXV (October, 1974), 44.
Meinke, Peter. *New Republic*, November 24, 1973, p. 25.
Stumpf, Thomas. *Carolina Quarterly*, XXVI (Spring, 1974), p. 101–107.
Times Literary Supplement, March 29, 1974, p. 340.

The Gates, 1976

Coles, Robert. *American Poetry Review*, VII (May/June, 1978), 15.
Cotter, James Finn. *America*, April 2, 1977, p. 297.
Stone, Elizabeth. *Village Voice*, November 22, 1976, p. 93.
Wagner, Linda. "Song of the Sun." *Nation*, March 19, 1977.
Webster, Lee. *Win*, May 12, 1977.

Other Sources Cited

Aaron, Daniel. *Writers on the Left: Episodes in American Literary Communism.* New York: Harcourt, Brace, and World, 1961.

Allen, Donald M., ed. *The New American Poetry.* New York: Grove Press, 1960.

Altieri, Charles. "From Symbolist Thought to Immanence: The Ground of Postmodern American Poetics." *Boundary* 2 (Spring, 1973), 605–41.

Altizer, Thomas J. J., and William Hamilton. *Radical Theology and the Death of God.* Indianapolis: Bobbs-Merrill, 1966.

Antin, David. "Modernism and Postmodernism: Approaching the Present in American Poetry." *Boundary* 2 (Fall, 1972), 98–146.

Auden, W. H. "As it Seemed to Us." *New Yorker,* April 3, 1965, p. 159.

————. *The Collected Poetry of W. H. Auden.* New York: Random House, 1945.

————. *Collected Shorter Poems.* New York: Random House, 1967.

————. *Epistle to a Godson.* New York: Random House, 1972.

————. *Journey to a War.* London: Faber, 1939.

————. *Letters from Iceland.* London: Faber, 1937.

————. *On This Island.* New York: Random House, 1937.

————. *Poems.* New York: Random House, 1934.

Benardete, M. J., and Rolfe Humphries, eds. *And Spain Sings: Fifty Loyalist Ballads Adapted by American Poets.* New York: Vanguard, 1937.

Bergman, Alexander. Review of Kenneth Fearing's *Collected Poems. New Masses,* XXXVII (November 19, 1940), 26.

Blake, William. *The Poetry and Prose of William Blake.* Edited by David V. Erdman. Garden City, N.Y.: Doubleday, 1965.

Bogan, Louise. *The Blue Estuaries: Poems 1923–1968.* New York: Ecco Press, 1977.

————. *Selected Letters of Louise Bogan 1920–1970.* Edited by Ruth Limmer. New York: Harcourt, Brace, Jovanovich, 1973.

Bowles, Gloria. "Louise Bogan: To Be (Or Not To Be?) Woman Poet." *Women's Studies,* V, 2 (1977), 131–35.

Brinnin, John Malcolm. Letter to Rukeyser, January 5, 1941, in the Berg Collection, New York Public Library.

Brooks, Van Wyck. *Letters and Leadership.* New York: Huebsch, 1918.

Burke, Kenneth. *Attitudes Toward History.* 2 vols. New York: New Republic, 1937.

Cooper, Jane. Letter to the author, July 10, 1978.

Cowley, Malcolm. "Matty for One." *New Republic,* April 24, 1950, p. 21.

Crane, Hart. *The Collected Poems of Hart Crane.* Edited by Waldo Frank. New York: Liveright, 1933.

Crowder, Richard. *Carl Sandburg.* New York: Twayne, 1964.

Dembo, L. S. *Hart Crane's Sanskrit Charge: A Study of "The Bridge."* Ithaca: Cornell University Press, 1960.

Drew, Elizabeth. *Directions in Modern Poetry.* New York: Norton, 1940.

Eisenstein, Sergei. *The Film Sense.* New York: Harcourt, Brace, 1942.

Eliot, T. S. *The Complete Poems and Plays.* New York: Harcourt, Brace, and World, 1962.

Emerson, Ralph Waldo. *The Selected Writings of Ralph Waldo Emerson*. New York: Random House, Modern Library, 1940.

Fair, Charles M. "The Poet as Specialist." *American Poetry Review*, IV (November–December, 1975), 20.

Falk, Signi L. *Archibald MacLeish*. New York: Twayne, 1965.

Fearing, Kenneth. *Angel Arms*. New York: Coward McCann, 1929.

———. *Collected Poems of Kenneth Fearing*. New York: Random House, 1940.

———. *Dead Reckoning*. New York: Random House, 1938.

———. *Poems*. New York: Dynamo, 1935.

Frank, Waldo. *Our America*. New York: Boni & Liveright, 1919.

Frye, Northrop. *Anatomy of Criticism*. Princeton: Princeton University Press, 1957.

Ginsberg, Allen. *Howl and Other Poems*. San Francisco: City Lights Books, 1956.

Goldstein, Malcolm. *The Political Stage: American Drama and Theater of the Great Depression*. New York: Oxford University Press, 1974.

Gornick, Vivian. Letter to Muriel Rukeyser, March 17, 1976, in Berg Collection, New York Public Library.

Gregory, Horace. *Chorus for Survival*. New York: Covici, 1935.

———. *No Retreat*. New York: Harcourt, Brace, 1933.

Halpern, Daniel, ed. *American Poetry Anthology*. New York: Avon, 1975.

Heilbrun, Carolyn. *Toward a Recognition of Androgyny*. New York: Knopf, 1973.

Hicks, Granville. *The Great Tradition*. New York: Macmillan, 1968.

———[*"M. Mather"*]. "Der Schöne Archibald." *New Masses*, X (January 16, 1934), 26.

Hicks, *et al*, eds. *Proletarian Literature in the U.S.* New York: International Publishing Co., 1935.

Levertov, Denise. *Footprints*. New York: New Directions, 1972.

———. *The Freeing of the Dust*. New York: New Directions, 1975.

———. *The Jacob's Ladder*. New York: New Directions, 1961.

———. Letter to the author, June, 1977.

———. *O Taste and See*. New York: New Directions, 1964.

———. *The Sorrow Dance*. New York: New Directions, 1966.

Levy, Alan. "In the Autumn of the Age of Anxiety." *New York Times Magazine*, August 8, 1971, pp. 10–11, 29–43.

Lewis, Anthony. "We Have Really Seen the Future and It Works." *New York Times Magazine*, July 4, 1976, pp. 24–27.

Lowell, Robert. *Life Studies and For the Union Dead*. New York: Farrar, Straus, 1967.

———. *Notebook*. New York: Farrar, Straus, 1971.

MacDiarmid, Hugh. *Selected Essays of Hugh MacDiarmid*. Edited by Duncan Glen. Berkeley: University of California Press, 1970.

Macdonald, Dwight. Letter to the author, October 18, 1976.

MacLeish, Archibald. *The Human Season: Selected Poems, 1926–1972*. Boston: Houghton, Mifflin, 1972.

———. "In Challenge Not Defense." *Poetry*, LII (July, 1938), 212–19.

———. *New Found Land*. Boston: Houghton, Mifflin, 1930.

———. *Streets in the Moon*. Boston: Houghton, Mifflin, 1929.

Marcuse, Herbert. *Eros and Civilization*. Boston: Beacon Press, 1966.

Marx, Jane and Leo. Interview, February 4, 1976.

Merideth, Robert. "Homage to a Subversive: Notes toward Explaining John Beecher." *American Poetry Review*, V (May/June, 1976), 45–46.

Millay, Edna St. Vincent. *The Buck in the Snow*. New York: Harper, 1928.

———. *Make Bright the Arrows*. New York: Harper, 1940.

Morison, Samuel Eliot. *The Oxford History of the American People*. New York: Oxford University Press, 1965.

Mumford, Lewis. *Herman Melville*. New York: Harcourt, Brace, 1929.

———. Letter to Rukeyser, September 28, 1958. Berg Collection, New York Public Library.

Nadir, Moishe. Review of Horace Gregory's *Chorus for Survival*. *New Masses*, XIV (January 22, 1935).

North, Mary Baldwin. Letter to the author, September 12, 1978.

Olson, Charles. "Projective Verse." *The New American Poetry*. Edited by Donald M. Allen. New York: Grove Press, 1960, pp. 387–8.

Partisan Review. Symposium: "The State of American Writing, 1948." XV (August, 1948), 855–94.

Patchen, Kenneth. *Before the Brave*. New York: Random House, 1936.

———. *First Will and Testament*. Norfolk, Conn.: New Directions, 1939.

Phillips, William. Letter to the author, June 23, 1976.

Quinn, Vincent. *Hart Crane*. New York: Twayne, 1963.

Reik, Miriam. Letter to the author, August 23, 1978.

Rexroth, Kenneth. *The Alternative Society*. New York: Herder and Herder, 1970.

———. *Assays*. Norfolk, Conn.: New Directions, 1961.

———. *The Collected Shorter Poems of Kenneth Rexroth*. New York: New Directions, 1966.

———. *The Dragon and the Unicorn*. Norfolk, Conn.: New Directions, 1952.

———. Letters to the author, August, 1977, and October 25, 1977.

Rich, Adrienne. *Diving into the Wreck*. New York: Norton, 1974.

———. *Poems: Selected and New, 1950–1974*. New York: Norton, 1975.

Ridge, Lola. *Dance of Fire*. New York: H. Smith and R. Haas, 1935.

———. *The Ghetto*. New York: Huebsch, 1918.

———. *Red Flag*. New York: Viking Press, 1927.

———. *Sun-up*. New York: Huebsch, 1920.

Rosenfeld, Paul. *Port of New York: Essays on Fourteen American Moderns*. New York: Harcourt, Brace, 1924.

Schacht, Marshall. Review of Marya Zaturenska's *Cold Morning Sky*. *Poetry*, LI (February, 1938), 266–67.

Schneider, Isidor. *Comrade Mister*. New York: Equinox Cooperative Press, 1934.

———. "Poetry: Red-baiting Victim." *New Masses*, L (January 18, 1944), 24–25.

———. *The Temptation of Anthony*. New York: Boni and Liveright, 1928.

Schwartz, Delmore. *Shenandoah*. Norfolk, Conn.: New Directions, 1941.

Scott, Winfield T. "The Dry Reaction." *Poetry*, LVIII (1941), 86–90.

Sexton, Anne. Letter and postcard to Rukeyser, November 1 and December 19, 1967, in Berg Collection, New York Public Library.

Shapiro, Karl. *The Poetry Wreck*. New York: Random House, 1975.

———. *V-Letter and Other Poems*. New York: Reynal, 1944.

Shirley, John W., ed. *Thomas Harriot, Renaissance Scientist*. Oxford: Clarendon Press, 1974.
Simpson, Louis. Review of *American Poetry Anthology*. *New York Times Book Review*, January 4, 1976, p. 17.
Smith, Cyril Stanley. Letter to the author, April 6, 1976.
Snyder, Gary. *Earth House Hold*. New York: New Directions, 1969.
———. *Turtle Island*. New York: New Directions, 1974.
Spears, Monroe K. *Hart Crane*. University of Minnesota Pamphlets on American Writers, XLVII. Minneapolis: University of Minnesota Press, 1965.
Spector, Herman, and Joseph Kalar. *We Gather Strength*. New York: Liberal Press, 1933.
Spender, Stephen. *Poems*. London: Faber, 1933.
———. *The Thirties and After*. New York: Random House, 1978.
Spiller, Robert. *The Cycle of American Literature*. New York: Mentor, 1957.
Sutton, Walter. *Modern American Criticism*. Englewood Cliffs, N.J.: Prentice-Hall, 1963.
Taggard, Genevieve. *Collected Poems*. New York and London: Harper, 1938.
———. *Long View*. New York and London: Harper, 1942.
Thompson, D'Arcy Wentworth. *On Growth and Form*. Cambridge: Cambridge University Press, 1917.
Viereck, Peter. "The Crack-up of American Optimism: Vachel Lindsay, the Dante of the Fundamentalists." *Modern Age*, IV (Summer, 1960), 269–84.
Waggoner, Hyatt. *The Heel of Elohim: Science and Values in Modern American Poetry*. Norman, Oklahoma: University of Oklahoma Press, 1950.
Wasson, Richard. "From Priest to Prometheus: Culture and Criticism in the Post-Modernist Period." *Journal of Modern Literature*, III (July, 1974), 1188–1202.
Wheeler, Lynde Phelps. *Josiah Willard Gibbs*. New Haven: Yale University Press, 1952.
Whitman, Walt. *Complete Poetry and Selected Prose*. Edited by James E. Miller, Jr. Boston: Houghton, Mifflin, Riverside Editions, 1951.
Williams, Oscar. *New Poems, 1943*. New York: Howell, Soskin, 1943.
Wright, George. *W. H. Auden*. New York: Twayne, 1969.
Zabel, Morton Dauwen. "The Poet on Capitol Hill." *Partisan Review*, VIII (January, 1941), 1–17.
Zaturenska, Marya. *Cold Morning Sky*. New York: Macmillan, 1937.
———. *Threshold and Hearth*. New York: Macmillan, 1934.

Index